Digital Governance and Decentralisation

About the Editors

Prof. (Dr.) M.R. Biju is currently Dean, School of Social Sciences, Dean, School of Legal Studies and Head Department of Public Administration and Policy Studies, Central University of Kerala, Kasaragod. He is also serving as Chairperson of Board of Studies, Public Administration and Policy Studies. He is also working as Member of the Court of the University. He is the Editor of *South Asian Journal of Socio-Political Studies* (SAJOSPS) and Editor-in-Chief of *International Journal of Political Science* (IJOPS). He is a prolific writer on socio-political and developmental issues and published Thirty books, One Hundred and Seventy research papers, Seventeen book chapters, and has reviewed over Nine Hundred books for South Asian Journal of Socio-political Studies.

His teaching and research experience, spanning more than 26 years, includes several achievements such as completion of three major research projects funded by Ministry of Panchayati Raj, Government of India and University Grants Commission, New Delhi and the Post-doctoral fellowship awarded by the UGC in 2004. He has successfully guided doctoral students of the University of Kerala.

He is consistently making professional academic contributions in the capacity of an Associate Board member of Economics and Management, a prestigious journal published by the Technical University of Liberec, Czech Republic, as the Director and Member Secretary of the Asian Institute of Development Research (AIDR), and as a life Member of several Academic and Professional Bodies. He is also serving on the Editorial Board of International Journal of Business and Innovation Administration. He is a member of the PG Board of Studies Political Science and Public Administration of the Central University of Rajasthan and Gandhigram Rural Institute, Dindigul.

M.R.B. Anantha Padmanabha is working as Deputy Editor of *South Asian Journal of Socio-Political Studies* (SAJOSPS) has to his credit a few books (co-author) and research papers published in International and national journals. He has also presented papers in National Seminars. Currently, he is studying Political Science and International Relations at Pondicherry University.

Digital Governance and Decentralisation

Edited by

M.R. Biju
M.R.B. Anantha Padmanabha

CONCEPT PUBLISHING COMPANY PVT. LTD.
NEW DELHI-110059

ISBN: 978-93-5439-029-6

First Published 2021

Published and Printed by

Concept Since 1974

Concept Publishing Company Pvt. Ltd.
A/15-16, Commercial Block, Mohan Garden,
New Delhi-110059 (India)
T : 91 11 41101460, 91 11 25351460, 91 11 25351794
E : publishing@conceptpub.com, *W*: www.conceptpub.com

Cataloging in Publication Data--Courtesy: D.K. Agencies (P) Ltd. <docinfo@dkagencies.com>

Digital governance and decentralisation / edited by M.R. Biju, M.R.B. Anantha Padmanabha.
pages cm
Contributed articles.
Includes bibliographical references and index.
ISBN 9789354390296

1. Internet in public administration—India. 2. Decentralization in government—India. 3. Panchayat—India. I. Biju, M. R., 1965- editor. II. Anantha Padmanabha, M. R. B., editor.

LCC JQ229.A8D54 2021 | DDC 352.3802854678 23

Preface

In India E-Governance originated during the seventies with a focus on in house government applications in the areas of defence, economic monitoring, planning and the deployment of ICT to manage data intensive functions related to elections, census, tax administration etc. The efforts of the National Informatics Centre (NIC) to connect all the district headquarters during the eighties was a watershed. From the early nineties, e-governance has seen the use of IT for wider sectoral applications with policy emphasis on reaching out to rural areas and taking in greater inputs from NGOs and private sector as well. There has been an increasing involvement of international donor agencies such as DFID, G-8, UNDP, and WB under the framework of e-governance for development. While the emphasis has been primarily on automation and computerization, state endeavours to use IT include forays into connectivity, networking, setting up systems for processing information and delivering services. At a micro level, this has ranged from IT automation in individual departments, electronic file handling, and access to entitlements, public grievance systems, service delivery for high volume routine transactions such as payment of bills, tax dues to meeting poverty alleviation goals through the promotion of entrepreneurial models and provision of market information. The thrust has varied across initiatives, with some focusing on enabling the citizen-state interface for various government services, and others focusing on bettering livelihoods.

In short, e-Governance is the application of Information and Communications Technology to government functioning in order to create 'Simple, Moral, Accountable, Responsive and Transparent' (SMART) governance. The revolution in Information and Communications Technology (ICT) has brought a whole new agenda for governance for wider participation of citizens in public affairs. The purpose of implementing e-Governance is to improve governance processes and outcomes with a view to improving the delivery of public services to citizens. Some authors have defined e-Governance as the e-business of the State. This seems appropriate as both e-Governance and e-business use similar technologies, infrastructure and hardware. However, the market models are widely different thus justifying e-Governance as a separate area of research (Gisler, 2001).

India, being the largest democracy in the world, has much to gain from e-Governance, especially when citizen participation in governance is one of the features of the fully evolved stage of e-government. Many e-readiness assessments have been carried out at the global level that shows the current state of India's e-readiness. e-Governance further refers to the use by government agencies of Information Technologies (such as Wide Area Networks, the Internet and mobile computing) that have the ability to transform relations with citizens, businesses, and various arms of government resulting in better delivery of government services to citizens, improved interactions with business and industry, citizen empowerment through access to information, or more efficient government management. The resultant benefits are less corruption, increased transparency, greater convenience, revenue growth, and cost reductions.

The primary purpose of governance is the welfare of citizens. While one aspect of governance relates to safeguarding the legal rights of all citizens, an equally important aspect is concerned with ensuring equitable access to public services and the benefits of economic growth to all.It is expected that e-Governance would enable the government to discharge its functions more effectively. However, this would require the government to change itself-its processes, its outlook, laws, rules and regulations and also its way of interacting with the citizens. It would also require capacity building within the government and creation of general awareness about e-Governance among the citizens.

During the initial stages of introduction of ICT in governance there was resistance from some quarters. Some felt that computerization cannot work in the complex government system and that introduction of computers would lead to unemployment. There were also serious doubts whether government employees at all levels would be able to handle computers. Fortunately, all these misgivings have proved wrong. Today, new software tools have enough flexibility, to accommodate the most complex situations. The new technology makes the machine human interface very user-friendly. The Information Technology (IT) and Information Technology Enabled Services (ITES) sectors have created millions of jobs besides improving vastly on the services provided by government undertakings like banks, Airlines, Railways etc. Thus e-Governance is no longer a far-fetched dream.

As government organizations function at varying degrees of IT-preparedness, there is first of all a need for building an environment within government organizations at various levels which is conducive to e-Governance. This would require computerization of the lowest possible unit, as well as building capacity at the individual level which recognizes the need for reforms in processes using modern technology. The essential elements in this phase are as follows:

- Decades of following a particular mode of governance procedure tends to develop inertia and resistance to change. Further, old skills and habits will require to be replaced with new skills and new processes if e-Governance is to sustain. There has to be a strong will from within the government itself to crossover from the present system to e-Governance.
- The vast scope of e-Governance combined with the enormous task of process re-engineering which will be necessary at various levels and the infrastructural and financial requirement necessarily call for commitment to the vision of e-Governance at the highest political level. A bottom-up approach will not suffice.
- Weaning government entities from the mechanical application of technology to adoption of e-Governance tools will require incentivising e-Governance among different entities and individuals. These incentives need to be reflected in the budgetary allocations.
- Apart from building capabilities within the government, there is need for generating widespread awareness among the public at large. The success of e-Governance lies in increasing the number of electronic interactions between citizens and the government and not merely in building the infrastructure of e-Governance. In addition to governmental measures, a proactive approach from civil society groups would also generate greater demand and acceptance for e-Governance initiatives. Further, this would also require the adoption of 'quality' as a mission of governance, as was done in Japan.
- e-Governance has to be a collective effort. However, in every organization, there are people who would not be convinced about its benefits or who would perceive it as a challenge to certain entrenched interests. Such resistance would need to be overcome by demonstrating the potential benefits of e-Governance; how it strengthens the organization internally, creates goodwill externally and above all, enhances citizens' satisfaction.

- Training would have to be imparted to government officials starting right from the cutting edge level so that any apprehensions of intrusive technology is removed and e-Governance is accepted as an achievable and desirable target.

India's e-Governance experience shows a plethora of pilot projects with varying rates of success but with the common characteristic that the majority of them are not up-scaled or widely replicated. It is essential to learn from such experiences and each pilot project should be taken to its logical end. For this to happen, emphasis has to be on there forms in government procedures, structures and systems and must take precedence over mere technological solutions. Ultimately, the success of an e-Governance initiative lies in how efficiently it has enhanced people's participation in government functioning through wide ICT access, bringing government and the services it offers closer to its citizens, promoting accountability, transparency and responsiveness in government functioning and ensuring that government works better at lesser costs. These are the signs for good governance and a vibrant democracy.

Keeping this background in view, an attempt has been made in his volume to address the issues pertaining to a wide-ranging areas and aspects of Digital Governance in the context of Decentralised Governance. The topics covered include e-Governance in India with focus on Second ARC Report, Role of Digital Technology in the Governance for Local Development with Special Focus on Smart Cities, Social Welfare and its Linkages with Digital Governance and Digital India, Importance of Gender Digital Divide, Knowledge Management and e-Governance, e- Government Development Index, Digi-Locker in Transforming e-Governance, Delivering Justice at the Grassroots, Decentralisation and Healthcare, Micro-Analysis of the Life and Livelihood of MayanaVettiyan Community, CSR and its role in LSGs, Functioning of Ombudsman, Village Adoption and Transforming Rural World, Economic Status of De-Notified Tribes, Marketing Methods in Women Enterprises, m-Commerce and Legal Configuration of GST in the Indian e-Commerce Industry. The chapters are contributed by senior academics and development experts with rich experience on the core areas of the study. In their submission, the authors have high lightened the existing issues and problems connected with the subject and put forward solid suggestions to revamp the system.

M.R. Biju
M.R.B. Anantha Padmanabha

Acknowledgements

We would like to express our deep sense of gratitude to those who have been kind enough to help us in the preparation of this volume. We wish to express our heartfelt thanks to the esteemed contributors to this anthology of articles. The views and opinions expressed by the contributors are of great value for the researchers, academics and administrators for framing policies and strategies on grassroots democracy in India. Also thankful to Shri Ashok Kumar Mittal of Concept Publishing Company Pvt. Ltd., New Delhi, who brought out this book in an elegant form.

M.R. Biju
M.R.B. Anantha Padmanabha

Contents

Introduction

In India E-Governance originated during the seventies with a focus on in-house government applications in the areas of defence, economic monitoring, planning and the deployment of ICT to manage data-intensive functions related to elections, census, tax administration etc. The efforts of the National Informatics Centre (NIC) to connect all the district headquarters during the eighties was a watershed. From the early nineties, e-governance has seen the use of IT for wider sectoral applications with policy emphasis on reaching out to rural areas and taking in greater inputs from NGOs and private sector as well. There has been an increasing involvement of international donor agencies such as DFID, G-8, UNDP, and WB under the framework of e-governance for development. While the emphasis has been primarily on automation and computerization, state endeavours to use IT include forays into connectivity, networking, setting up systems for processing information and delivering services. At a micro level, this has ranged from IT automation in individual departments, electronic file handling, and access to entitlements, public grievance systems, service delivery for high volume routine transactions such as payment of bills, tax dues to meeting poverty alleviation goals through the promotion of entrepreneurial models and provision of market information. The thrust has varied across initiatives, with some focusing on enabling the citizen-state interface for various government services, and others focusing on bettering livelihoods.

In short, e-Governance is the application of Information and Communications Technology to government functioning in order to create 'Simple, Moral, Accountable, Responsive and Transparent' (SMART) governance. The revolution in Information and Communications Technology (ICT) has brought a whole new agenda for governance for wider participation of citizens in public affairs. The purpose of implementing e-Governance is to improve governance processes and outcomes with a view to improving the delivery of public services to citizens. Some authors have defined e-Governance as the e-business of the State. This seems appropriate as both e-Governance and e-business use similar technologies, infrastructure and hardware. However, the market models are widely different thus justifying e-Governance as a separate area of research (Gisler, 2001).

India, being the largest democracy in the world, has much to gain from e-Governance, especially when citizen participation in governance is one of the features of the fully evolved stage of e-government. Many e-readiness assessments have been carried out at the global level that show the current state of India's e-readiness. e-Governance further refers to the use by government agencies of Information Technologies (such as Wide Area Networks, the Internet and mobile computing) that have the ability to transform relations with citizens, businesses, and various arms of government resulting in better delivery of government services to citizens, improved interactions with business and industry, citizen empowerment through access to information, or more efficient government management. The resultant benefits are less corruption, increased transparency, greater convenience, revenue growth, and cost reductions.

e-Governance needs to transform all levels of Government but the focus should be on local governments since local governments are the closest to citizens, and constitute for many, the main interface with government. The advances in information and communications technologies and the internet provide opportunities to transform the relationship between governments and citizens and business in new ways that contribute to the attainment of good governance. They provide opportunities for people and business to involve themselves in the process of governance at all levels. They facilitate better service delivery to clients, in terms of timelines and quality, thus making governance more efficient and effective. In addition, the use of ICT may lower transaction costs both for citizens and government operations and public services can be made more affordable to the people at large.

The primary purpose of governance is the welfare of citizens. While one aspect of governance relates to safeguarding the legal rights of all citizens, an equally important aspect is concerned with ensuring equitable access to public services and the benefits of economic growth to all. It is expected that e-Governance would enable the government to discharge its functions more effectively. However, this would require the government to change itself–its processes, its outlook, laws, rules and regulations and also its way of interacting with the citizens. It would also require capacity building within the government and creation of general awareness about e-Governance among the citizens.

During the initial stages of introduction of ICT in governance there was resistance from some quarters. Some felt that computerization cannot work in the complex government system and that introduction of computers would lead to unemployment. There were also serious doubts whether government employees at all levels would be able to handle computers. Fortunately all these misgivings have proved wrong. Today, new software tools have enough flexibility, to accommodate the most complex situations. The new technology makes the machine human interface very user-friendly. The Information Technology (IT) and Information Technology Enabled Services (ITES) sectors have created millions of jobs besides improving vastly on the services provided by government undertakings like banks, Airlines, Railways etc. Thus, e-Governance is no longer a far-fetched dream.

e-Governance has to be implemented across different departments and organizations with a wide spectrum of activities and with varying levels of readiness for e-Governance. Achieving the desired results would, therefore, require the fullest political backing, a determined and resolute approach by all organizations and departments of Government as well as active and constructive participation by the public. It would require providing institutional and physical infrastructure for taking e-Governance initiatives across our cultural and regional diversities; more importantly it would require the creation of an environment that would encourage the adoption of ICT. Thus, apart from the technical requirement, success of e-Governance initiatives would depend on capacity building and creating awareness within government and outside it.

As government organizations function at varying degrees of IT-preparedness, there is first of all a need for building an environment within government organizations at various levels which is conducive to e-Governance. This would require computerization of the lowest possible unit, as well as building capacity at the individual level which recognizes the need for reforms in processes using modern technology. The essential elements in this phase are as follows:

- Decades of following a particular mode of governance procedure tends to develop inertia and resistance to change. Further, old skills and habits will require to be replaced with new skills and new processes if e-Governance is to sustain. There has to be a strong will from within the government itself to crossover from the present system to e-Governance.

- The vast scope of e-Governance combined with the enormous task of process re-engineering which will be necessary at various levels and the infrastructural and financial requirement necessarily call for commitment to the vision of e-Governance at the highest political level. A bottom-up approach will not suffice.
- Weaning government entities from the mechanical application of technology to adoption of e-Governance tools will require incentivising e-Governance among different entities and individuals. These incentives need to be reflected in the budgetary allocations.
- Apart from building capabilities within the government, there is need for generating widespread awareness among the public at large. The success of e-Governance lies in increasing the number of electronic interactions between citizens and the government and not merely in building the infrastructure of e-Governance. In addition to governmental measures, a proactive approach from civil society groups would also generate greater demand and acceptance for e-Governance initiatives. Further, this would also require the adoption of 'quality' as a mission of governance, as was done in Japan.
- e-Governance has to be a collective effort. However, in every organization, there are people who would not be convinced about its benefits or who would perceive it as a challenge to certain entrenched interests. Such resistance would need to be overcome by demonstrating the potential benefits of e-Governance; how it strengthens the organization internally, creates goodwill externally and above all, enhances citizens' satisfaction.
- Training would have to be imparted to government officials starting right from the cutting edge level so that any apprehensions of intrusive technology is removed and e-Governance is accepted as an achievable and desirable target.

India's e-Governance experience shows a plethora of pilot projects with varying rates of success but with the common characteristic that the majority of them are not up-scaled or widely replicated. It is essential to learn from such experiences and each pilot project should be taken to its logical end. For this to happen, emphasis has to be on the reforms in government procedures, structures and systems and must take precedence over mere technological solutions. Ultimately, the success of an e-Governance initiative lies in how efficiently it has enhanced people's participation in government functioning through wide ICT access, bringing government and the services it offers closer to its citizens, promoting accountability, transparency and responsiveness in government functioning and ensuring that government works better at lesser costs. These are the signs for good governance and a vibrant democracy.

Summary of Contents

In the inaugural chapter Prof. Neelima Deshmukh examines the role of digital technology in governance for the local development. She has carefully narrated issues in Local Government administration of Smart Cities in India based on Nagpur. According to the author, Digital India is a latest flagship programme of Government of India to transform India into complete digitally empowered as well as IT enabled and knowledge economy of the world. The main aim of this brainchild of PM Narendra Modi is to provide Indian citizens electronic government services by reducing the paper work and reducing the corruption and red tapism saving the manpower and time. No doubt it is a very good technique of good governance which was launched on 1st July, 2015 to ensure that the government services are made available to the citizens electronically by improving online infrastructure and internet connectivity. The digital India provides intensified impetus for further momentum and the progress for e-governance and would promote inclusive growth that covers electronic services, products, devices manufacturing and the job opportunities. The main aim is to reform governance through technology. This three-dimensional vision of this programme is to provide digital utility to every citizen Governance and Services on demand and Digital empowerment of the citizens. Prof. Neelima further adds that laying emphasis on universal digital literacy, and availability of the digital resources/services in Indian language, which would facilitate to meet the challenges of LPG era, upcoming Smart Cities, Metro cities, and other infrastructural development of the nation at world class level. It assumes greater relevance and importance in the context of Smart City wherein every household and the individual will be digitally empowered having the thrust on IT the great enabler for empowerment, equity and efficiency. It focuses on the broad banding villages, participative governance, digital learning, telemedicine, mobile health care, e-learning tools, skills development, jobs creation, open source and open standards, e-bhasha and others.

- This time bound project is to be completed by 2019. Today till November 2018 there is no visible movement and impact of the programme and hardly only few elites know about it and the ordinary common man is totally ignorant and unaware about his programme for whom it is meant. But looking at the grim picture, administrative issues, other complexities, very slow and tardy growth of this upcoming Smart City of Nagpur there is an acute need to create awareness and sensitize public to accept, welcome and handle this change in their progressive life, But at this moment it is very disheartening and disappointing to witness performance of the local government institutions at zero development rate, very slow non-noticeable at grassroots level the needs to be expedited at multiple levels with the corrective measure to overcome the lacunae to improve the present scenario.
- More precise, perfect, electronic instruments, equipments and logistics along with high precision trouble free citizen friendly computerisation, digitalization procedure should be developed and adopted for the easy access.
- With the effective and strong powerful ruling Bhartiya Janata Party's existence from local to central level headed by its committed strong willed leadership for the nation's development, the administration is running smoothly streamlining its objectives, and overcoming all hurdles, difficulties, and the constraints thereby delivering the desired visible results to the last man of this city leading to the Vidarbha's holistic development.

In chapter Two the **volume** editors have made an enquiry on the evolution of e-Governance in the Indian context based on the second Administrative Reforms Commission (ARC) Report. According to the authors, e-Governance is the application of Information and Communications Technology to government functioning in order to create 'Simple, Moral, Accountable, Responsive and Transparent' (SMART) governance. The revolution in Information and communications Technology (ICT) has brought a whole new agenda for governance for wider participation of citizens in public affairs. The purpose of implementing e-Governance is to improve governance processes and outcomes with a view to improving the delivery of public services to citizens. Some authors have defined e-Governance as the e-business of the State. This seems appropriate as both e-Governance and e-business use similar technologies, infrastructure and hardware. However, the market models are widely different thus justifying e-Governance as a separate area of research. India, being the largest democracy in the world, has much to gain from e-Governance, especially when citizen participation in governance is one of the features of the fully evolved stage of e-government. Many e-readiness assessments have been carried out at the global level that show the current state of India's e-readiness. e-Governance further refers to the use by government agencies of Information Technologies (such as Wide Area Networks, the Internet and mobile computing) that have the ability to transform relations with citizens, businesses, and various arms of government resulting in better delivery of government services to citizens, improved interactions with business and industry, citizen empowerment through access to information, or more efficient government management. The resultant benefits are less corruption, increased transparency, greater convenience, revenue growth, and cost reductions.

The authors further states that

- e-Governance needs to transform all levels of Government but the focus should be on local governments since local governments are the closest to citizens, and constitute for many, the main interface with government. The advances in information and communications technologies and the internet provide opportunities to transform the relationship between governments and citizens and business in new ways that contribute to the attainment of good governance. They provide opportunities for people and business to involve themselves in the process of governance at all levels. They facilitate better service delivery to clients, in terms of timelines and quality, thus making governance more efficient and effective. In addition, the use of ICT may lower transaction costs both for citizens and government operations and public services can be made more affordable to the people at large.
- The primary purpose of governance is the welfare of citizens. While one aspect of governance relates to safeguarding the legal rights of all citizens, an equally important aspect is concerned with ensuring equitable access to public services and the benefits

of economic growth to all. It is expected that e-Governance would enable the government to discharge its functions more effectively. However, this would require the government to change itself–its processes, its outlook, laws, rules and regulations and also its way of interacting with the citizens. It would also require capacity building within the government and creation of general awareness about e-Governance among the citizens.

- During the initial stages of introduction of ICT in governance there was resistance from some quarters. Some felt that computerization cannot work in the complex government system and that introduction of computers would lead to unemployment. There were also serious doubts whether government employees at all levels would be able to handle computers. Fortunately all these misgivings have proved wrong. Today, new software tools have enough flexibility, to accommodate the most complex situations. The new technology makes the machine-human interface very user-friendly. The Information Technology (IT) and Information Technology Enabled Services (ITES) sectors have created millions of jobs besides improving vastly on the services provided by government undertakings like banks, Airlines, Railways etc. Thus, e-Governance is no longer a far-fetched dream.

The authors conclude their study by stating that India's e-Governance experience shows a plethora of pilot projects with varying rates of success but with the common characteristic that the majority of them are not up-scaled or widely replicated. It is essential to learn from such experiences and each pilot project should be taken to its logical end. For this to happen, emphasis has to be on the reforms in government procedures, structures and systems and must take precedence over mere technological solutions. Ultimately, the success of an e-Governance initiative lies in how efficiently it has enhanced people's participation in government functioning through wide ICT access, bringing government and the services it offers closer to its citizens, promoting accountability, transparency and responsiveness in government functioning and ensuring that government works better at lesser costs. These are the signs for good governance and a vibrant democracy.

Digital Governance and its linkage with social welfare is the topic of discussion in the third chapter. This study is an enquiry and assessment of Digital India programme by **Dr. C. Jeevan Kumar**. The chapter critically examines the impact of neo-liberal reforms on the Indian state. While doing so, it assesses the impact of technology on social welfare administration. It discusses the benefits and opportunities created by Digital India Programme. It critically examines digital divide in India and issues surrounding this phenomenon. According to the author,

- ICTs brought in managerial changes in Indian government in the 1990s. They caught the imagination of both administrators and politicians. While other sections of society are adapting themselves to these changes, it became imperative for the administration to respond to these changes (Mathur, as cited in Mehta, 2000, p. 55). It is an internal change communicated by ICT revolution. It was advocated that extensive usage of ICTs would redefine administrative process and improve the efficiency of the government. ICTs are expected to reduce administrative cost as well as corruption.
- Increased use of ICTs has altered public service delivery in the public domain. At the policy level, Fifth Pay Commission has recommended the use of ICTs for automation of service provision and paperless government (GoI, 1997). Besides enhancing speediness in service delivery, technologies facilitate the interface between government-citizen; citizen-market and state-market. Y.K. Alagh Committee on civil service reforms identified a variety of skills required by a civil servant of the twenty-first century (GoI, 2001, p. 71). Technological revolution afforded the opportunity to civil servants to adapt themselves to these changes. This committee suggested that civil servants should be able to interface with modern technology and provide a cutting edge to many solutions.

In a nutshell, e-governance has been construed as a means to attain transformational improvement in quality, efficiency, and effectiveness of governance. The focus is laid on reduction in administrative costs, redefining administrative process, and enhancing the efficiency in public service delivery. Convinced by these arguments, e-governance has been promoted in India in the post-1990s. Institutional measures were taken by setting up of National Institute for Smart Government (NISG) in India in 2002. Having discussed the advantages of e-governance, let us turn to the e-government initiatives undertaken by the government. After making a detailed enquiry C. Jeevan Kumar concludes his enquiry by stating that India adapted itself to ICT revolution in tandem with the neoliberal reforms in the post-1990s. Technology is expected to offer many solutions to problems such as administrative inefficiency and corruption. ICTs provide tremendous opportunities to governments for improving administrative transparency, efficiency, and effectiveness of governmental performance. It also opens up more ways for the public to be involved and participate in the policy-making processes. Studies showed that use of ICTs had reduced corruption including improved service delivery. If we evaluate India against Baumi and Di Maio's model, the country remains at the third stage. The relationship between citizens and government did not go beyond limited transactions. In other words, it is transaction driven rather than transformation. Though India is technologically advanced, it has to do more. E-governance is a journey, but not a destination (GoI, 2008, p. 64).

There have been several issues that hinder digital inclusion, such as, infrastructure, skills, and censorship. More importantly, freedom of the internet and political will are prerequisites of achieving the goals of Digital India. When the citizens are not provided with enough access to the web, it is tantamount to social exclusion from participatory democracy. Unless these problems are addressed, it is impossible to achieve the goals of Digital India. There is a bottom line to the implementation of this programme. Technology neither replaces human beings nor democracy. Mobile connectivity cannot address country's hunger and basic needs with India ranking 55 in the Global Hunger Index (Nissim Mannathurkkaren, 2015). People are central to all these digital initiatives. Necessary steps have to be taken by the government in this direction.

Dr. B. Madhusudhan has contributed a chapter (four) on Gender-Digital Divide with special emphasis on Mobile Penetration in India. To him the digital divide is growing in many of the least developing nations. One of the reasons for the digital divide is the gender divide where women lag behind men in using and accessing digital technology. Many of the developing nations including India are in the process of addressing digital gender divide. Infrastructural and technical problems could be resolved by consensus efforts. However, certain social norms and practices also act as an obstacle to bridging digital divide. The study examines the digital gender divide with special reference to use and access of mobiles in India. B. Madhusudhan is of the firm opinion that the digital divide has become a global phenomenon and is even visible in developed nations. The developing and least developed nations are striving hard to tide over the challenges posed by digital divide. Apart from infrastructural and technical issues, cultural and social issues come in the way of bridging digital divide. One such social issue is the growing gender disparity in using ICT. The study examines the digital gender divide in developing nations with a focus on India. The Indian scenario reveals that the gender gap predominant by analyzing the various dimensions of the use of mobile handsets. Several issues hamper women in accessing mobiles. These include—issues of ownership, lack of autonomy, cost of handsets, and lack of technical know-how, lack of confidence and social norms and practices. The GSMA studies expose that among the emerging nations as well, the gender digital divide is noticeable. The Indian situation of digital gender divide is really challenging to the policy makers. To tide over such barriers are difficult in the context of persisting maladies women suffer in the current Indian scenario.

In chapter five, the volume editors have made an investigation on the relationship between Knowledge Management and e-Governance. According to the authors, knowledge has always been a cornerstone of all decision-making. It is essential when we set out to achieve goals as individuals, communities, countries or regions, because decisions made are based on what is known at the time the action is taken. In order to make the best decisions possible it is necessary to ensure that those with the responsibility have or have access to the needed skills, experiences, understandings and values, when and where it is required, to do so. Knowledge management makes this possible. Managing knowledge is not an easy task. It is inherently part of all individuals, sectors, communities and organizations in a country. The role that knowledge plays in decision-making and the potential impact it has on the lives of all these carriers of knowledge and countries has made it necessary for governments to manage their knowledge and leverage it to further good governance so that they can effectively foster innovation and creativity geared towards development. Knowledge management is a tool that when implemented enables the availability and accessibility of knowledge through its distinct, but interdependent processes and activities of creation, capture, storage and retrieval and transfer. Broadly the processes and activities surrounding knowledge management can be divided into those that enable and ensure the creation of knowledge and those that enable and ensure the sharing of knowledge. Creation processes ensure that new knowledge is available and sharing processes makes it transferable.

The success of knowledge management activities and processes depends on the goals, practices and culture of an organization, and on the willingness of its employees to change their mindsets, perceptions and ways they work. Some knowledge processes can be implemented within the current government structure and hierarchies, but to be truly successful fundamental changes, such as flatter hierarchies, are necessary to ensure greater fluidity of skills, experiences, understandings within government as well as between government and its citizenry. KM is increasingly imperative as it is regarded as the key determinant of a firm, industry or country for survival and growth in knowledge era. Varieties of disciplines have contributed to knowledge and KM. Research focuses on one or more specific fields, but to understand which levels of knowledge processes KM should concentrate on, should be more fundamental than advocacy of KM. Knowledge management is not just about creating and storing knowledge so that we can access it when and where it is needed, it also brings about fundamental changes in the way government processes are designed and executed, and the way national policies, plans and strategies are developed and implemented. Promoting KM in Government Knowledge Management is essentially about facilitating the processes by which knowledge is created, shared and used in organizations. It is not about setting up a new department or getting in a new technology. It is about making changes to the way individuals in organisations function. There are many ways of looking at Knowledge Management and different organizations will take different approaches. Generally speaking, creating a knowledge environment usually requires changing organizational values and culture, changing people's behaviours and work patterns, and providing people with easy access to each other and to relevant information resources. The authors sum up their study by stating that all governments should strive to achieve good governance, as this will help in the eradication of poverty, combating corruption and ensuring that economic, social and environmental development goals are met, while improving the wellness of citizens. In order to achieve good governance the best decisions possible should be taken. This is only possible when governments, citizens and communities have access to knowledge that can inform their decisions and actions. Knowledge management is a tool that can ensure the availability and accessibility of knowledge when and where it is needed, but it should be planned and integrated into the national strategies of a country to ensure success. ICT is an enabler of knowledge management initiatives, and not knowledge management itself. The implementation thereof should, therefore, be carefully considered and aligned with strategies and national development goals. This will ensure that ICT implementations are effective and efficient. Before concluding the authors would like to add the recommendation made by Second ARC Report (December 2008) in this regard. The Commission has recommended that "Union and State Governments should take proactive measures for establishing knowledge management systems as a pivotal steps for administrative reforms in general and e-governance in particular."

In chapter six, an attempt has been made by **Dr. Yudhishthira Sapru** to analyse e-Government Development Index by using Socio-Economic indicators. According to the author, the current methodology for calculation of this index and availability of data in public domain makes it difficult and costly for effective calculation of this index at country or at state level. This study is aimed at understanding the association of this Index with commonly identifiable socio-economic indicators. It has been found that the Index has high level of association with the income levels and Human Development Index. A regression model has been proposed in this chapter in terms of socio-economic factors to calculate and compare the index which can be used to find relative ranking of Indian States on e-Governance. The study indicates that it would be useful for the governments to concentrate on improving the health and urban infrastructure to achieve higher levels of e-Governance. The author further states:

- that one of the most comprehensive and popular surveys to access readiness on e-Governance is the United Nations E-Government Survey which is published every two-years by the Department of Economic and Social Affairs of the United Nations (United Nations, 2014). The survey assesses the E-Government development status of all the United Nations Member-States. It serves as a tool for policy makers to identify their areas of strength and challenges in e-Governance and to guide e-Government policies and strategies.
- e-Government rankings have joined the likes of other famous indices such as the Human Development Index (HDI) and the Gini coefficient in helping to define the conditions within a country (Whitmore, 2012).
- India has been ranked quite low in the index reflecting poor levels of e-Government in the country. In the latest edition of the Survey (2014), India has been ranked at mere 118 despite country's huge thrust on making electronic public service delivery. The National e-Governance Plan (NeGP) was initiated in 2006, has received only moderate success. Though some

initiatives like National Passport and eBiz portal have been a huge success, other initiatives have failed to take off especially at the State level in the country.

Dr. Sapru conducted the enquiry with three key objectives–(i) to analyse whether EGDI of countries varies with income levels, (ii) To analyse the correlation between Human Development Index and EGDI, and (iii) To create a regression model for EGDI in term of socio-economic indicators. After making a detailed scientific analysis the author brought out a few interesting results.

- Firstly, out of the three constituents whose weighted score form the EGDI, the index has highest correlation with the Telecommunication Infrastructure Index. Thus, an important implication for the policy-makers would be to concentrate more on providing universal access to mobiles which is reflected in the Telecommunication Infrastructure Index. Needless to say other factors are also important.
- Secondly, Human Development Index (HDI) can also be treated as proxy measure of the EGDI. Countries high on Human Development Index are also likely to be high on EGDI. The Human Development Index (HDI) is a composite statistics of life expectancy, education, and per capita income indicators, which is used to rank countries into four tiers of human development. Indian States have been ranked high on the Human Development Index, as per the India Human Development Report (Mehrotra, 2011). With its own version of Human Development Index in the report (based on data of 2007-08), Kerala, Delhi and Himachal Pradesh were the top three states on the Index. Thus, as per the analysis, these states are also expected to be high on EGDI.
- The third analysis reflected that countries with higher per capita income are likely to be rated higher on EGDI. Thus, it is imperative for Indian States to work towards increasing their respective GDP levels so that per capita income increases. e-Government then will be an obvious consequence of such an improvement in GDPs.
- Lastly, the regression analysis has presented us with a model to quickly arrive at Index scores for a group of countries in a region, at state or even district levels. The model clearly reflects that

primarily life expectancy at birth and urban population to some an extent can help in arriving at EGDI. For a country like India where health and urban infrastructure are not developed, it calls for a rethinking in efforts towards better governance. For Indian states, it is reflective of where they stand and how they can provide better governance. Kerala for instance is high on life expectancy at birth can be benchmarked by other states.

- For policy-makers it would be useful to concentrate on improving the health and urban infrastructure in the country. An improvement in health and urban utility services would be likely accompanied by investment in IT infrastructure and other e-Governance initiatives which are crucial and critical to improving public service delivery or e-Government. This will go a long way making an effective government which will also be high on EGDI rankings.

The **same author** in chapter Seven came out with a chapter on DigiLocker. To him, DigiLocker facilitates issuance and verification of documents and certificates digitally. Very quickly, this platform has touched the lives of Indian citizens. It provides an access to billions of documents to its large number of registered users. DigiLocker offers a plethora of opportunities especially in a developing country where government involvement with citizens is almost on a daily basis and where most of the government databases are working in silos and in heterogeneous environments. This chapter attempts to throw light on the evolving concept of DigiLocker from a usage perspective and provides a clear understanding of the DigiLocker concept despite a dearth of systematic literature on the subject. Further, innovative use-cases where DigiLocker is currently and can be prospectively used have also been presented. Besides, the paper also discusses the current challenges and way forward which can be useful not only for the academicians but government organisations both in India and in countries where governments are facing similar challenges.

Dr. Y. Sapru is of the opinion that

- huge data sets of citizen information stored in fragmented government systems which operate in varied environments and involving multiple public agencies is a common dilemma which government heads usually face while realizing the vision of a single government. There lies an immense potential in using this data for the benefit of both the governments and citizens for a seamless service delivery, but the technology, resources and commitment required for bringing various government departments is an uphill task. This is especially challenging in countries where number of government departments providing citizen services is large, a federal structure is in place or various government departments are at varied stages of digitization. In India the scenario is no different but through an innovative use of technology, Government of India has created a platform–DigiLocker or the Digital Locker which is not resource intensive, easy to integrate with and allows multiple government organisations to work in synergy in spite of their diverse nature.

- Although, e-Governance transformation in India started in the late 1990s only with certain initiatives which were undertaken in silos, the country has made significant progress as regards IT-enabled working of government is concerned. Two major national level initiatives which have helped in creating digital infrastructure across the country have been the National eGovernance Plan (NeGP) which was started in 2006 and the Digital India Programme which was launched in 2014. While, NeGP had the vision of making all government services accessible to the common man (Sapru & Sapru, 2014), Digital India taking a broader view has been envisioned at transforming India into a digitally empowered society and a knowledge economy (Ministry of Electronics and IT, 2014).
- With the changing demographics, expectation of citizens in terms to efficiency, burden reduction and personalization are on the rise (López-De-Ipiña, Emaldi, Aguilera, & Pérez-Velasco, 2016). Both the programmes can be seen to be in line with the 'open government movement' which is being witnessed world over since the beginning of the 21st century to provide citizens with open access to information and thereby increasing transparency and accountability (Henninger, 2017). Utilizing the digital infrastructure created under these two programmes, complemented with the growing mobile reach especially to the rural India and success of unique identification programme–Aadhaar[1], Government of India launched the DigiLocker platform in 2015.
- Very quickly, the DigiLocker initiative has grown in importance for both citizens and government organisations. Within a short

> span of its launch, both the number of users and access to the documents has increased manifold. However, despite being a highly transformational initiative, the literature available on the subject is minimal and insufficient. Thus, the objective of this chapter is to familiarize the academicians and governments across the world with the concept of DigiLocker. The chapter aims to explain the DigiLocker's ecosystem, its benefits and its usage in practical government scenarios. The chapter is also aimed to present the challenges DigiLocker faces. The object of the chapter is also to sensitize government organisations that are in the midst of digitization, i.e. where certain level of digitization is available but due to lack to standardisation, various government departments are working in silos and data sharing is a challenge.

Regarding DigiLocker ecosystem, the author further states that it consists of four major stakeholders.

- First and primary among them are the citizens which are at the centre of this digital service. Citizens are the owners of the DigiLocker accounts where documents issued to them or uploaded by them reside. In fact, DigiLocker only hosts the links (using a unique document URI number) to these documents, which can be downloaded from the electronic repository of the issuing organisation. Thus, DigiLocker is a decentralized repository. Citizens can access their account which can be created online or through a mobile-app. Citizens can optionally link their account to their Aadhaar number which is a unique identification number issued to Indian citizens. This linking facilitates fetching of documents which are usually linked with the Aadhaar number. However, DigiLocker also facilitates linking of documents using other identifiers where Aadhaar number is not present. These identifiers could be basic user demographics like date of birth, gender or personal information like mobile number or unique identifier of the document like certificate number which is only known to the owner of the document.
- Secondly, there are the 'Issuers', primary being the Government organisations, who issue documents to the citizens. Examples include a Regional Transport Office which issues a driving licence or a registration certificate of a vehicle or a municipal

office issuing birth certificate. The documents issued by the issuers, once linked to a citizen's locker account can be accessed through Issuer's database. The documents issued are differentiated from the documents 'uploaded' by the citizens which is also facilitated by the DigiLocker. The upload feature allows citizens to keep a scanned copy of their documents (like mark sheets etc.) in the digital repository but being not issued on DigiLocker by a verified 'Issuer', the uploaded documents are treated somewhat less authentic than the issued ones. Issuers are registered organisations which can only become part of DigiLocker after thorough verification only.

- Thirdly, there are 'Requestors' which require secure access to a particular document issued or uploaded on the DigiLocker. A requestor, for instance, can be a private firm which is hiring a person and requires mark sheets for verification of educational qualifications. This is where DigiLocker obviates need for providing physical copy or scanned copy of the document which can be counterfeited easily.
- Finally, another category of stakeholders is coming up which are the 'Verifiers'. DigiLocker allows Verifiers to use the DigiLocker repository to verify users' documents (subsequent to user's consent). This verification feature is primarily for the organisations which do not have an electronic database of their own but intend to verify users' records.

After the submission of DigiLocker ecosystem he further moves to present the benefits of DigiLocker. In the concluding part of his study Dr. Sapru presents the challenges of DigiLocker in a solid way. To him DigiLocker has the potential of transforming India to a truly digitally driven country where government, industry and citizens interact in a paperless ecosystem. This is especially crucial in a developing economy where resources are limited and a majority of the population interacts with the government almost on a daily basis. However, challenges still remain to truly realise this potential.

The second part of the volume (**Chapter Eight**) starts with a chapter on Gram Nyayalayas in India contributed by the volume editors. According to the authors, the preamble of the Gram Nyayalaya Act envisages access to justice to the citizens at their doorsteps with the assurance that opportunities for securing justice are not devised to any citizen by season of any disability whatsoever. Hence, the success of these institutions should not only be measured by the number of courts in the whole nation but in terms of the extent and depth of reaching out to deprived sections and its role in the overall reduction in the number of pending cases. Over 72 years after Independence, the search for acceptable and accessible legal institution for those living in rural India is still a faraway dream. However, whatever things which are available at our hands should be used and utilized with a new professional legal touch, which may give a new light to the Indian Judicial System in the days to come. The areas covered in the chapter include the evolution of Gram Nyayalayas, its constitutional status, composition, jurisdiction and functioning. The Law Commission Report on Gram Nyayalayas, Gram Nyayalaya Act, 2008, Working of Gram Nyayalayas in Kerala, Inadequacies of the Act were also discussed in detail. Thereafter, the authors conclude their study by saying that Administration of Justice is one of the Primary responsibilities of a Nation. It is also the fundamental duty of the State to ensure its citizens equal access to legal services. The problem of inequality in accessing justice at minimum cost has been a widespread problem across almost all democracies of the world. India is certainly not an exception. Since independence, the country has consistently taken serious initiatives in fulfilling its emotional obligation of making legal services available to all citizens, through different mechanisms. Certainly the Gram Nyayalaya Act, 2008 is an appreciable step in this direction. But the pace of the implementation of this Act has been unfortunately carried out in an exceptionally slow manner. Besides that certain apprehensions and objectives have been raised from various corners regarding the efficiency of certain provisions of the Act, which need classification from higher ups. However, the real test of any legislation takes place at the execution phase. Therefore, the first and foremost priority of the government should be to give prominence to these areas which can genuinely protect the interests of the needy people. Therefore, remedial measures can be taken to resolve the limitations. Till then the entire Indian society should extend or keep faith in this Act, which can throw light to the millions of downtrodden who genuinely work for a transparent and judicious justice delivery system at their doorsteps. An analysis on the working of this Act from 2009 to 2018 shows that it requires a thorough revision in several key areas. The citizens at their doorsteps with the assurance that opportunities for securing justice are not devised to any citizen by reason of any disability whatsoever. The success of these institutions should not only be measured by the number of courts in the whole nation but in terms of the extent and depth of reaching out to deprived sections and its role in the overall reduction in the number of pending cases. Over 72 years after Independence, the search for acceptable and accessible legal institution for those living in rural India is still a faraway dream. However, whatever things which are available at our hands should be used and utilized with a new professional legal touch, which may give a new light to the Indian Judicial System in the days to come.

In chapter nine, **Dr. Nisha Velappan Nair** and **Prof. M.S. John** made a study on the application of decentralisation in health care sector of Kerala with special focus on Gender. According to the authors, Decentralised Planning which initiated in the state of Kerala way back in 1997 resulted in the transfer of substantial resources to local bodies. The local bodies were expected to spend money for services rendered by the transferred institutions such as Public Health Centres. In view of the high morbidity of Kerala and the growth in lifestyle-related ailments, the local bodies were encouraged to invest considerably in the health sector. After a faltering start, most local bodies now allocate money for infrastructure and various services provided by the health centres for allopathic, ayurvedic and homeopathic systems of treatment. It has also been found that most of those who use the public health system are women. This chapter looks at the allocation and expenditure in the health sector in Thiruvarpu Gram Panchayat in Kottayam district from 2009 to 2016. It then seeks to make an analysis of the gender dimensions of this allocation and expenditure by dividing the projects carried out in the health sector into three categories, namely women-specific, women-friendly and women-neutral and undertakes a gender benefit incidence analysis. The authors further add that, women's health projects are of least priority both under women component plan and general health sector. The data show that nutrition constituted the largest chunk of both allocation and expenditure in the health sector. Only two health projects were implemented under WCP. The panchayat does not have any health policy of its own. Investing in women's health can be based only on a conscious policy or design. In this case, not much investment has been made by design. However, whatever investment has been made, has yielded, by default, some outcomes that are beneficial for women. The foray made into sectors like palliative care has implications for women in the sense that they constitute more than 50 per cent of the beneficiaries as well as because it has helped reduce to some extent the burden of the informal care economy is now borne by women. It can also be seen that any further investment in the health sector is likely to benefit women more than men since they constitute the majority or single largest group of the patients who frequent the dispensaries.

A micro-analysis of the life and livelihood of Mayana Vettiyan Community in Tamil Nadu is made by **Prof. G. Palanithurai** in chapter ten. Mayana Vettiyan is a Scheduled Caste Community who perform the task of burying and burning the dead human and animal bodies in the villages of Tamil Nadu. It is an assigned function to Dalit families by the dominant communities through the practices evolved historically over a period of time. It is being practiced in the rural areas of the State without much opposition or resistance. After a detailed enquiry on the issue connected with the subject, Prof. Palanithurai came to the conclusion that Vettiyans have to be relieved from such hazardous works and they have to be rehabilitated. The Government Order passed by the Government of Tamil Nadu has to be implemented in letter and spirit. Till government finds alternative to this practice of burning and burying the dead bodies, the grievances of the Vettiyans have to be redressed. Protective measures have to be taken by giving instruments and safety equipments for the works they do. The wage has to be hiked by doubling the wage of unskilled workers. Minimum wage has to be fixed for the work and that can be done by the government. Burial and burning ground should have some basic facilities and the place should be maintained as clean as the divine place. An electric light provision has to be made in the burning ground. Water and toilet facilities have to be created there. Shade giving trees have to be planted in the premises of the burial and burning ground. The graveyard has to be maintained neatly and cleanly. Compound walls have to be constructed. All the above facilities have to be created by the Gram Panchayat. Professional training has to be conducted for them to perform the task more scientifically. There are modern cemeteries constructed by various civil society organisations. These cemeteries never use firewood to burn the bodies. After performing the religious rites, the dead bodies will be inserted into the cemetery. The body will be burnt in the natural heat generated in the cemetery. Government of Tamil Nadu can think of alternative mode of disposal of dead bodies as devised by civil society organisations. Considering the quantum of firewood used for this purpose, an alternative mode can be thought of. Thus, for every five panchayats one cemetery could be created and they can be managed professionally by the local bodies. User fee can be levied from the users. Cost of maintenance can be met from the user fee collected from the users. Thus, this Vettiyans can be liberated from this unscientific task and modernize the very process of burning the dead bodies.

Prof. Palanithurai's second chapter (eleven) is on the functioning of Ombudsman in Tamil Nadu. According to the author, Ombudsman is an institutional mechanism to redress the grievances of the people. Though it originated for public institutions, it has expanded to both public and private institutions and organisations. It is an alternate dispute settlement mechanism. It has to enable the poor to get their grievances redressed without much complication and expenses.[8] It should have simplified procedures and access to the institutions to get their grievances to be redressed. Generally ombudsman in public sector institutions has to supervise the administrative activities of the executive branch. The ombudsman has to receive complaints from the public and investigate the same and resolve the problem. Mostly it is related to conduct of government administration.[9] Essentially the basic objective is to enhance efficiency of public administration and effectiveness of service delivery to the public. It has to ensure government accountability to the public. It has to enhance the transparency of governance and administration. In a democracy governance institutions have to instill confidence among the citizens. There should not be trust deficit. In order to enhance the trust of the people over public institutions efficiency and effectiveness of service delivery has to be monitored and supervised. Basically it is a democratic deepening process.[10] All investigations will exclude judiciary and legislative bodies. Its jurisdiction covers mostly the government departments and other public agencies. It has got powers to make recommendations to bring change in the laws of the country. Basically, the framework of ombudsman relies on its autonomy, adequate powers, adequate institutional facilities, easy procedures, access to public, cost effective, timely delivery, and impartial conduct.[11] The ombudsman should be established through law and it should be made independent. It should have needed autonomy. It should have needed powers to investigate the grievances. It should handle cases with all fairness and sense of justice. Ombudsman should have balance and equipoise to deliver decisions fairly. Hence, it is neither anti-state and anti-people or citizen. Basically, the ombudsman should have power to act and independent from the government. The institutional framework, powers and process of investigation vary from country to country in context. Now, it has to work for the poor as judiciary works above their level of reach as they do not have adequate resources to go to judicial system. Further, basic services are being provided by the local institutions. When the services are not reaching the poor, poor have to have an institutional mechanism to sort out their grievance within their resource capacity. For this purpose even the rich countries have created such mechanism and it also vary from country to country. In India, at present a governance mechanism has been created at the grassroots level constitutionally and the same institutions are delivering basic services to the communities. There is a provision in the institutional arrangement to have a redressal of mechanism through the participation of people in the meetings of Gram Sabha. Apart from the above, there is yet another arrangement created called ombudsman for local bodies. Against this background, the ombudsman created for local bodies in Tamil Nadu is being investigated.

In order to understand the functioning of Ombudsman in the state, the author relied on the documents supplied by the Office of the Ombudsman, Chennai and interacted with the officials of the Ombudsman including the Chief of the Ombudsmen. The interactions on wide range of subjects and for most of the issues, the Chief responded as he is the person to set up the entire office from scratch. Officials have supplied the documents. After examining the varied issues of the subject the author concludes the study by stating that ombudsman for local bodies in Tamil Nadu is new and it is in a nascent stage. For any objective evaluation of the performance of any institution that too on governance, administration and service delivery it requires at least a minimum of five years. Officially, it came into being only on 14th December, 2014. Primarily, it is an investigating agency to inquire into the allegations against the elected representatives, officers and employees of local bodies of Tamil Nadu. Still, it is in the process of establishing itself as a vibrant functional unit to discharge the assigned responsibilities. It is a known fact that Tamil Nadu is always a state prompt in adhering to the mandates of the Constitution. It is not lacking behind any state in compliance with the mandates of the Constitution of India. Whether the state is performing all the activities in line with the spirit of the Constitution of India is a debatable question. It is also a reality in Tamil Nadu many of the institutions have excelled in performance only because of the efficient leadership of the institutions. Thus, leadership plays a crucial role in determining the quality of performance. Against this background, a cursory assessment is undertaken to understand the functioning of the ombudsman in Tamil Nadu. For many of the aspects in local bodies, generally opinion makers used to quote the experience of the Kerala state as it is a pioneering state in establishing a vibrant local buy system in Kerala. Though, it wanted to follow the state of Kerala, Tamil Nadu has not fully followed the state of Kerala. The Gram panchayats and the block panchayats have not included in the ombudsman jurisdiction and they are under the jurisdiction of the inspector of panchayats (District Collector). Many do not know the role of inspector of panchayats. Many are not aware of the ombudsman role of the inspector of panchayats.

Afseer, K.P., Sonny Jose and **Gopakumar, K.** have jointly submitted a chapter (twelve) on the role of local self-governments in the effective implementation of Corporate Social Responsibility. According to the authors, CSR has been considered to be an important principle of corporate governance. It is presumed that such contributions will indeed enrich the social development of the country especially in the nine major areas like education, community health that have been specifically mentioned in the Schedule VII of the Act. Corporate social responsibility is about the role of the business community, about preventing companies from contributing to exacerbation of the problems or, conversely, about the contribution companies can make to solving problems in society.

Although many companies do have CSR projects, the successful accomplishment of each project depends on the identification of real problem, i.e. felt-need. However, serious efforts are seldom taken by the companies to identify the felt need. This dilemma can be rectified to a great extent with the support of local governing institutions working in the lower strata of society. Local Self Government (LSG) Institutions plays an important role in reaching public services to all citizens in India in their respective areas. The bottom-up approach of development is very well applicable with a systematic involvement of LSGs in all development areas for better results especially in social responsibility initiatives of the companies.

The research study is an attempt to portrait the perceived role, expectations and implementation strategy requirements for effectiveness CSR projects execution with the mutual participation of the LSGs. The methodology followed in the study is case studies of experts from various domain including LSGs and corporates are included. The researchers summed up their study by pin-pointing the following facts and findings:

- The concept of Corporate Social Responsibility (CSR) is a company's sense of responsibility towards the community and environment in which it operates. The current perception has grown to acknowledge that the companies achieving good performance in their social, ethical and environmental fields will also perform well in their financial matters. The enactment of New Companies Act in 2013 has mandated CSR in India, and this has led to a very strong discussion on CSR in the country last decade.
- Here CSR is defined as a principle stating that corporations should be accountable for the effects of any of their actions on

their community and environment. Which intend the need of having a healthy relationship for corporates with other social stakeholders of the business organisation. The study is based on the assumption of having a better relationship and involvement for LSGs with corporates, local community and society at large to understand as well as to design an effective solution for the problems, i.e. for felt needs and problems.

- The study is based on the Freemans Stakeholder Management theory in which the role and expectation of different social and non-social stakeholder in the contexts of CSR have very well explained. The methodology followed is case study design in which expert discussions are very well applied.
- The expert discussion with a various segment of people includes academician, policy-maker, NGO professional, LSG official and corporate representative has given a cross-sectional dimensions on perceived role of LSGs in CSR. The areas suggested for CSR projects in the context of state has classified under 10 heads, which all are cross-verified the important to suggest in the socio-cultural and business contexts.
- The major concerns highlighted by many experts are on the inclusion of very specific guidelines on CSR projects undertaking model in the upcoming Panchayat Manual of the state. Also, recommends taking up effective measures and training sessions for LSG officials to increase the awareness level of CSR and future possibilities.

In chapter thirteen, **Prof. M. Sarngadharan** made a study on the legal configuration of GST in the Indian e-Commerce industry. E-Commerce industry according to the author is a broad term that evinces the exchange of services and products online, inclusive of services of all kinds as well as affiliate, physical, and digital products that involve an exchange of funds online. The Goods and Services Tax (GST) has subsumed various indirect taxes in India, like Service Tax, VAT, and Excise Duty and so on, since its introduction in the commencement of July 2017. This has fortified the indirect tax mechanism of both central and state governments in simplifying the taxation system in India with the displacement of multiple taxes. This chapter attempts to assess: (a) the structure of e-commerce industry in India; (b) the salient provisions of the GST Act, 2017 pertaining to the e-commerce industry; and (c) apparent after-effect of the unravelled by GST rules on the e-commerce industry.

Secondary data available in research reports and periodicals were collected and used for the work. The e-commerce sector has been still under preparation by focusing on provisions specific to this sector in the GST Act. The success of e-commerce sector is largely dependent on the increasing number of retail entrepreneurs, who fall in the unorganized retail sector category. The government has included such players in the ambit of GST with an intention of broadening the tax base and has introduced specific provisions for the e-commerce companies.

The author has made a detailed investigation connected with the subject which is quite new to the commerce and management fields. His areas of enquiry include the structure of e-Commerce Industry, models of e-Commerce deals, prospects of e-Commerce, GST in Indian e-Commerce sector, Legal disposition etc. Thereafter the author concludes his study by stating that with the inclusion of retail entrepreneurs in the ambit of GST and the introduction of specific provisions for e-commerce companies, certain areas of GST will impact the e-commerce sector. Every company in India, be it a multinational company or a small/medium enterprise, is gearing up for the implementation of GST. The e-commerce sector would follow suit in its preparation by focusing on provisions specific to this sector in the GST law. The success of the e-commerce sector is largely dependent on the increasing number of retail entrepreneurs, who fall in the unorganized retail sector category. The government has included such players in the ambit of GST with an intention of broadening the tax base and has introduced specific provisions for the e-commerce companies.

After a study on GST, **Dr. Shahir Bhatt** and **Amola Bhatt** made a study on M-Commerce (chapter fourteen) and its influence on the consumer's perceptions. According to the authors, inclusive growth means ensuring that India's economic development lifts all boats; which is a critical national priority. One kcy focus has been on the role of Indian companies in enabling inclusive growth. The explosive growth of penetration and usage of mobile devices is frequently noted in research studies. Mobile commerce is the subset of e-commerce, which includes all e-commerce transactions, carried out using a mobile (hand held) device. Mobile commerce can be used to tackle the issues of productivity and sustainability. So the chapter tries to explore the perceptions of consumers towards M-commerce. The authors are of the contention that Mobile is becoming the dominant means for accessing communications primarily because deploying mobile network is not only more cost-efficient but also mobile provides greater flexibility and convenience to its subscribers than landline telephone. Mobile Commerce is the subset of e-commerce, which includes all e-commerce transactions, carried out using a mobile (hand held) device. Mobile commerce, which is commonly referred to as m-commerce, has become an important concept in today's business environment. The research design for the study is descriptive in nature and the sampling unit consists consumers who are aware of M-commerce. The questionnaire constructed for the study included several questions which were continuous and categorical in nature. A scale was constructed with five point Likert type statements in which respondents were asked to indicate their level of agreement (1 = strongly disagree to 5 = strongly agree). For this study, the scale constructed by Bhatti (2007) was used which comprised 20 Likert scale statements. The final study involved a survey conducted in Ahmedabad between January and February 2014. The sampling technique used for the study was convenient sampling. Reponses were obtained from 179 respondents. SPSS 19 was used to analyze the data. Factor Analysis along with Cluster Analysis was used to analyse the data collected.

The authors while summing up their study state that the prolific usage of mobile devices and the growth in the mobile sales has opened an array of opportunities as far as payment and settlements are concerned. Following e-commerce and its success story, m-commerce has also paved its way to success. Hence, the current study investigates the factors which influence people in resorting to m-commerce transactions and further also segregates the consumers according to their characteristics.

The factors which erupted from the study which influence the usage of M-commerce were Attitude towards M-commerce, Perceived Benefits, Adventure, Perceived Risk and Idea. Further, three segments of M-commerce users were brought out from the study, which included Reserved Shoppers, Utilitarian Shoppers, and Assured Shoppers. Assured shoppers were the ones who were already using M-commerce and were contented with the same, utilitarian shoppers used M-commerce when they perceived it to be beneficial while reserved shoppers showed inhibitions in resorting to M-commerce.

In Chapter fifteen, **Nishamol, M.** and **Rajesh, K.** have presented a study on reproduction of marginality through developmentalism. It is a case study carried out at Attapadi Tribal belt of Kerala. According to the authors, the discourses on development is closely linked with the progress in the lives of human beings which lies in the attainment of socio-economic stability and quality of life through the effective usages of natural resources and human capabilities. Similarly, as the promotion of the socio-economic and cultural development of tribal population, the governments have been implementing lot of projects in the tribal areas. Attappady is one among the marginalised tribal belts in Kerala, so as the governments distribute lot of fund for the welfare of tribes in this area through various projects. Attappady is a good example of how the distorted development projects of government affect the way of life of tribal communities without considering the necessities of the end users of projects. Among these, the tribal economy was worse affected by the AWCEC project of AHADS. They attempted to implement the activities of eco-restoration project to the affected areas in the name of donor-recipient concept, especially among the tribal lands. This negatively affected the tribal population in Attappady in such a way of destruction in agriculture culture as well as agriculture land and also their traditional livelihood sources. The lack of proper exit policies and failure of proper planning for long-term livelihood assistance are the noted drawbacks of AHADS. Through the direct or indirect intervention of AHADS, the tribal communities unrooted from their traditional cultural capabilities.

In chapter sixteen, **Dr. Md. Ayub Malik** presented a study on location of democracy and governance in India with special reference to the participation among tribals in Burdwan district of West Bengal. After making a detailed empirical study covering varied issues the author concludes his study by stating that the success of parliamentary democracy depends upon willingness of the minority to accept the majority rule, agreement on fundamental rules of the game and eternal vigilance of the public. Otherwise, it will weaken democracy, what Norberto Bobbio (1987) calls 'broken promises' of democracy. Bobbio warns about the defects in inherence that without proper application and operation democracy might result in discordance, irregularities, disorder and instability. So, due respect to the rules of the game, both constitutive and regulatory should there be. The simple fact of the matter is that the world has never built a multi-ethnic democracy in which no particular ethnic group is in majority and where political equality, social equality and economies that empower all have been achieved. Representation is public, therefore, no secret session, secret agreements be committed to ensure democracy educative, creative, logical and comprehensive, in essence, harmless and idyllic. Today's parliamentary democracy drifts away from its purposes and goals abolishing separation of powers between executive, legislature and judiciary, freedom of the individuals and parliamentary privileges and immunities, thereby public suffers from terrible disillusionment about parties and parliaments as of close-door politics of party coteries and formality politics of parliamentarians. Therefore, openness and discussion are two main pillars of parliamentarism, i.e. truth and justice. Here, participation in politics and participation in the development process are also important. Further, according to the author, there are four measures of protecting democracy, namely following the rules of the game of democracy, giving the opportunity and legitimacy to political opponents or opposition parties, toleration of political violence and giving the political opponents to flourish to take part in socio-political dialogue.

Dr. S.N. Rao contributed a chapter (seventeen) captioned 'Village Adoption: Transforming Rural World–A Case Study of Jorandajhariya'. This chapter depicts the stages and sagas of development mission carried out in a backward underdeveloped village, named Jorandajhariya.

In chapter Eighteen **Swapna Aji** made an enquiry on the methods and measures followed by Scheduled Caste women enterprises in the state of Kerala for marketing their products and services. This is against the backdrop that the main bane confronted by small and medium enterprises in the State is found to the problems in respect of marketing the products both in local external markets. Marketing strategies differ with respect to rural areas and urban areas and from business to business. There are caste differences in the sphere of marketing opportunities and also with respect to various avenues that linked entrepreneurship with marketing. Development of scheduled caste women owned enterprises through strategic interventions in various realm of marketing helps in accelerating entrepreneurship among scheduled caste women. The scheduled caste women owned industries in the State were identified for the present study and classified based on the nature of business into nine categories for the analysis and interpretation of the data. The data required for the research paper was collected from both primary sources and secondary sources.

In chapter Nineteen **Akhil, K.O**. has made a study on the economic status of de-notified tribes in Palakkad District of Kerala. The chapter inspects economic status of Denotified Tribes (DNTs) of Kerala. The study is based on primary data collected from Palakkad District. The only one DNT people group in Kerala is Domban. The investigation results demonstrate that DNTs in Kerala are marginalised from the standard advancement process. They are the marginalised among the marginalised. These individuals linger behind in accomplishing least instructive dimension. The vast majority of the families are compelled to stop their traditional occupation on account of inadequate income. Families from these network holds just little land. Their living condition is very poor. Some of them do open defecation even today. The vast majority of the families are compelled to stop their traditional occupation on account of inadequate income. In the concluding chapter the **volume editors** presents a paper on the relevance of Sarvodaya Approach of Decentralisation in the present day national context.

Keeping this background in view, an attempt has been made in his volume to address the issues pertaining to a wide-ranging areas and aspects of Digital Governance in the context of Decentralised Governance. The topics covered include e-Governance in India with focus on Second ARC Report, Role of Digital Technology in the Governance for Local Development with Special Focus on Smart Cities, Social Welfare and its Linkages with Digital Governance and Digital India, Importance of gender Digital Divide, Knowledge Management and e-Governance, e-Government Development Index, DigiLocker in Transforming e-Governance, Delivering Justice at the Grassroots, Decentralisation and Healthcare, Micro-Analysis of the Life and Livelihood of Mayana Vettiyan Community, CSR and its role in LSGs, Functioning of Ombudsman, Village Adoption and Transforming Rural World, Economic Status of De-Notified Tribes, Marketing Methods in Women Enterprises, m-Commerce and Legal Configuration of GST in the Indian e-Commerce Industry. The chapters are contributed by senior academics and development experts with rich experience on the core areas of the study. In their submission the authors have highlighted the existing issues and problems connected with the subject and put forward solid suggestions to revamp the system.

REFERENCES

Flak, L.S., Olsen, D.H. and Wolcott, P. (2005). "Local E-Government in Norway", *Scandinavian Journal of Information Systems*, Volume 17, No. 2, pp. 41–48.

Second Administrative Reform Commission Report, Promoting E-Governance; the Smart way Forward, Government of India, New Delhi, 2008, https://darpg.gov.in/arc-reports

https://shodhganga.inflibnet.ac.in/bitstream/10603/5433/9/09_chapter% 204.pdf

http://www.ignou.ac.in/upload/B2U2cit-002.pdf

http://unpan1.un.org/intradoc/groups/public/documents/un/unpan038851. pdf (19/11/2011)

http://www.apdip.net/projects/e-government/capblg/casestudies/India-Chandrashekhar.pdf (20/3/2011) http://www.it.iitb.ac.in/~prathabk/egovernance/egov_ict.html (20/6/2011)

http://www.unescap.org/pdd/prs/ProjectActivities/Ongoing/gg/governance.asp (16/7/2011)

More than most IT systems, e-Governance applications need to be secured by Trivedi Pujya published in http://www. Express computeronline.com (7/6/2008)

The Working Group on E-Government in the Developing World, "Roadmap for E-government in the Developing World, 10 Questions E-Government Leaders Should Ask Themselves", April 2002.

http://ictanddevelopment.blogspot.com/2009/06/ict-and-e-governance.html (14/7/2011)

http://arc.gov.in/11threp/ARC_11thReport (10/3/2011)

http://www.indg.in/e-governance (15/3/2011)

http://www.indg.in/e-governance/e-governance/egov-plan (17/7/2011)

http://www.mit.gov.in/content/mission-mode-projects (20/9/2011)

http://www.tulip.net/Product_Service/EGovernance.htm (19/10/2011)

http://en.wikipedia.org/wiki/E-readiness (19/11/2011)

http://www.csi-sigegov.org/E-Governence/e_Governance.pdf (9/2/2011)

http://omec.uab.cat/Documentos/mitjans_dem_gov/0138.pdf (17/7/2011)

PART ONE
Digital Governance

1

Role of Digital Technology in Governance for the Local Development: Issues in Local Government Administration of Upcoming Smart Cities in India

A Case Study of Nagpur District

Neelima Deshmukh

Digital India is a latest flagship programme of Government of India to transform India into complete digitally empowered as well as IT enabled and knowledge economy of the world. The main aim of this brainchild of PM Narendra Modiji is to provide Indian citizens electronic government services by reducing the paper work and reducing the corruption and red tapism saving the manpower and time. No doubt it is a very good technique of good governance which was launched on 1st July, 2015 to ensure that the government services are made available to the citizens electronically by improving online infrastructure and internet connectivity. The digital India provides intensified impetus for further momentum and the progress for e-governance and would promote inclusive growth that covers electronic services, products, devices manufacturing and the job opportunities. The main aim is to reform governance through technology. This three dimensional vision of this programme is to provide digital utility to every citizen Governance and Services on demand and Digital empowerment of the citizens.

E-Governance, Good Governance and Smart Governance

The practice of good governance has been widely facilitated with the use of Information and Communication Technology (ICT) is globally used to deliver services to its citizens in most effective, efficient and transparent manner. India being a land of diversity spanning across culture, traditions, languages and uneven economic conditions needs effective governance as a tool particularly for the rural population for all-round development of Rural Society. It is no more technological innovation available only to few elites, but it is a need of hour and has become vital necessity for efficient, transparent and democratic governance and public service delivery too. India too has been successfully incorporating e-governance techniques for service delivery and building citizen-centric administration but still there is a need to develop more holistic, easily accessible participative approach to e-governance. The issues of equality and development in socioeconomic fields still remains farfetched but equality, empowerment, participation and transformation seems to be achievable through virtual world of internet which has become a powerful tool of shaping the public opinion as well as good governance through the use of digital and ICT tools leading to real empowerment of the people. All the more its importance increases many fold when it aims at development at grassroots base levels of the local bodies which are committed to the public empowerment in letter and spirit for its face-lifting.

Thus, e-governance in its essence is application of Information Technology to government functioning in order to create simple, Moral, Accountable, Responsive, and Transparent (SMART) Governance. While e-governance is defined as mere a delivery of government services and information to public using electronic means, e-governance allows for direct participation of the constituents in government activities. E-governance is the development, deployment and enforcement of the policies, laws, and regulations necessary to support the functioning of knowledge society as well as e-governance. Application of e-governance in the recent past have demonstrated surprising results in terms of quality services, data bank creation, tracking and monitoring system, interacting with departments and related organizations. If the attributes of good governance are transparency, efficiency, responsiveness and accountability, e-governance is the means to attain these attributes through application of technology.

Importance of Good Governance

Good Governance conceptualized in the past as ideal state of Ramrajya has suddenly entered into the vocabulary of Public Administration since 1990s. Traditionally the governance refers to the form of political system and the manner in which the power is exercised in utilizing country's economic and social resources for the development. Good governance is associated with efficient and effective administration in a democratic framework. It is purposive and the development oriented administration which is committed to the improvement of the quality of life of the people. It implies high level of organisational effectiveness and also relates to the capacity of centre of power of political and administrative system to cope with the emerging challenges of the society. It refers to the adoption of new values of governance to establish the efficiency, legitimacy and credibility of the system. In simple terms good governance can be considered as citizen friendly, citizen caring and responsive administration.

Good and humane governance is the most important issue faced by the country today which is tottering under the weight of political and bureaucratic corruption. Good governance implies gearing up of the government machinery and administrative structure to provide, responsive, transparent, clean, and people friendly administration. Further it is also considered as an act or manner of governing the way of control. It is linked up with the role of the state what it can do or cannot do matching its capacity and the resources to undertake the task assigned for itself.

Good Governance from the Systems Perspectives

Administration *vis-à-vis* does not function in isolation, it has to respond to the changing situation every now and then responding to the public demands and the call of nation and need of the hour effectively and the governance operates under the fluctuating scenario of currents, undercurrents, cross-currents etc. coping up with the constant change hence needs to be seen from the systems perspectives facing various problems and challenges from various aspects for delivering the goods and services to the public as an end product.

E-Governance and Smart Governance

With the global advent of Good Governance, Structural Adjustment Programme introducing New Economic Policies, in 1991 India was facing new challenges of Liberalization, Privatization, and Globalization, posed a challenge to respond to the process of development which was governed by market as a principal factor across the international borders inviting attention of the scholars, policy-makers, administrators to the struggle for existence and the survival of fittest. In this process extremely technocracy situation aroused which was effectively contributing to handling the change successfully. In order to respond to the tenets of New Public Management (NPM) philosophy to ensure the speedy delivery of the results through latest technology-oriented computer era emerged on the scene giving rise to e-Governance system which was totally a new concept and venture for the Indian society to adopt but there was no choice other than to respond to this challenge particularly in the rural development background as majority of Indian population hails from the rural background.

Smart Cities

The ambitious project of Smart Cities in India came into an existence on 15th August, 2015 when the Prime Minister Shri Narendra Modiji made this announcement from the Red Fort of India on the historical occasion. The objectives of the smart cities Mission is to promote cities that provide core infrastructure and give a decent quality of life to its citizens, a clean and sustainable environment and applications of the smart solutions. The focus is on the sustainable environment and inclusive development. The idea is to look at compact areas, create a replicable model which will act like a light house to other aspiring cities. Smart Cities Mission of Government of India is a bold initiative meant to set the examples that can be replicated both within and outside the Smart City catalyzing the creation of similar Smart Cities in various regions and the part of the country.

Accordingly the purpose of Smart Cities Mission is to drive economic growth and improve the quality life of the people by enabling the local area development and harnessing the technology that leads to the smart outcomes. Area based development will transform the existing areas (retrofit and redevelop) including the slums into the better planned ones, thereby improving the liveability of the whole city. New areas Greenfield would be developed around the cities in order to accommodate the expanding population in urban areas, application of the smart solutions will enable the cities to use technology information and the data to improve infrastructure and services. Comprehensive development in this way will improve the quality of life, create employment and enhance the incomes for all, especially the poor and disadvantaged leading to inclusive cities. The data to improve infrastructure and services. Comprehensive development in this way will improve the quality of life, create employment and enhance the incomes for all, especially the poor and disadvantaged leading to inclusive cities.

1. "Total Winning Projects Proposals: 100
2. Total urban population impacted: 99,630,0639
3. Total Area Based Development Cost: 1,64,204 crore
   Total PAN city solution; 38,914 crore."[1]

According to the Ministry of Housing and Urban Affairs, till now 97 SVPs have been constituted to execute the Projects selected under Smart Cities Mission. Tenders have been issued for 1686 Projects worth 63,000 crore in various Smart Cities while 1200 projects more than Rs. 38000 crore are under the implementation.[2] Smart Cities Mission is the largest mission with citizen consultations ever undertaken and has a long incubation programme. Every city took about 12-15 months to establish SVPs and identify Project Management Consultants, but now with 97 Special Purpose vehicle and 82 PMCs in place the mission is going well and truly on its way, (Ministry Tweeted) Each Smart City will have an SVP headed by full time CEO and have nominees of Central Government, State Government and Urban local bodies on its Board. Additionally in order to provide safety and better services to the citizens 11 States of the Art Command and Control centres have been operationalised and another 17 centres are on their way. Tenders have been called for additional 31 centres across the country.[3] Under the mission cities propose to take up various projects including Smart roads, rejuvenation of water bodies, cycle tracks, walking paths, Smart Classrooms, Skills Development Centres, upgrading health facilities and Pan city project like integrated command and control centre.

E-governance issues assumes greater importance in the context of Nagpur district as it is one of the 100 cities included in the list of Smart cities aimed at the all-round development throughout the country and it is emerging very fast as not only as Metro city but also the smart city working for its holistic development on war footing for meeting the parameters of global standards, with huge infra structure coming up to cater to needs of the globalization and the citizen of this new era. With the advent of international ambitious project of MIHAN (The Multi-modal International Hub Airport at Nagpur):

In order to attract the foreign investors all the plans, programmes and strategies are being implemented through local institutions such as Nagpur Municipal Corporation, Nagpur Improvement Trust, Zilla Parishad and other Panchayat Raj Institutions effectively and efficiently. Further due to the continuous migration of people from neighbouring and other various areas, the population has grown up to the large extent and the city limits have been extended to the additional radius of 25 KMs. including 721 villages. Naturally, the existing setup of local government institutions is finding it difficult to cope up with the situation and are facing the problems of various nature such as administrative, financial, legal, social which are hindering the process of development. Nagpur being the seat of political power, with committed leadership, and tremendous support from ruling party, is expected to deliver the results in effective and measurable terms but the various factors are hampering the growth and the development of this sub-capital of Maharashtra. One needs to study what are those factors.

Why Case Study of Nagpur?

I. Nagpur District: The Evolving Metro Region of Vidarbha: Nagpur is a third largest city of Maharashtra and is a sub-capital of state. It is the 13th largest urban agglomeration in India and the largest city in Vidarbha Region which comprises of 11 districts. It has one of the highest literacy rate of 91.92 per cent among all the urban agglomerations in India and one of the proposed Smart Cities from Maharashtra.[4]

Since 1990s the agglomeration of the city has rapidly expanded beyond the municipal boundaries. The unplanned growth has posed certain challenges for the future growth of the city and its fringes in an organized manner. With a view to achieve balanced development within the region, the Nagpur Improvement Trust (NIT) has been notified as the Special Planning Authority (SPA) for the Nagpur Metropolitan Area (NMA) and entrusted with preparation of a Statutory Development Plan as per provisions of the MRTP Act, 1966. The notified NMA comprises areas outside the Nagpur city and includes 721 villages under 9 tehsils of the Nagpur District spreading across an area of 3,567 km^2.

In 1999, the Government of Maharashtra declared that the Nagpur Metropolitan Area shall comprise all of Nagpur city, Nagpur Gramin (rural areas near Nagpur), Hingna, Parseoni, Mauda and Kamptee Taluka and parts of Savner, Kalmeshwar, Umred and Kuhi. The boundaries of the "Metro region" around the municipal corporation limits of the city have been defined as per the notification with the addition of almost 721 villages around the city.

In 2002, the government extended the jurisdiction of the Nagpur Improvement Trust (NIT) by 25 to 40 kilometres. This new area was defined under clause 1(2) of NIT Act,1936 as "Nagpur Metropolitan Area"[5].

Area of Nagpur region/District	9810 km^2
Area proposed for Metroregion	25 to 40 km
Area around Nagpur Municipal limit	3780 km^2
Area Under NMC limit	218 km^2

NIT has proposed the Metro region plan in two phases:

Phase I	area 1520 km^2
Phase II	area 2260 km^2

II. Nagpur Metro Rail: The Nagpur Metro Rail project is announced by the state government of Maharashtra for the city with the expenses of Rs. 4,400 crore and Rs. 3,800 crore for its two phases of 25 km (from Sitabuldi to MIHAN and Butibori via Airport) and 20 km (Sitabuldi to Automotive Square in Kamptee) respectively.

The site inspection has already begun in March 2012 with the initiatives from Nagpur Improvement Trust. The project will be executed by a new company called Nagpur Metro Rail Co. Ltd. (NMRCL) formed under the NIT. In July 2015, the project has been approved by Government of Maharashtra and has been given "In Principle" nod by MoUD of Government of India. The Bhoomipujan for Metro rail work has been performed on 21 August, 2014 at the hands of prime minister Shri Narendra Modi.

III. The Multi-modal International Hub Airport at Nagpur (MIHAN): It is a project for the Dr. Babasaheb Ambedkar International Airport, Nagpur. It is the biggest economical development project currently underway in India in terms of investments. The project aims to exploit the central location of Nagpur and convert the airport into a major cargo hub with integrated road and rail connectivity. This project consists of two parts:

- An international airport to act as a cargo hub, and
- A Special Economic Zone (SEZ) with residential zone covering an area of 40.25 km^2 on the southern end of Nagpur.

The Government of Maharashtra formed a special purpose entity, Maharashtra Airport Development Company, for the development of MIHAN. The project is financed by Indian banks with a loan of INR 3,000 million along with investment from the state government and Airports Authority of India. With a projected target of serving 14 million passengers and handling 0.87 million tonnes of cargo, this is one of the largest aviation projects in India. The estimated capital cost of the project is INR 2581 crore (by the year 2035) and it is supposed to generate revenues INR 5280 crore.

With the growing challenges of modernization and the expected response of the government to meet those, the government of Maharashtra has its commitment for the development it has undertaken two ambitious programmes for world-wide connectivity for free trade according to new terms of globlisation providing facilities for its economic activities from local to global level raising not only the standards of living of a common man but bettering the job opportunities and achieving the international standards. Since India has adopted the model of Britain for all its practical purposes this evolving metro city is expected to be more or less on the line of London city. Needless to say that it is a Herculean task creating a landmark in the Indian history facilitating the very fast transition of development phase which was a day dream for all of us. India being a signatory to Millennium Development Programme along with the newly introduced happiness Index, creation of infrastructural facilities as a way bridge to respond to the achievement of developed state is its established priority.

Nagpur Metropolitan Area comprises all Nagpur city and the rural area including 721 villages under the 9 tehsils of the district. Therefore, e-governance as an instrument to the local to global level development and coping up of the challenges of LPG the local government has face many challenges and overcome the problems and the issues of administration responding to change of paradigm of New Public Management. Also while launching such a extra-big venture it would be appropriate to visualize its prospects as well to have clear picture and blueprint of the committed vision and mission. Therefore, this topic has been of immense importance with its practical relevance and the need of the hour from the from the systems perspectives. If very thing goes as per plans the Nagpur city located at zero mile distance would be seeing the new modern era meeting the needs of new generation with a sustainable development, Although the crucial role of digital technology cannot be undermined at any point of time in the context of Smart Governance it is a very tough proposal to implement the same on the gigantic level of building Smart Cities of international standards with a progressive vision on account various administrative, financial, technical, legal, and social issues which are intermingling with each other from the Systems Perspective indeed. Out of the many few problem areas are enumerated as follows:

Issues and the Problem Areas

1. Rural-Urban Divide: A lopsided Development: The infrastructural development work like constructions of roads, flyovers, bridges, commencement of Metro Mono Rail project, facilities and development of facilities for attracting the international companies through its MIHAN project is going on in its full swing throughout the city is creating lot of inconveniences to the citizens in terms of distorted traffic at times leading to the loss of lives agreed its all part of the game. By now the Nagpurians are used to this life. True to the slogan today's pain is tomorrow's gain. But there is a huge discrepancy observed while delivering the performances, the urban area/city is coming up very fast but at the same time the rural area seems to be neglected and devoid of any mentionable work. So the rift urban-rural continues to grow instead of bridging the gap.

2. NMC's e-Governance modules are not in working conditions: Since most of the work is focused in city area, mainly Nagpur Municipal Corporation is playing pivotal role in supplying the very basic amenities to the citizen of upcoming smart city. But it is observed that contrary to the expectations NMC's e-Governance modules are not in working conditions proving the sheer negligence of officers of NMC around 90 per cent modules are not in working conditions.[6] NMC conferred with the national level "Skoch gold award 2014 for introducing comprehensive e-Governance programme has failed in its implementation of modules. The Civic body has spent Rs. 17 crore on the development of those e-government modules. E-Government Foundation TCS and Aryansh Company had developed 64 different modules for the paperless and transparent system which were reduced to 37 for its convenience. Further it is also learnt that senior level officers are not user friendly with the online system as they have not undergone any type of training to handle the operations. Recently the NMC has decided to engage Project Management Unit (PMU) to manage its e-governance system which will comprise one Principal Consultant, Senior Consultant and Consultants. These experts will be hired Deloitte, Ernest and Young, Grant Thornton, PWC, KPMG and Wipro. However, this decision is long pending and the file is not cleared by the Municipal Commissioner who is on leave for more than one month. The leave is just an eyewash but in reality the non-cordial relations between the officials and non-officials are the underlying cause for this delay. On account of this situation property tax department is most affected due to the failure of e-Governance system as a data of more than 2 lakh properties is not uploaded in the system which is ultimately leading to the non-collection of revenue to the desired levels. The modules like Birth and Death Management System, Works Management System, Property Tax Grievances, PWD Contractor Licence Management System, Finance Management System, Fire Services and Emergency Departments, Marriage Registration Document Management System, City Web Portal, and Hospital Management Systems are in working conditions. As far as building permission is concerned the Planning Department has moved on Maharashtra Government's system to grant permission to building Plans, sanitation and the drainage system is also not working as NMC is using Fleet Vigil System, while in the Education Department its using Ahalarath System of the State Government. Trade Licence Management System, Hospital Licence Management System, Veterinary Licence Management System and the Electrical Contractor Licence Management Systems are not in use due to various other reasons. The Systems are vulnerable to huge corruption and the Department is not ready to mark the System transparent has been the allegations of the contractors whose huge outstanding dues are long pending and the NMC is not paying much attention and seriousness to it.

In addition to it other Departments like Land and Estate, and Market Management System, Social Welfare, Library, Legal Case Management System, Garden Records, slums, Workshop Roads, Quality Control System, Hot Mix plant, Cattle Pond Committee, Sports and Cultural Committee, Special desk office, Pench and other major projects, Dashboard and Enforcement Departments are not functioning on e-Government modules. No doubt the local body is implementing several innovative ideas to improve the system. However, officers and employees do not want to use it for their own convenience and the vested interest making the mockery of Prop people concept of the Government.

3. Shortage of Funds and strained relations of officials and non-officials: With multiple huge developmental on going activities in the city, the due and legitimate payments for the various tenders executed on behalf of the local bodies, are unpaid for years together and the contractors are not getting their bills and payments released on time to continue further stages of their assigned project works. And there is too much of discontent over the issues, and the they have formed a chain, all of them together refusing to undertake any work with the NMC. Majority of the construction works has been outsourced to outsider venders who have been engaging the local petty contractors for minor work. Even for the regular work of NMC the same situation continues as there is always a paucity of funds and the proportionate quantum of funds are never available. Due to the non-functioning of e-governance modules, the targeted revenue from the taxation has not been raised and NMC is struggling with the poor financial conditions of cash strapped NMC, the Municipal Commissioner has issued a directive to clip the wings of Corporators and the officers of the local bodies. As per the directions, now every Corporator will get Rs. 1.25 lakh per month for the development work in his/her ward, meaning 20 lakh per month to every zone for the development[7] as per the directives of the Corporator which is a very meagre amount to talk about. This has triggered resentment amongst the Public representatives who are planning to undertake various development works in their *prabhag*. The Commissioner has also applied brakes over the distribution of the funds from additional Municipal Commissioner to Assistant Municipal Commissioner level.

It may also be mentioned here that the Chairman of Standing Committee presented a 2018-19 budget of Rs. 2900 crore before the general body which didn't match the targets.[8] Therefore, the Commissioner took this strong decision to maintain a balance between committed and development expenditure. Previous Municipal Commissioners have also applied such measure to maintain the financial balance in the local body. The Commissioner has further fixed financial and administrative approval limits of 50 lakh per month for the subordinate officers, and 20 lakh for the Assistant Municipal Commissioner and departmental heads per month. Four Deputy Municipal Commissioners will be having the powers to sanction works up to Rs. 40 lakh. Total Financial powers delegated to the officers is up to Rs. 6 crore per annum and the Assistant Municipal Commissioner will spend Rs. 2.40 crore per annum. This curtailing of financial powers have irked the elected representatives who were very enthusiastic about starting new projects in their area before 2019 elections, which has led to the confrontation between official and non-officials' powers leading to chaos and non-cooperation leading to the stranded and tardy growth of development when the city has been included in the ambitious Project of Smart Cities Mission deserves much more than this.

(a) Sanction of Special Grants of Rs. 150 crore by the State Government: After the hue and cry, followed by the threats of the civil, electrical contractors, and the bus operators have issued the warning to NMC to release their funds immediately or face the stir, totally stopping ongoing development work. The Government of Maharashtra on the initiative of the Chief Minister intervened into the matter as a result of which a special grant of Rs. 150 crore was sanctioned and released immediately to meet the requirement of stalled payments of ongoing work of the city. Be it mentioned here that the Urban Development Department in its order stated that the earlier government had released Rs. 15 crore per annum from 1995-2000 for the special development of second capital of Maharashtra which later on was not released by the successive governments. Now the present BJP lead government with their strong political lobby headed by the Chief Minister Shri Devendra Fadnavis has revived the pattern and decided to release this special fund of Rs. 150 crore for undertaking the special development of orange city. Further considering its financial crises, the Finance department of NMC suggested to the local body to request the government to release the special grants of Rs. 25 crore to suffice the requirement for undertaking the developmental work. Since the Corporation doesn't have its own resources to continue with the development work at this pace, therefore, they need special financial assistance justifying their demand for the special grants.

The committed expenditure of the local body over the salary, pension grants, electricity, raw water bill, payment to orange city water body, petrol, diesel, telephone bills, security, repayment of loan, garbage lifting etc. is around Rs. 92 crore.[8] In addition to this abolition of octroi and Local Body Tax (LBT) the civic body is receiving only Rs. 52 crore against Goods and Service Tax (GST) from the state government which is very meagre as compared to income generated from the octroi in the past. In addition to these constraints, the recovery from the property tax is also very poor mainly due to failure of ineffective performance of e-Governance module aimed at smooth paperless, transparent and Smart governance in the institution. Therefore, the civic body is facing many difficulties in contributing towards the development work as well as to maintain public transport system efficiently.

(b) Collection of Goods and Services Taxes from the Contractors:

Additional Revenue: Focusing attention to the financial crunch of the civic body the strict measures to collect 2 per cent GST from the contractors as tax deducted at source from the bills of the contractors and suppliers were adopted from October 2018. Till now this TDS was not deducted at source for last 15 months. According to the directions issued by the government under section 51 of GST Act, 2017 to deduct 2 per cent TDS against GST from the bills of the contractors and suppliers for the due payment of more than Rs. 2.50,000 not otherwise. The local body will have to issue the TDS certificate within 5 days of crediting the amount to the government treasury. In case of failure to make the payment before due date then 18 per cent per annum interest will be charged, delay in filing TDS will also attract the penalty. Earlier local body deducted value added tax (VAT) from the bills of contractor and suppliers but after the enforcement of GST the government deferred the deduction of GST from the bills of the contractor. This strict vigilance and the measure adopted proved effective because of which the revenue to the tune of Rs. 52 crore was raised additionally[9].

(c) State Government relaxes the condition for the utilization of Rs. 150 crore: Special Fund: It was within the span of one week the Government of Maharashtra issued 2 government resolutions, which is a very rare phenomenon otherwise. It permits NMC to release outstanding payments of the development work. As per the directive of the earlier GR dated December 12, 2017 imposed the condition to spend money only for the new work which created hurdles for the Municipal corporation to release the payments to the contractors and the ongoing development work which has already been done.[10] Ultimately the ruling party pleaded with the Chief Minister to revise the said GR and remove this condition in the interest of the prevailing situation. The new GR was issued immediately relaxing the earlier conditions and authorized Nagpur Municipal Corporation to spend the released fund of Rs. 150 crore as per its requirement and priority. So as on today the civic body has more than Rs. 200 crore in their treasury to carry on the development work in full swing.[11] The State Government in its order clearly mentioned that Nagpur is a second capital of Maharashtra, therefore, the Government has released special financial assistance to the civic body, of course, because of its status as the upcoming metro city of the State.

Conclusion

Laying emphasis on universal digital literacy, and availability of the digital resources/services in Indian language, which would facilitate to meet the challenges of LPG era, upcoming Smart Cities, Metro cities, and other infrastructural development of the nation at world class level. It assumes greater relevance and importance in the context of Smart City wherein every household and the individual will be digitally empowered having the thrust on IT the great enabler for empowerment, equity and efficiency. It focuses on the broad banding villages, participative governance, digital learning, telemedicine, mobile health care, e-learning tools, skills development, jobs creation, open source and open standards, e-bhasha and others.

(a) This time-bound project is to be completed by 2019. Today till November 2018 there is no visible movement and impact of the programme and hardly only few elites know about it and the ordinary common man is totally ignorant and unaware about his programme for whom it is meant. But looking at the grim picture, administrative issues, other complexities, very slow and tardy growth of this upcoming Smart City of Nagpur there is an acute need to create awareness and sensitize public to accept, welcome and handle this change in their progressive life. But at this moment it is very disheartening and disappointing to witness performance of the local government institutions at zero development rate, very slow non-noticeable at grassroots level the needs to be expedited at multiple levels with the corrective measure to overcome the lacunae to improve the present scenario.

(b) More precise, perfect, electronic instruments, equipments and logistics along with high precision trouble free citizen friendly computersation, digitalization procedure should be developed and adopted for the easy access.

(c) With the effective and strong powerful ruling Bhartiya Janata Party's existence from local to central level headed by its committed strong willed leadership for the nation's development, the administration is running smoothly streamlining its objectives, and overcoming all hurdles, difficulties, and the constraints thereby delivering the desired visible results to the last man of this city leading to the Vidarbha's holistic development.

REFERENCES

1. https://enwikipedia.org/wiki/Smart_city
2. Ministry of Housing and Urban Affairs: Tweet, quoted by "*the Hitvada, Nagpur*", dated: August 24, 2018.
3. *Ibid.*
4. https://enwikipedia.org/wiki/Nagpur#citi _note 15
5. https://enwikipedia.org/wiki/Nagpur#citinoteMetroRegion88
6. *The Hitvada*, Nagpur Dated City line page No. 5, dated 08 July, 2018.
7. *The Hitvada*, Nagpur Dated page No. 1 City line. 2nd August, 2018.
8. *Ibid.,* page 1 City Line. 23 October, 2018.
9. *Ibid.,* page 1 City Line. 25 October, 2018.
10. *Ibid.,* page 1 City Line. 30 October, 2018.
11. *Ibid.,* page 1 City Line. 2 November, 2018.

2

E-Governance in India

The Second Administrative Reforms Commission Perspective

M.R. Biju and *M.R.B. Anantha Padmanabha*

E-Governance originated in India during the seventies with a focus on inhouse government applications in the areas of defence, economic monitoring, planning and the deployment of ICT to manage data intensive functions related to elections, census, tax administration etc. The efforts of the National Informatics Centre (NIC) to connect all the district headquarters during the eighties was a watershed. From the early nineties, e-governance has seen the use of IT for wider sectoral applications with policy emphasis on reaching out to rural areas and taking in greater inputs from NGOs and private sector as well. There has been an increasing involvement of international donor agencies such as DFID, G-8, UNDP, and WB under the framework of e-governance for development. While the emphasis has been primarily on automation and computerization, state endeavours to use IT include forays into connectivity, networking, setting up systems for processing information and delivering services. At a micro level, this has ranged from IT automation in individual departments, electronic file handling, and access to entitlements, public grievance systems, service delivery for high volume routine transactions such as payment of bills, tax dues to meeting poverty alleviation goals through the promotion of entrepreneurial models and provision of market information. The thrust has varied across initiatives, with some focusing on enabling the citizen-state interface for various government services, and others focusing on bettering livelihoods.

In short, e-Governance is the application of Information and

Communications Technology to government functioning in order to create 'Simple, Moral, Accountable, Responsive and Transparent' (SMART) governance. The revolution in Information and Communications Technology (ICT) has brought a whole new agenda for governance for wider participation of citizens in public affairs. The purpose of implementing e-Governance is to improve governance processes and outcomes with a view to improving the delivery of public services to citizens. Some authors have defined e-Governance as the e-business of the State. This seems appropriate as both e-Governance and e-business use similar technologies, infrastructure and hardware. However, the market models are widely different thus justifying e-Governance as a separate area of research (Gisler, 2001).

India, being the largest democracy in the world, has much to gain from e-Governance, especially when citizen participation in governance is one of the features of the fully evolved stage of e-government. Many e-readiness assessments have been carried out at the global level that show the current state of India's e-readiness. e-Governance further refers to the use by government agencies of Information Technologies (such as Wide Area Networks, the Internet and mobile computing) that have the ability to transform relations with citizens, businesses, and various arms of government resulting in better delivery of government services to citizens, improved interactions with business and industry, citizen empowerment through access to information, or more efficient government management. The resultant benefits are less corruption, increased transparency, greater convenience, revenue growth, and cost reductions.

A. The Goals of E-Governance

E-Governance goals are:

(i) Better service delivery to citizens,
(ii) Ushering in transparency and accountability,
(iii) Empowering people through information,
(iv) Improved efficiency within Governments, and
(v) Improve interface with business and industry.

E-Governance needs to transform all levels of Government but the focus should be on local governments since local governments are the closest to citizens, and constitute for many, the main interface with government. The advances in information and communications technologies and the internet provide opportunities to transform the relationship between governments and citizens and business in new ways that contribute to the attainment of good governance. They provide opportunities for people and business to involve themselves in the process of governance at all levels. They facilitate better service delivery to clients, in terms of timelines and quality, thus making governance more efficient and effective. In addition, the use of ICT may lower transaction costs both for citizens and government operations and public services can be made more affordable to the people at large.

The primary purpose of governance is the welfare of citizens. While one aspect of governance relates to safeguarding the legal rights of all citizens, an equally important aspect is concerned with ensuring equitable access to public services and the benefits of economic growth to all. It is expected that e-Governance would enable the government to discharge its functions more effectively. However, this would require the government to change itself–its processes, its outlook, laws, rules and regulations and also its way of interacting with the citizens. It would also require capacity building within the government and creation of general awareness about e-Governance among the citizens.

During the initial stages of introduction of ICT in governance there was resistance from some quarters. Some felt that computerization cannot work in the complex government system and that introduction of computers would lead to un-employment. There were also serious doubts whether government employees at all levels would be able to handle computers. Fortunately all these misgivings have proved wrong. Today, new software tools have enough flexibility, to accommodate the most complex situations. The new technology makes the machine-human interface very user-friendly. The Information Technology (IT) and Information Technology Enbled Services (ITES) sectors have created millions of jobs besides improving vastly the services provided by government undertakings—like banks, Airlines, Railways etc. Thus, e-Governance is no longer a far-fetched dream.

B. Definition—E-Government and E-Governance

According to the World Bank,

> "E-Government refers to the use by government agencies of information technologies (such as Wide Area Networks, the Internet, and mobile computing) that have the ability to transform relations with citizens, businesses, and other arms of

government. These technologies can serve a variety of different ends: better delivery of government services to citizens, improved interactions with business and industry, citizen empowerment through access to information, or more efficient government management. The resulting benefits can be less corruption, increased transparency, greater convenience, revenue growth, and/or cost reductions."

UNESCO defines e-Governance as:

"Governance refers to the exercise of political, economic and administrative authority in the management of a country's affairs, including citizens' articulation of their interests and exercise of their legal rights and obligations. E-Governance may be understood as the performance of this governance via the electronic medium in order to facilitate an efficient, speedy and transparent process of disseminating information to the public, and other agencies, and for performing government administration activities."

C. Stages of E-Governanance

(a) *Computerisation:* In the first phase, with the availability of personal computers, a large number of Government offices got equipped with computers. The use of computers began with word processing, quickly followed by data processing.

(b) *Networking:* In this phase, some units of a few government organizations got connected through a hub leading to sharing of information and flow of data between different government entities.

(c) *On-line presence:* With increasing internet connectivity, a need was felt for maintaining a presence on the web. This resulted in maintenance of websites by government departments and other entities. Generally, these web-pages/web-sites contained information about the organizational structure, contact details, reports and publications, objectives and vision statements of the respective government entities.

(d) *On-line interactivity:* A natural consequence of on-line presence was opening up of communication channels between government entities and the citizens, civil society organizations etc. The main aim at this stage was to minimize the scope of personal interface with government entities by providing downloadable Forms, Instructions, Acts, Rules etc. In some cases, this has already led to on-line submission of Forms. Most citizen-government transactions have the potential of being put on e-Governance mode.

D. Types of e-Governance

1. G2G (Government to Government): In this case, Information and Communications technology is used not only to restructure the governmental processes involved in the functioning of government entities but also to increase the flow of information and services within and between different entities. This kind of interaction is only within the sphere of government and can be both horizontal, i.e. between different government agencies as well as between different functional areas within an organisation, or vertical, i.e. between national, provincial and local government agencies as well as between different levels within an organization. The primary objective is to increase efficiency, performance and output.

2. G2C (Government to Citizens): In this case, an interface is created between the government and citizens which enables the citizens to benefit from efficient delivery of a large range of public services. This expands the availability and accessibility of public services on the one hand and improves the quality of services on the other. It gives citizens the choice of when to interact with the government (e.g. 24 hours a day, 7 days a week), from where to interact with the government (e.g. service centre, unattended kiosk or from one's home/workplace) and how to interact with the government (e.g. through internet, fax, telephone, email, face-to-face etc). The primary purpose is to make government, citizen-friendly.

3. G2B (Government to Business): Here, e-Governance tools are used to aid the business community–providers of goods and services–to seamlessly interact with the government. The objective is to cut red tape, save time, reduce operational costs and to create a more transparent business environment when dealing with the government. The G2B initiatives can be transactional, such as in licensing, permits, procurement and revenue collection. They can also be promotional and facilitative, such as in trade, tourism and investment. These measures help to provide a congenial environment to businesses to enable them to perform more efficiently.

4. G2E (Government to Employees): Government is by far the biggest employer and like any organisation, it has to interact with its employees on a regular basis. This interaction is a two-way process between the organisation and the employee. Use of ICT tools helps in making these interactions fast and efficient on the one hand and increase satisfaction levels of employees on the other.

E. Positive Aspects of e-Governance

1. Better Access to Information and Quality Services for Citizens

ICT would make available timely and reliable information on various aspects of governance. In the initial phase, information would be made available with respect to simple aspects of governance such as forms, laws, rules, procedures etc. later extending to detailed information including reports (including performance reports), public database, decision-making processes etc. As regards services, there would be an immediate impact in terms of savings in time, effort and money, resulting from online and one-point accessibility of public services backed up by automation of back end processes. The ultimate objective of e-Governance is to reach out to citizens by adopting a life-cycle approach, i.e. providing public services to citizens which would be required right from birth to death.

2. Simplicity, Efficiency and Accountability in the Government

Application of ICT to governance combined with detailed business process re-engineering would lead to simplification of complicated processes, weeding out of redundant processes, simplification in structures and changes in statutes and regulations. The end result would be simplification of the functioning of government, enhanced decision making abilities and increased efficiency across government–all contributing to an overall environment of a more accountable government machinery. This in turn, would result in enhanced productivity and efficiency in all sectors.

3. Expanded Reach of Governance

Rapid growth of communications technology and its adoption in governance would help in bringing government machinery to the doorsteps of the citizens. Expansion of telephone network, rapid strides in mobile telephony, spread of internet and strengthening of other communications infrastructure would facilitate delivery of a large number of services provided by the government. This enhancement of the reach of government—both spatial and demographic—would also enable better participation of citizens in the process of governance.

4. Clarity of Purpose

There needs to be a clear understanding and appreciation of the purpose and objectives to be achieved through e-Governance. In the past, a large number of projects appear to be based on what technology can achieve rather than what the citizens need. A corollary to this would be a precise definition of the parameters against which any future evaluation would be done. e-Governance should not be taken up merely to demonstrate the capability of an existing technology, but the technology should be adopted to solve an existing problem. Citizen-centricity should be at the heart of all e-Governance initiatives.

5. Environment Building

There is need to change the mind-set of all the stakeholders involved, i.e. politicians, government officials and civil society at large. This would require a strong will to change among various stakeholders in the governance system. As the task involves redesigning of governmental processes at various levels, implementing e-Governance would require political support at all levels. On the other hand, government personnel would have to be incentivized to change old habits and acquire new skills. In the public, awareness needs to be created so that there is a constant demand for reforms in governance through implementation of e-Governance. In the end, the environment should be such that the perceived threat to entrenched interests is removed and resistance to change is addressed by dealing with actual grievances. Thus, the positive approach of government personnel towards the needs of citizens would be the necessary elements for creating a conducive environment. Raising public awareness, forming partnerships with academic institutions–public and private, Public-Private Partnerships (PPPs), exchange of best practices including with the private sector and involvement of citizen-groups should all form part of this process.

6. E-Governance as an Integral Part of Reform in Governance

E-Governance cannot be separated from governance as a whole. Further, it cannot be taken as an adjunct of governance. It has to be an integral part of the governance structure and processes. Thus, every government organization or entity, every government programme or policy and every law and regulation would have to integrate e-Governance modules within itself rather than brought-in as an afterthought or introduced as an adjunct.

7. E-Preparedness and Step-wise Approach

E-Governance cannot be introduced in the whole country across government organizations at one go. As mentioned above, e-Governance is an integral part of reforms in governance and each organization needs to embed e-Governance systems within the organization in a seamless way. However, different organizations are not, presently, at the same level of e-preparedness. There has to be a step-wise approach to e-Governance so that outcomes are maximized and citizens reap early benefits from e-Governance. These steps are mentioned below.

a. E-Preparedness

A certain level of preparedness is essential for any e-Governance project, in the form of existence of basic infrastructure and human resource capabilities of the organizations. A clear assessment of actual e-preparedness of an organization should be first carried out while conceptualizing any project. Efforts should be made to enhance the e-preparedness to the desired levels.

b. Identification of e-Governance Projects by Each Organization/ Entity

Each organization would have to identify areas/activities falling under its functional domain which could benefit from e-Governance. This identification has to be based on the needs of the citizens.

c. Prioritization

Once the e-Governance projects to be undertaken by an organization have been identified, they would require to be prioritized. This should be based on simplicity of the project, ease in implementation and benefits to the citizens. However, capacity building for the more complex projects should remain in focus. Simple projects serve to bring out the potential benefits of e-Governance. These create a demand for more such initiatives. However, the more complex initiatives have the potential of bringing the larger benefits of good governance to citizens.

d. Business Process Re-Engineering

Whether it be for providing information and services to the citizens or for streamlining the internal functioning of government organizations, each e-Governance initiative would have to be accompanied by a step-by-step analysis of the governmental processes involved and tested on the anvil of simplicity and desirability. This would lead to redesign of processes using technology. The process would result in, if required, changes in forms, processes, structures and laws and regulations. The exercise should centre around the needs of the citizens. Business process re-engineering in government organizations is a complex task because, as opposed to private organizations, governmental processes and structures are designed or regulated by various statutes, rules, regulations, instructions etc. changing them would require a complete understanding of the functioning of individual government organizations and laws and regulations associated with them on the one hand and technological applications and the needs of the citizens on the other. This exercise would form the backbone of e-Governance initiatives.

e. Developing Technological Solutions

Every e-Governance initiative would require its own technological solution. However, there would be commonalities across Union, State and local government levels. Further, there would be need for sharing of information and establishing connectivity across organizations at different levels. This would require standardization of basic requirements, adoption of interoperable platforms and creation of data storage and retrieval systems. In the end, the technological solution would have to be modified according to the specific needs of the organization with the help of field experts. However, care has to be taken to ensure that the country does not follow the beaten path in adopting technological solutions. Due to rapid strides in the development of information and communications technology (ICT), there is a strong case for 'leap-frogging' in the selection of technology and applications to achieve better results. Applications mounted on mobile telephone sets and other hand-held devices are examples of such advancements. The technological solution should be able to provide a simple interface to the citizens, be cost-effective, promote efficiency, be sustainable and reliable and lend itself to scalability. Implementation of e-Governance projects: Only when the above-mentioned steps have been undertaken should e-Governance projects be implemented. This may be in the form of a pilot project initially, testing the technological solution and the procedural and functional inputs. However, the business process re-engineering should be such that once the e-Governance project has been successfully tested on a pilot basis, the scaled up system should be able to make e-Governance irreversible, i.e. it should not relapse into the pre-e-Governance mode. In the past, there have been numerous instances of successful projects not being scaled up and also of lessons not being learnt from failed projects. Thus, each pilot project should invariably be evaluated and the lessons learnt including why it did not lead to scaling up. Failed projects should be redesigned to remove shortcomings, this would ensure that organizations do not become a graveyard of pilot projects. As e-Governance is expected to touch all aspects of governance–economic, social and administrative, identification and prioritization of e-Governance projects assumes great significance. E-preparedness and a step-wise approach is a recipe for starting small but building up on successes.

8. Disciplined Way of Working

e-Governance requires a disciplined and systematic way of working in organizations. Most technologies pre-suppose a set of rational behaviour on the part of users. It is element needs to be emphasized during the capacity building as well as in the life cycle of the project.

9. Monitoring and Evaluation

Close monitoring of e-Governance projects is necessary in both the pilot phase as well as during the actual working of the up-scaled project. This helps in early detection of problems and hence facilitates prompt corrective action. However, apart from periodic monitoring of e-Governance initiatives in the post-implementation stage, there would also be need for evaluation of the impact of such initiatives through independent agencies against parameters which would determine whether the objectives have been achieved or not.

10. Developing Secure, Fail-safe Systems and Disaster Recovery Systems

Given the scale of potential e-Governance applications in the country and the prospective mammoth flow of data involved, the technological architecture on which such applications are mounted would need to be made not only secure but also fail-safe. Mechanisms would have to be incorporated which would put the systems in the 'safe mode' in times of crisis. Further, depositories and 'mirrors' would need to be created with sound disaster recovery modules with adequate security features to prevent loss of data and collapse of the system.

Unless security features are properly implemented, electronic transactions are more prone to fraud and abuse than traditional paper-based transactions. As governments move towards providing the full range of government services online with the capability to conduct sensitive transactions, it needs to be ensured that these transactions are secure and the privacy of citizens is not compromised. Over and above, these systems would also need to be insulated from the possibility of cyber-attacks, hacking etc.

11. Sustainability

In the end, e-Governance initiatives need to be sustainable. Once it has been established that any particular initiative is the better way of providing services or information to the people or conducting the business of government, it should not be allowed to relapse on grounds of expediency. Reforms are always harder to implement and sustain, but once they take root, they deliver the best results. Sustainability could be addressed in many ways–some initiatives may require designing in a way that they are financially sustainable. Others may be driven by administrative objectives or simplicity of use. Saving of time and money may be the driving force in case of some projects. All these are objectives, which on their own merit, justify the continuance of any particular initiative. If projects have been able to achieve any of these objectives, their sustainability should not be allowed to be jeopardized on some other grounds.

12. Allowing for Horizontal Applicability

A coordinating mechanism is needed to prevent cases of re-inventing the wheel. Different States across India face similar types of challenges. Past experience has shown that a number of States have undertaken e-Governance projects to address similar concerns. To make e-Governance more cost effective and successful, successes need to be adopted across States and organizations thereby minimizing costly repetitions and in many cases, failures.

13. Development of Local Language Interfaces

As India is a multilingual society, e-Governance initiatives need to provide citizen interfaces in the respective local language. Thus, displays and keys should be based on localized interfaces and multi-media instructions should be commonly used to make the interface accessible in rural areas, where low literacy rates can be an obstacle.

14. E-Governance: A Continuing Process

E-Governance represents a paradigm shift in the field of governance reforms. Bringing it about would have to be a continuing process which would require many adjustments. It has been well said that e-Governance is a journey and not a destination.

F. Challenges of e-Governance in India

Implementation of e-governance has changed the way of living of the people in many countries. The Government of India has embraced e-governance as a trigger and means to redefine and streamline outdated, inefficient processes and procedures while simultaneously exploiting the full power of modern ICT. The aim is to provide citizens with easier and faster access to government services. India has recognized the benefits of e-governance and through it, ushered in a paradigm of citizen-centric service delivery. Governance is reforming the way government manages and shares information with external and internal clients. Specifically, it harnesses ICT to transform relations with citizens, businesses and the various arms of government. There are, however, numerous challenges. Some of the key areas needing attention are as follows:

1. *Clarity in objective setting:* Project approval and funding of projects through multiple departmental budgets lead to wide variations in the approach to project objective setting, without a clear focus on outcomes or on building sustainable services.

The service needs of citizens/businesses and those of other departments are often either overlooked or accorded lower priority in relation to internal needs. Very often, objective setting is purely in ICT terms such as computers, networks and so on which are specified in great detail, while government business process outcomes are either not defined or are defined in vague terms that do not lend themselves to measurement post-implementation.

2. *Ensuring service delivery:* E-governance projects have primarily focused on internal process automation and generally are hardware and infrastructure driven with little focus on citizen service delivery or outcomes.
3. *Awareness:* There is a general lack of awareness regarding benefits of e-governance as well as the process involved in implementing successful G2C, G2B and G2G projects. The administrative structure is not geared for maintaining, storing and retrieving governance information electronically. The general tendency is to obtain the data from the files as and when required rather than using document management and workflow technologies.
4. *Awareness of government officials about ICT:* More than anything else, it is the mindset of government officials that poses the biggest bottleneck to e-government. There are a number of reasons why they resist the use of computers beyond the usual typing of letters and documents. The primary reasons are that they are resistant to any kind of change in their familiar working environment; they fear that computerization of different government activities may make some people redundant and think that computers are meant for low-level typist kind of work.
5. *Public Awareness about ICTs:* Although there is much hype about IT among the younger generation, there is not a high level of awareness among the general public about how ICTs may be useful to their lives. Also, there is a cultural inhibition about the use of PCs in this country. From a cultural context, people are generally not familiar with the concept of using computers. ICTs are still generally perceived as catering to the rich and the elite. As a result, there is no demand or pressure from the public for service delivery through the use of ICTs.
6. *Non-acceptability of IT systems:* It is often seen that even after an IT system is implemented in a government office, it becomes hard

for government officials to convince themselves to use it. Besides the general lack of awareness about ICTs and the fears discussed earlier, some other factors also play a part in the non-acceptability of IT systems. They fear that important data may get lost or they are doubtful about the security features of computers.

7. *Leveraging private capital:* The experience of successful e-governance initiatives indicates that well structured service-oriented projects can attract private capital linked to explicit service-linked revenues from users or from government. The current system of project formulation, i.e. based on budgetary allocation/grants places little or no pressure on departments to develop project structures that can attract private capital, a goal that necessitates additional rigour and complexity at the project formulation and development stage.
8. *Resistance to re-engineering of departmental processes:* Successful implementation of e-governance projects requires a lot of restructuring in the administrative processes and redefining of administrative procedures and formats. This meets with resistance in almost all departments at all levels. Additionally there is a lack of expertise among departmental MIS executives in exploiting data mining techniques, updating of and collection of real time content in the website etc. Therefore, the content collected or maintained by various e-governance portals is unreliable or full of gaps. In such a scenario, it is difficult for any e-governance solution to achieve its intended results. Hence, it is essential to undertake process re-engineering as an integral part of e-governance project implementation in order to ensure increased efficiency and reduced costs.
9. *Standardization:* A departmental approach and the absence of a national framework for common standards has resulted in the adoption of different technical standards and varied architectures. This has significant implications for designing effective integrated applications and also entails long-term costs and sub-optimal results.
10. *Independent Impact Assessment:* In the current system, there is no requirement or institutional mechanism for an independent assessment of projects post-implementation to determine whether they have achieved the set objectives, except in purely financial terms. Further, very few projects have formal

performance metrics defined at the start of the project to measure outcomes.

11. *Localization/Multi-language support:* E-governance has an impact only when the services to citizens are made available in their respective language. However, this is a challenge that needs to be addressed by formulating clear standards and guidelines with respect to the fonts, storage, input etc. ICT solutions were mostly developed with an English language interface. However, in India vast majorities (95%) of the citizens do not know English and use the local language. The fact is that India has 22 official languages; for the success of e-governance, this reality needs to be reflected in the implementation strategy.
12. *Internal Capacity/Project Management Expertise:* Departments/states have limited access to any institutional mechanisms for building capacities in the areas of e-governance project development and design, bid process management, professional project management, development of contractual frameworks and service level agreements.
13. *Underutilization of existing ICT infrastructure:* To a larger extent, the computers in the department are used for the purpose of word processing only, resulting in the under-utilization of the computers in terms of their use in data mining for supporting management decisions. The time gap between the procurement of the hardware and development of the custom applications is so large that by the time the application is ready for use, the hardware becomes obsolete.
14. *Lack of coordination between the government department and solution developers:* Designing of any application requires a very close interaction between the government department and the agency developing the solutions. At present the users in the government departments do not contribute enough to design the solution architecture. Consequently the solutions developed and implemented do not address the requirements of an e-governance project and hence do not get implemented.
15. *Lack of infrastructure for sustaining e-governance projects on a national level:* Infrastructure to support e-governance initiatives does not exist within government departments. The agony is that government departments are not equipped to be in a position to project clear requirements nor are there any guidelines for involving the private sector. Whatever efforts

have been made by various government organizations may be defined as islands of computerization. The infrastructure creation is not guided by a uniform national policy, but is dependent on the needs of individual officers championing a few projects. Therefore, the required networking and communication equipment is either nonexistent in government departments, or if it exists at all, it does not serve any tangible purpose as far as the requirement of a e-governance project is concerned. The use of connectivity options provided by government agencies like NICNET etc. are used in a very limited manner for the purpose of data transmission between various locations, viz. district, state, centre etc. and are mainly utilized for e-mail and internet purposes only.

16. *Sharing of data across various e-governance implementations:* One of the key benefits that a citizen is looking at from e-governance initiatives is a single window access to various government services no matter which department is responsible for giving the service. To achieve this, there is a need to be able to seamlessly share data across the applications.
17. *Security Issues:* While there are clear standards like ISO for IT securities and IT service management which are presently being used by various e-governance applications, it has been seen however, that the concerns of the respective departments with regard to data and application security and control are still not adequately addressed. The reasons include the lack of adequate knowledge and understanding of the various management controls on these standards by the departments. Policies like access control and security are not made very comprehensive, and the controls in international standards need to be made more prescriptive for our requirements. The RFP should also highlight the concerns of the government department with respect to the requisite strategic controls clearly.
18. *Lack of adequate training programmes:* Many e-government or computerization projects suffer gravely from a lack of adequate training programmes. Training is of vital necessity in familiarizing users with computers and overcoming their fears. Some officials go through unplanned 'IT Training', often in another country, and then come back not getting any scope for utilizing their newly gathered knowledge of IT and forgetting it all in due time. The training programmes are mostly not need-based. They are

arranged at arbitrary periods, and not during the implementation phase of an e-government project.

Lack of reliable maintenance: Another significant problem is that generally there is no in-house maintenance personnel. It is of vital necessity that computers get fixed as soon as they malfunction or users very easily lose confidence in the IT systems. Most offices have contracts with local hardware companies for maintenance, but their services are often not immediate.

G. The Way Forward

E-Governance has to be implemented across different departments and organizations with a wide spectrum of activities and with varying levels of readiness for e-Governance. Achieving the desired results would, therefore, require the fullest political backing, a determined and resolute approach by all organizations and departments of Government as well as active and constructive participation by the public. It would require providing institutional and physical infrastructure for taking e-Governance initiatives across our cultural and regional diversities; more importantly it would require the creation of an environment that would encourage the adoption of ICT. Thus, apart from the technical requirement, success of e-Governance initiatives would depend on capacity building and creating awareness within government and outside it.

As government organizations function at varying degrees of IT-preparedness, there is first of all a need for building an environment within government organizations at various levels which is conducive to e-Governance. This would require computerization of the lowest possible unit, as well as building capacity at the individual level which recognizes the need for reforms in processes using modern technology. The essential elements in this phase are as follows:

a. **The will to change:** Decades of following a particular mode of governance procedure tends to develop inertia and resistance to change. Further, old skills and habits will require to be replaced with new skills and new processes if e-Governance is to sustain. There has to be a strong will from within the government itself to crossover from the present system to e-Governance.

b. **Political support at the highest level:** The vast scope of e-Governance combined with the enormous task of process re-engineering which will be necessary at various levels and the infrastructural and financial requirement necessarily call for commitment to the vision of e-Governance at the highest political level. A bottom-up approach will not suffice.

c. **Incentives:** Weaning government entities from the mechanical application of technology to adoption of e-Governance tools will require incentivising e-Governance among different entities and individuals. These incentives need to be reflected in the budgetary allocations.

d. **Awareness:** Apart from building capabilities within the government, there is need for generating widespread awareness among the public at large. The success of e-Governance lies in increasing the number of electronic interactions between citizens and the government and not merely in building the infrastructure of e-Governance. In addition to governmental measures, a proactive approach from civil society groups would also generate greater demand and acceptance for e-Governance initiatives. Further, this would also require the adoption of 'quality' as a mission of governance, as was done in Japan.

e. **Overcoming resistance to change:** E-Governance has to be a collective effort. However, in every organization, there are people who would not be convinced about its benefits or who would perceive it as a challenge to certain entrenched interests. Such resistance would need to be overcome by demonstrating the potential benefits of e-Governance; how it strengthens the organization internally, creates goodwill externally and above all, enhances citizens' satisfaction.

f. **Training and capacity-building:** Training would have to be imparted to government officials starting right from the cutting edge level so that any apprehensions of intrusive technology is removed and e-Governance is accepted as an achievable and desirable target.

Conclusion

India's e-Governance experience shows a plethora of pilot projects with varying rates of success but with the common characteristic that the majority of them are not up-scaled or widely replicated. It is essential to learn from such experiences and each pilot project should be taken to its logical end. For this to happen, emphasis has to be on the reforms in government procedures, structures and systems and must take precedence over mere technological solutions. Ultimately, the success of an e-Governance initiative lies in how efficiently it has enhanced people's participation in government functioning through wide ICT access, bringing government and the services it offers closer to its citizens, promoting accountability, transparency and responsiveness in government functioning and ensuring that government works better at lesser costs. These are the signs for good governance and a vibrant democracy.

REFERENCES

Flak, L.S., Olsen, D.H. and Wolcott, P. (2005). "Local E-Government in Norway", *Scandinavian Journal of Information Systems*, Vol. 17, No. 2, pp. 41–48.

More than most IT systems, e-Governance applications need to be secured by Trivedi Pujya published in http://www. Express computeronline.com (7/6/2008).

Second Administrative Reform Commission Report, Promoting E-Governance; the Smart way Forward, Govt. of India, New Delhi 2008, https://darpg.gov.in/arc-reports

The Working Group on E-Government in the Developing World, "Roadmap for E-government in the Developing World, 10 Questions E-Government Leaders Should Ask Themselves", April 2002.

https://shodhganga.inflibnet.ac.in/bitstream/10603/5433/9/09_chapter% 204.pdf

http://www.ignou.ac.in/upload/B2U2cit-002.pdf

http://unpan1.un.org/intradoc/groups/public/documents/un/unpan038851. pdf (19/11/2011)

http://www.apdip.net/projects/e-government/capblg/casestudies/India-Chandrashekhar.pdf (20/3/2011)

http://www.it.iitb.ac.in/~prathabk/egovernance/egov_ict.html (20/6/2011)

http://www.unescap.org/pdd/prs/ProjectActivities/Ongoing/gg/governance. asp (16/7/2011)

http://ictanddevelopment.blogspot.com/2009/06/ict-and-e-governance.html (14/7/2011)

http://arc.gov.in/11threp/ARC_11thReport (10/3/2011)

http://www.indg.in/e-governance (15/3/2011)

http://www.indg.in/e-governance/e-governance/egov-plan (17/7/2011)

http://www.mit.gov.in/content/mission-mode-projects (20/9/2011)

http://www.tulip.net/Product_Service/EGovernance.htm (19/10/2011)

http://en.wikipedia.org/wiki/E-readiness (19/11/2011)

http://www.csi-sigegov.org/E-Governence/e_Governance.pdf (9/2/2011)

http://omec.uab.cat/Documentos/mitjans_dem_gov/0138.pdf (17/7/2011)

3

Digital Governance and Social Welfare

An Assessment of Digital India Programme

C. Jeevan Kumar

Introduction

In the post-Independent India, State's intervention permeates all walks of life of citizens. Indian state pledged to become a welfare state. State designed and implemented programmes, such as Public Distribution System (PDS) and poverty reduction programmes to promote socio-economic development of its people. Sunil Khilnani (2004) aptly sums up state's intervention during the planning period:

> "During the Nehruvian era, Indian state was enlarged, its ambitions inflated, and it was transferred from a distant, alien object into, the imagination of Indians, proclaiming itself responsible for everything they could desire: jobs, ration cards, educational places, security, cultural recognition. The state etched itself into the imagination of Indians in a way that no previous political agency had ever done."

However, state and its role began to undergo change since the mid-1970s. Simultaneously, state's commitment to the welfare of citizens also underwent change. During the 1980s, the then Prime Ministers, both Indira Gandhi and later her son Rajiv Gandhi made attempts to introduce economic reforms in India. In the guise of socialist approach, Rajiv Gandhi-led government introduced economic reforms to liberalize the economy and relax controls and regulations in doing business. The private sector was encouraged in investment to boost economic growth.

By 1990s, there was a shift in the model of development, i.e. from a centralized planning model to a private sector/market-based model. Contours of social welfare administration began to change due to state's withdrawal from the social sphere. The information, communication, and technologies (ICTs) facilitated by digital revolution became a catalyst for the creation of sprawling information and communication networks that enmesh individuals, state and business alike (Steger and Roy, 2010).

The Internet is a ubiquitous and powerful media. It has been at the leading edge of industrial change across the globe. Since 1982, one can see a rise in the number of internet users from few people to the billion by 2007. Antony Rutkowski, First Director of Internet Society, says "Internetworking is one of the most revolutionary technologies of the twentieth century…indeed it may perhaps be the most revolutionary human communications medium that has ever emerged" (as cited in Mathiason, 2009, p. 2). It is not exaggerating to say that access to technology has become one of the core needs of society.

The chapter critically examines the impact of neo-liberal reforms on the Indian state. While doing so, it assesses the impact of technology on social welfare administration. It discusses the benefits and opportunities created by Digital India Programme. It critically examines digital divide in India and issues surrounding this phenomenon.

I. Neoliberalism and Changing Role of the State

Globalization resulted in the free movement of capital and goods across borders. Heightened flows of goods, capital, labour, and information are believed to have moved effortlessly across national frontiers. By shrinking the world, globalization facilitated companies moving from one place to another in search of markets. The governments had to keep tax rates as low as possible to attract new businesses. The market gained the upper hand in deciding where to invest and set up the industry, leaving little scope for governmental interference. It is apprehended that any interference on the part of the government became a hindrance to market. It would lead to industries moving out to other convenient place resulting in job losses, loss of taxes, and thereby posing serious constraints for the government. It is argued that nation-states have been replaced with a borderless globe and undermined the role of national governance. It led to 'hollowing out of state' (Robert Reich and Kenichi Ohmae as cited in Marsh *et al.*, 2006).

A paradigm shift took place in government with increasing role of multiple actors, such as private sector, market, and social networks. The state has to share its control with these actors in policymaking. For instance, the state can no longer use command and monitoring instruments to get things done. These developments influenced operations of the public sector. In place of command and control, the state plays the role of 'facilitator' (Peters and Pierre, 2006). The state has become a regulatory state instead of commanding one. It favoured de-bureaucratization and alteration in the forms of service delivery.

Farazmand (1999) argues that there has been a shift from being a welfare state to that of a corporate one. States began to gain from the information-age advantages by processing information for all functions of governance and administration. Technology caused changes in government due to the use of ICTs in day-to-day management. Countries that possessed technological capability became dominant states in the international arena (United States of America), and other nations became dependent.

Changing Contours of Social Welfare

Bell and Hindmoor (2009) discuss the role of the state in the modern society. They outline, globally, governments have taken measures to cut the expenditure. Cut-back management manifested in government's withdrawal from financial subsidies, exchange and credit controls and tariffs; loosening of regulatory restrictions on capital creation; privatization of enterprises and deregulation of markets. Obinger and Zohlnofer (as cited in Bell and Hindmoor, 2009, p. 73) illustrate that Organization for Economic Co-operation and Development (OECD) countries have reduced the total economic subsidies as a percentage of Gross Domestic Product (GDP) from 1980 and 2004 (See the Table 3.1 below).

World Bank in its Report entitled, 'The State in a Changing World' mentions that states have increasingly come under pressure to perform well. ICT revolution inspires the role of the state. New technologies meant new and different roles for government. Technologies brought in competition among different service providers, particularly between the public and private sectors. ICTs opened new opportunities for unbundling of services and allowing a larger role for markets (World Bank, 1997). These changes were evident in the changing nature of Indian state. It is pertinent to examine the impact of these changes on social welfare in India.

Table 3.1: Total Economic Subsidies as Percentage of Gross Domestic Product, Selected OECD Countries, 1980 and 2004

Country	*Total Economic Subsidies*		*% change, 1980-2004*
	1980	*2004*	
Australia	1.44	1.32	0.13
Canada	2.74	1.17	1.57
France	2.13	1.29	0.84
Germany	2.08	1.27	0.81
Italy	2.70	1.07	1.63
Japan	1.50	0.86	0.64
Norway	5.15	2.25	2.90
Portugal	4.60	1.64	2.96
United Kingdom	1.96	0.53	1.43
United States	0.35	0.34	0.01
Total (20–country OECD average)	**2.37**	**1.24**	**1.02**

Source: Adapted from Bell and Hindmoor (2009, p. 73).

State's Withdrawal in Social Sector

The role of Indian state has been redefined with the adoption of neoliberal policies. Social welfare has come under strain with state's retreat in the social sector. India's national debt was 50 per cent of the GDP in the early 1990s (Steger and Roy, 2010, p. 93). The government had introduced neoliberal reforms to reduce this burden. The then Finance Minister, Manmohan Singh believed in the adoption of fiscal austerity and strict monetary policies in conjunction with sizeable Structural Adjustment Programme (SAP) to unleash India's entrepreneurial potential. These reforms have brought in change in the nature of state and its commitment to welfare in India.

Atul Kohli (2012) argues state's approach to help the poor has undergone a drastic change in the recent past. The Indian state has become pro-business over last three decades. He avers, in contrast to Nehruvian socialist era, state in neoliberal times, does not attempt to address inequalities. Instead of attacking substantial disparities, it is promoting equality of opportunity. One can observe a paradox here. On the one hand, the State claims to provide entitlements for its citizens. On the other hand, it is reducing government's total expenditure to GDP over the years (See Table 3.2). It is reducing subsidies as part of GDP (See Table 3.3).

Table 3.2: Government's Total Expenditure as Percentage of India's GDP

Year	Percentage of total expenditure to GDP
1950-51	5.2
1980-81	16.93
1990-91	20.07
2000-01	17.25
2007-08	16.35

Source: Government of India, *Economic Survey, 2008-09*, Ministry of Finance, A-3 and A-39.

Table 3.3: Subsidy as Percentage of India's GDP (2002-03 to 2014-15)

Year	Subsidies Percentage of total expenditure to GDP
2002-03	1.72
2003-04	1.56
2004-05	1.42
2005-06	1.29
2006-07	1.33
2007-08	1.42
2008-09	2.30
2009-10	2.19
2010-11	2.22
2011-12	2.53
2012-13	2.31
2013-14	2.25
2014-15	2.02

Source: Government of India, *Economic Survey, 2014-15*, p. 35.

Subsidies and Social Welfare

State's withdrawal from the social sector has had a negative impact on social welfare. Social welfare services are designed for weaker sections of society or particular groups of individuals. Those services are provided to enable them to be part of mainstream society. Provision of such services and transforming social policy into social services are the responsibilities of social welfare administration (Kidneigh, 1950). It is a two-way process: (i) turning policy into concrete social services and (ii) the use of experience in recommending modification of policy. According to Harleigh Trecker (1971), social welfare administration works for providing needed community services and programmes. In the post-Independent India, subsidies were provided to people in social sector such as health, education, and environment. They aimed to promote welfare of the society beyond the targeted sections. However, subsidies became a major area of contestation in neoliberal times. Subsidies have been questioned on the ground of rationality.

Ministry of Finance, Government of India, in its discussion paper on Subsidies in May 1997, argued that subsidies in India are unduly large, non-transparent, input-based, poorly targeted, and regressive. They induce waste and misallocation of resources. In the same year, the Government of India appointed Subsidies Committee to study the existing subsidy regime and make recommendations (Srivatsava *et al.*, 2003). The Subsidies Committee argued that subsidies often promote inefficiencies in public sector including State Electricity Boards, State Irrigation Departments, Food Corporation of India. The report proposed limiting subsidies to only Merit I and Merit II categories[1]. It aimed to make subsidy system transparent and explicit to avoid multiple subsidies to serve a single objective. Subsidies were sought to be result-oriented (*Ibid.*, p. 71). These recommendations have had a significant impact on the equity and efficiency concerns of the fiscal regime (*Ibid.*, p. 21).

The other dimension of neoliberal reforms is that new opportunities were created for developing countries through greater access to and transfer of technologies (Deepak Nayyar, 2006). ICTs opened up new vistas of economic and social transformations in both the developed and developing countries. ICTs have had brought a profound change in the administrative system in India, particularly in the implementation of social policies and delivery of social services. Against this backdrop, the government had to look for means to reduce expenditure on administration. When states are withdrawing from the social sector, it was viewed that ICTs could play a major role in reducing the administrative costs in running the government. It began with the automation of the service delivery. The implementation and use of ICT solutions can support governance reforms. Governments have resorted to ICTs as new technologies are seen as an opportunity to implement neoliberal agenda. Let us see how ICTs impact governance in India in the subsequent paragraphs.

II. New Technologies and Governance

Technology and Human Development

United Nations Development Programme in its Report 2001 titled, 'Making new technologies work for human development' underlines that both technology and human development are mutually reinforcing and increase people's ability to participate more actively in the social, economic and political life of a community. Secondly, technological innovation is a means to human development because of its impact on economic growth through the productivity gains it generates. It raises the crop yields of farmers, the output of factory workers and the efficiency of service providers and small businesses. It also creates new activities and industries such as the ICT sector which will enhance economic growth and contribute to employment creation. The linkage between technology and human development is multidimensional (See Figure 3.1). The governments across the world have started harnessing technology through policy as it will enable new technologies to become a tool for human development everywhere.

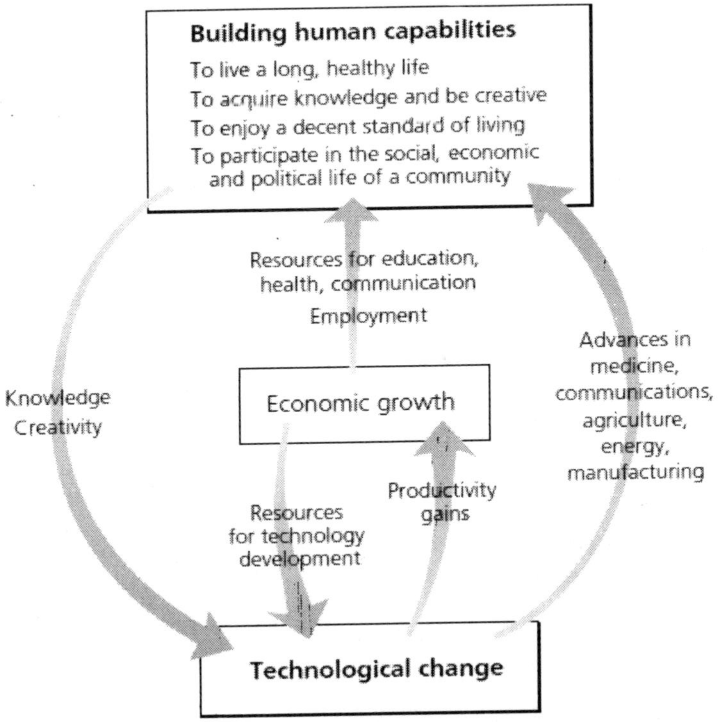

Fig. 3.1: Link between Technology and Human Development
Source: United Nations Development Programme (2001, p. 28).

Internetworking

Technologies have become a tool for networking among state, citizens and market. They provide three possible relations in terms of the interface between (i) the government and citizens (G2C), (ii) government to government (G2G), and (iii) government to business (G2B). It is diagrammatically shown in Figure 3.2.

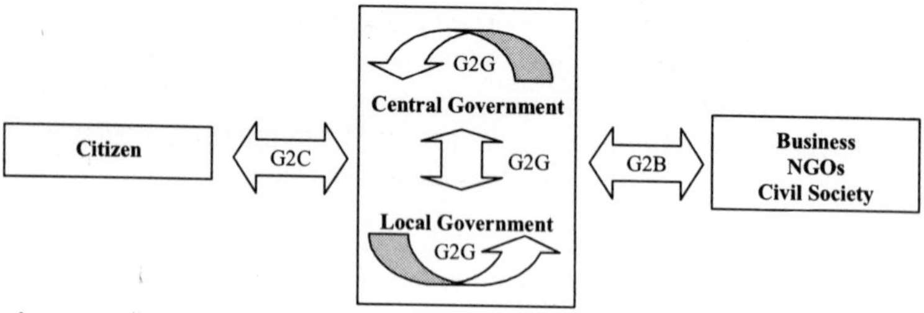

Fig. 3.2: Technology and its Interface

Source: Michiel Backus (2001, p. 4).

Heeks (2001) argues that e-governance is more than providing information to the citizens. It should be able to transform the landscape of service delivery. E-governance encompasses all ICTs which creates a wealth of new digital connections:

- Connections within government (G2G)–permitting 'joined-up thinking'.
- Connections between government and NGOs/citizens (G2B)–strengthening accountability.
- Connections between government and business/citizens (G2C)–transforming service delivery.
- Connections within and between NGOs–supporting learning and concerted action.
- Connections within and between communities–building social and economic development.

Digital Empowerment

Baumi and Di Maio (2000) belonging to Gartner Group have developed a model of e-government. Four stages are identified in the evolution of e-governance as illustrated in Figure 3.3.

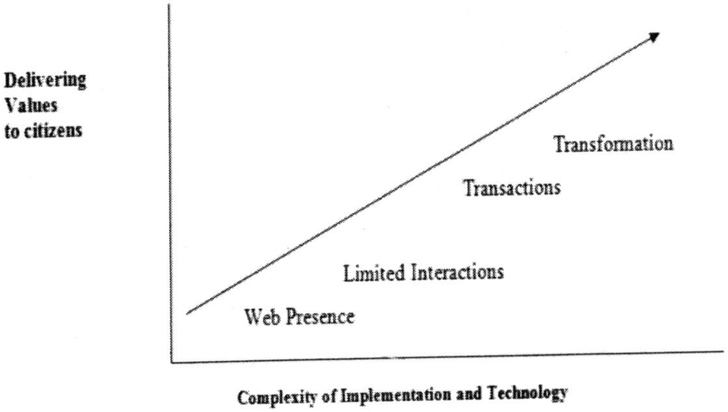

Fig. 3.3: Stages in e-Governance
Source: Baumi and Di Maio (2000)

According to Baumi and Di Maio, in the first phase, the government will provide essential information to citizens on the websites. In the second stage, the government provides limited interaction with the government and officials online. This will be followed by a transactional phase in which citizens will be able to conduct business online with government. The final stage witnesses a relationship between the government and citizens in a sustained manner. The government will respond to the citizens' needs for their queries online thereby gaining the trust from the citizens.

Impact of ICT on Administration

ICTs brought in managerial changes in Indian government in the 1990s. They caught the imagination of both administrators and politicians. While other sections of society are adapting themselves to these changes, it became imperative for the administration to respond to these changes (Mathur, as cited in Mehta, 2000, p. 55). It is an internal change communicated by ICT revolution. It was advocated that extensive usage of ICTs would redefine administrative process and improve the efficiency of the government. ICTs are expected to reduce administrative cost as well as corruption.

Increased use of ICTs has altered public service delivery in the public domain. At the policy level, Fifth Pay Commission has recommended the use of ICTs for automation of service provision and paperless government (GoI, 1997). Besides enhancing speediness in service delivery, technologies facilitate the interface between government-citizen, citizen-market and state-market. Y.K. Alagh Committee on civil service reforms identified a variety of skills required by a civil servant of the twenty-first century (GoI, 2001, p. 71). Technological revolution afforded the opportunity to civil servants to adapt themselves to these changes. This committee suggested that civil servants should be able to interface with modern technology and provide a cutting edge to many solutions.

In a nutshell, e-governance has been construed as a means to attain transformational improvement in quality, efficiency, and effectiveness of governance. The focus is laid on reduction in administrative costs, redefining administrative process, and enhancing the efficiency in public service delivery. Convinced by these arguments, e-governance has been promoted in India in the post-1990s. Institutional measures were taken by setting up of National Institute for Smart Government (NISG) in India in 2002. Having discussed the advantages of e-governance, let us turn to the e-government initiatives undertaken by the government.

III. Digital Initiatives in India

In the post-1990s, several e-governance reforms have been introduced at both Central as well as State governments. Some of these initiatives and their advantages have been discussed below.

Service Delivery at One Stop

ICTs can be applied to deliver services efficiently. For instance, Mee-Seva (In your service) in Andhra Pradesh provides a single window system where bills for telephone, income tax, water tax, electricity, house tax, can be paid. This saves the time of citizens in locating different offices. Besides, this system enables the government to interact with citizens; establish arrangements to share revenue; and also channelize necessary funds at the appropriate time to the different agencies. Scholarships, health, banking and ration items services are also being provided to weaker sections.

Poverty Reduction

ICTs are being leveraged in the public distribution system to provide the poor with subsidized items in a transparent manner. For instance, Chhattisgarh and Tamil Nadu have used ICTs extensively in tracking the beneficiaries of PDS. It prevented diversion of foodgrains from the targeted population and delivered them in a transparent manner (Mudgal, 2014). Better provision of foodgrains, in turn, improved the livelihood of the rural poor. Jean Dreaze and Reetika Khera (2013) in their study found that PDS has significantly reduced the poverty gap index of the rural poor.

Unique Identification Project (Aadhaar)

One of the recent e-governance initiatives of the government is creating the unique identity to each person in the country. This identification card, known as Aadhaar, becomes a basis for receiving various services from the government. Aadhaar card represents a sharp transition from paper-based identity system to IT enabled identification system. Aadhaar card is linked to biometric and demographic information to ensure their uniqueness. It is stored in a secure central database. It allows citizens to access resources quickly in both urban and rural areas (Nilekani, 2011). This has been entrusted with the Unique Identification Authority of India (UIDAI). The Aadhaar number supports remote verification of the identity of citizens and creates the possibility for the remote delivery of services across the country. Accordingly, the government can design welfare programmes and deliver services more efficiently and transparently.

National e-Governance Plan

During United Progressive Alliance (UPA-I) rule, Government of India launched National e-Governance Plan (NeGP) on May 18, 2006. NeGP envisions 'making all government services accessible to the common man in his locality, through common service delivery outlets and ensure efficiency, transparency, and reliability of such services at affordable costs to realize the basic needs of the common man.'[2] Accordingly, 31 Mission Mode Projects covering various domains were initiated. Despite the successful implementation of many e-Governance projects across the country, e-Governance as a whole has not been able to make the desired impact and fulfil all its objectives.

Digital India

The Bharatiya Janata Party-led National Democratic Alliance (NDA) government introduced 'Digital India' (DI) in the year 2014 to bridge the rural-urban divide through communications, broadband connectivity, building the skills of the rural youth. E-kranti is part of the DI for good governance and service delivery. DI is an initiative to prepare the country for a knowledge future and transform it. It weaves together a large number of ideas and thoughts into a single and comprehensive vision. The weaving together makes the mission transformative in totality. The existing e-governance programmes are pulled together and merged with Digital India Programme. It restructures, re-focuses and implements them in a synchronized manner. It is coordinated by Department of Electronics and Information Technology (DeitY), executed by the entire government.

DI programme is centred on three key vision areas: (i) Digital infrastructure as a core utility to every citizen, (ii) Governance and services on demand, and (iii) Digital empowerment of citizens.[3] Digital empowerment of citizens gains significance here. Empowering digitally implies imparting digital literacy to citizens individually. It requires that government makes at least one person in every household e-literate. Digital literacy assumes paramount importance for fully leveraging the potential of DI. It enables citizens to exploit the digital technologies fully; seek better livelihood opportunities and become economically secure. Common Service Centres (CSCs) set up by Central and State governments play the critical role in taking digital literacy to the remotest locations in the country. National Institute of Electronics and Information Technology (NIELIT), an autonomous society under DeitY, has identified more than 5000 facilitation centres across the country for training citizens on courses. They will equip a person to undertake e-governance transactions through computers and other essential activities, like e-mail, browsing the internet, etc. NIELIT has also signed Memorandum of Understanding (MoU) with industry partners to conduct courses and online examinations on digital literacy jointly.

As part of Digital Initiative, Government of India launched National Scholarships Portal on 1st July, 2015 as 'one stop solution' for an end to end scholarship process right from submission of student application, verification, sanction and disbursal to end beneficiary for all the scholarships provided by the Government of India[4]. Students have to register once on this portal. According to the eligibility criteria, the system itself suggests the schemes for which a student is eligible. Online portal resulted in a simplifying process for the students' applications. It led to improving transparency as scholarship amount is directly transferred to bank accounts of students through Direct Benefit Transfer (DBT). Registered students will get Short Message Service (SMS) and E-Mail alerts at every step of the scholarship process. The online scholarship portal eliminated duplicate applications; and served as a Decision Support System (DSS) as up-to-date information is available on demand. So far 6828397 applications have been submitted to this portal. Despite these digital initiatives, the digital divide is a major issue that hampers digital penetration in every nook and corner of the society.

IV. Issues in Digital Divide

Sapru and Sapru (2014) in their critical analysis of e-governance highlight the challenges to DI initiative. They include limited availability of internet infrastructure, the high cost of access and usage, lack of awareness and low digital literacy, narrow range of applications and services and an unfavourable business environment.

Understanding Digital Divide

OECD (OECD, 2001, p. 1) defines digital divide as "the gap between individuals, households, business and geographical areas at different socio-economic levels about both their opportunities to access information and communication technologies and to their use of the internet for a wide variety of activities." Socio-economic background determines the access to the digital devices. For instance, the OECD report finds, income and education have a positive correlation in the digital divide. Educational attainment and income are strongly related and explain much of the difference in uptake. Accordingly, higher the level of education, the more likely individuals have access to and use ICTs in both the home and the workplace. Moreover, at the same income level, those with higher educational attainment will have higher rates of access. There are large differences in Personal Computer (PC) penetration and internet access between those with tertiary education and those with the lowest education levels, though the latter group is growing more rapidly from a small base.

Digital divide prevents digital activism of individuals in society. It precludes their free expression of thoughts and participation in democracy. According to Brodock (2010), digital divide manifests in three ways: unequal access, different skills, and censorship. The article examines India's status on these parameters.

(a) Unequal Access

Technology provides an opportunity to Dalits to occupy their space in the cyber domain, and articulate their cause as well as that of the country by using social media. The Internet opened up vistas for Dalits in modern society to participate in the national discourse of the civil society and to develop dialogues among themselves. Through the use of the internet, they have tried to overcome the barriers imposed by the upper castes. However, access to IT determines their digital inclusion in society. Access to technology is contingent on the socio-economic status of Dalits (Tirumal and Tartakov, 2013).

As has been mentioned, access to digital devices like computers and tablets is determined by social and economic background. Gaurav Mishra, in his study, explores that a low number of Dalit communities are active on social media. Referring to socio-economic aspects of the digital divide, Mishra says, "Higher, more dominant castes like Brahmins, Rajputs, and Yadavs tend to have more money and better access to the internet. Old disparities are further accentuated by the net."[5] Existing inequalities permeate the digital life of the lower castes in India.

(b) Infrastructure

Problems about IT infrastructure hamper digital access. To ensure high-speed connectivity to all panchayats in the country, the Department of Telecom (DoT) established Bharat Broadband Network Ltd. (BBNL) during UPA-II rule in 2011. It rolled out the National Optical Fiber Network (NOFN) (now known as BharatNet) to digitize and connect local institutions, such as panchayat office, schools, health centres, libraries, etc. When the project was launched, it aimed to connect 2.5 lakh village panchayats with 100 Mbps link. By doing so, it is expected to ensure that digital inclusion reaches all communities across the country by 2013. A review of the progress of this project tells that it could not be materialized as the deadline is extended to March 2016 (Mudgal, 2014). Unaccomplished BharatNet makes Digital India a distant reality to millions of people.

(c) Unequal Skills

Though attempts are made to promote e-literacy through National Digital Literacy Mission, they are not complemented by adequate skills of individuals. For instance, 40 per cent of the population in India is illiterate.

3 per cent of them cannot afford to pay telephone bills. One cannot imagine that they own a PC and get it connected to the internet. According to Freedom House (2015), only 18 per cent of the Indian population (out of 1.29 billion) has got access to the web. Bridging digital divide requires building the capacities of the users who intend to take advantage of DI, such as farmers and illiterate persons. The Prime Minister, Narendra Modi, is reported to have said that 'DI is not meant for the wealthy, but for those who are poor'.[6]

(d) Censorship

Global surveys reveal a gloomy picture about internet usage in India. On the one hand, the government is trying to promote access to digitalization. On the contrary, there has been a declining freedom of netizens concerning the use of the internet. According to Freedom House (2013), India stands 35 in the ranking of internet freedom enjoyed by netizens in the year 2013 (i.e. 35) (*Economic Times of India*, 2 November, 2011, Jaipur, p. 11). See Figure 3.4. This has been further worsened in 2015 wherein India was ranked 40th among the 88 countries on internet freedom. It is attributed to the increasing surveillance of the state over the use of internet and its censorship.

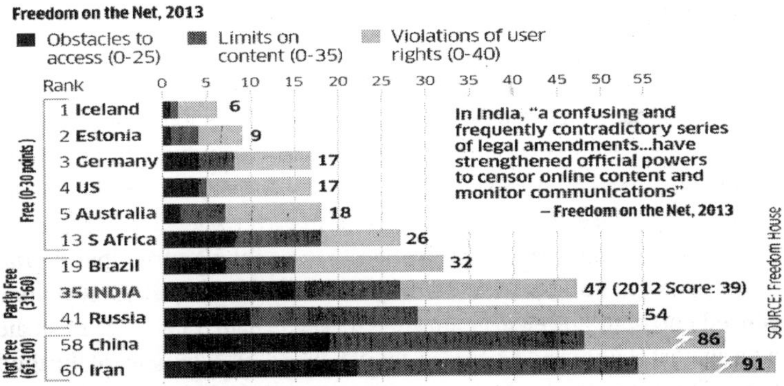

Fig. 3.4: Freedom on the Internet to Netizens

E-government Readiness

India is ranked 118 (out of 193 countries) in providing online services to the citizens according to the latest UN Department of Economic and Social Affairs (DESA) Index 2014. It is not enough to have the availability of gadgets to access the Internet. Connection speed matters more than just the availability of these devices. According to a recent report of Akaimi, a content delivery network, the average speed of Internet is just 2.3 Mbps against that of South Korea (23.6 Mbps) (*Times of India*, 24 October, 2015, Jaipur, p. 6).

Political Will

In a study carried out by Jennifer Bussell (2012a) across Indian states during 1999-2009, it was found that scope of implementation of e-governance initiative depends on the political expediency. The study finds that digitization of services is not uniform, rather selective across states. She analyzed that politicians tend to restrict access to information if hiding it provides them an opportunity to collect their bribes. Where there is scope for bribery in public service delivery, there politicians are less likely to be supportive of policies to increase transparency in administration. For example, when citizens and it necessary to pay "speed money" to access services, politicians tend to hide information. Another study by Jennifer Bussell (2012 b) found limitations of digitization. The quality of public utilities cannot be improved unless the public institutions are revamped.

Conclusion

India adapted itself to ICT revolution in tandem with the neoliberal reforms in the post-1990s. Technology is expected to offer many solutions to problems such as administrative inefficiency and corruption. ICTs provide tremendous opportunities to governments for improving administrative transparency, efficiency, and effectiveness of governmental performance. It also opens up more ways for the public to be involved and participate in the policy-making processes. Studies showed that use of ICTs had reduced corruption including improved service delivery. If we evaluate India against Baumi and Di Maio's model, the country remains at the third stage. The relationship between citizens and government did not go beyond limited transactions. In other words, it is transaction driven rather than transformation. Though India is technologically advanced, it has to do more. E-governance is a journey, but not a destination (GoI, 2008, p. 64).

There have been several issues that hinder digital inclusion, such as, infrastructure, skills, and censorship. More importantly, freedom of the internet and political will are prerequisites of achieving the goals of Digital India. When the citizens are not provided with enough access to the web, it is tantamount to social exclusion from participatory democracy. Unless these problems are addressed, it is impossible to achieve the goals of Digital India. There is a bottom line to the implementation of this programme. Technology neither replaces human beings nor democracy. Mobile connectivity cannot address country's hunger and basic needs with India ranking 55 in the Global Hunger Index (Nissim Mannathurkkaren, 2015). People are central to all these digital initiatives. Necessary steps have to be taken by the government in this direction.

NOTES

1. The report suggests a three-tier hierarchy of Government social and economic services:
   Merit I–Elementary education, primary healthcare, prevention and control of diseases, social welfare and nutrition, soil and water conversation, ecology and environment.
   Merit II–Education (other than elementary), sports and youth services, family welfare, urban development, forestry, agricultural research and education, other agricultural programmes, special programmes for rural development, land reforms, other rural development programmes, special programmes for north-eastern areas, flood control and drainage, non-conventional energy, village and small industries, ports and light houses, roads and bridges, inland water transport, atomic energy research, space research, oceanographic research, other scientific research, census surveys and statistics, and meteorology.
   Non-Merit–All others.
2. http://deity.gov.in/content/national-e-governance-plan, accessed on 23 November, 2015.
3. http://www.digitalindia.gov.in/content/vision-and-vision-areas, accessed on 23 November 2015.
4. http://scholarships.gov.in/main.do, viewed on 18 December 2015.
5. http://timesofindia.indiatimes.com/India/Social-networking-sites-have-become-caste-wide/articleshow/5729775.cms, accessed on 10 December 2015.
6. www.ndlm.in, accessed on 24 November 2015.

REFERENCES

Atul Kohli, (2012), *Poverty amid Plenty in the New India*, Cambridge, New Delhi.

Baumi, Christopher, H. and Andrea Di Maio (2000). *Gartner's Four Phases of e-government model*. www.gartner.com.

Bell, Stephen and Hindmoor, Andrew (2009). *Rethinking governance: The centrality of the state in modern society*, Cambridge University Press, UK.

Brodock, Katharine (2010). "Economic and social factors: The digital (activism) divide", In Joyce, Mary (editor), *Digital activism coded: The new mechanics of change*, Idebate Press, New York.

Bussell, Jennifer (2012a), "E-Governance and corruption in the states can technology serve the aam aadmi?" *Economic and Political Weekly*, Vol. XLVII, No. 25, p. 78.

Bussell, Jennifer, (2012b), *Corruption and reform in India: Public services in the digital age*, Cambridge University Press, London.

Deepak Nayyar (2006). Globalization, History and Development: A Tale of Two Centuries, *Cambridge Journal of Economics*, 30(1): 137-159.

Dreze, Jean and Reetika Khera (2013). "Rural poverty and the public distribution system", *Economic and Political Weekly*, 16 November, Vol. XLVIII, Nos. 45-46.

Farazmand, Ali (1999). "Globalisation and public administration", *Public Administration Review*, 59(6): 509-522.

Freedom House (2015). Freedom on the net 2015, accessed from freedomhouse.org, 31 October, 2015.

Government of India, (1997). *Report of Fifth Central Pay Commission*, Vol. II, All India Railwaymen's Federation, New Delhi.

—— (2001). *Report of Civil Service Examination Review Committee*, Union Public Service Commission, New Delhi.

—— (2008). Second Administrative Reforms Commission (ARC), Promoting e-governance–the smart way forward, Ministry of Personnel, Public Grievances and Pensions, Department of Administrative Reforms and Public Grievances, 2005.

Heeks, Richard (2001). Understanding e-governance for development, http://www.iimahd.ernet.in/egov/ifip/dec2001/article3.htm, accessed on 14 December, 2015.

Khilnani, Sunil (1997). *The idea of India*, Hamish Hamilton, UK.

Kidneigh, John C. (1950). "Social work administration: an area of social work practice?", *Social Work Journal*, April, Vol. XXXI, No. 2.

Marsh, David; Smith, Nicola; Smith, J. and Hothi, Nicola (2006). "Globalisation and the state", In Colin Hay (eds.), *The state: theories and issues*, Palgrave Macmillan, New York.

Mathiason, John (2009). *Internet governance: The new frontier of global institutions*, Routledge, New York.

Mehta, Vinod (ed.) (2000). *Reforming administration in India*, Har-Anand, New Delhi.

Michiel Backus (2001). E-governance and developing countries: Introduction and examples, Research Report, No. 3, April, International Institute for Communication and Development (IICD), Hague.

Mudgal, Vipul (2014). "Union budget and the 'digital divide': Old wine in new bottle", *Economic and Political Weekly*, Vol. XLIX, No. 3.

Nilekani, Nandan (2011). "The possibilities of the Aadhaar Number", *Yojana*, June.

Nissim Mannathurkkaren (2015). "The grand delusion of Digital India", *The Hindu*, Noida/New Delhi, 26 October, 2015, p. 11.

OECD, 2001, *Understanding the digital divide*, OECD, Paris.

Peters, B.G. and Pierre, J. (ed.) (2004). *The politicisation of civil service in comparative perspective: a quest for control*, Routledge, London.

Sapru, R.K. and Sapru, Yudhishthara (2014). "Good governance through e-governance with special reference to India", *Indian Journal of Public Administration*, Vol. LX, No. 2, April-June.

Srivastava, D.K.; Rao, Bhujanga; Chakraborty, Pinaki and Rangamannar, T.S. (2003). *Budgetary subsidies in India: subsidising social and economic services*, National Institute of Public Finance and Policy, New Delhi.

Steger, Manfred B. and Roy, Ravi K. (2010). *Neoliberalism: A very short introduction*, Oxford University Press, New York.

Tirumal, P. and Tartakov, Gary Michael, (2013). "India's dalit search for democratic opening in the digital divide", In Johnson, Lindsay (ed.), *Digital literacy: concepts, methodologies, tool, and applications*, Vol. I, Information Resources Management Association, USA.

Trecker, H.B. (1971). *Social work administration principles and practice*, Association Press, New York.

World Bank (1997). *World Development Report 1997, The state in a changing world*, World Bank, Washington D.C.

United Nations Development Report (2001). *Making new technologies work for human development*, Oxford University Press, New York.

4

Gender Digital Divide

A Study of Mobile Penetration in India

Madhusudhan, B.

In today's world, the technological revolution and its advancements should be inclusive in nature particularly gender sensitive. This would enable women in rural and urban areas in reaping the various benefits provided by the Information and Communication Technology (ICT). The crucial benefit the women enjoy from information revolution is social capital and social networking which ultimately paves the way for women's empowerment. As information technology is a common parameter that connects people, irrespective of caste, class, sex, religion, race, or political alignments, it is pertinent to evaluate and assess the role of communication technology in empowering women, particularly from the point of view of access and utilisation (Kumari, 2016, p. 31). Gender equality explains that all forms of discrimination against women need to be eliminated and information technology acts as a catalyst in realising such an ideal situation. One of the challenging issues in women's empowerment is the dissemination of information on various aspects of women's life such as information on immunisation, child mortality, maternal mortality, sanitation, nutritional awareness, and causes, prevention, and treatment of diseases (Kumari, 2016, p. 32). The gender and technology interplay consist of numerous dimensions:

- Technology to facilitate women's productivity.
- Technology to reduce women's drudgery.
- Technology to empower women.
- Technology to remove hurdles to women's growth.

- Role of women in technological fields.
- Familiarity of women in handling technology.
- Decision-making capacity of women in technology-related issues.
- Exposure of women to technological scenarios at national and international levels.
- Gender sensitivity in technological aspects (Kumari, 2016, p. 33).

The technology and gender equality interplay reveals that information technology could contribute meaningfully to women's empowerment. However, access to information technology is cardinal to women's empowerment. Women consequent to various factors are excluded from the external information sphere, both deliberately, and because of factors leading to their disadvantage such as lack of freedom of mobility or low levels of formal education (Kumari, 2016, p. 34). Kumari (2016) argues that 'women's access to and use of ICT is constrained not only by technological infrastructure, but also by socially constructed gender roles and relations'. In contemporary times, ICT could provide tremendous information to women. This is quite discernible in the context of the use and access to mobile phones. The use of mobile phones proves how technology can be used to benefit women's lives, by reducing travelling time between market and suppliers, by allowing women to call for product prices and by facilitating the constant managing of paid and unpaid family activities (Kumari, 2016, p. 34).

In India, the role of women in contributing to socio-economic development is still constrained by the patriarchal societal norms which impose certain restraints on their involvement with socio-economic realms. Such norms prevent women to have meaningful access to various socio-economic sectors. The right to self-determination and sovereignty in women's lives are still a distant dream in many parts of the country. Arrawatia (2012) argues that women's empowerment has got five dimensions such as women's sense of self-worth; their right to have and to decide their choices; their right to have access to chances and resources; their right to have the power to control their own lives, both within and outside the home; and their aptitude to influence the direction of social conversion to create a more just social and economic order, nationally and universally. The Indian women have seldom been able to come out of the rigid social structure.

The technological development focusing on Information and Communication Technologies (ICTs) has introduced several kinds of initiatives in the form of mobiles, information kiosks, call centres so on and so forth. However, these endeavoures are seldom accessed by women. Several reasons could be attributed to the hesitance on the part of women to access Information and Communication Technologies (ICT).

1. The ICT tools and their application are generally introduced for providing information for rural people which are not gender sensitive and not taking into account the constraints to access them.
2. It is also found that men are invariably involved and targeted in these IT initiatives since they take decisions on inputs, farm operations, marketing, accessing government schemes etc.
3. The information disseminated through these tools is generic. Hence, it lacks contextualisation.
4. Paucity of research on women's access and utilisation of ICT has made it difficult for policy makers to formulate a gender sensitive IT policies and initiatives (Arrawatia, 2012, p. 101).

Digital Divide: Emerging Issues

In the last several years, the world has undergone revolutionary changes in technology particularly Information and Communication Technology (ICT). This revolution is coined as 'the Information Age'. The information age has become a reality in the wake of rapid development and proliferation of computer software and hardware in the world on account of globalization and liberalization processes beginning from the 1970s onwards. As Keniston (2004) opined 'the revolution has been as dramatic, rapid, and far reaching as the agricultural revolution, the first industrial revolution (around factory production and steam engine), and its sequel, based on the chemical and electrical industries' (Keniston, 2004, p. 11). The most striking aspect of the information technology is the rapid speed in which the technology penetrates into the various walks of human life than earlier technology-based revolutions. Similar to all other kinds of technological developments, the Information and Communication Technology has evoked certain hopes and aspirations in the day-to-day life of the citizens in the form of transparency, efficiency of services, and rapid spread of information, culture so on and so forth. The democratic culture and economic prosperity have also enhanced in a big manner by information revolution.

However, the benefits of Information Age cannot be reaped by all nations of the world in uniform manner. This could be of various reasons which include technological lagging, educational backwardness, inability in acquiring IT devices etc. All these maladies in realizing a digital society in a developing country or even in a developed country is commonly referred as a situation of 'Digital Divide'. It has been argued by Chinn and Fairlie (2004) that the gulf in computer and Internet use can be attributed to differences in per capita income followed by 'disparity in telecommunications infrastructure' causing in differences in tele-connections; ownership and/or access to computers; density of mobile phones and higher generation of information-communication instrumentation; density of the Internet subscription and use; and volume of indicators, e-commerce transactions (as cited in Saith, 2008, p. 139). Digital divide is all pervasive in various degrees, but developing and least developing countries are in a deplorable condition in their efforts to bridge the digital divide. Many empirical studies had revealed the fact that huge differences could be found in accessing to ICTs even in economically advanced countries like the US and Australia, differences between the rich and poor, whites and non-whites, the educated and uneducated (Keniston, 2004, p. 12). However, some of the so-called emerging nations including India and China have made tremendous progress in the level of Internet penetration, digital revolution and ultimately to bridge the digital divide to a greater extent. Despite the endeavours of these nations, digital divide persists in various forms such as rural-urban divide, digital gender divides etc. It has been identified that there are three digital divides and the fourth one gradually appearing in several nations.

The first divide is visible in almost all nations. It is measured in terms of economic capacity-income, affordability to access ICT devices etc. This divide is more apparent in developing countries rather than in developed countries. The second divide is linguistic and cultural. In several countries, this divide brings out cleavage in speaking English or other Western European languages and those who do not. It is also significant that a cultural difference in accessing ICT exists where there is no thrust on developing local language. This is particularly noticeable in a developing or emerging nation like India.

The third divide emanates from the first two—the growing digital disparity between rich and poor nations. There is an increasing gap between the information rich nations of the North and information-poor nations of the South (Keniston, 2004, p. 16). The Northern countries such as US, Sweden, Iceland, Finland could be the leaders of bridging the digital divide where the tele-density is over 90 per cent, computer saturation over 50 per cent, and household internet connectivity averages over 50 per cent (Keniston, 2004, p. 16).

In addition to the above divides, a fourth one is identified in US and India where the ICT explosion has enabled the creation of a new software development parks, and cyber parks. The emergence of IT savvy people in these regions is characterized by money power and expertise in handling information needs of the society. While the earlier generations may not have benefited from IT revolution in terms of financial stability and skills, the new human resource in IT sector is advancing despite the ups downs of the sector.

In the first category of digital divide, the gender divide in digital technology is less studied and analysed. The digital gender divide is alarming in developing and emerging nations. The digital gender inequality is a reality that it exacerbates the already challenging aspect of women's life.

Digital Gender Divide

Despite the tremendous potentiality of ICT, in fostering gender equality and empowerment of women, a gender digital divide is a reality across the world in which women's access to information technology is found to be less that of men. The lagging on the part of women can be attributed to numerous factors as one study suggests that many things can come between women and new technology: social norms about appropriate behaviour of women, cultural attitudes, gendered division of labour, gender stereotypes and gender based violence. Hafkin (2013) contends that women may also have more to gain from ICT than men, in time, freedom and opportunities' (as cited in Devaki, 2018, p. 9). Women who have several constraints in socio-economic milieu of developing countries have similar challenges in accessing information technology as well. The socio-economic challenges and cultural norms impose restrictions on women in accessing information technology space. Women in India have to confine themselves to the private space of family thereby sidelining the skill improvement processes. Culture, media and society determine the role of women and they are not invariably motivated to fulfil their individual needs, or pursue self-growth even in socially advanced societies (Antonio, 2014, p. 674).

Theoretical Postures Gender Digital Disparity

Majority of the feminist scholars try to approach the issue argue that there is a structural inequality and the role played by technology in mitigating the inequality. Henwood contends that technology is a culture. He believes that technological meanings are not "given", they are made (Devaki, 2018, p. 32). Mies prescribes a model called 'subsistence Perspective' on technology which indicates that technology is not capable in resolving the gender inequalities but suggests a multi-dimensional approach that makes the way for ecologically sound, grassroots knowledge systems in which women have an active role, in understanding that such systems do not reinforce existing inequalities, but rather will enhance social justice (Mies, 1986). Another significant contribution to the social dimensions of technology is techno-feminism which perceives gender and technological relations averting the determinism of technophobia and techno-enthusiasm and contends that feminist politics paves the way for gender equality (Devaki, 2008, p. 32). A group of feminists assert the role of women particularly from the bottom of social and economic structure in democratisation of communication by way of augmenting participation and representation where transmission of message is democratic.

Feminists who are more radical in nature expostulate that computers are hegimonised by male values and the women has to make endeavours to create pertinent technological resources for them. The inference is that women need to play significant roles in leadership positions in the context of an alternative model of ICTs and Internet is to be created (Wood, 2005, pp. 41-53).

Internet Penetration among Women in Developing Countries

The ICT penetration among women in developing countries especially internet penetration is found to be low. It is fact that internet would provide women greater capability to participate in the digital world. Although their lower starting point provides for greater possible gains, these women continue to face gender-related discrimination that prevents them from accessing the full benefits of ICTs (Hilbert, 2011, pp. 479-489).

Moolman, Primo and Shackleton (2007) opine that the gender digital divide is one of the most significant inequalities created by the digital revolution. Some of the few studies that focus on Internet use particularly most have revealed that women in developing countries are significantly less likely to use the Internet than men. Women are found to constitute 25 per cent or less of Internet users in Africa, 22 per cent in Asia, 38 per cent in Latin America, and a meagre 6 per cent in the West Asia (Halfkin, 2001). Dugdale (2013) reports that a study conducted by Intel brought out that 25 per cent of women in developing countries had no access to internet and the figure is increased by 45 per cent in Sub-Saharan countries (as cited in Antonio, 2014, p. 677). According to Elizabeth Weingarten, there are two crucial factors that influence the digital inclusion of women—availability and affordability and one of the suggestions putting before in the report was the policymakers and technology companies to make the internet more accessible and affordable on mobile phones (Weingarten, 2013).

Obstacles to Internet Access for Women in Developing Countries

In the developing world, it is perceived that that a sizable number of women are not accessing the Internet to the same level as men and, even if access to a computer and the Internet is available, women are not necessarily utilising it. Now it is pertinent to evaluate some of the barriers to Internet penetration among women in developing countries. Gill et al. (2010) propose four barriers that prevent women's access to and use of ICTs: Exclusion from technology education and design; restrained free time; social norms favouring men; and financial and/or institutional constraints.

(a) Exclusion from Technology Education and Design

Melhem, Morrell and Tandon (2009) believe that "women and girls are poorly placed to benefit from the knowledge society because they have less access to scientific and technical education specifically and to education in general." Education is an important prerequisite for accessing technology especially Information Technology. The unfamiliarity and lack of skills in using the internet has emanated from lack of education and literacy.

(b) Restrained Free Time

Women irrespective of the class and caste factor, carries a heavy burden of household and family responsibilities. On account of a blend of domestic responsibilities and their role as primary caretakers, women have very little free time to experiment with new technologies (Antonio, 2014, p. 679). Woman's use of internet is limited by several factors such as lack of access, family engagements, negative family responses etc.

(c) Social Norms Favouring Men

Hafkin and Taggart (2001) believes that technologies are invariably the arena of men and gender norms with regard to men's control of technology, information and knowledge limit women's opportunity to learn, use and benefit from technology (as cited in Antonio, 2014, p. 679). The social stigma in using technology is found more among women than men. The lack of educational opportunities and restrictive gender norms hamper the digital inclusiveness of women.

(d) Financial and/or Institutional Constraints

Chadwick *et al.* (2013) remark that, 'due to its role as a means of information gathering and sharing, use of ICT corresponds to having increased power and control within society. The digital divide draws attention to how disempowered groups with limited economic resources have reduced access to ICTs'. The financial independence and autonomy of women are restricted to a greater extent which prevents them from accessing to ICT.

The above aspects of barriers to internet for women could be addressed by the widespread use of mobile technology. The mobile technology can tackle various challenges the women encounter such as affordability, freedom of use, time saving etc.

Mobile Phones Scenario in India

There has been a phenomenal growth of mobile phones in India from the late 1990 onwards. The reasons for the growth of mobile phones in India can be attributed to several reasons such as falling tariffs and increasing competition (Thomas, 2012, p. 44). It is a reality that in 2008, fixed density penetration ratios, after more than four decades of investment, was 3: 100, while mobile densities, in less than a decade, was already 27:100, brings out the extent of this growth (Thomas, 2012, p. 44). In the early 2008 owing to government's liberalised policies, three services including Bharathi Airtel, Reliance Communications and Tata Teleservices constitute over 50 per cent of the new mobile customers. In the same year in some of the major cities in India including Mumbai and Chennai had overwhelming rate of mobile connections.

Mobile Access and Utilization among Women

Access to mobile technology has been enhanced significantly in developing countries, as more and more cheap handsets are easily available. It has been proved that the use and access of mobile phones are beneficial for women. Women can have several advantages such as security, information, connectivity etc. Several studies reveal the fact that Mobile phones are found to empower women. A study by GSMA (Global System for Mobile Communications) a European Trade body that represents the interests of mobile network operators reveals that:

- 89 per cent of women in every country believe that mobile phones help them stay in touch with friends and families.
- 74 per cent in every country remarked that it saves time.
- 68 per cent believes that women feel safer with a mobile phone.
- 58 per cent responded that they felt more autonomous and independent.
- 60 per cent of women remarked that mobile phone saves money (GSMA, 2015).

Despite the phenomenal growth of mobile phones globally, the women are not able to utilize it properly owing to many factors including the inability in obtaining them and owner of the handsets. In Low and Middle income countries, 3 billion people still do not own mobile phones of which 1.7 billon comprise women (GSMA, 2015). Majority of them lives in South Asia, East Asia and Pacific. In Sub-Saharan Africa also, a large number of females are still to be connected. Studies reveal that mobile phone ownership gap stands at 14 per cent in Low and Middle income countries and among these countries the gender divide in South Asia is 38 per cent (GSMA, 2015). It was also found that wealthier nations among the Low and Middle income countries are better in bridging the digital gender gap such as China, Turkey, Mexico etc.

Mobile Phone Utilisation: The Indian Scenario

The study is based on a secondary data collected from GSMA Report, 2015 which analyses various dimensions of mobile usage. The mobile usage by women is studied by taking into consideration the utilization of SMS facility by both men and women in India.

Table 4.1: Mobile Phone Users in India who Report Never Sending an SMS (Mobile phone owners %)

Mobile Phone Owners who report never sending SMS	*Mobile Phone Owners from poorer households who report never sending SMS*	*Mobile Phone Owners from wealthier households who report never sending SMS*
Male—33% Female—55%	Male—48% Female—69%	Male—20% Female—44%

Source: GSMA Report, 2015.

The study indicates that women are lagging behind men in sending SMS. This could be of variety of reasons—lack of education, value appreciation of mobile phones, lack of technical knowledge so on and so forth. This challenge on the part of women could be resolved by providing sufficient technical skills to females and make handsets cheaper in its price.

Social Media Attraction to Women

Another significant dimension of usage of mobiles is the attraction towards new social media. New Social Media often appeals women, however, women lags behind men in using new social media. A 2017 study of Face book penetration in India by age and gender-wise data points out those women of various age groups are hesitant to use Facebook.

Table 4.2: FaceBook Users by Gender and Age (2017)

Age-wise Data	*FaceBook Users by Gender (Million)*
13-17 Years	4 Million Female 14 Million Male
18-24 Years	20.8 Million Female 61.8 Million Male
25-34 Years	13.3 Million Female 44.7 Million Male
45-54 Years	2.1 Million Female 5.3 Million Male

Source: statista.com

GSMA report reveals that social media appeals are significantly favourable to men rather than women. The following are certain significant findings:

Table 4.3: Smart Phone and Feature Phone Owners Who Report Using Facebook or We Chat, Twitter or Weibo in India

Facebook or Wechat	*Twitter or Weibo*
Male—50 % Female—26%	Male—22 % Female—14 %

Source: GSMA (2015).

Women in developing countries do not possess mobile phones on their own, they tend to borrow mobile phones from their close relatives. This particular dimension is a significant indication of women falling behind men in using mobile phones. In South Asia as a whole phone sharing and borrowing are common phenomena. Those women, who live at the bottom of the society, may give priority to other pressing needs of the society over purchasing mobile phones. India is not an exception to this. In India, 29 per cent of women tend to borrow mobile phones from their close relatives, while 6 per cent of men borrow from others (GSMA, 2015). The proportion of rural and urban woman in borrowing handsets and SIM exhibit the pattern that 18 per cent of urban women tend to borrow, whereas 34 per cent rural women borrow in India (GSMA, 2015). It is also found that women in India have a propensity to buy handsets and SIM more from household and friends.

Barriers Encountered by Women to Mobile Ownership and Usage

There are several barriers to mobile ownership and usage. Some are technical and infrastructural issues and others are social and family norms. Women often encounter numerous barriers which include—cost, security and harassment, and technical literacy and confidence (GSMA, 2015). These factors can be justified by social norms and practices.

Table 4.4: Cost Factor as a Barrier for Women to Use Mobile Phones (%)

Cost	*Men*	*Women*
Handset Cost	51	57
SIM Cost	25	29
Credit Cost	36	39
Battery Charging Cost	17	16

Source: GSMA (2015).

Cost factor shows that except in the case of battery charging cost, all other cost factors are really a challenge for women.

With regard to network quality 45 per cent women felt that it was a barrier and only 35 per cent of men find it difficult cope with poor network quality (GSMA, 2015).

The third significant barrier for women to use mobile phones is the perception of security and harassment. It means the security issues pertaining to the use and ownership of mobile phones and harassment from strangers. In India, 37 per cent of women responded that they are concerned about the security issues related to mobile phones including theft (GSMA, 2015). On the other hand, only 35 per cent of men worried about security concerns. Women are concerned about strangers misusing the handset and in India 33 per cent of women included in that segment which acts as barrier. Harassment comes from Facebook, WhatsApp and also mobile calls from strangers. Some women are concerned about the misuse of their profile photos in WhatsApp.

A barrier which is a combination of technical, cultural and psychological factors is technical literacy and confidence. Technical literacy denotes an individual's capacity to use mobile phones in all its aspects. Confidence assumes that a sense of self-confidence in handling the mobile phones. The study discerns that 34 per cent of women in India had no awareness regarding the use of mobile and its complex features. As far as men are concerned the technical literacy as a barrier is only 23 per cent. Women also encounter cultural barrier of trouble of reading content and language particularly English language. Lack of confidence also poses as a challenge to women accessing mobiles and 38 per cent women in India comprise that category.

Social Norms and Practices

Women encounter a plethora of discriminatory practices both conscious and unconscious which prevent them from using mobiles. In households there is deliberate attempt to give preferential consideration for men and boys (GSMA, 2015). In India gender disparity exists in financial independence of women in purchasing and possessing mobile phones and even a SIM.

In India only 19 per cent of women make decisions themselves to purchase handsets as compared to 72 per cent of men and 41 per cent of women had no role in choosing the handset (GSMA, 2015). It is also an alarming situation that a mere 44 per cent of women spend their own money to purchase the handsets as against 83 per cent of men handset owners (GSMA, 2015). Even the social norms prevent female mobile owners to visit mobile shops alone for credit purposes. In some parts of the country particularly in rural areas, there is a tendency to check young women's mobile phones to prevent unwanted calls by family members.

A comparative analysis of emerging and Less Developed countries unveil a dismal scenario of digital gender gap. GSMA studied three emerging nations such as China, India and Mexico and one Less Developed country—Tanzania for deciphering the grim reality of gender digital divide in mobile phone utilisation. Table 4.5 indicates the level of utilisation of mobile phones for various purposes.

Table 4.5: Mobile Utilisation in Various Countries (Gender Based)

Country	*Make/Receive calls*	*Send/Receive SMS/MMS*	*Use Mobile Internet*
China	Male—99% Female—99%	Male—89% Female—85%	Male—77% Female—74%
India	Male—77% Female—78%	Male—46% Female—35%	Male—31% Female—13%
Mexico	Male—94% Female—94%	Male—78% Female—80%	Male—79% Female—75%
Tanzania	Male—78 % Female—75%	Male—50% Female—42%	Male—36% Female—13%

Source: GSMA Intelligence Consumer Survey, 2017.

The GSMA study suggests that India is lagging behind the emerging nations in terms of mobile utilisation by women and even Tanzania is in the forefront in the arena of mobile internet use and making and sending mobile calls. The digital gender divide is very much manifest in India when compared to the two emerging and one less developed nations.

Online activity of mobile internet users in selected countries including India reveals that gender divide is still a pernicious issue (Table 4.6).

Conclusion

The digital divide has become a global phenomenon. Digital divide is even visible in developed nations. The developing and least developed nations are striving hard to tide over the challenges posed by digital divide. Apart from infrastructural and technical issues, cultural and social issues

Table 4.6: Online Activity of Mobile Internet Users in Selected Countries

Country	*Use Instant Messaging*	*Use Social Media*	*Browse the Internet*	*Download/ Use Apps*	*Make/Receive Video Calls*
China	M—95% F—95%	M—86% F—85%	M—81% F—74%	M—58% F—53%	M—74% F—74%
India	M—70% F—51%	M—54% F—49%	M—53% F—51%	M—42% F—44%	M--57% F—57%
Mexico	M—90% F—85%	M—86% F—79%	M—73% F—65%	M—60% F—62%	M—45% F—51%
Tanzania	M—59% F—55%	M—63% F—65%	M—52% F—41%	M—38% F—29%	M—25% F—31%

Source: GSMA Intelligence Consumer Survey, 2017.
M—Male, F—Female

come in the way of bridging digital divide. One such social issue is the growing gender disparity in using ICT. The study examines the digital gender divide in developing nations with a focus on India. The Indian scenario reveals that the gender gap is predominant by analysing the various dimensions of the use of mobile handsets. Several issues hamper women in accessing mobiles. These include—issues of ownership, lack of autonomy, cost of handsets, and lack of technical knowhow, lack of confidence and social norms and practices. The GSMA studies expose that among the emerging nations as well, the gender digital divide is noticeable. The Indian situation of digital gender divide is really challenging to the policy-makers. To tide over such barriers are difficult in the context of persisting maladies women suffer in the current Indian scenario.

REFERENCES

Antonio, Amy and David Tuffley (2014). "The Gender Digital Divide in Developing Countries", *Future Internet*, 6.

Arrawatia, Mini Amit and Pankaj Meel (2012). "Information and Communication Technologies and Women Empowerment in India", *International Journal of Advanced Research in Computer Engineering and Technology*, 1(8).

Chadwick Darren; Carroline Wesson; and Chris Fullwood (2013). "Internet Access by People with Intellectual disabilities, inequalities and opportunities", *Future Internet*, 5(3).

Devaki, Konstantina (2018). The Underlying Causes of Digital Gender Gap and Possible Solutions for Enhanced Digital Inclusion of Women and Girls,

Policy Department for Citizens' Rights and Constitutional Affairs, Directorate General for Internal Policies of the Union, European Parliament, Brussels.

Gill, K.; Brooks, K.; McDougall, J.; Patel, P. and Kes, A (2010). *Gender Divide: How Technology can advance Women Economically*. International Centre for Research on Women. Washington DC.

GSMA (2015). Connected Women Bridging the Gender Gap: Mobile Access and Usage in Low and Middle Income Countries. Accessed from https://www.gsma.com/mobile for development/wp-content/uploads/2016/02.

GSMA (2017). Connected Women, Mobile Gender Gap Report (2018). Accessed from https://www.gsma.com/mobilefordevelopmenty/connected-women/the-mobile-gender-gap report-2018/

Halfkin, N. (2001). *IT and Developing Countries: An Analytic Study*, Washington D.C.: Centre for Education Innovations.

Hilbert, M. (2011). Digital Gender Divide or technologically empowered women in developing countries? A typical case of lies, damned lies and statistics, *Women's Studies International Forum*, 34(6). Retrieved from http://www.martinhibert.net/Digital Gender Divide.

Keniston, Kenneth (2004). "The Four Digital Divides", In Kenneth Keniston and Deepak Kumar (Eds.), *IT Experience in India: Bridging the Digital Divide*, New Delhi: Sage.

Kumari, Priti and Prabhas Kumar (2016). "ICT-A Road Map of Women Empowerment", In Ashutosh Vyas (Ed.), *Gender Issues and Women Empowerment: Dimension and Development*, Jaipur, Book Enclave.

Melhem, S.; Morrel, C.; and Tandon, N. (2009). *Information Communications Technologies for Women's Socio-Economic Empowerment*. Retrieved from http://elibrary.worldbank.org/doi/book/10.1596/978-0-8213.8133-5.

Mies, M. (1986). *Patriarchy and Accumulation on a World Scale: Women in the International Division of Labour*. London: Zed Books.

Moolman, J.; Primo, N.; and Shackleton, S. (2007). Taking a byte of Technology: Women and ICTs. Empower. Women Gender Equity.

Saith, Ashwani (2008). "ICTs and Poverty Alleviation: Hope or Hype", In Ashwani Saith; M. Vijayabaskar; and V. Gyathri (Eds.). *ICTs and Indian Social Change: Diffusion, Poverty, and Governance*, New Delhi: Sage.

Thomas, Pradip Ninan. (2012), *Digital India: Understanding Information, Communication and Social Change*, New Delhi: Sage.

Weingarten, E. (2013). The Developing World needs more Internet Users 2013. Retrieved fromhttp://www.slate.com/articles/technology/technology/2013/01/

Woods, P. (2005). "Gender and Information and Communication Technology: Towards an Analytical Framework". In APC WNSP (2005), *Gender Evaluation Methodologies for Internet and ICTs: A Learning Tool for Change and Empowerment*. Association for Progressive Communications Women's Networking Support Programme.

5

Knowledge Management and E-Governance

M.R. Biju and *M.R.B. Anantha Padmanabha*

Knowledge has always been a cornerstone of all decision-making. It is essential when we set out to achieve goals as individuals, communities, countries or regions, because decisions made are based on what is known at the time the action is taken. In order to make the best decisions possible it is necessary to ensure that those with the responsibility have or have access to the needed skills, experiences, understandings and values, when and where it is required, to do so. Knowledge Management (KM) makes this possible. Managing knowledge is not an easy task. It is inherently part of all individuals, sectors, communities and organizations in a country. The role that knowledge plays in decision-making and the potential impact it has on the lives of all these carriers of knowledge and countries has made it necessary for governments to manage their knowledge and leverage it to further good governance so that they can effectively foster innovation and creativity geared towards development. Knowledge management is a tool that when implemented enables the availability and accessibility of knowledge through its distinct, but interdependent processes and activities of creation, capture, storage and retrieval and transfer. Broadly the processes and activities surrounding knowledge management can be divided into those that enable and ensure the creation of knowledge and those that enable and ensure the sharing of knowledge. Creation processes ensure that new knowledge is available and sharing processes makes it transferable.

The success of knowledge management activities and processes depends on the goals, practices and culture of an organization, and on the willingness of its employees to change their mindsets, perceptions and ways they work. Some knowledge processes can be implemented within the current government structure and hierarchies, but to be truly successful fundamental changes, such as flatter hierarchies, are necessary to ensure greater fluidity of skills, experiences, understandings within government as well as between government and its citizenry. KM is increasingly imperative as it is regarded as the key determinant of a firm, industry or country for survival and growth in knowledge era. Varieties of disciplines have contributed to knowledge and KM. Research focuses on one or more specific fields, but to understand which levels of knowledge processes KM should concentrate on, should be more fundamental than advocacy of KM. Knowledge management is not just about creating and storing knowledge so that we can access it when and where it is needed, it also brings about fundamental changes in the way government processes are designed and executed, and the way national policies, plans and strategies are developed and implemented.

Significance of Knowledge Management

Knowledge management, is defined as "a discipline that promotes an integrated approach to identifying, capturing, evaluating, retrieving and sharing enterprise information assets." (Gartner Group). Knowledge Management is a process that, continuously and systematically, transfers knowledge from individuals and teams, who generate them, to the brain of the organisation for the benefit of the entire organisation. It is the systematic, explicit, and deliberate building, renewal, and application of knowledge to maximize an enterprise's knowledge-related effectiveness and returns from its knowledge assets. Knowledge Management in an organization involves the following steps:

- Development of these knowledge assets,
- Capturing and preservation of the knowledge, and
- Using and sharing of the knowledge.

Knowledge Management is often perceived as merely a technological solution; in fact it has a much wider connotation since it is aimed at enabling people to efficiently perform their functions. For citizens, the benefits to be reaped from KM include better services, more choices, more personalization and greater accountability of how their money is spent. For the organization, KM provides the major benefit of improving the organization's performance through increased efficiency and innovation. But for these benefits to occur, the back office processes must be in place. KM is founded on most valuable resource is the knowledge of its people. This year's Survey therefore looks at the issue of connected governance from the perspective of how governments manage and how they should manage their back office processes. The steps of a KM process can be summarized as:

- Knowledge creation,
- Knowledge capture,
- Knowledge application, and
- Knowledge impact measurement.

Governments across the globe are the biggest source of information and knowledge by virtue of their size and complexity of processes. Inadequate or no knowledge management practices within the Government generally lead to loss of opportunity as a result of lost institutional memory, knowledge gaps and non-availability of appropriate inputs for decision-making. Although, Government has lagged behind a bit in realizing the importance of knowledge management, but with the tremendous investment in KM in the private sector leading to substantial benefits, governments too have started to appreciate the benefits of KM. The motivation for the Government to adopt KM practices are factors like existence of a vast knowledge pool, shrinking Government budgets and the need to promote knowledge sharing within and across government organizations leading to achievement of better governance.

In India, governments, both at the Union and State levels, have witnessed the intervention of KM initiatives albeit in a sporadic manner these efforts have been initiated either because of the interest of some Government officials or due to a push from technology/consulting companies to sell their products/services. There have been no instances of KM initiatives undertaken as a matter of policy.

Promoting KM in Government: Knowledge Management is essentially about facilitating the processes by which knowledge is created, shared and used in organizations. It is not about setting up a new department or getting in a new technology. It is about making changes to the way individuals in organisations function. There are many ways of looking at Knowledge Management and different organizations will take different approaches. Generally speaking, creating a knowledge environment usually requires changing organizational values and culture, changing people's behaviours and work patterns, and providing people with easy access to each other and to relevant information resources.

Knowledge Management: Varied Points of View

Niki Frasheri has brought out the varied points of view of Knowledge Management. It can be summarized as under:

1. Cultural Point of View

We will use three of cultural dimensions developed by Hofstede to focus the attention in main cultural aspects that have to do with KM.

Uncertainty avoidance (UAI)—How comfortable people feel towards ambiguity (high if ambiguity creates stress, non-acceptance of conflicts and need for regulations). Low ranked cultures feel more comfortable with the unknown.

Power distance (PDI)—extent to which less powerful members of organizations accept that power is distributed unequally (high if there is a need of dependence and hierarchy, inequality is accepted and superiors are inaccessible). Individualism versus collectivism (IDV, high if conscious "I" instead of "we", obligations "to self" instead of "to group", loss of "self-respect" instead of "face/shame").

Values of cultural dimensions vary in different countries, and we need to take into account potential differences related with the degree of development of the country. The key question is "how easy people may give away his personal tacit experience and accept that of others?"

KM implies formalization of explicit and tacit knowledge within complex IS and increasing the regulation of an organization. That means to reduce the degree of ambiguity of the organization's system. Communities characterized by lower values of UAI feel better with higher ambiguity and may not easily accept reducing of ambiguity.

Knowledge is power, in the same way as information but of higher value. Deployment of KM systems means direct access to the knowledge for decision-makers, that otherwise would have to directly address to lower levels staff to prepare it. Links between different levels of hierarchy become more invisible and work of personnel more regulated. Communities characterized by lower values of PDI would feel uneasy with the idea of strengthening the hierarchy.

The value of knowledge assets is higher that those of information due to the component of experience. Knowledge gives power to each individual. Communities characterized by higher values of IDV would not easily accept the idea of giving away personal experiences. In this context it is important to consider individualism as missing of "team spirit" necessary for the personnel of an organization to work together. The same "dimensions" can be mapped in political, managerial and technical "spaces".

2. Political Point of View

KM implies creation of a "central repository to share and evaluate captured knowledge". "Centrality" is a necessity for development of a dense mesh of links between different pieces of information as a substratum for storing of captured experience. This concept of "centrality" does not match with the principle of decentralization, which is an important component of political agendas today, both in administration and SME businesses.

On the other hand, formalization and management of knowledge implies application of complex regulations as guide for daily operations of organizations and decision making. Such requirements do not match with practices followed in developing countries, characterized by lack of structured information systems in public administration and dominance of personal preferences of decision-makers instead of professionalism.

3. Managerial Point of View

An important policy in today's management of organizations is promotion of individual and small group initiatives as an effective way for better use of resources, opening of new perspectives and markets, and sustainability. On the other hand, deployment of KM implies formalization of the knowledge and application of regulations to force people to use captured knowledge. In such context it is necessary to define a delicate balance between applications of existing experiences versus creation of new experiences.

How may we realize such balance in daily work of employees? Considering the complexity of society's problems, it cannot be done simply through regulations, particularly in developing context. It is well-known that forcing deployment of IS in some organizations, even in developed countries, may dramatically fail if end-user preferences are not considered. The goodwill of employees and decision-makers to evaluate positively with "team spirit" different constraints and optimize the ratio between existing and new experiences is a necessity (it smells like "Confucism").

4. Technical Point of View

"Centrality" seems to be a principal issue for KM. On the other hand, considering the decentralization policies, we may expect development of separate IS and the use of telecommunication means for their interconnection and exchange of data. KM requires much more—a distributed IS to function as a centralized one. We need to design distributed systems (to match with decentralization) that may run as a centralized easily accessible system (to match with KM requirements). It goes beyond actual web-based technologies; probably grid technologies may give a hand, but anyway it means considerable investments and in this point new problems and ambiguities emerge.

As summary, we have to deal with a complex of political, managerial and social factors that are specific for different countries, especially when developed and developing worlds come together. The main idea is that we need to consider this "difference of rationalities".

Application of ICT in Knowledge Management

The advent of information and communication technologies (ICT) has for ever changed the ways that knowledge, information and data are stored, accessed and shared and therefore forms an integral part of decision-making processes and the road to achieve good governance. It should therefore be an important component of any knowledge management strategy that is developed and implemented by governments.

When discussing the implementation of knowledge management the conversation more often than not focuses on ICT solutions, applications and infrastructures. It is important to understand that ICT, although important, are not the main actors in knowledge management. Rather, ICT is there to support the knowledge processes employed. ICT provide for faster knowledge flows through systems, ensuring that it reaches its targets faster so that faster and effective decision-making is possible.

In the Caribbean, where the national boundaries are often characterised by multi-island classification, ICT is essential for effective knowledge management. The Internet, mobile technologies and the advent of faster connections and applications make it possible for governments to connect with citizens in large geographical areas and efficiently deliver products and services to them.

ICT not only makes the government accessible to people, but also make the knowledge, information and data held by citizens accessible for the national government. In the same way that the government uses ICT to deliver services it can use it to gather needed understandings, experiences and skills from citizens and other groups to inform their decision-making for good governance.

The use of ICT also enables the achievement of good governance as it encourages transparency and the effectiveness in the delivery of services and thus helps to combat corruption. Providing citizens with access to information from the government and participation in the government democratic governance and the protection of human rights can be furthered.

In order for ICT to be an effective underlying infrastructure for knowledge management and decision-making practices in government and a supporter in the achievement of good governance, its development and implementation should be carefully planned alongside the national development goals of a country. Dysfunctional ICT initiatives will only cause frustration for citizens and eventually harm the relationship between the citizenry and the government and impact negatively on good governance goals.

Importance of Knowledge Management in e-Government

Knowledge management provides the overall strategy to manage the e-content of e-government by providing knowledge organization tools and techniques, monitoring updatedness of knowledge contents and availing all necessary information to citizens. Zhou & Gao (2007) have identified three benefits of knowledge management in e-government as being conducive to enhance governments' competence, to raise governments service quality, and to promote healthy development of e-government. Knowledge needs to be managed time and cost effectively in order to connect citizens to citizens and citizens to government and vice versa to make participative government policies and decisions. That brings government transparency and citizen empowerment and buys in of government projects and policies and consequently results in a more citizen-centric government. So, the success of e-government depends heavily on knowledge management. "Knowledge management for e-government is no longer a choice but an imperative if economies have to survive in the unfolding era of privatization, liberalization and globalization" (Misra, 2007). Thus e-government is not merely a transformation from manual to digital; it is a collective vision of all government activities, vision and mission. Since e-government is largely knowledge-intensive, it requires knowledge management applications and techniques to represent government. This raises several issues of concern in e-government.

Major Issues of Concerns in e-Government

There are a number of major issues of concern faced in e-government, identified below:

- E-government content is haphazard.
- Information is not updated regularly, which hinders informed decision-making in all sectors of government and non-government.
- All necessary information is not available, that leaves an e-portal incomplete.
- Use of obsolete information technology: often the latest information technologies are not used or embraced quickly enough to keep the pace with the global society.
- Government portals are often designed by 'non-professionals', who are not trained in knowledge application tools and techniques. They do not know how to adequately create, capture, store, share and update the site information.
- Knowledge is presented in a standard format, which may not be suitable for all citizens and stakeholders.
- Budgetary constraints obstruct the affordability of infrastructure for e-government.
- There is a lack of good policies and legislation to provide a roadmap and action plan to manage knowledge on government e-portals.
- A lack of understating of ethical behaviour in e-government is another issue.

E-Governance based on KM

E-governance has not made enough impact on the people as e-commerce and e-learning have done. There are several barriers on the roads of e-governance. From the software engineering point of view, e-governance has a lot of characteristics, which are different from e-commerce and e-learning. Unlike e-commerce and e-learning, e-governance needs to be proactive. While e-commerce and e-learning involve information management, e-governance involves KM. KM is the management of information, skill, experience, innovation, and intelligence. E-governance mostly based on Knowledge Management System (KMS) is built on KM cycle of knowledge capturing, knowledge sharing, knowledge enhancing, and knowledge preserving. The development model of e-governance, based on information management system, applies a cycle-based process such as waterfall, spiral or iterative process. E-governance is a combination of interaction and integration. It is also a path-based process.

Conclusion

All governments should strive to achieve good governance, as this will help in the eradication of poverty, combating corruption and ensuring that economic, social and environmental development goals are met, while improving the wellness of citizens. In order to achieve good governance the best decisions possible should be taken. This is only possible when governments, citizens and communities have access to knowledge that can inform their decisions and actions. Knowledge management is a tool that can ensure the availability and accessibility of knowledge when and where it is needed, but it should be planned and integrated into the national strategies of a country to ensure success. ICT is an enabler of knowledge management initiatives, and not knowledge management itself. The implementation thereof should, therefore, be carefully considered and aligned with strategies and national development goals. This will ensure that ICT implementations are effective and efficient. Before conclude, the authors would like to add the recommendation made by Second ARC Report (December 2008) in this regard. The Commission has recommended that "Union and State Governments should take proactive measures for establishing knowledge management systems as a pivotal steps for administrative reforms in general and e-governanace in particular."

REFERENCES

Asoh, D.; Belardo, S. and Neilson, R. (2002). *Knowledge Management: Issues, Challenges and Opportunities for Governments in the New Economy.*

Bangemann M. et al. (1994). "Europe and the global information society Recommendations to the European Council". Brussels.

Chakraborty, Arun Kumar (2008). "Symbiosis between Knowledge Society and E Governance", *DESIDOC Journal of Library and Information Technology*, 28(5): 27-34, DESIDOC.

Cong and Pandya (2003). *Issues of Knowledge Management in the Public Sector*. Accessed 4 May, 2009: http://www.ejkm.com/volume-1/volume1-issue-2/issue-2-art-3-cong-pandya.pdf.

Frasheri, N. (2001), E-Governance, International Cooperation and Security: New Millennium Challenges for a Small Country. *SSRC ITIC Work Paper*.

Frasheri, Neki, *Knowledge Management for E-Governance*, http://itc.upt.al/nfra/papers/informatics/BCI2-knowledge-management-for-egovernance.pdf

Gupta, Rachna and Jasvinder Singh (2014). "Knowledge Management and Innovation in (e)Government", *International Journal of Information and Computation Technology*. Volume 4, Number 16, pp. 1637-1645, International Research Publications House. http://www. irphouse.com

Halsey, W.D. (ed.) (1986). *Collier's Dictionary*, Macmillan Publishing,

Heeks R. (2001). Building e-Governance for Development: A Framework for National and Donor Action. *I-Government Working Paper Series*, IDPM, University of Manchester, UK.

Heeks R. (2004). *e-Government for Development: Using ICT-s for Government Transparency*, IDPM, University of Manchester, http://www. egov4dev.org/topic2smry.htm

Heeks, R. (2008). *What is E-Government?* Accessed 14 March, 2009: http://www. egov4dev.org/success/definitions.shtml.

https://repositorio.cepal.org/bitstream/handle/11362/38381/1/LCCARL413_en.pdf

Institute for Development Policy and Management (2008). *What is e Government?* Accessed 23 March, 2009: http://www. egov4dev. org/success/definitions. shtml#definition.

Margetts, H. (1991). "The Computerization of Social Security: the Way Forward or a Step Backwards?", *Public Administration*, Vol. 69, No. 3.

Nath, V. (2000). Networking Networks for Empowerment and Governance, *Global Development Network*, World Bank, Japan. http://www.cddc.vt.edu/digitalgov/gov-menu.html

Prytherch, R. (comp.), *Harrod's Librarians' Glossary and Reference* (2000)., Gower, London, 9th Ed.

Second Administrative Reform Commission Report (2008), *Promoting E Governance: The Smart Way Forward*, Govt. of India, New Delhi. https://darpg.gov.in/arc-reports

Wriston W. (1997). "Bits, Bytes, and Diplomacy", *Foreign Affairs*, Vol. 76, No. 5.

6

Analysis of E-Government Development Index (EGDI) Using Socio-Economic Indicators

Yudhishthira Sapru

E-Government is unquestionably one of the most crucial developments which has changed the way governments deliver information and services to their citizens. It holds the promise to promote democracy, reduce fraud, improve efficiency and increase citizen participation in government. These facts have prompted government officials and academics to attempt to benchmark or rank these programmes in order to set the standard for best practice, to acknowledge top performers, and to motivate lagging countries to invest in IT infrastructure and e-Governance initiatives.

One of the most comprehensive and popular surveys to access readiness on e-Governance is the United Nations E-Government Survey which is published every two-years by the Department of Economic and Social Affairs of the United Nations (United Nations, 2014). The survey assesses the E-Government development status of all the United Nations Member States. It serves as a tool for policy-makers to identify their areas of strength and challenges in e-Governance and to guide E-Government policies and strategies.

E-Government rankings have joined the likes of other famous indices such as the Human Development Index (HDI) and the Gini coefficient in helping to define the conditions within a country (Whitmore, 2012).

India has been ranked quite low in the index reflecting poor levels of e-Government in the country. In the latest edition of the Survey (2014), India has been ranked at mere 118 despite country's huge thrust on making electronic public service delivery. The National e-Governance Plan (NeGP) was initiated in 2006, has received only moderate success. Though some initiatives like National Passport and eBiz portal have been a huge success, other initiatives have failed to take off especially at the State level in the country.

The conceptual framework of the United Nations E-Government Survey has rested on three dimensions—(i) the availability of online services, (ii) telecommunication infrastructure, and (iii) human capacity—only while the constituent measures of each of these dimensions has varied over the years. Although, these dimensions provide a good measure for overall E-Government readiness, these dimensions do not directly relate to the commonly used socio-economic indicators. The current methodology for calculation of EGDI and availability of data in public domain makes it difficult and costly for effective calculation of this index at country level, state or even district levels. UN undertakes a comprehensive exercise every two-years to calculate this index. It was deemed worthy to investigate and find indicators which have high level of association with the EGDI. The aim was to come up with a model which expresses EGDI in terms of commonly identifiable socio-economic indicators. This model will be useful for economically poor countries and a federal country like India to access the E-Government readiness at State level also. The model will give the policy-makers a handy tool to see where each state stands so that the states can be ranked and benchmarked against the state which is performing the best.

Accordingly, this research includes three objectives—(i) to analyse whether EGDI of countries varies with income levels, (ii) To analyse the correlation between Human Development Index and EGDI, and (iii) To create a regression model for EGDI in term of socio-economic indicators.

E-Government Development Index (EGDI)

Since its inception in 2003, the conceptual framework of the United Nations E-Government Survey has adopted a holistic view of E-Government development resting on three important dimensions: (i) the availability of online services, (ii) telecommunication infrastructure, and (iii) human capacity. Each year, data on the availability of online government services, the telecommunications infrastructure of each country, and various aspects of country's human capital are collected. The data are then combined into aggregate indices which are further combined into a top level EGDI (called E-Government Readiness Index prior to 2010). This index is then used to rank the UN Member States' E-Government programmes.

Mathematically, the EGDI is a weighted average of three normalized scores on three dimensions: scope and quality of online services (Online Service Index, called OSI), development status of telecommunication infrastructure (Telecommunication Infrastructure Index, called TII) and inherent human capital (Human Capital Index, called HCI). Each of these sets of indices is in itself a composite measure that can be extracted and analyzed independently.

The 2014 Survey covered 193 Member States. For the first time, all 193 United Nations Member States had the national websites which where were reviewed, but a majority of countries remain at the low or intermediate levels of E-Government development.

Review of Literature

E-Government is unquestionably one of the most critical developments in government information over the last several decades. It holds the promise to promote democracy, reduce fraud, improve efficiency and increase citizen participation in government (Whitmore, 2012).

Given the importance of E-Government, academics have started to attempt to benchmark or rank E-Government programmes in order to set the standard for best practice, to acknowledge top performers, and to motivate lagging countries to invest in this critical area.

Several researchers have attempted to evaluate E-Government programmes at various levels of the government. Some researchers have focused on making methodological recommendations by comparing and contrasting qualitative and quantitative approaches to E-Government programme evaluation. Baker (2009) has suggested a content-analysis methodology utilizing Guttman-type scales refine usability assessments of E-Government websites. He has identified six dimensions to portray the aggregate influence on website usability, viz. Online Services, User-help, Navigation, Legitimacy, Information Architecture, Acessibility accommodations. Similarly, Gupta & Jana (2003) have suggested a flexible framework to choose an appropriate strategy to measure the tangible and intangible benefits of E-Government.

Potnis (2010) has made certain recommendations for developing better informed, more balanced, and more powerful EGDI and E-Government Participation Index for the future. The first recommendation underlined the need to balance criteria assessing hard and soft components of e-

Governance. The second recommendation offered a solution to better equip the UN for assessing capabilities of Member States, which are shaped by their willingness for empowering their citizens with knowledge and information required for e-Participation. The third recommendation has a message of elevating the equity in the UN e-Readiness rankings. The fourth recommendation includes applications of NPV, BEV, and ROI as criteria to evaluate the success in terms of efficiency of E-Government initiatives. Since effective and efficient knowledge management is the backbone for any Knowledge-based Society, the fifth recommendation expects the survey to build a metric for assessing effectiveness and efficiency of knowledge management achieved through e-Governance. The sixth recommendation focuses on maintaining a consistency among a series of Surveys in order to maintain the current position of the Indices as a point-of-reference in the digital government community.

There is debate among scholars about what constitutes E-Government success, what method is best for measuring it, and which variables best describe it. This lack of consensus naturally leads to disagreement about the best approach for ranking the E-Government programmes of different countries. Whitmore (2012) has evaluated the current standard in E-Government ranking—the United Nations EGDI, by performing a confirmatory factor analysis on the data reported in the 2010 United Nations E-Government Survey. He has identified several technical issues with the index and pointed to the need for a statistical tool that can be used to evaluate and guide the development of E-Government ranking systems. The author has recommended that researchers need to develop a new paradigm for quantitative E-Government ranking that uses factor analysis to aid in the selection of variables, the organization of aggregate constructs, and the determination of weights.

Gauld, Goldfinch, & Horsburgh (2010) have examined the use of and support for E-Government measures. The study found that while respondents were generally supportive of E-Government on a number of measures, but a majority was reluctant to use some of the more sophisticated 'transactional' E-Government measures, and less than half had even visited a government website. High users of information and communication technologies (ICT) were more likely to use E-Government measures, and are more positive towards E-Government in general across several measures.

Ojo, Janowski, & Estevez (2005) have compared different E-Government ranking systems to synthesize a set of "core indicators" and have suggested ways to determine the weights for them that can be used to rank E-Government programmes. These include number of PCs, Internet Users, Online population, mobile subscription, TVs, e-Information, e-Consultation etc. An important core indicator which is also an important socio-economic factor is the 'adult literacy'. Rorissa, Demissie, & Pardo (2011) have compared different frameworks for E-Government ranking and discussed ways to offset the limitations of the different approaches.

Existing studies of E-Government concentrate on the supply-side by focusing on the availability and level of sophistication of online services and usage. Graafland-Essers & Ettedgui (2003) have addressed the demand-side of E-Government—not only usage, but also perceptions and barriers to utilisation that have not been treated previously. The results indicated that a familiarity with using the Internet tended to correlate with a higher interest in online services.

This EGDI, though rich in depth and breadth of data collection, relies on a method that is a simple mathematical average of the values of the variables measured. Ayanso, Chatterjee & Cho (2011) have proposed alternative indices based on principal components analysis (PCA).

Farooquie (2011) has investigated the E-Government readiness scenario in India and UAE vis-à-vis other countries in Asia. He has found that the economic structure of a country also matters in its E-Government readiness.

The review of literature indicates that authors above have done a good job at identifying the diverse perspectives on E-Government and the conceptual and methodological challenges surrounding the question of how to measure E-Government success. However, the literature on using proxy measures for measuring EGDI is much less developed than the more general literature on E-Government. This literature gap highlights the need for the identification of proxy measures to evaluate the EGDI.

The Department of Electronics and Information Technology (DEIT) of the Government of India and the National Council for Applied Economic Research (NCAER) have collaborated in producing the India e-Readiness Reports since 2003 (DEIT, 2011). The focus of these reports has been to evaluate the ability of the State Governments and Union Territories Administration to pursue value creation opportunities and accompanying inclusive economic development. The e-Readiness index is a Relative Index and includes three sub-components, namely (i) the ICT environment of a given state or community, (ii) the readiness of the community's key stakeholders to use ICT and (iii) the actual usage of ICT among these stakeholders. Although, the index appears to be a right step in the direction, however, it is not as popular as the United Nations EGDI.

Method

An empirical analysis was conducted on the data available from various sources. The data from United Nations E-Government Survey, 2014 was primarily used as the base data.

A definition of World Bank was used to categorize countries into low, medium and high income economies. As of 1 July, 2014, low-income economies are defined as those with a GNI per capita, calculated using the World Bank Atlas method, of $1,045 or less in 2013; middle-income economies are those with a GNI per capita of more than $1,045 but less than $12,746; and high-income economies are those with a GNI per capita of $12,746 or more.

In addition, Human Development Index data for the year 2014 was used in the analysis and was assessed through the website of United Nations Development Programme (http://hdr.undp.org/en/data).

The data about socio-economic factors pertaining to various countries was taken from World Bank database (http://data.worldbank.org/). The latest data available was for the year 2013. It was considered valid to compare socio-economic data of 2013 with United Nations E-Government Survey of 2014 on account of two reasons. Firstly, United Nations E-Government Survey is conducted only once in two years and therefore, 2014 data pertained to analysis conducted during 2013 and 2014. Secondly, it was safe to assume that socio-economic indicators would not have changed much over a period of one year.

The commonly used socioeconomic factors which were considered useful to interpret were chosen for the analysis. These were (i) GDP (current Billion US $), (ii) GDP growth (annual %), (iii) GNI per capita, Atlas method (current US $), (iv) Life expectancy at birth, total (years), (v) Unemployment, total (% of total labour force) (modeled ILO estimate), (vi) Urban population (% of total), (vii) Health expenditure per capita (current US $), and (viii) Internet users (per 100 people).

Since Internet users was directly used in the calculation of the EGDI, it was decided that this variable be kept out of the model. Also, since data pertaining to certain literacy rate were not available for large number of countries it was not made part of the analysis. For the final regression analysis 152 data points were complete.

Results

As a first step, an analysis was undertaken to see the correlation between the EGDI and its constituent indexes. Although, a significant correlation between EGDI and each of its three constituent indexes was expected, it was considered insightful to access as which index holds maximum correlation with the EGDI. EGDI was found to be strongly correlated with HCI ($r=0.877, p<0.01$) and OSI ($r=0.897, p<0.01$), the correlation with TII ($r=0.938, p<0.01$) was the highest, indicating strong relationship. Table 6.1 presents the results of the correlation analysis.

Table 6.1: Correlation Matrix

Index	*E-Government Index*	*Online Service Index*	*Human Capital Index*	*Telecommunication Infrastructure Index*
E-Government Index	1	.897**	.877**	.938**
Online Service Index	.897**	1	.644**	.751**
Human Capital Index	.877**	.644**	1	.792**
Telecommunication Infrastructure Index	.938**	.751**	.792**	1

A correlation analysis of 185 countries was also undertaken to see if significant correlation exists between EGDI and HDI. EGDI and HDI were found to be significantly correlated, $r=0.914, p<0.05$. Thus, HDI could be used a proxy indicator for EGDI.

The EGDI computation in the UN Surveys does not take into account the socio-economic factors of the participating countries. It was deemed research worthy to enquire if these factors are related to EGDI in some way or the other. An ANOVA analysis was undertaken so if EGDI varied with income level of the countries. Analysis of variance showed that EGDI varied significantly over the three groups, $F(2,148) = 181.90$, $p <.001$. Post hoc analyses using the Scheffé post hoc criterion for significance indicated that EGDI for Low Income economies was significantly lower ($M = 0.204$, $SD = 0.072$) than in the other income groups–Medium Income ($M=0.435$, $SD=0.126$) and High Income ($M= 0.734$, $SD=0.128$). (See Table 6.2).

In order to further investigate the relationship between key economic factors, a regression analysis was undertaken. The socio-economic factors chosen were: (i) GDP (current US$), (ii) GDP growth rate, (iii) GNI per capita, (iv) Life expectancy at birth, (v) Unemployment, (vi) Urban

Table 6.2: Income Group Descriptive

Income Level	N	Mean	Std. Deviation
Low Income	28	.203551	.717908
Medium Income	79	.435335	.1263567
High Income	44	.733505	.1275352
Total	**151**	**.479239**	**.2192252**

population, (vii) Health expenditure per capita, and (viii) Internet User per 1000 users.

Since number of Internet users was already an important component of the EGDI and the variable already has high-correlation with the EGDI, $r = 0.886$, $p < 0.001$, it was decided that the variable be removed from the analysis. As, Health Expenditure and GNI per capita also had high correlation, $r = 0.926$, $p = 0.000$, it was decided to remove the health expenditure per capita from the analysis. According to Field (2005) "If there is no multicollienarity in the data then there should not be substantial correlations ($r > 0.9$) between predictors."

The step-wise regression analysis (4 steps involved) on the above stated socio-economic indicators as Independent variables led to a strong model which was able to explain 75.7% [$R^2 = 0.757$, $F(1,150) = 8.75$, $p < 0.05$] of variance in the EGDI. (Refer Table 6.3 for results).

Table 6.3: Regression Model Stepwise Summary

Model	R	R Square	Adjusted R Square	Std. Error of the Estimate
1	.811a	.657	.655	.13246032
2	.847b	.717	.713	.12079762
3	.862c	.743	.738	.11554471
4	.870d	.757	.750	.11268855

a. Predictors: (Constant), Life expectancy at birth, total (years).
b. Predictors: (Constant), Life expectancy at birth, total (years), Urban population (% of total).
c. Predictors: (Constant), Life expectancy at birth, total (years), Urban population (% of total), GNI per capita, Atlas method (current US $).
d. Predictors: (Constant), Life expectancy at birth, total (years), Urban population (% of total), GNI per capita, Atlas method (current US $), GDP (in Billions) (current US $).

All variables were included in the final model except GDP growth rate and unemployment. The variable having the strongest impact on the model was Life Expectancy at Birth which accounted for 65.7% [R^2 =

better governance. For Indian states, it is reflective of where they stand and how they can provide better governance. Kerala for instance is high on life expectancy at birth can be benchmarked by other states.

For policy-makers it would be useful to concentrate on improving the health and urban infrastructure in the country. An improvement in health and urban utility services would be likely accompanied by investment in IT infrastructure and other e-Governance initiatives which are crucial and critical to improving public service delivery or e-Government. This will go a long way making an effective government which will also be high on EGDI rankings.

REFERENCES

Ayanso, A., Chatterjee, D., and Cho, D.I. (2011). "E-Government readiness index: A methodology and analysis", *Government Information Quarterly*, 28(4): 522–532. http://doi.org/http://dx.doi.org/10.1016/j.giq.2011.02.004

Baker, D.L. (2009). "Advancing E-Government performance in the United States through enhanced usability benchmarks", *Government Information Quarterly*, 26(1): 82-88. http://doi.org/http://dx.doi.org/10.1016/j.giq.2008.01.004

Deit, Y. (2011). e-Readiness Assessment of States and Union Territories. Retrieved on June 28, 2015, from http://deity.gov.in/content/e-readiness-assessment-states-and-union-territories

Farooquie, J.A. (2011). "A Review of E-Government Readiness in India and the UAE", *International Journal of Humanities and Social Science*, 1(1): 6-13.

Field, A. (2005). *Discovering Statistics Using SPSS*. SAGE Publications.

Gauld, R., Goldfinch, S. and Horsburgh, S. (2010). Do they want it? Do they use it? The "Demand-Side" of E-Government in Australia and New Zealand. *Government Information Quarterly*, 27(2), 177–186. http://doi.org/10.1016/j.giq.2009.12.002

Graafland-Essers, I., and Ettedgui, E. (2003). Benchmarking E-Government in Europe and the US. RAND. Santa Monica, CA.

Gupta, M.P. and Jana, D. (2003). "E-Government evaluation: A framework and case study". *Government Information Quarterly*, 20(4): 365-387. http://doi.org/http://dx.doi.org/10.1016/j.giq.2003.08.002

Mehrotra, S. (2011). *India Human Development Report 2011: Towards Social Inclusion*. New Delhi, India.

Ojo, A.; Janowski, T. and Estevez, E. (2005). "Determining progress towards E-Government: What are the core indicators?" In *Proceedings of the European Conference on E-Government, ECEG* (pp. 313–322).

Potnis, D.D. (2010). "Measuring e-Governance as an innovation in the public sector". *Government Information Quarterly*, 27(1): 41-48. http://doi.org/10.1016/j.giq.2009.08.002

Rorissa, A., Demissie, D. and Pardo, T. (2011). "Benchmarking E-Government: A comparison of frameworks for computing E-Government index and ranking", *Government Information Quarterly*, 28(3): 354-362. http://doi.org/http://dx.doi.org/10.1016/j.giq.2010.09.006

United Nations (2014). United Nations E-Government Survey 2014 "E-Government for the Future We Want." New York.

Whitmore, A. (2012). "A statistical analysis of the construction of the United Nations E-Government Development Index". *Government Information Quarterly*, 29(1): 68-75. http://doi.org/http://dx.doi.org/10.1016/j.giq.2011.06.003

7

DigiLocker: Transforming e-Governance in India

Yudhishthira Sapru

Introduction

Huge data sets of citizen information stored in fragmented government systems which operate in varied environments and involving multiple public agencies is a common dilemma which government heads usually face while realizing the vision of a single government. There lies an immense potential in using this data for the benefit of both the governments and citizens for a seamless service delivery, but the technology, resources and commitment required for bringing various government departments is an uphill task. This is especially challenging in countries where a number of government departments providing citizen services is large, a federal structure is in place or various government departments are at varied stages of digitization. In India the scenario is no different but through an innovative use of technology, Government of India has created a platform–DigiLocker or the Digital Locker which is not resource intensive, easy to integrate with and allows multiple government organisations to work in synergy in spite of their diverse nature.

Although, e-Governance transformation in India started in the late 1990s only with certain initiatives which were undertaken in silos, the country has made significant progress as regards IT enabled working of government is concerned. Two major national level initiatives which have helped in creating digital infrastructure across the country have been the National e-Governance Plan (NeGP) which was started in 2006 and the Digital India Programme which was launched in 2014. While, NeGP had the vision of making all government services accessible to the common man (Sapru & Sapru, 2014), Digital India taking a broader view has been envisioned at transforming India into a digitally empowered society and a knowledge economy (Ministry of Electronics and IT, 2014).

With the changing demographics, expectation of citizens in terms to efficiency, burden reduction and personalization are on the rise (López-De-Ipiña, Emaldi, Aguilera, & Pérez-Velasco, 2016). Both the programmes can be seen to be in line with the 'open government movement' which is being witnessed world over since the beginning of the 21st century to provide citizens with open access to information and thereby increasing transparency and accountability (Henninger, 2017). Utilizing the digital infrastructure created under these two programmes, complemented with the growing mobile reach especially to the rural India and success of unique identification programme–Aadhaar[1], Government of India launched the DigiLocker platform in 2015.

Very quickly, the DigiLocker initiative has grown in importance for both citizens and government organisations. Within a short span of its launch, both the number of users and access to the documents has increased manifold. However, despite being a highly transformational initiative, the literature available on the subject is minimal and insufficient. Thus, the objective of this chapter is to familiarize the academicians and governments across the world with the concept of DigiLocker. The chapter aims to explain the DigiLocker's ecosystem, its benefits and its usage in practical government scenarios. The chapter is also aimed to present the challenges DigiLocker faces. The object of the chapter is also to sensitize government organisations that are in the midst of digitization, i.e. where certain level of digitization is available but due to lack to standardisation, various government departments are working in silos and data sharing is a challenge.

Literature Review

Electronic Documents vs. Printed Documents

A key objective of securing a government document especially an important document like an identity document is to avoid identity fraud, i.e. to ensure that the document and the document holder belong to each other and maintain the data integrity and authenticity of the document throughout its life (Buchmann, Rathgeb, Baier, Busch, & Margraf, 2017). Ironically, physical or printed documents are seen more prone to forgery by falsification of information. More so, these can be easily used by non-genuine persons to obtain other documents (Kalvet, Tiits, & Laas-Mikko, 2018).

As compared to the physical documents, Electronic documents do have their immediate advantages. They have a life till eternity and do not get lost or damaged like physical documents. With the legislations providing backing, a digitally-issued certificate is more authentic than a physical document. A physical document can be easily be counterfeited. Likewise, a fabricated identity can be created easily using physical documents whereas in electronic ones, a lot of trace is to be created, thus making it a difficult and a time consuming process to forge electronic documents (Mason, 2004).

While, establishing the authenticity of a physical record may take months as Government organisations prefer to check their records in files, a document which is directly fetched from an (authentic) electronic database is always a true copy. Also, there is no need to get the electronic document attested or verified from any designated government officer. Further, sharing of documents, besides being more authentic, requires no further creation of copies of the original document. Clearly, digital documents have an advantage over physical documents in terms of life, verification, storage and audit etc. (Porey, 2016). Consequently, we have examples of countries like Estonia and Uganda which have completely done away with printed documents like birth certificates (Kalvet et al., 2018).

However, the dependence upon electronic documents has its own share of issues. Problems may relate to validation, verification and authentication of identity (Mason, 2004). Thankfully, technology and processes have evolved over time, giving edge to the electronic documents. Moreover, presence of structural assurances like legal backing and addressing privacy concerns builds higher level of trusts in the electronic environment (McKnight, Choudhury, & Kacmar, 2002; Park, Choi, Kim, & Rho, 2015; Zucker, 1986).

Government Issued Documents

Adoption of technology by a government organisation has the potential to reduce the barriers that exist in enabling the citizens to engage for a participatory governance (Yavuz & Welch, 2014). The government departments thus are gradually adopting technology and are getting their processes and records digitized. These organisations have started providing multiple access channels for service delivery including websites, social media or mobile-apps. While, the adoption of technology has helped in bringing the citizens closer to the government but at the same time there still needs a lot of ground to be covered. There usually exists a gap between how the government feels about provisioning service access and what users expect (Henninger, 2017).

Madariaga, Nussbaum, Marañón, Alarcón, and Naranjo (2019) have highlighted the issue of below par and fruitless use of government documents. The authors attribute it to barriers involved in adopting technology, misfit online service delivery modes, lack of digital inclusion, lack of awareness among users and behavioural tendencies of the users. The authors assert that user experience of government documents is impacted by issues both at the information provider end, i.e. the government and the information user end, i.e. the citizens. Based upon the literature review provided in their research, the authors assert that information provider specific barriers include reliability, transparency, preservation, quality and accessibility of information. Whereas, the barriers from the information seeker end include channels of preference, source selection, user awareness, information seeking behaviours, user expectations and motivations for using government documents. Thus, it is imperative for the government that while provisioning online access to the government documents, the barriers from both the sides be brought down if not completely removed.

With a federal structure envisaged in the Constitution of India, there are a large number of government agencies at central, state and local levels which are issuing documents and certificates to the citizens for services pertaining to them. Prime among those are the Passport, Driving Licence, Birth Certificate, Permanent Account Number (PAN card is a unique identity card for tax related purposes in India), Caste Certificate and the list has simply no end. These are primarily used as "Proof of Address" (commonly referred to as PoA) or as "Proof of Identity" (commonly referred to as PoI). These documents traditionally have been issued in physical form only but the advent of technology has added altogether a new dimension to it. While the Government organisations have at their own pace started adopting digital technologies, issuance of documents in electronic forms has nearly become a norm. The Information Technology Act of 2000 and subsequent Information Technology (Amendment) Act, 2008 passed by the Indian Parliament addresses multiple areas and more importantly gives legal recognition to electronic documents and digital signatures.

Literature Survey on DigiLocker

As highlighted in the above sections, the research on the subject has been very limited. However, a few researchers have attempted to throw light on this important initiative through their research. Arvind, Vitthalrao, and Mukund (2015), have attempted to explain thc Digilocker concept and its objectives along with an example to open a DigiLocker account. Using DigiLocker as a platform, Khandekar and Devadiga (2016) have proposed a system that allows the voters to know about prospective candidates during elections and make a more informed decision. Ghodke and Dagade (2018) have proposed a secured verification system for vehicle registration using QR codes and DigiLocker.

Recognizing the privacy and security concerns related to personal information consequent upon linking of Aadhaar and DigiLocker, Kumar, Chaturvedi, and Dave (2018), have proposed a framework for securing the document using authentication. They also recommend the owner's consent and accessibility of document should be for a limited time only.

George, Viswambharam, and Scholar (2019) have attempted to understand the awareness levels about DigiLocker in a South Indian city and found that most citizens were aware of this initiative.

DigiLocker: A Mode for Securely Keeping Documents

In order to create a citizen-centric public service ecosystem, new technological platforms are required which create value through sharing, interaction and collaboration between stakeholders (López-De-Ipiña *et al.*, 2016). A DigiLocker is one such initiative.

DigiLocker is a technological platform for Indian citizens which enables issuance and verification of documents in the digital mode and thus obviating requirement of physical documents. It is basically a citizen data vault (Dais, Nikolaidou, & Anagnostopoulos, 2009; Poelmans, 2006) where personal and government related documents can be added and linked. DigiLocker users also get a personal account with a dedicated cloud storage space that is linked to their Aadhaar number where they can upload documents and also electronically sign them using the 'eSign' facility. eSign is an online electronic service which allows the users to digitally sign a document using certain authentication techniques and without the use of 'Digital Signature Certificate' (DSC) physical tokens (NSDL e-Governance Infrastructure Limited, 2016). Further, organizations can link electronic copies of documents and certificates (e.g. driving licence, Voter ID, School certificates) directly into the citizens' lockers. Users can access their lockers on the move through mobile app and also share their documents wherever required (National e-Governance Division, 2019a).

DigiLocker is not a private managed or a domain-specific electronic vault, like we have a health vault ("Microsoft HealthVault-Wikipedia," 2019) for storing health information or a financial information vault. It encompasses documents of multiple government agencies and is managed by a government organisation only.

DigiLocker Ecosystem

From the usage purposes, the DigiLocker ecosystem consists of four major stakeholders. First and primary among them are the citizens which are at the centre of this digital service. Citizens are the owners of the DigiLocker accounts where documents issued to them or uploaded by them reside. In fact, DigiLocker only hosts the links (using a unique document URI number) to these documents, which can be downloaded from the electronic repository of the issuing organisation. Thus, DigiLocker is a decentralized repository. Citizens can access their account which can be created online or through a mobile-app. Citizens can optionally link their account to their Aadhaar number which is a unique identification number issued to Indian citizens. This linking facilitates fetching of documents which are usually linked with the Aadhaar number. However, DigiLocker also facilitates linking of documents using other identifiers where Aadhaar number is not present. These identifiers could be basic user demographics like date of birth, gender or personal information like mobile number or unique identifier of the document like certificate number which is only known to the owner of the document.

Secondly, there are the 'Issuers', primary being the Government organisations, who issue documents to the citizens. Examples include a Regional Transport Office which issues a driving licence or a registration certificate of a vehicle or a municipal office issuing birth certificate. The documents issued by the Issuers, once linked to a citizen's locker account can be accessed through Issuer's database. The documents issued are differentiated from the documents 'uploaded' by the citizens which is also facilitated by the DigiLocker. The upload feature allows citizens to keep a scanned copy of their documents (like mark sheets etc.) in the digital repository but being not issued on DigiLocker by a verified 'Issuer', the uploaded documents are treated somewhat less authentic than the issued ones. Issuers are registered organisations which can only become part of DigiLocker after thorough verification only.

Thirdly, there are 'Requesters' which require secure access to a particular document issued or uploaded on the DigiLocker. A requester, for instance, can be a private firm which is hiring a person and requires mark sheets for verification of educational qualifications. This is where DigiLocker obviates need for providing physical copy or scanned copy of the document which can be counterfeited easily.

Finally, another category of stakeholders is coming up which are the 'Verifiers'. DigiLocker allows Verifiers to use the DigiLocker repository to verify users' documents (subsequent to user's consent). This verification feature is primarily for the organisations which do not have an electronic database of their own but intend to verify users' records.

Currently, there are more than 31.69 million people who have a registered DigiLocker account. More than 3.68 billion documents are available through DigiLocker a figure which is growing everyday (National e-Governance Division, 2019b). These numbers are highly significant given the level of digitations in a country like India is far from those achieved by developed nations. However, there are only 142 Issuers and 42 Requesters registered with DigiLocker (National e-Governance Division, 2019b), a figure which the Government of India aspires to increase manifold to realise the true potential of DigiLocker.

DigiLocker Benefits

While on one hand the technology has enabled government organisations to improve service delivery, but on the other hand, lack of access to technology increases the digital divide. As per the United Nations E-Government Survey of 2018, a negative correlation between digital use and social exclusion has been found (United Nations, 2018). This poses a challenge to developing countries to find solutions which increase service access with use of technology but do not create or deepen the digital divide. A solution like DigiLocker is one such initiative which is accessible to a majority of Indian citizens having a minimal access to internet and a smart mobile phone. While the DigiLocker does not completely replace the physical documents, it provides an efficient and more reliable mechanism of sharing documents by the citizens who have access to internet. In India, users having access to internet were more than 450 million by March 2019 (Internet and Mobile Association of India, 2019) and thus has the potential to change lives of a large population.

Government departments usually work in silos and sharing of documents require huge amount of efforts and resources. While it may be easier for two departments to share data by setting up of a single linkage, the number of such linkages quickly increases with more number of departments requiring exchange of information. In such a case, having a central repository helps. DigiLocker serves as a common platform that brings various departments on a common platform that increasing efficiency in service delivery.

The most apparent advantage which the DigiLocker offers is the elimination of physical documents which benefits both the government organisations and citizens. Governments save on paper while citizens save on time and resources required to securely store the documents. Being directly issued by the authorised agencies and fetched from their databases, the platform facilitates easier validation of documents. In a big country like India, without the availability of digital means, verification of documents has always been a time and a money consuming process. Another, key advantage which the DigiLocker offers is the privacy concern it addresses. It is only after the owner of the document gives consent to share, the documents are made available to the agencies requiring documents.

In their research on the subject, Kumar, Chaturvedi, and Dave (Kumar et al., 2018) have identified multiple benefits of DigiLocker including reduction of administrative overhead, reduced paper work, reduced need for original physical document, ease of sharing, ease of updating, ease of access, centralization of all the important documents of the individual, legal backing and government authorisation, online validation, free of cost (till now), secure backup and digital empowerment of the citizens.

Use Cases for DigiLocker Applications

With more and more Government agencies becoming part of this Digital infrastructure, the true potential of DigiLocker is slowly and slowly being realised. Researchers have also started to propose use cases where DigiLocker can be useful. For instance, Khandekar and Devadiga (2016), suggest its application to enable voters to verify the credentials of election candidates.

While, common applications include use by Indian Railways as 'Proof of Identity' of travellers (First Post, 2018) or India's Central Board of Secondary Education[2] (CBSE) issuing marksheet for secondary and higher secondary results on DigiLocker (News Heads, 2018), the latest thrust area has been its application for transport related enforcement.

Across the globe, it is usually compulsory to carry an original physical copy of key driving related documents like driving licence, registration certificate, pollution check and vehicle insurance, which many a times are forgotten by the drivers (Ghodke & Dagade, 2018). In order to overcome this issue, Ministry of Road Transport and Highways[3] (MoRTH), Government of India has already linked its records of Driving Licences and Vehicle Registration with DigiLocker. People no longer need to carry physically their Driving Licence or Vehicle Registration Certificate (RC) documents. These documents are very difficult to obtain and in the event of their theft, it requires lengthy procedure for re-issuance. Requirement of enforcement agencies like Traffic Police is sufficed by authentic records available on DigiLocker of the driver. MoRTH and many state governments of Indian states have already issued notifications in this regard wherein requirement of carrying physical documents has been eliminated (National e-Governance Division, 2019c). While, enforcement agencies and vehicle users are slowly realising the benefit, some new and prospective applications of DigiLocker can be as below:

For Land Transactions

One of the major issues that Indian citizens face is dealing with land transactions. Since, land ownership information is usually not easily available, most people fear entering into land transactions. With little information available about land titles, the risk involved is very high. In some cases, buyers fall into the trap and end up buying property from non-genuine owners, losing hard earned money and precious time in resolving land disputes. This is where DigiLocker can prove to be a panacea. A digital land record document can be linked to the DigiLocker account of the owner by a local land registrar's office. This document or ownership details can be shared by the owner to the prospective buyer through a QR code who can satisfy herself or himself about the ownership rights. The DigiLocker can thus help in alleviating fears of the buyers and genuineness of the buyer is easily established. Similarly, DigiLocker can be used for transactions like vehicle sale or purchase etc.

For Background Verification of Employees

It is a general myth that DigiLocker is useful for only Government Organisations. On the contrary it has a huge potential for private entities also. Background checks during hiring process are commonly employed by private organisations, as it is important to verify past records of the prospective employees to know if they had previously been engaged in wrongful activities or have misrepresented facts about employment history or educational qualifications etc. (Aamodt, 2015). Organisations usually spend huge amount of money and resources on hiring third party agencies to undertake background check of the prospective employees including verifying their criminal records, credit history, educational qualifications, work experience, passport etc. Backgrounds checks which were earlier limited to only senior management have been extended to all employees, be it any level and even new joiners (Economic Times, 2009). With a digital repository like DigiLocker, access to such documents becomes very easy and it can be done at a much cheaper cost. Further, records coming directly from government databases represent true information.

In Events of Natural Disasters

The unfortunate floods of 2018 in the southern state of India—Kerala, left many of the people displaced from their homes whose belongings were destroyed in the deluge. Nonetheless, losses also included important identity and other Government documents which left people devoid of basic things including subsidized food which was available through fair price shops (FPS) on production of ration cards. DigiLocker proved to be bane and soon the Government undertook massive efforts to bring most government documents on DigiLocker. Thus, this unexpected catastrophe showed how DigiLocker can help people in event of a disaster.

For Credit Loans and Banking Facilities

DigiLocker has opened up new avenues to banks and financial institutions. In a typical scenario, an SME borrower can securely share its documents to the banks for availing loans. Funds Tiger[4] which operates an online lending marketplace for 'Small and Medium-Sized Enterprises' (SMEs), 'Micro, Small and Medium Enterprises'(MSMEs) and, retail borrowers has already integrated with DigiLocker where loan seekers can share their documents through DigiLocker online only (FundsTiger, 2018). Similarly, a popular Non-Banking Financial Company (NBFC) in India, India Bulls[5] has integrated with the platform for home loans (National e-Governance Division, 2017b). Users can easily share their identity proof, address proof, and tax returns details to the banks.

For Maintaining Health Records

In a vast country like India, where Health infrastructure is evolving, standardisation of Health records is still a distant reality. Although efforts are on, private hospitals and government organisations, till date, have different standards for storing patient health records (wherever digital) which limits sharing of crucial patient information. An infrastructure like DigiLocker can eliminate this drawback as all patient records can be stored centrally in patient's account. Also, DigiLocker can enable consent based access to the health records to hospitals, insurance companies and other third parties agencies. This also is important in a big country like India where patients move from geographic locations in search of better health amenities.

Challenges

DigiLocker has the potential of transforming India to a truly digitally driven country where government, industry and citizens interact in a paperless ecosystem. This is especially crucial in a developing economy where resources are limited and a majority of the population interacts with the government almost on a daily basis. However, challenges still remain to truly realise this potential.

First and foremost is adoption of DigiLocker system. This is where lack of number of issuers, requesters and citizens utilizing DigiLocker offer hindrance to development of the DigiLocker ecosystem. Simply explained, lesser number of issuers would mean lesser number of documents issued, which translates to still lesser number of documents shared by the citizens and even lesser number of documents used by requesters. Take for example, a passport document is an important document and is the most widely used document as proof of identity and address also. Absence of a passport like document on the DigiLocker significantly limits its application usage by a wide variety of requesters. Thus, Government of India's thrust over the last few years have been on on-boarding of maximum number of issuers and requestors and also creating awareness among the citizens.

Another major challenge is the cyber-security related issue which is much heightened in this case where critical documents of the citizens of the whole of the country are accessible. Although, DigiLocker system, in itself is not a repository of government issued documents but it does hold URI[6] for the documents which can enable access to the documents.

Further, uploaded documents are already on DigiLocker which need to be secured. Also, DigiLocker is a gateway application which facilitates sharing of documents across various databases. Any attack like a DDOS[7] attack can impact the whole system. Further, as the system will grow, many related 'Phishing'[8] sites are likely to come up. There can be multiple actors who may attempt to exploit (known or unknown) vulnerabilities but DigiLocker needs to be ahead of hackers all the time and build strong defence walls. There is also need to secure document repositories of the issuers because many a times vulnerability in a linked system is exploited to damage the main system.

Another issue is related with the enforcement part. As long as there is no recognition among government agencies, the DigiLocker can do little to benefit the citizens. Take for example, a typical scenario, where a regional transport office has issued a Driving Licence on DigiLocker and the citizens produces the same (in electronic form) to a traffic enforcement officer. However, due to lack of legal backing regarding recognition of DigiLocker issued documents to be treated at par with physical document in the court of law, a citizen is fined for want of physical documents. This also holds true when the enforcement officer is completely unaware of the DigiLocker system. This may have a very negative impact on the citizens towards the system. This issue has been recognised by Government of India, which has already notified "Information Technology (Preservation and Retention of Information by Intermediaries Providing Digital Locker Facilities) Rules, 2016", under its IT Act. Similarly, many state governments in India have issued notifications to provide legal backing (National eGovernance Division, 2017a). Also efforts are on to sensitize those involved with enforcement.

As highlighted in the literature review above, any government online service provision should cross barriers that exist both at the government side and the citizen side. While, best efforts should be made to make information available through digital locker reliable, transparent and accessible. Although, DigiLocker stands good on these parameters but the real challenge is to make sustainable efforts to meet the changing and ever increasing expectations of the citizens. Also, efforts should be made to reduce barriers that exist on the citizens' side. The challenges relate to citizen awareness about existence of DigiLocker, ease of use of technology and user behaviours while transacting online.

Discussion

While, Government of India is already working hard to onboard new users, new issuers and new requesters into the DigiLocker ecosystem, a way forward for better uptake of DigiLocker is suggested.

Under the ambitious Digital India Programme, various Central Ministries and State Governments in India are undertaking rapid digitalization of crucial citizen services. For better uptake of the DigiLocker, it needs to be mandated that integration with DigiLocker must be part of software architecture of all existing and up-coming eGovernance applications of the Government of India. Unnecessary requirement of physical production of documents must be completely done away with through regulatory or statutory provisions. Government can also consider it making mandatory for all organisations under its purview to use issue and seek document through DigiLocker only.

Technology Acceptance Model (TAM) which was propagated by Davis (1989) is one of the most used model which explains what factors influence user's adoption of a new technology. Although, the model has been duly extended as TAM-2 (Venkatesh & Davis, 2000) and Unified Theory of Acceptance and Use of Technology (UTAUT) (Venkatesh, Morris, Davis, & Davis, 2003) and many others, the base model provides two factors which govern users acceptance of technology. These are: (i) Perceived usefulness (PU) and (ii) Perceived ease-of-use (PEOU). Thus, the most simplistic action items for the practitioners are to concentrate on these two factors for a wider acceptance and propagation of the technology. The perceived usefulness will only increase when the DigiLocker ecosystem grows and especially when more and more organisations start to accept DigiLocker documents. There is a need that Government of India must concentrate on not only on-boarding more issuers but more requesters also. Also, DigiLocker is available online and through mobile apps on popular app-stores. However, from the user point of view the system needs to be upgraded regularly. User actions linked to opening of new account, linking of issued documents, sharing of documents with the requestors and eSigning must be made more users friendly to aid ease-of-use.

As highlighted earlier, security of the system must be accorded utmost priority. There is already a 'two-factor' authentication in place at crucial junctures and the application talks securely to various document repositories. However, needless to say, the system must be upgraded to keep ahead of potential attacks. Although, DigiLocker provisions seeking of user's consent before sharing of document, it is important that the implications of sharing user data with other government and non-government agencies be apprised to the users, to enable them to make more informed decisions (O'Connor, Rowan, Lynch, & Heavin, 2017). While, currently standard electronic consent is being obtained from the citizens by 'ticking' a checkbox, there is a definite case for introducing 'consent levels'(Coiera & Clarke, 2004) as DigiLocker grows and more sensitive information (like health information) becomes available to the users. This also becomes important as countries worldover embrace stricter privacy laws (Greig, 2019).

It is also proposed that on similar lines, DigiLocker may also be extended to Business organisations where all the key documents issued to any business entity like registration certificate, tax related documents (like GST number and returns), environment clearances and various other permits can be provided. The documents issued on such a non-citizen based DigiLocker can be shared with other Government agencies for compliance purposes or for sharing organisational credentials for public procurement purposes.

Governments across the globe can also use these platforms to exchange information related to their citizens. For example, DigiLocker opens up a huge box of opportunities for students seeking admission to foreign universities as it obviates physical verification of students' degrees etc. Similarly, passport and visa related information can be easily shared and authenticated.

DigiLocker has opened up new avenues for the government organisations, citizens and other service providers. It is high time that the uptake speed is increased by concentrating on key stakeholders of DigiLocker ecosystem, viz. Citizens, Issuers, Requesters and Verifiers. Once fully utilized, this digital infrastructure of the Government of India has the potential to fulfil the long-lasting digital repository requirement of all the Indian citizens and to bridge the digital divide that currently exists in the society. If adopted in other developing countries, it will pave the way for making governments more responsive to citizens' needs and truly 'citizen-centric' organisations.

[Acknowledgements

The author is thankful to President and CEO, National eGovernance Division (NeGD) and DigiLocker team, Ministry of Electronics and Information Technology (MeitY), Government of India for their help and valuable insights on the DigiLocker platform.]

NOTES

1. Aadhaar is a 12-digit unique identity number that is given to Indian residents on the basis of their demographic and biometric data. The details of Aadhaar can be found at https://uidai.gov.in/.
2. http://cbse.nic.in/
3. http://morth.nic.in/
4. https://www.fundstiger.com/
5. http://www.indiabulls.com/
6. "A URI is a Uniform Resource Identifier generated by the issuer department, which is mandatory for every e-document of the DigiLocker system. This unique URI can be resolved to a full URL (Uniform Resource Locator) to access the actual document in its appropriate repository." Source: https://digilocker.gov.in/faq.php
7. A distributed denial-of-service (DDoS) is a cyber threat which refers to a coordinated cyber attack where multiple IT systems (called 'bots') from distributed locations flood and choke the bandwidth or resources of a targeted system, thus rendering the target system unavailable for intended users.
8. Phishing is a form of cyber threat where a cyber criminal fraudulently obtains sensitive information during electronic transactions from users by posing as a trustworthy or authentic source.

REFERENCES

Aamodt, M.G. (2015). "Using Background Checks in the Employee Selection Process", In *Practitioner's Guide to Legal Issues in Organizations* (pp. 85-110). https://doi.org/10.1007/978-3-319-11143-8_4

Arvind, P.P., Vitthalrao, M.P. and Mukund, J.M. (2015). "Digilocker (Digital Locker-Ambitious Aspect of Digital India Programme)". *GE-International Journal of Management Research*, 3(6): 299-308.

Buchmann, N., Rathgeb, C., Baier, H., Busch, C. and Margraf, M. (2017). Enhancing Breeder Document Long-Term Security Using Blockchain Technology. *Proceedings—International Computer Software and Applications Conference*, 2, 744–748. https://doi.org/10.1109/COMPSAC.2017.119

Coiera, E. and Clarke, R. (2004). "e-Consent: The Design and Implementation of Consumer Consent Mechanisms in an Electronic Environment", *Journal of the American Medical Informatics Association*, 11(2): 129-140. https://doi.org/10.1197/jamia.M1480

Dais, A., Nikolaidou, M. and Anagnostopoulos, D. (2009). "Facilitating Business to Government Interaction Using a Citizen-Centric Web 2.0 Model". *IFIP Advances in Information and Communication Technology*, 305: 134-147. https://doi.org/10.1007/978-3-642-04280-5_12

Davis, F.D. (1989). "Perceived Usefulness, Perceived Ease of Use, and User

Acceptance of Information Technology", *MIS Quarterly*, 13(3): 319-340. Retrieved from http://www.jstor.org/stable/249008

Economic Times (2009). Companies step up background checks of prospective employees: The Economic Times. Retrieved November 11, 2019, from https://economictimes.indiatimes.com/jobs/companies-step-up-background-checks-of-prospective-employees/articleshow/5269650.cms ?from=mdr

First Post. (2018). Railways to accept soft copies of Aadhaar and driving licence in your DigiLocker-Technology News, Firstpost. Retrieved November 2, 2019, from https://www.firstpost.com/tech/news-analysis/railways-to-accept-soft-copies-of-aadhaar-and-driving-license-in-your-digilocker-4676971.html

Funds Tiger. (2018). Funds Tiger becomes First FinTech Company to Integrate with GoI's DigiLocker-FundsTiger-Fast Loans for India. Retrieved November 2, 2019, from https://www.fundstiger.com/fundstiger-first-fintech-digilocker/

George, M.A., Viswambharam, A.M. and Scholar, M. (2019). "Digi-Locker: An Overview", *International Journal of Research and Analytical Reviews*, 6(1).

Ghodke, A.V. and Dagade, R.V. (2018). Electronic Secure Vehicle Verification System Using Advanced Digi-Locker System. 2018 3rd International Conference for Convergence in Technology (I2CT), 1–4. https://doi.org/10.1109/I2CT.2018.8529450

Greig, J. (2019). How more countries plan to pass stringent privacy laws in 2019-TechRepublic. Retrieved November 11, 2019, from https://www.techrepublic.com/article/how-more-countries-plan-to-pass-stringent-privacy-laws-in-2019/

Henninger, M. (2017). "Government information: Literacies, behaviours and practices", *Government Information Quarterly*, 34(1): 8-15. https://doi.org/10.1016/j.giq.2016.12.003

Internet and Mobile Association of India (2019). India Internet 2019.

Kalvet, T., Tiits, M. and Laas-Mikko, K. (2018). Public acceptance of advanced identity documents. ACM International Conference Proceeding Series, 429-432. https://doi.org/10.1145/3209415.3209456

Khandekar, C. and Devadiga, N. (2016). "VoteItRight: Digital Empowerment of Citizens", *International Journal of Computer Applications*, 154(5): 6-9. https://doi.org/10.5120/ijca2016912131

Kumar, V., Chaturvedi, A. and Dave, M. (2018). "A Solution to Secure Personal Data When Aadhaar is linked with DigiLocker", *International Journal of Computer Network and Information Security*, 10(5): 37-44. https://doi.org/10.5815/ijcnis.2018.05.05

López-De-Ipiña, D., Emaldi, M., Aguilera, U. and Pérez-Velasco, J. (2016). Towards citizen co-created public service apps. Lecture Notes in Computer Science (Including Subseries Lecture Notes in Artificial Intelligence and Lecture Notes in Bioinformatics), 10070 LNCS, 469–481. https://doi.org/10.1007/978-3-319-48799-1_51

Madariaga, L., Nussbaum, M., Marañón, F., Alarcón, C., and Naranjo, M.A. (2019). "User experience of government documents: A framework for informing design decisions", *Government Information Quarterly*, 36(2): 179-195. https://doi.org/10.1016/j.giq.2018.12.005

Mason, S. (2004). "Validating identity for the electronic environment". *Computer Law and Security Report*, 20(3): 164-170. https://doi.org/10.1016/S0267-3649(04)00031-7

McKnight, D.H., Choudhury, V. and Kacmar, C. (2002). "The impact of initial consumer trust on intentions to transact with a website: A trust building model", *Journal of Strategic Information Systems*, 11(3-4), 297-323. https://doi.org/10.1016/S0963-8687(02)00020-3.

Microsoft HealthVault-Wikipedia. (2019). Retrieved November 11, 2019, from https://en.wikipedia.org/wiki/Microsoft_HealthVault

Ministry of Electronics and IT, G. of I. (2014). Vision and Vision Areas of Digital India Programme. Retrieved November 2, 2019, from http://digitalindia.gov.in/content/vision-and-vision-areas

National eGovernance Division. (2017a). Digital Locker Rules and Amendment. Retrieved November 2, 2019, from https://digilocker.gov.in/resource/rules-and-Amendment.html

National eGovernance Division. (2017b). IndiaBulls showcases how NBFCs can integrate with DigiLocker for digitised document verification | DigiLocker Blog. Retrieved November 2, 2019, from https://blog.digitallocker.gov.in/indiabulls-showcases-how-nbfcs-can-integrate-with-digilocker-for-digitised-document-verification/

National eGovernance Division. (2019a). About DigiLocker. Retrieved November 2, 2019, from https://digilocker.gov.in/about.php

National eGovernance Division. (2019b). DigiLocker National Statistics. Retrieved November 2, 2019, from https://digilocker.gov.in/public/dashboard#!

National eGovernance Division. (2019c). DigiLocker Resource Centre. Retrieved November 2, 2019, from https://digilocker.gov.in/resource/departmental_circulars.html

News Heads. (2018). CBSE opens 80 lakh digital lockers for class 10, 12 students. Retrieved November 2, 2019, from https://www.newsheads.in/education/news/cbse-opens-80-lakh-digital-lockers-for-class-10-12-students-article-17462

NSDL e-Governance Infrastructure Limited. (2016). NSDL e-Governance Infrastructure Limited. Retrieved November 3, 2019, from https://www.egov-nsdl.co.in/e-sign.html

O'Connor, Y., Rowan, W., Lynch, L., and Heavin, C. (2017). Privacy by Design: Informed Consent and Internet of Things for Smart Health. *Procedia Computer Science*, 113, 653–658. https://doi.org/10.1016/j.procs.2017.08.329

Park, M.J., Choi, H., Kim, S.K. and Rho, J.J. (2015). Trust in government's social media service and citizen's patronage behaviour. *Telematics and Informatics*, 32(4), 629–641. https://doi.org/http://dx.doi.org/10.1016/j.tele.2015.02.006

Poelmans, M. (2006). The e-Citizen Charter as an Instrument to boost e-

Government. *Exploiting the Knowledge Economy: Issues, Applications and Case Studies*, Pts 1 and 2, 3(1–2): 531–538.

Porey, J.D. (2016). "Digital locker system in India". *International Journal of Commerce and Management Research*, 2(12): 80–81.

Sapru, R.K., and Sapru, Y. (2014). Good governance through e-governance with special reference to India. *Indian Journal of Public Administration*, 60(2): 313–331. Retrieved from http://www.iipa.org.in/New Folder/8—Sapru.pdf

United Nations. (2018). E-Government Survey 2018: Gearing E-Government to support transformation towards sustainable and resilient societies. New York, 270. https://doi.org/e-ISBN: 978-92-1-055353-7

Venkatesh, Morris, Davis, and Davis. (2003). "User Acceptance of Information Technology: Toward a Unified View", *MIS Quarterly*, 27(3): 425. https://doi.org/10.2307/30036540

Venkatesh, V. and Davis, F.D. (2000). A Theoretical Extension of the Technology Acceptance Model: Four Longitudinal Field Studies. *Management Science*, 46(2): 186–204. https://doi.org/10.1287/mnsc.46.2.186.11926

Yavuz, N. and Welch, E.W. (2014). "Factors affecting openness of local government websites: Examining the differences across planning, finance and police departments", *Government Information Quarterly*, 31(4): 574–583. https://doi.org/10.1016/j.giq.2014.07.004

Zucker, L.G. (1986). "Production of trust: institutional sources of economic structure, 1840-1920", In B.M. Staw and L.L. Cummings (Eds.), *Research in Organizational Behaviour* (Volume 8, pp. 53–111). Greenwich, CN: JAI Press.

PART TWO

Decentralisation and Transforming Rural India

8

Delivering Justice at the Grassroots

The Case of Gram Nyayalayas in India

M.R. Biju and *M.R.B. Anantha Padmanabha*

1. Introduction

Justice and equality are two key concepts which constitute the foundation of any civilized society and polity. Both these principles are realised by the State apparatus through the business of administration of justice.

Article 39A of the Constitution of India, mandates justice for all on the basis of equal opportunity. Over the years successive Governments have tried in their own ways to strengthen the judicial system. As a result, procedural laws have been simplified, Lok Adalats and Fast Track Courts were introduced at the national and state level. Similarly an alternative dispute resolution mechanisms such as arbitration, conciliation and mediation have been incorporated into the legal system. However, despite these initiatives, a large percentage of population, mostly of the rural and the disadvantaged sections, has been excluded from the ambit of justice delivery.

In order to dispense justice in the rural and the remotest of areas in the country, the Gram Nyayalaya Act was enacted in 2008. The Act was designed to bring speedy, affordable and substantial justice for these citizens who are denied access to justice in the formal system (This Act has added the lowest tier of courts of subordinate judiciary in addition to the regular civil and criminal courts). One of the objectives was also to reduce pendency in courts and to improve India's dismal judge to population ratio. In this chapter we will try to make sense of the Act, its principal features and provisions, some of which had also been recommended by the Law Commission (114th Report, 1986), and suggest stops to plug in the leakages/loopholes in the Gram Nyayalaya setup.

The Preamble to the Gram Nyayalaya Act envisages access to justice to the citizens at their doorstep with the assurance that opportunities for securing justice are not denied to any citizen by reason of any disability whatsoever. Hence, the success of these institutions should not only be measured by the number of courts established in different states, but also in terms of reaching out to deprived sections of the society and its role in the overall reduction in the pendency of cases. However, data analysed for Gram Nyayalayas in MP and Rajasthan indicate a not so positive outcome in respect of the latter.

When we begin to analyse the reasons for this failure, we see that there are a number of fault-lines in the functioning of these institutions in these two states. These range from procedural aspects such as ambiguity about its jurisdiction, absence of alternative methods of dispute resolution like conciliation or plea etc., to substantive issues like part-time nature of Gram Nyayalayas, absence of a separate cadre of Gram Nyayadhikari, inadequate infrastructure and security, lack of seriousness and lukewarm response of the Public Prosecutors and lawyers, reluctance of police officials and other State functionaries to invoke the jurisdiction of Gram Nyayalayas etc.

Also, the state-wise responses detailed above, reveal that many of the states have been procrastinating, citing reasons such as absence of sufficient work for Gram Nyayalayas and some even expressing their apprehensions about increased work load in the District and Session Courts. Most of the states have expressed their dissatisfaction at the inadequate amount of funds and land allocation for the establishment of Gram Nyayalayas. Other issues include the non-availability of notaries and stamp vendors and problem of concurrent jurisdiction of regular courts. Further, majority of States have now set up regular courts at Taluk level, thus reducing the demand for Gram Nyayalayas.

Interestingly, a recurring question during various discussions prior to the passing of the Act was that whether speedy disposal meant speedy and effective justice for the poorer litigant. An emphasis on speedy disposal alone raised concerns about the objective of these institutions—whether to manage the arrears of the cases or to enable better access to the litigants?

However, despite these shortcomings, the institution of Gram Nyayalayas has been a positive step. Above everything else they need concrete, well-planned and continuous efforts to make them work. The policy makers need to review, reflect and act upon the suggestions offered by stakeholders and firmly resolve to fulfil the mandate of Section 39A. This may need an amendment to the Act in order to iron out ambiguities on the basis of experiences of the past 10 years. Failing this, the dispensation of inexpensive and 'effective' justice to each person in the farthest and the remotest rural corners will remain a distant dream.

2. The Evolution: From Nyaya Panchayats to Gram Nyayalayas

While Article 40 of the Constitution enjoins the state to organize village panchayats, another Directive Principle (Article 50) directs it to take steps to separate the judiciary from the executive. Apart from the states which already had a system of village courts at the time of the adoption of the Constitution (Madras, Mysore, Kerala), only a few states (Madhya Pradesh, Uttar Pradesh) implemented Article 50 upon the adoption of the Constitution by creating separate Nyaya Panchayats. In the period following the adoption of the Balwant Rai Mehta Committee Report (1959) and the reorganization of the village institutions both as local government and developmental agencies, many more states established Nyaya Panchayats as separate judicial bodies, thus fulfilling the Directive Principle of separation of the judiciary from the executive (Rakesh Chandra, 2017).

The ideology of separation of judicial from the executive power, embodied in Article 50, was clearly one impulse that led to the creation of Nyaya Panchayats in States which did not have such separate bodies. But the creation of judicial panchayats was not entirely a function of this ideology. It was also kept in mind that in order to increase the efficiency of village panchayats in performance of developmental and governmental tasks, relief from the judicial workload was necessary (Rakesh Chandra, 2017).

Law Commission's Fourteenth Report testified to the volume of this work in the years following independence. In U.P., for example, judicial panchayats heard, for the period 15 August, 1949 to 31 March, 1956, 1,914,098 cases, of which 1,894,440 cases were disposed. Clearly, then, as a measure of planning efficient allocation of work-load, the establishment of Nyaya Panchayats must have been felt essential. However, apart from the ideology of separation and consideration of efficient division of labour, the creation of Nyaya Panchayats can be seen as illustrating two other concerns. First, their creation testifies to concern for providing easy legal access to the village population. Second, at the same time, it also represents a massive attempt by the State to displace (as effectively as it could) the existing dispute processing institution in village areas—be they Jati (Caste) institutions, territorially based secular institutions or special dispute processing institutions established under the auspices of social reformers (such as the Rangpur People's Court). The Nyaya Panchayats seek to do this by retaining procedural flexibility and lay adjudicators, thus co-opting the very features of the institutions they seek to displace. On the other hand, the Nyaya Panchayats, as integral part of the administration of justice are characterized by principles of formal organization and of judicial oversight and control which donot 'mesh in' with the organization of justice by village communities.

Although the establishment of Nyaya Panchayat derived symbolic support from an appeal to the virtues of traditional panchayats, it should be emphasized that these new tribunals are in many ways very different from their traditional counterparts:

(a) Their membership is fixed rather than flexible and is based, indirectly, on popular election rather than social standing;
(b) Their constituencies are territorial units rather than functional or ascriptive groups;
(c) They decide by majority vote rather than by rule of unanimity;
(d) They are required to conform to and to apply statutory law;
(e) They are supported by the government in the compulsory execution of their decrees; these decrees may be tested in regular courts.

Nyaya Panchayats: Constitution and Composition

Nayaya Panchayats are established for a group of villages, usually an area covering 7 to 10 villages. Nyaya Panchayat usually cover a population of 14,000 to 15,000 villagers. A member of a Nyaya Panchayat must be able to read and write the State Language, must not suffer from any disqualification described in the statute, and must not hold an office of Sarpanch or be a member in the Samiti, parishad, or State or Union Legislature. The rules regarding appeals in disputed elections are the same as those which apply to gram panchayats. The Nyaya Panchayat has a chairman and secretary elected by its members, One-third of its members retire every second year.

Almost all States have adopted election as a method of constituting Nyaya Panchayat. Each gram panchayat. (Itself an elected body) elects members for Nyaya Panchayats. Some states combine the method of elections with nomination for example, in The Law Commission, in its Fourteenth Report, however, expressed itself against the principle of government nomination of nyaya panchayats.

Jurisdiction

Nyaya Panchayats have civil and criminal jurisdiction, but the former is more limited than the latter. Civil jurisdiction is normally confined to pecuniary claims of the value of Rs. 100 which may by agreement among parties be raised to Rs. 200 involving money due on contracts not affecting interests in immovable property, compensation for wrongfully taking or damaging property and recovery of movable property. In some states the civil jurisdiction extends to the recovery of minimum wages or arrears for maintenance (e.g. Kerala). The criminal jurisidiction is comparatively extensive and covers a substantial range of offences under the Indian Penal Code as well as the special statutes (e.g. Cattle Trespass Act, Gambling Acts, Prevention of Juvenile Delinquency Act). The Nyaya Panchayats are authorized to levy fines (ranging from Rs. 25 to 100), but they have no power to sentence offenders to imprisonment, substantively or in default of fine. Emphasis on the amicable settlement of disputes is an important aspect of the Nyaya Panchayat ideology. Accordingly, conciliation is emphasized over adjudication in some State legislation.

Evaluation of Nyaya Panchayats' Functioning

While the Law Commission (1958) and the Study Team on Nyaya Panchayats (1962) saw a bright future for Nyaya Panchayats, two evaluations, namely, the Maharashtra Committee's Report on Panchayati Raj (1971) and the Rajasthan Committee Report (1973) had recommended the abolition of Nyaya Panchayats altogether. 'The pathos of the Nyaya Panchayats is that they have achieved neither the impartiality of the regular courts (at their best) nor the intimacy, informality and ability to conciliate of traditional Panchayats (at their best). Instead Nyaya Panchayats seem in large measure to have achieved a rather unpalatable combination of the mechanical formalism of the courts with the political malleability of traditional dispute processing." As Catherine Meschievitz summed it up, "the Nyaya Panchayat is thus a body of men.... that handles disputes without regard to applicable rules and yet appears to villagers as formal and incomprehensible."

Nevertheless, the Panchayat idea continued to exert a powerful attraction on legal intellectuals. The 1973 report of the Expert Committee on Legal Aid, chaired by (and consisting of) Justice Krishna Iyer, a report that viewed itself as a radical critique of Indian legal managements, speaks glowingly of nyaya panchayats as part of a larger scheme of legal aid and access to the courts. Panchayats are endorsed as a method of incorporating lay participation into the administration of justice. But it is clear that the justice in mind is "legal justice," the law of the land, and not that of the villagers or their spiritual advisers. Panchayats are commended as inexpensive, accessible, expeditious and suitable to preside over conciliatory proceedings. The panches envisioned by the report are not village notables but supersaturated Judges and retired advocates.

The follow-up report of the Bhagwati Committee, charged with proposing concrete measures to secure access to justice for the poor, endorses a system of "law and justice at the panchayat level with a conciliatory methodology." The argument was that panchayats would remove many of the defects of the British system of administration of justice, since they would be manned by people with knowledge of local customs and habits, attitudes and values, familiar with the ways of living and thought of the parties before them. Yet again the proposed panchayats donot depart from established notions of law. There was to be a presiding Judge having knowledge of law, and the lay members were to receive rudimentary legal training. There would be no lawyers and the tribunal would proceed informally, its decisions subject to review by the district court. What is proposed is an informal, conciliatory, non-adversarial small claims court with some lay participation. This follow-up report-written by distinguished activist Judges dedicated to enlarging access to justice—thus registered the appeal of the locally based "indigenous" forum under the guidance of an educated and beneficial outsider (Rakesh Chandra, 2017).

3. Law Commission of India 114th Report on Gram Nyayalaya

The Gram Nyayalaya should consist of a legally trained Judge belonging to the cadre of Judges to be specifically set up for this purpose. In order to select legally trained Judges for Gram Nyayalaya, the State shall form a Panchayati Raj cadre of Judges. They would ordinarily form part of the Subordinate Judiciary of the State. The Judge must have all those qualifications which he should have for being recruited as Munsif Magistrate or Civil Judge (Junior Division) and Judicial Magistrate, First Class.

As the Panchayati Raj Judge is to be drawn from the cadre of Munsif Magistrate/Civil Judge (Jr. Division), Judicial Magistrate First Class, for the time being the same method of selection will apply which, the Commission is informed, is that the selection is done by the State Public Service Commission in which a Judge nominated by the Chief Justice of the concerned High Court participated for the time being: the same method may be adopted. It is desirable that a Member of the State Judicial Service at the lowest level with three years experience should be selected for this cadre. The selection must be made by the High Court.

In the selection of the lay Judges, a Selection Committee of District Magistrate and District Judge of the concerned district should be constituted in each district for this purpose. To begin with, the District Magistrate and District Judge should separately draw up a panel up to a number far exceeding the minimum required. Thereafter, they must exchange their panels. A few days later, they must assemble, interact and finalise the panel. The panel of laymen should, as far as possible, be an agreed one, failing which the District Magistrate and the District and Sessions Judge may recommend their separate lists and also record their objections to the names suggested by the other members of the selection committee. The entire panel whether it is drawn up on consensus, or partly agreed or wholly separate, should be submitted to the Chief Justice of the High Court having jurisdiction. The Chief Justice, in consultation with two of his colleagues, shall finalise the panel. It would be open to him to call for additional information about the persons figuring in the panel on separate lists submitted by the members of the selection committee. The selection must be confined to the residents of the district. While preparing a panel a member of the selection body may have recourse to his subordinates to collect the antecedents of the proposed persons. The members of the selection body should have first-hand information as far as possible, through authentic sources enabling checking of the antecedents of the persons proposed by one member or by the other of the selection committee.

Adequate representation should be ensured to members of the weaker sections of the society, Scheduled Castes, Scheduled Tribes, women and backward classes. Panel members must represent the cross-section of the village community.

It is desirable that the lay Judges possess some educational qualifications. The safe middle course is to prescribe a graduate degree as a qualification failing which those who have obtained Higher Secondary School Examination Certificate would be eligible. Educational qualifications may be prescribed as a desirable, and not as minimum, qualification. In the matter of selection of persons from Scheduled Castes, Scheduled Tribes, backward communities and women, educational qualifications may be dispensed with if adequate number of persons with educational qualifications are not available. Persons to be selected should preferably be within the age group of 30-65.

Active political party workers, elite wealthy persons, rich and big farmers, high pay bracket service personnel and moneylenders must be excluded from consideration. So also persons convicted of an offence involving moral turpitude, economic offenders, undischarged insolvents and the like.

The Judges should be Persons of Character and Integrity

It is imperative that the Panchayat Raj Judges as also the members of the panel are imparted basic training in creating a new atmosphere in the forum where all formal technical approach must be eschewed. The Panchayati Raj Judges should assist in imparting information about the relevant point of law, social justice approach, non-formal disposal of causes and deprofessionalised atmosphere. Members of the panel should be imparted training in decision-making process free from prejudices of caste, community, colour, sex or religion. They must be acquainted with the fundamental approach to justice, namely, that the weak and less fortunate should not be the victims of class exploitation. The training may extend to a period of three months. A re-orientation course about the change in pattern of law, sociology of law, object and purpose behind justice system would be of immense assistance to the members of the proposed forum.

Training

The training could comprise subjects like method of hearing cases, attempted conciliation and resolution of disputes by compromise and training in the decision-making process. The lay Judges in particular should be taught that they should conform to the principles of natural justice. Panchayati Raj training centres have been started and they are located in different parts of the country. It is only necessary to expand these training centres and to provide adequate facility for training of the lay Judges.

The approach of the Gram Nyayalaya should be mediatory at the initial stages except in regular criminal proceedings where, save the compoundable offences, trial has to be held. Offence being an injury to society there is hardly any question of conciliation.

Nothing should be done to impair the relative equality among the three Judges composing the court. Therefore, while providing that it would be the primary duty of the Panchayati Raj Judges, who would be presiding over the Gram Nyayalaya to give effective guidance to the two lay Judges on questions of law, in the matter of decision, the majority view in the absence of an unanimous decision will be the decision of the court.

The Commission would favour conferment of civil jurisdiction of Gram Nyayalaya in respect of disputes covered by the subject-matter herein delineated:

I. **Civil Disputes**: Disputes arising out of implementation of agrarian reform and allied statutes
   1. Tenancies—protected and concealed and contested.
   2. Boundary disputes and encroachment.
   3. Right to purchase.
   4. Use of common pasture.
   5. Entries in revenue records.
   6. Regulation and timing of taking water from irrigation channel.
   7. Disputes as to assessment.

II. **Property Disputes**:
   1. Village and farm houses (possession).
   2. Sobas.
   3. Easements: Right of way for man, cart and cattle to fields and courtyards.
   4. Water channels.
   5. Right to draw water from a well or tubewell.

III. **Family Disputes:**
   1. Marriage.
   2. Divorce.
   3. Custody of children.
   4. Inheritance and succession—share in property.
   5. Maintenance.

IV. **Other Disputes:**
   1. Non-payment of wages and violation of Minimum Wages Act.
   2. Money suits either arising from trade transaction or money lending.

3. Disputes arising out of partnership in cultivation of land.
4. Disputes as to use of forest produce by local inhabitants.
5. Complaints of harassment against local officials belonging to police, revenue, forest, medical and transport departments.
6. Disputes arising under the Bonded Labour System (Abolition) Act, 1976 and the Protection of Civil Rights Act, 1955.

The Gram Nyayalaya must have jurisdiction to try all offences which can be tried under the Code of Criminal Procedure, 1973, by the Judicial Magistrate First Class. Though undoubtedly, the Family Courts Act, 1984 has been enacted and brought into operation, since custody of children has a distinct local flavour, the Gram Nyayalaya must have jurisdiction to deal with matrimonial disputes arising in rural areas. The Gram Nyayalaya would be a body for administration of justice, and a legislation for the same would squarely fall under Entry 11-A of the Concurrent List (Usha Vaidyanathan: EBC, Practical Lawyer).

4. Gram Nyayalaya Act, 2008

Discussing about the need of entrusting Federal judicial power to hybrid tribunals in reference to United States of America, Professor Lawrance Tribe, in his monumental work "Constitutional Choices" has stated: "… In a series of cases spanning more than a century and a half, the (Supreme) Court has upheld the constitutionality of several such hybrid tribunals while fervently endorsing the principle of Judicial independence. The Court's quest for a principled distinction between Article III adjudicative power and all other kinds of dispute-resolving authority, like Diogenes' search for an honest man, has taken many roads. The Court has enjoyed little more success than Diogenes." The Gram Nyayalaya Act, 2008 is not the first legislative attempt at establishing a hybrid or informal tribunal like system (in India) ostensibly located in some version of an indigenous system of dispute resolution. Nyaya Panchayats and Lok Adalats were created with the same objective of dispensing speedy justice in informal settings. Both forums, derived "sentimental and symbolic support from appeal to the virtues of the indigenous system." They note that the informalism of the Lok Adalat with its emphasis on compromise and speedy disposal could disadvantage weaker parties.

The Lok Adalats are not bound by of Civil Procedure Code, 1908

(CPC) and the Indian Evidence Act, 1872. According to the authors, Lok Adalat judges appeared to be "overbearing and coercive" to the parties before them—especially poor and unrepresented parties. The authors observe that critics of the look adalats "see in these moves portents of a dismantling of legality in favour of paternalistic, intuitive kadi justice for the poor."

The gram nyayalayas capture all the weaknesses of the Nyaya Panchayats, and Lok Adalats, and the problems associated with these forums would apply equally to this most recent version of the ostensible indigenous dispute resolution forum.

Intent and Jurisdiction

The Act provides for the establishment of gram nyayalayas for the purpose of providing access to justice and to ensure that speedy justice is not denied to any citizen for reasons for social, economic or other disabilities. The gram nyayalaya will be the lowest court of subordinate judiciary in a State and shall be in addition to the regular civil and criminal courts. The Act is broadly based on the recommendations of the Law Commission of India, which had in its 114 the Report (August 1986) suggested the establishment of such courts in order to "provide speedy, inexpensive and substantial justice to the common man. The Report recommended the concept of the Gram Nyayalaya with two objectives. While addressing the pendency in the subordinate courts was the major objective, the other objective was the introduction of a participatory forum of justice. To make it participatory the Law Commission recommended that the Magistrate be accompanied by two lay persons who shall act as Judges, that the legal training of the Magistrate will be complemented by the knowledge of the lay persons who would bring in the much required socio-economic dimension to adjudication. It was proposed that such a model of adjudication will be best suited for rural litigation. The Law Commission also observed that such a court would be ideally suited for the villages as the nature of disputes coming before such a court would be "simple, uncomplicated and easy of solution" and that such disputes should not be enmeshed in procedural claptrap. The report suggests that such a litigation is expensive both for the State as well as the litigant. However, the participatory aspect has been set aside in the current Act and we find the Gram Nyayalaya manned by the regular First Class Magistrate.

The Gram Nyayalaya Act, 2008 received the assent of the President on the 7th January, 2009. The Act came into force on October 2, 2009, i.e. the birth anniversary of Mahatma Gandhi. More than 5000 Nyayalayas were expected to be set up under the Act. Around 194 such Courts have been set up as on March 2015.

The Salient features of the Gram Nyayalayas Act, 2008 are as follows:

1. Gram Nyayalayas are aimed at providing inexpensive justice to people in rural areas at their doorsteps;
2. the Gram Nyayalaya shall be court of Judicial Magistrate of the first class and its presiding officer (Nyayadhikari) shall be appointed by the State Government in consultation with the High Court;
3. the Gram Nyayalaya shall be established for every Panchayat at intermediate level or a group of contiguous Panchayats at intermediate level in a district or where there is no Panchayat at intermediate level in any State, for a group of contiguous Panchayats;
4. the Nyayadhikaris who will preside over these Gram Nyayalayas are strictly judicial officers and will be drawing the same salary, deriving the same powers as First Class Magistrates working under High Courts;
5. the Gram Nyayalaya shall be a mobile court and shall exercise the powers of both Criminal and Civil Courts;
6. the seat of the Gram Nyayalaya will be located at the headquarters of the intermediate Panchayat, they will go to villages, work there and dispose of the cases;
7. the Gram Nyayalaya shall try criminal cases, civil suits, claims or disputes which are specified in the First Schedule and the Second Schedule to the Act;
8. the Central as well as the State Governments have been given power to amend the First Schedule and the Second Schedule of the Act, as per their respective legislative competence;
9. the Gram Nyayalaya shall follow summary procedure in criminal trial;
10. the Gram Nyayalaya shall exercise the powers of a Civil Court with certain modifications and shall follow the special procedure as provided in the Act;
11. the Gram Nyayalaya shall try to settle the disputes as far as possible by bringing about conciliation between the parties and for this purpose, it shall make use of the conciliators to be appointed for this purpose;

12. the judgment and order passed by the Gram Nyayalaya shall be deemed to be a decree and to avoid delay in its execution, the Gram Nyayalaya shall follow summary procedure for its execution;
13. the Gram Nyayalaya shall not be bound by the rules of evidence provided in the Indian Evidence Act, 1872 but shall be guided by the principles of natural justice and subject to any rule made by the High Court;
14. appeal in criminal cases shall lie to the Court of Sessions, which shall be heard and disposed of within a period of six months from the date of filing of such appeal;
15. appeal in civil cases shall lie to the District Court, which shall be heard and disposed of within a period of six months from the date of filing of the appeal;
16. A person accused of an offence may file an application for plea bargaining.

The Central Government has decided to meet the non-recurring expenditure on the establishment of these Gram Nyayalayas subject to a ceiling of Rs. 18.00 lakh out of which Rs. 10.00 lakh is for construction of the court, Rs. 5.00 lakh for vehicle and Rs. 3.00 lakh for office equipment. Government has also estimated that the Gram Nyayalayas upon establishment would incur a recurring expenditure of Rs. 6.4 lakh per annum on salaries etc. and proposes to share such recurring expenditure with the State Government for the first three years within this ceiling (Rakesh Chandra, 2017).

Working of Gram Nyayalayas in Kerala–Picture in Kollam District–December 2018

Sl. No.	*Name of Gram Nyayalaya*	*Areas/Panchayats of Jurisdiction*	*Areas of Police-station Jurisdiction*	*Year-wise*	*No. of Cases*
1.	Chavara (Started functioning on 19 November, 2016)	Chavara, Panmana, Thevalakkara, Thekkumbhagom, Neendakara	Chavara Thekkumbhagom	2018	568
				2017	2764 (Including cases transferred)
				2016	1062

(*Contd.*)

Sl. No.	*Name of Gram Nyayalaya*	*Areas/Panchayats of Jurisdiction*	*Areas of Police-station Jurisdiction*	*Year-wise*	*No. of Cases*
2.	Perinad (Started functioning on 19 November, 2016)	Munroethuruthu East Kallada Perayam, Kundara Perinad Panayam Thrikkaruva	East Kallada Kundara Anchalummoodu	2018	221
				2017	2367 (Including cases transferred)
				2016	1714
3.	Chadayamangalam (Started functioning on 20 February, 2016)	Chadayamangalam Chithara Kummil Kadakkal Ittiva Nilamel Elamadu Velinalloor	Chadayamangalam Kadakkal Pooyappally	2018	519
				2017	748 (Including cases transferred)
				2016	3899

Source: Discussions with Sri Kochupodiyan, Smt. George Elizabeth and Sri Shahul Hameed, Secretaries of Gram Nyayalayas of Chavara, Perinad and Chadayamangalam respectively by the authors on 26th December, 2018 at their respective offices.

6. Inadequacies of the Gram Nyayalaya Act

In a study by Menaka Guruswamy and Aditya Singh pointed out several inadequacies in the Act, which are likely to result in the unjust exclusion of the impoverished from just legal processes thereby restricting access to justice. Their findings can be summed up as under:

- **(i) Nature of Offences within the Domain of Gram Nyayalayas:** Schedule I of the Act lists those offences which can be adjudicated by the gram nyayalayas. Within its criminal jurisdiction, theft; concealment, disposal and receiving of stolen property; and insult with intent to provoke a breach of the peace are some of the offences that can be decided by these courts. Vitally, offences which are not punishable with death, imprisonment for life or imprisonment for a term exceeding two years are also included within the scope of its jurisdiction.
- **(ii) Circumscribed Right of Appeal:** The most problematic part of the Act–Part VII deals with appeals. Section 33 provides for appeals in criminal cases. Sub-section (1) provides that

> notwithstanding anything contained in the CrPC or any other law, no appeal shall lie from any judgment, sentence or order of a gram nyayalaya except as provided hereunder.

The Act already prevents appeals in cases where the "accused person has pleaded guilty" or where the gram nyayalaya has passed a sentence only of fine not exceeding Rs. 1,000. This leads up to the legally unjustifiable, Section 34(2) that provides that no appeal shall lie from any judgment or order passed by the gram nyayalaya (a) with the consent of the parties; (b) where the amount or value of the subject matter of a suit, claim or dispute does not exceed Rs 1,000; (c) except on a question of law, where the amount or value of the subject matter of such suit, claim or dispute does not exceed Rs 5,000.

It is crucial to note that Sections 33 and 34 provide for appeals in certain cases to the court of sessions and the district court, respectively. Hence, a party can appeal the nyayadhikari's decision to a sessions court for criminal matters which must be decided in that forum by that judge within six months. For civil matters the appeal should be directed to district court which must decide it within six months.

Summary Procedure and Plea Bargaining: Gram nyayalayas shall follow summary trial procedure in criminal cases. This runs contra to the CrPC that normally governs all criminal trials in the formal court system. Section 20 provides that any person accused of an offence may file an application for plea-bargaining in the gram nyayalaya in which such offence is pending trial and the gram nyayalaya shall dispose of the case in accordance with the provisions of the CrPC. This provision for plea-bargaining must be read in the context of Section 33(2) (a) which provides that no appeal shall lie where an accused person has pleaded guilty and has been convicted on such plea.

(i) **'Interests of Justice':** While the scheme of the Act which details the special procedure in civil disputes is not entirely undesirable, it is worthwhile to appreciate that Section 24 (7) provides that the proceedings shall, "as far as practicable", be consistent with the interests of justice. This provision employs non-binding language and is conditional while dealing with an issue of prime importance. Any proceeding in a court of law must be consistent with the interests of justice in all circumstances; however, this provision allows for non-compliance when it is not "practicable".

(ii) **Civil Court sans Civil Procedure:** In terms of civil suits, the gram nyayalaya has the power of a civil court, and the judgment passed by it shall be executed as if it were a decree of a civil court. However, the forum shall not be bound by the procedure in respect of execution of a decree as provided in the CPC and it shall be guided by the principles of natural justice. Section 30 of the Act dealing with the application of the Indian Evidence Act, 1872, provides that a gram nyayalaya may receive as evidence any report, statement, document, information or matter that may, in its opinion, assist it to deal effectually with a dispute, whether or not the same would be otherwise relevant or admissible under the said Act. The Act envisages day-to-day hearing with summary procedure and pronouncement of judgment within 15 weeks from the date of the last hearing. The proceedings shall be in one of the official languages of the state other than English, as far as practicable. The parties may argue their own case but they also reserve the right to engage a lawyer to represent them. The Act also places a duty on the gram nyayalayas to provide for conciliation and settlement of civil disputes for which they shall follow the procedure prescribed by the High Court.

Concluding Observations

Administration of Justice is one of the primary responsibilities of a Nation. It is also the fundamental duty of the State to ensure its citizens equal access to legal services. The problem of inequality in accessing justice at minimum cost has been a widespread problem across almost all democracies of the world. India is certainly not an exception. Since independence, the country has consistently taken serious initiatives in fulfilling its emotional obligation of making legal services available to all citizens, through different mechanisms. Certainly the Gram Nyayalaya Act, 2008 is an appreciable step in this direction. But the pace of the implementation of this Act has been unfortunately carried out in an exceptionally slow manner. Besides that certain apprehensions and objectives have been raised from various corners regarding the efficiency of certain provisions of the Act, which need classification from higher ups. However, the real test of any legislation takes place at the execution phase. Therefore, the first and foremost priority of the government should be to give prominence to these areas which can genuinely protect the interests of the needy people. Therefore, remedial measures can be taken to resolve the limitations. Till then the entire Indian society should extend or keep faith in this Act, which can threw light to the millions of downtrodden who genuinely works for a transparent and judicious justice delivery system at their doorsteps. An analysis on the working of this Act from 2009 to 2018 shows that it requires a thorough revision in several key areas. Notable among them include the following:

Training of Gram Nyayadhikari

This is imperative keeping in mind the objectives of Gram Nyayalayas. Apart from the legal and procedural requirements of Gram Nyayalayas, training may also include the local language of the community amongst whom they are posted.

Infrastructure and Security

Separate building for the functioning of the Gram Nyayalaya as well as for the accommodation of the Gram Nyayadhikaris and other staff need to be constructed. Provision also has to be made for providing adequate security.

Creation of Awareness Among Various Stakeholders

Suitable steps may be taken for creating awareness among various stakeholders including the revenue and police officers.

Creation of a Regular Cadre of Gram Nyayadhikari

Officers recruited to this service ought to have a degree in social work apart from a law degree. However, some of the Gram Nyayadhikaris opined that creation of such a separate cadre might not be advisable due to the absence of chances of promotion. Instead, this could be made a compulsory service for a certain period for a newly recruited judicial officer to the regular cadre of first class judicial magistrates or civil judges.

Establishment of Permanent Gram Nyayalayas

Gram Nyayalayas may be established in every Panchayats at intermediate level or group of contiguous Panchayats at intermediate level depending upon the number of disputes which normally arise from that area. While determining the location of the Gram Nyayalayas the location of courts having parallel jurisdiction may also be considered.

The jurisdiction of the Gram Nyayalayas may be redefined in order to remove the ambiguities regarding the jurisdiction of Gram Nyayalayas, and the Act amended.

To conclude, the preamble of the Gram Nyayalaya Act envisages access to justice to the citizens at their doorsteps with the assurance that opportunities for securing justice are not devised to any citizen by season of any disability whatsoever. Hence, the success of these institutions should not only be measured by the number of courts in the whole nation but in terms of the extent and depth of reaching out to deprived sections and its role in the overall reduction in the number of pending cases. Over 72 years after independence, the search for acceptable and accessible legal institution for those living in rural India is still a far away dream. However, whatever things which are available at our hands should be used and utilized with a new professional legal touch, which may give a new light to the Indian Judicial System in the days to come.

REFERENCES

1. P. Baxi, (2007), *Access to Justice and the Role of (Good) Law*, Institute of Human Development, New Delhi 2007.
2. Mare Galanter (1972). "The Aborted Restoration of Indigenous Law in India", *Comprehensive Studies in Society and History* 53.
3. Law Commission of India, 14th Report, *Reform of Judicial Administration*, 1958.
4. Government of India, Central Publication Branch, Civil Justice Commission, 1924-25 Reports.
5. Menaka Guruswamy, Aditya Singh, (2010). Accessing Injustice, The Gram Nyayalayas Act, 2018, *EPW*, Vol. XIV, No. 43, October 23.
6. Anumeha, (2016). Why are we floundering, Eight years after getting the New Act, *Common Cause*, Vol. XXXV, No. 1, Jan-March.
7. Usha Vaidyanathan, Salient Features of Law Commission of India, 114th Report an Gram Nyayalaya, www.ebc-india.com/lawyer/articles/87 2aa.html.
8. Rakesh Chandra, Gram Nyayalaya, (2017). *International Journal of Academic Research and Development*, Vol. 2, Issue 3, May, pp. 217-230, www.academicsjournal.com
9. Shishir Bail, *From Nyaya Panchayats to Gram Nyayalayas: The Indian State and Rural Justice*.
10. https://resturumlegal.com/journal/discourse on access to justice in India rise of gram Nyayalayas at Grassroot

11. Government of India, The Gram Nyayalayas Act, 2008.
12. Government of Kerala, *Kerala Gazette* No. 18, Dated 4th May 2010 No. 9831/Leg.Pbn.3/2009/Law
13. PRS, Legislative Research, Centre for Policy Research, New Delhi, The Gram Nyayalaya Bill, 2007.
14. Government of India, Public Information Bureau, Ministry of Law and Justice, Gram Nyayalayas, 9 March, 2015.
15. Government of India, Ministry of Law and Justice Dept. of Justice, No. J-12021/5/2009-JR, New Delhi, 16.12.2009.
16. Government of India, Ministry of Law and Justice, Dept. of Justice, File No. J.12021/61/297-JR/610 dated 27.10.2017.
17. Government of India, Ministry of Law and Justice, Dept. of Justice, File No. J.12021/10/2009/JR dated 21 May, 2018.
18. Government of India, Ministry of Law and Justice, File No. J-12021/10/2009-JR/398 dated 9.10.2018.
19. *Common Cause*, Vol. 35, No. 1, Jan.-Mar. 2016.
20. Nyaya Panchayats in India, www.shodhaganga.com
21. Ashwini Obulesh, *Institutionalising justice: Gram Nyayalayas and Consumer Courts*, www.dakshindia.org
22. PRS Legislative Research, Centre for Policy Research, New Delhi, The Gram Nyayalaya Bill, 2007, Sept. 4, 2007.
23. Government of India, Press Information Bureau, Gram Nyayalayas, dated. 9 March, 2015.
24. Government of Kerala, *Kerala Gazette* No. 18 dated 4th May, 2010.

9

Decentralisation and Healthcare in Kerala

A Gender Perspective

Nisha Velappan Nair and *M.S. John*

From 1997 onwards, Kerala introduced participatory planning at the local level with the original goal of transferring 35 to 40 per cent of the state's plan (development) funds to local bodies to be spent by them having regard to broad sector guidelines issued by the state government. It resulted in the transfer of an average of around 25 per cent of the plan funds to local bodies, which is the highest in India. The process started from needs appraisal in the local assemblies and ended with the granting of approval to the plan by the District Planning Committee consisting mainly of District level elected functionaries. Many scholars have hailed the scale of Kerala's effort comparing it as a case in "empowered deliberative democracy" akin to the experiment in Porto Alegre (Fung and Wright, 2003; Heller, 2003).

Primary and secondary healthcare institutions were transferred to the Local Self Governments (LSGs) as part of the decentralisation process in the state. A significant budget allocation was also made with the People's Planning Campaigns to equip the LSGs to assume these responsibilities. Decentralisation was expected to strengthen the public healthcare network all over the state to address the new challenges emerging in the healthcare sector. Health reformists argue that decentralization can enhance the participation of local communities in decisions regarding health policy objectives, goals, strategies, planning, financing, implementation and monitoring, which are important to improve the health outcomes (Lieberman, 2002).

In Kerala, by the middle of the 1990s, administrative decentralisation and decentralised planning paved the way for transfer of health care institutions up to the district level to the Panchayati Raj Institutions (PRIs). All health care institutions except General Hospitals, Women and Children Hospitals and Speciality Hospitals have been transferred to the three tier PRIs and up to 40 per cent of the plan fund of various sectors including that of health sector is being disbursed through these institutions. Thus, Kerala became the first state in the country to initiate administrative decentralisation in an extensive way including in the health sector. A government level expert committee has identified some of the lacunae such as the lack of technical support from the department, the absence of a public health perspective in planning, unnecessary construction work at the Primary Health Centre (PHC)/CHC levels and repetitive nature of most projects with a focus on field level medical camps and drug purchases (GOK, 2013:18).

Kerala is known for the prevalence of 3 systems of medical treatment starting at the grassroots level. Hence each panchayat has been entrusted with the responsibility of overseeing the functioning of a PHC under each of the three systems manned by a qualified medical practitioner. This allows a range of choices for the patients. For treating children, homeopathy is often preferred. Elderly persons with mobility-related problems invariably go to the ayurvedic doctor. For ailments requiring quick relief, allopathy is preferred.

Review of Literature

There are studies related to decentralisation and health but lacks studies relating to gender health and decentralisation. And those exist are cursory in nature.

A study on decentralization of health sector identified some problem-areas such as benefit spillover effect, which means the benefits being made use of by people belonging to another panchayat, and the continuation of a pre-existing body like Hospital Development Committee in the new panchayat set-up (Narayana and Hari Kurup, 2000). Another study reveals the close relationship between women's health and intersectionality. Caste interacts with socioeconomic variables on health by magnifying or buffering their effect on health. Small household landholdings, which are linked with poor health, yielded high level of health problems among SC/ST women, and to a lesser extent among OBC. Forward caste women are buffered from the negative effect of small household landholdings. Caste and socioeconomic position are two inter-related sources of inequality that can reinforce each other; being from an upper caste can buffer women from the poor health effects related to low socioeconomic status, whereas being from a lower caste can magnify these effects. The study shows that both being from a lower caste and of low socioeconomic status can trap people into poor health more than either inequality on its own (Mohindra et al., 2006: p. 1025).

Another study on public health and health care delivery suggests that the decentralised plan campaign created conditions for a more effective and efficient extension of needed public health facilities such as latrines and safe drinking water, as well as improvements in PHCs and taluk hospitals. Projects at the different government levels reflected the capacities of those levels; so a positive functional division of health sector tasks developed. Projects mostly reflected the will of the communities as decision-making shifted from bureaucrats in line departments to participants in democratic assemblies. Equality of access to public health and health care improved as below-poverty-line households, scheduled caste and scheduled tribe communities, and women benefited proportionally more (Elamon et al., 2004: p. 706).

Yet another study on Political Decentralization and the Primary Health Care System suggest that there should be some role demarcation between the PHCs and the panchayats. It would be better if the administrative matters were left to the health care centres and the financial matters rested with the panchayats. At the PHC level, many of the Medical Officers recognize the opportunities that the PRIs present to improve the material conditions of the PHCs and this can be used as a basis of forging better relationships between the two. There are some tensions that exist between the PRIs and the Health sector particularly with higher levels of functionaries including the Medical Officer. At the level of the PHC health workers these tensions are minimal and in many cases the study found the PRI functionaries are to be more than willing to respect the health functionaries as professionals and not interfere with their professional duties, but request their assistance with the due processes of decentralization (Ramanathan et al., 2005, pp. 108-109).

During the early stages of the decentralised plan campaign, the PHC was functioning primarily as an adjunct of the health department. In that stage of the PPC, there was conflict between panchayat representatives and PHC staff. Later, the clashes came down and both of them now work together with some kind of broad agreement. The constitution of Standing Committee on Health and Education implies that the body play a more active role on health matters. Likewise, some degree of pressure was exerted by the PHC doctor and supporting staff on the panchayat to invest more money in the health sector, and since then funds starting flowing into the health sector. Women component plan (WCP) is a plan for women at the local level for which ten of plan funds are mandatorily set apart. WCP funds were rarely allocated for women-focused health projects. A rather elaborate study on WCP carried out in 2011 showed that the only investment in the health sector made under the programme was for generating health awareness among the women (Nair, 2012).

John and Jacob (2016) study found that developing countries can learn from Kerala's experience of collaborative governance at local level where the local government and staff of public health institution shares joint responsibility. 'Collaborative governance' is crucial for strengthening and tackling problems of public health delivery system. 'Comprehensive Health Planning' is needed for effective utilisation of fund in the health sector at LSGs (Ali & Kumar, 2015). The local health needs are not addressed by local government as per mandate due to the inefficiency of leaders at local level who lack of skills and exposure (Nair & Naidu, 2016).

A study on Kerala remonstrate that Local-self Governments are coerced to implement centrally sponsored schemes by not taking into account of the local facilities and needs. The study points out excluding NRHM, all other central schemes 'continued as a parallel activity that worked against the spirit of decentralisation'(Thomas and Rajesh, 2011:15). Chathukulam (2016) says that the performance of local government in the health sector is directly related to the level of autonomy and decentralisation. Investment with more autonomy and financial devolution is the only way by which a local government can make greater achievement.

Eapen (2012) asserted that NHRM, an engendered health programme would go beyond technical service in the case of women health issues and it would address 'practical' need of women in a way that challenges existing gender roles and stereotypes transforming women's situation with respect to men'.

Methodology

This paper looks at the allocation and expenditure in the health sector in Thiruvarpu, a Gram Panchayat in Kottayam, Kerala relating to the period from 2009 to 2016. It then seeks to make an analysis of the gender dimensions of this allocation and expenditure by dividing the projects carried out in the health sector into three categories, namely, women-specific, women-friendly and women-neutral and undertakes a gender benefit incidence analysis. The projects which benefit women alone are categorised as women-specific, projects whose benefits for women range between 50 per cent and 99 per cent are called women-friendly and those which benefit the community as whole are categorised as women-neutral (less than 50). Both primary and secondary data are used. Primary data were collected through interviews, focused group discussion and perusal of outpatient register.

Table 9.1: Demographic Profile of Thiruvarpu Panchayat

Area (Kms)	39.59
Density of population	714
No. of wards	18
Population	28274
Sex ratio	1026
SC population	1779
ST population	82
Literacy rate	96.92
Male work participation %	51.99
Female work participation %	13.58

Source: Panchayat Level Statistics 2006, Kottayam.

Thiruvarpu panchayat in Kottayam District was formed in 1953. It is located in a low-lying region of the District prone to water-logging. Politically, the panchayat is dominated by the Marxist party. After several years, a rightist-led coalition came to power in 2010. Presently LDF is the ruling party. Ezhavas, a backward caste, constitute the single largest social group. Other major social groups are Christians (mainly Jacobites), Muslims and Hindu Nairs. Pulayas who belong to the Scheduled Caste (SC), the lowest group in caste ranking entitled to quotas and protection, and Ulladan who are designated as a Scheduled Tribe (ST), with similar entitlements, are also found in this panchayat. Agriculture, particularly paddy cultivation and cattle rearing, are the main occupations of the people. Drinking water scarcity is one of the main problems experienced by the panchayat.

Table 9.2: Total Amount Envisaged, Spent and Expenditure Percentage in Health Sector in Thiruvarpu Panchayat (2009–2016)

Year	Per cent allocated from total fund for health	Per cent spent from total fund for health	Per cent of allocated amount actually spent in health sector
2009–10	17.5	15.9	58
2010–11	7.9	13.2	77.9
2011–12	8.6	12.2	80.6
2012–13	25.2	20.2	65.9
2013–14	20.8	16	70
2014-15	16.9	19.9	70.8
2015-16	16.8	15.1	85.6
Total	15.2	15.9	72.6

Source: Calculated from various plan documents.

Table 9.2 shows the percentage of fund flow in terms of allocation and expenditure from the total funds of the panchayat as well as the expenditure rate in health sector. If we take the total for all the seven years, it can be seen that there was higher expenditure as a share of the total expenditure of the panchayat in real terms compared to allocation. The average expenditure of the allocated funds for the seven years was 72.6 per cent.

Table 9.3 shows the share of fund allocation and expenditure under various categories in the health sector. The projects were divided into nine categories based on their nature. Nutritious food for anganwadi projects took up the highest amount of fund in health sector followed by distribution of medicine, equipment, furniture and building construction or maintenance for PHCs and clinics.

Table 9.4 shows the share of allocations in health sector under different categories. It is clear from the table that in the year 2011, 2013 and 2014 not even a single women-specific project was undertaken. Projects like Mothers' Association, girl-friendly toilet for Government Higher Secondary School, seminar for girls, women health check-up and treatment, and ladies public toilet in the panchayat are women-specific projects under the health sector. Only awareness class, medical check–up and treatment for women's diseases were implemented under Women Component Plan (WCP). WCP is a plan for women under which

Table 9.4: Year-wise Share of Funds Allocated in Health Sector Under Each Category in Thiruvarpu Panchayat

(in %)

Table 9.3: Distribution of Allocation and Expenditure in Health Sector in Thiruvarpu Panchayat During 2009–2016

Projects	*2009*		*2010*		*2011*		*2012*		*2013*		*2014*		*2015*	
	A	*E*	*A*	*E*	*A*	*E*	*A*	*E*	*A*	*E*	*A*	*E*	*A*	*E*
PHC and Hospital	15.16	14.29	14.36	11.94	14.74	18.3	8.93	13.55	30.98	44.03	31	44.03	9.51	13.44
Drainage waste disposal	4.07	0	5.05	6.48	0	0	33.74	0	33.42	5.72	33.4	5.72	30.24	13.98
Latrines	17.45	2.99	0	0	8.56	5.83	0	0	0	0	0	0	2.86	4.05
Nutrition	54.36	76.02	67.28	73.94	68.5	65.71	35.84	53.90	25.20	35.82	25.2	35.82	38.03	53.12
Eradiation or prevention (Rats, stray dogs, Mosquito etc.)	4.64	6.3	1.6S	2.05	1.72	2.12	2.26	3.43	1.68	2.39	1.7	2.39	0	0
Awareness class	0.10	0.18	0.22	28	0	0	0	0	0	0	0	0	0	0
Drinking water	4.08	0	5.05	0	0	0	11.88	18.02	2.32	2.95	2.32	2.95	7.78	0
Palliative Care	0	0	6.36	5.31	6.48	S.04	6.11	9.27	3.22	4.56	3.2	4.56	4.67	6.54
Others (Polio, Old age, women diseases etc.)	0.14	0.22	0	0	0	0	1.24	1.83	3.18	4.53	3.18	4.53	6.91	8.87
Total	**100**	**100**	**100**	**100**	**100**	**100**	**100**	**100**	**100**	**100**	**100**	**100**	**100**	**100**

Source: Calculated from various plan documents.

Year	Women Specific (100)	Women-Friendly (99–50)	Women-Neutral (50 <)
2009-10	0.4	73.7	25.9
2010-11	0.2	93.1	6.7
2011-12	0	89.7	10.3
2012-13	1.2	62.7	36.1
2013-14	0	60.4	39.6
2014-15	0	62.8	37.2
2015-16	1.9	71.9	26.2
Total	**0.6**	**70.6**	**28.8**

Source: Calculated from various plan documents.

ten per cent of plan fund is set apart which will exclusively benefit women. It is seen that rarely women health projects are implemented under WCP. Women-specific health projects are given the least amount of importance in health sector.

Table 9.5: Year-wise Share of Funds Spent in Health Sector Under Each Category in Thiruvarpu Panchayat

(in %)

Year	Women Specific (100)	Women-Friendly (99–50)	Women-Neutral (50 <)
2009-10	0.6	90.6	8.8
2010-11	0.3	91.2	8.5
2011-12	0	92.1	7.9
2012-13	1.8	94.7	3.5
2013-14	0	85.9	14.1
2014-15	0	77.1	22.9
2015-16	2	71.9	26.1
Total	**0.7**	**84.3**	**15**

Source: Calculated from various plan documents.

Table 9.5 shows the amount spent under health sector in each category. Women-specific projects constituted only 0.7 per cent and women-friendly projects had the lion's share with 84.3 per cent in the health sector expenditure, much higher than the 70.6 per cent allocated for such projects. It is apparent from Tables 9.4 and 9.5 that women-specific projects were totally neglected both in terms of allocation and expenditure. In contrast, women-neutral projects had a much lower share of expenditure, 15 per cent against the allocation of 28.8 per cent.

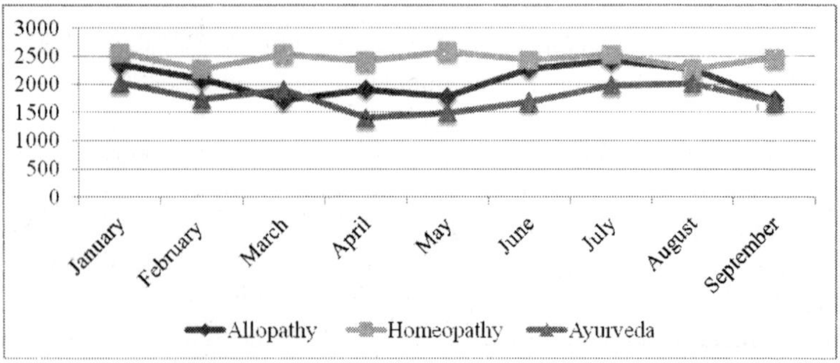

Fig. 9.1: Total number of Outpatients of Allopathy, Homeopathy and Ayurveda Hospital (January 2016 to September 2016)

Figure 9.1 shows the total number of outpatients visiting allopathy, homeopathy and ayurveda dispensaries. It is seen that homeopathy dispensary has highest number of outpatients every month and the number of such patients exceeds two thousand. The largest single share of children 27.6 per cent, use the outpatient facility of the homeo dispensary.

Table 9.6: Sex-wise Details of Outpatients in Different PHC/Clinics

	Allopathy	*Homeopathy*	*Ayurveda*
Male	38.5%	27.7%	27.3%
Female	60.0%	44.7%	68.6%
Children	1.5%	27.6%	4.1%
Total	**100%**	**100%**	**100%**

Source: Outpatient Registers.

Table 9.6 shows the sex-wise details of outpatients in allopathy, homeopathy and ayurveda dispensaries. It is clear from the table that women are the major or single largest group of beneficiaries of the three dispensaries. In the case of ayurveda, the percentage is the highest (68.6%) because the doctor serving in the hospital until recently was a specialist on women's reproductive health also. Men prefer to go for allopathic treatment and children who use the services of the homeopathy dispensary are several times higher than children who use the dispensaries of the other two systems of treatment.

Some Qualitative Information

The opening hours of both homeo and ayurveda hospitals is from 9 am to 2 pm and all outpatients are charged a nominal fee of rupees two. The working hour of Allopathy dispensary is from 9 am to 1 pm and one rupee is charged from the patients. The amount collected for outpatient services constitute the HMC fund. PHC is adjacent to the Thiruvarpu panchayat office. Ayurveda and homeo dispensaries are quite far away from the panchayat office, and both are located at the same place.

The PHC has a large number of outpatients on Mondays, Wednesdays and Fridays. There are three Junior Public Health Nurses, three Junior Health Inspectors, one Health Inspector and 32 ASHA workers in the panchayat. From 2015, the PHC was designated as a visual care centre where every Friday an optometrist comes and conducts eye check-up. There were very few patients when the service began, but the number increased gradually and recently they identified 30 patients with cataract. Such cases are referred to the district hospital for free surgery. On Mondays there is a clinic for Non-Communicable Diseases (NCD) where routine tests for determining blood sugar levels, blood pressure and cholesterol are conducted and medicines are freely given to the patients. People belonging to all classes, both male and female, use this facility.

The allopathy pharmacist says that the PHC space is very congested and according to government norms the medicine and store room in the PHC should be air conditioned. The doctor's room has no space and the fridge and other equipment are placed there. Electricity is erratic and the small inverter has very little back-up capacity. The space for check-up is also congested. The citizens have never raised any concern in the Gram Sabha over the limited facilities available in the PHC. JPHN and ASHA workers say that incidence of mental illness, cancer and infertility is very high in the panchayat.

The president of the panchayat is a woman. She won the election in 2005 and lost in 2010 because of local politics. The conflict between CPI and CPI(M) resulted in the panchayat going to the opposition UDF front after a period of 35 years of uninterrupted rule by the LDF. In 2015 both CPI and CPI(M) joined hands together and won the election. The President says that the panchayat does not have any health projects under WCP. The panchayat has no health policy as well.

From 2010 onwards, the panchayat had palliative care projects every year. Total number of persons registered is 789. Out of this 400 died and 300 are currently monitored. 40 patients are out patients and 24 of them have registered some improvement in their condition after medication. A nurse in charge of palliative care conducts house visits of bed-ridden patients. Water bed, wound dressing materials etc. are freely given to the patients. According to the palliative care nurse, most of the patients suffer from cancer and paralysis. 50 per cent of registered patients are women of whom 20 per cent suffer from breast cancer. The nurse makes a total of 9 visits a month.

Lack of staff is the major problem of Ayurveda dispensary according to the last grade staff. The doctor has to write the entries in the OP ticket herself and collect money from the patient. She has to maintain the pharmacist register at the same time. The newly appointed doctor says that every panchayat is expected to have two posts, namely, pharmacist and sweeper. A daily wage helper is there to help. The last grade staff says that earlier the hospital doctor was a specialist in gynaecology and she had taught them about medicine and treatments like massages etc. Both rich and poor women used to visit the doctor. Majority of the patients were women. The doctor says that Hospital Management Committee meeting is held on different dates and time for the three hospitals. Usually, it is conducted on the same day, say allopathy in the morning, homeopathy at noon and ayurveda in the evening. The committee members are the same for all the three systems of medicine. Majority of the patients who come to the ayurvedic hospital complained of arthritis.

The homeopathy health centre has sufficient staff. The homeopath says that most patients come from poor background. Asthma and allergic cases are brought to the homeopathic clinic for treatment. Currently, a temporary doctor is serving in the homeopathic health centre. People prefer homeopathy because they believe that it has no side effects and it is easier to make children adopt to it compared to ayurvedic or allopathy medicine.

Conclusion

To conclude, the study shows that women's health projects are of least priority both under Women Component Plan (WCP) and general health sector. The data shows that nutrition constituted the largest chunk of both allocation and expenditure in the health sector. Only two health projects were implemented under WCP. The panchayat does not have any health policy of its own. Investing in women's health can be based only on a conscious policy or design. In this case, not much investment has been made by design. However, whatever investment has been made, has yielded, by default, some outcomes that are beneficial for women. The foray made into sectors like palliative care has implications for women in the sense that they constitute more than 50 per cent of the beneficiaries as well as because it has helped reduce to some extent the burden of the informal care economy is now borne by women. It can also be seen that any further investment in the health sector is likely to benefit women more than men since they constitute the majority or single largest group of the patients who frequent the dispensaries.

REFERENCES

Ali, A., and Kumar, S.S. (2015). "Decentralized Health Planning–Lessons from Kerala State", *Academic Medical Journal of India*, 3(3): 75-78.

Chathukulam, J. (2016). "Reflections on Decentralised Health Delivery System in Kerala", *Mainstream*, Vol. LIV No. http://www.mainstreamweekly.net/article6189.html

Eapen, Mridul (2012). Engendering Health: The Experience of NRHM, available from http://www.cds.edu/wp-content/uploads/2012/09/Concept-Note-for-NC.pdf

Elamon, J., Franke, R.W., and Ekbal, B. (2004). Decentralization of health services: the Kerala people's campaign. *International Journal of Health Services*, 34(4), 681-708.

Fung, A., and E.O. Wright (2003). *Deepening Democracy: Institutional Innovations in Empowered Participatory Governance*, New York: Verso.

Government of Kerala (2013). *Health Policy Kerala draft, Health and Family Welfare Department*. http://dhs.kerala.gov.in/docs/draftpolicy.pdf

Heller, P. and T.M. Thomas Isaac (2003). "Democracy and Development: Decentralized Planning in Kerala", In Archon Fung and Erik O. Wright (eds.), *Deepening Democracy: Institutional Innovations in Empowered Participatory Democracy*. London, Verso Press.

John, J., and Jacob, M. (2016). *Local Governments and the Public Health Delivery System in Kerala: Lessons of Collaborative Governance*. Cambridge Scholars Publishing.

Lieberman, S. (2002). *Decentralisation and Health in the Philippines and Indonesia: An Interim Report*, World Bank, Washington, D.C.

Mohindra, K.S., Haddad, S. and Narayana, D. (2006). "Women's health in a rural community in Kerala, India: Do caste and socioeconomic position matter?", *Journal of Epidemiology and Community Health*, 60(12): 1020-1026.

Nair, Manju S., and V. Nagarajan Naidu. (2016). *Public Health Interventions by Local Governments in Kerala: An Effectiveness Analysis*: A19-A19.

Nair, Nisha, V. (2012). Mainstreaming gender in local development and governance: A study of selected panchayats in Kottayam district, Kerala. unpublished Ph.D Thesis, MG University, Kottayam.

Narayana, D., and Kurup, K.K. (2000). Decentralisation of the health care sector in Kerala: Some issues. Working paper: 298, Centre for Development Studies

Thiruvananthapuram. https://opendocs.ids.ac.uk/opendocs/bitstream/handle/123456789/3001/wp298-119994.pdf?sequence=1&is Allowed=y

Ramanathan, M., Vijayan, A., Varatharajan, D., and Sukanya, R. (2003, March). Political Decentralisation and the Primary Health Care System: Examining the Potential for Improving Women's Reproductive Health Care in Kerala. In National Seminar on 'Global Agendas, Local Realities: Implications of Health Sector Reforms on Woman's Access to Reproductive Health Services in India,' New Delhi (Vol. 7).

Shukla, A., Khanna, R., and Jadhav, N. (2014). Using community-based evidence for decentralized health planning: Insights from Maharashtra, India. Health Policy and Planning, czu099.

Thomas, M.B., and Rajesh, K. (2011). Decentralisation and interventions in health sector: A critical enquiry into the local self governments in Kerala. Working paper 271, The Institute for Social and Economic Change, Bangalore.

10

A Micro Analysis of the Life and Livelihood of Mayana Vettiyan in Tamil Nadu

G. Palanithurai

Introduction

"Mayana Vettiyan" is an individual designated by a community among the scheduled caste families to perform the task of burying and burning the dead human bodies and dead animals in the villages of Tamil Nadu. It is an assigned function to the Dalit families by the dominant communities through the practices evolved historically over a period of time. It is being practiced in the rural areas without any resistance. The same practices are in vogue in urban areas also. Yet the conditions with which the practices carried out in the urban areas are somewhat different in terms of the hardships undergone by the Mayana Vettiyans in the rural areas.[1] It is a task can be done by anyone provided it is done scientifically and professionally as it is being done in the western country. It can be made as a skilled work and this work has to be done by a skilled worker. If it is done through skilled worker, payment has to be made as fixed by the government. But assigning the work to a few Dalit families and the work carried out in an unscientific and hazardous way is really inhuman and condemnable in democratic governance arrangement. It was declared abolished in Tamil Nadu through a government order No. 74 dated 24th May, 2002. Despite the passage of the government order, this practice is being continued in rural Tamil Nadu. There are many progressive acts in India to facilitate the marginalised and deprived to empower them but they are not implemented in letter and spirit[2]. In the same way it is also not implemented in Tamil Nadu. There are innumerable hurdles and barriers in implementing such revolutionary reforms and acts in India. Enacting legislation is not a complicated task. Implementing the enacted legislation is the real task and achievement. It has been seen in independent India, how difficult it is to implement the provisions of the Constitution of India for the benefit of the poor[3].

Tracing the history of the practice of burying and burning dead bodies by a few individuals from a community hailing from the lowest strata of the society goes back to epic age. All the activities associated with burning and burying the dead bodies had been performed with varying degrees of rituals with differences from region to region. Rituals have been changed and yet the conditions with which the burial and burning have not been changed. As a result, the persons involved in burning and burying the dead bodies face volley of problems. The problems associated with burying and burning are also equivalent to that of the problem of the manual scavengers[4]. Neither the community nor the policy-makers are concerned about the plight of the graveyard workers called 'Mayana Vettiyan' in Tamil Nadu. Their pain and agony are not understood properly by the policy community. Their problems have not reached the corridors of decision-making bodies despite the earnest efforts of some of the civil society organisations. Even if they take decision at the state level to help them to redeem their problems, mostly it is cosmetic and it is not implemented letter and spirit. But in the urban areas, the conditions are somewhat better wherever they are assisted by the civil society organisations[5]. Wherever the civil society organisations have involved in helping the graveyard workers, the conditions of the work have been improved as they follow some scientific procedures. Civil society organisations help the graveyard activities only in the urban areas. The problems of the graveyard workers in the rural areas have not reached strongly the vicinity of the civil society organisations. Only a few civil society organisations are involved in the rehabilitation works of the graveyard workers. Organizing the manual scavengers, graveyard workers and cobblers are not the easy job as one finds in organizing other social groups. This may be one of the reasons why many civil society organisations have not evinced interest in organizing such marginalised groups. Since the number of people involved in this task is minimum in every village, their plight has not drawn the attention of the policy community. Even though there were ministers hailing from the same community, they have not come openly to support their cause. They are closer to power centre and they know the problem and yet they are not representing the problems of this category of people.

The graveyard workers are not a distinctive social group in the village setting to perform the above tasks of burying and burning the dead corps. They are also individuals from Dalit groups. They also live with other Dalit groups. No way, they are inferior or superior to the other Dalit families. "Vettumai" is a traditional job to be performed by the Vettiyans for the farming communities in the rural areas. Only a few designated families among the Dalits perform this task. This job has been conferred on certain families by the dominant caste groups in the rural areas. This job cannot be done by others. This is a common unwritten agreement among the communities. The individual families who perform the task of burying and burning the dead bodies and the communities in the rural areas on mutual consent carryout the tasks without having any conflict and disagreement even though there is no written agreement. Their operational units are not synchronized with either Gram Panchayat areas or revenue panchayat areas. Their area of operation is determined by the communities. It is also not decided by the communities now.

It is an age long practice followed in the rural areas for several centuries. They are not only burying the dead bodies and burning the same but also removing dead animals from the habitats of the higher caste groups. These activities are going on in Tamil societies over centuries. These jobs are difficult to carryout and yet they are being carried out by the dalit families. In the fast changing modern world, any activity can be carried out by any individual provided they are done professionally with adequate care attention and skill. If any work is professionalized through a formal system, that would attract the attention of everyone as it would help them to earn money. In India many of the manual works are unprofessionalised and they are earmarked for a few sections and they have to carry out all those activities as they are mandated by the community through a system of informal arrangement. 'Vettumai' is one such profession to be done by the dalits in the villages. What are all the problems they face and how they do the job are being investigated in this work.

To study any social problem or issue a well-formulated theory is an imperative need. Theory will be a goal post and it will enable the researcher to pursue the process of investigation more scientifically with precision to add value to the existing body of knowledge on this subject. Hence, to study this problem of marginalization the researcher has searched for a meaningful theory. On the search "Basic Grounded Theory" has been considered more suitable for this investigation and hence this theory has been adopted in this study.

Basic Grounded Theory

Basic grounded theory[6] is qualitative method adopted in social science to map up certain peculiar social realities which are unique and dissimilar to the general issues and problems. This theory helps the researcher to explore new area very deeply and the social phenomena are intricate and delicate which are to be investigated. Every aspect of the social phenomena has to be coded and is to be described, analysed and explained. It is applicable to the unique cases. The researcher can probe through any method and bring to light the realities. This method can be widely used in Indian and African social setting as differences, disparities, derivations, discriminations, and deprivations are abundantly explicit in the social constructions. Each segment of the society has peculiar character. They have the unique characteristic features which cannot be compared with any other in the same society. The grounded theory's canvas is wide and the freedom of the researcher and the integrity of the researcher is crucial[7]. For the investigation, the researchers need not depend on any conventional tool, framework or theory.

Methodology

To get to know the details, a focus group discussion was arranged. It was arranged in Alathambadi village in Thiruthuraipoondi Taluk in Thiruvarur district on 7th May, 2017. It is part of composite Tanjure district. In this district the left political parties have established their grip as they struggled for the emancipation of the working class in the rural areas and they have succeed in their attempts in considerable measure. Hence, this study was conducted in this area. This study is a preliminary one to launch a major study in Tamil Nadu. An extensive and elaborate discussion was held with a group mostly the Vettiyan family members. All are men. Of them three are 'Vettiyans' and others are only helpers. Mr. Radha (55), Gyanasambandam (49) and Thangavel (55) are the vettiyans performing the job since their earlier days. The participants who participated in the discussions had long year of experience and hence they had been chosen as respondents. They are performing this job as per community practices. In the focus group discussion, there were other members but they are not designated individuals for the job. But they perform the task as instructed by the designated individuals. But all the individuals have involved in the task of burying and burning the dead bodies. From the researchers perspective they are helpers and they also know the practices. The discussion went on for four hours. Though the helpers also participated, helpers have not spoken much as the Vettiyans handled the questions directly. Whenever, wherever the helpers are allowed to speak by the Vettiyans, the helpers have responded. They have been informed that the interview was only for research and not for anything.

Perception, Duties and Responsibilities

All the three respondents are "Vettiyans" designated by the community as perceived by them. While explaining it in the Focus group discussion, all the three categorically made a statement that they are the responsible persons to perform the task. This was considered as right conferred on them by the community traditionally. No other individual can perform this duty without their permission. They informed that whenever any death happens in any family, the family members immediately inform any of the three about the death. When it is communicated, it is the responsibility of the Vettiyan to go to the place immediately and ask for the details of the works to be carried out. To perform their duties and responsibilities they will prepare themselves and their team. They know the ritual pattern of each caste group and accordingly they take steps. They have not perceived that it is a job thrusted on them. They considered that it is a right. They are of the opinion that it is not confined to village panchayat area. Their area of operation is determined by the settlement of few cohesive communities. It is neither village panchayat area nor revenue panchayat area. They cover only community panchayat areas. Both communities and the Vettiyans know their area of jurisdiction. Neither the communities nor the Vettiyans feel any problem in the task and their relationship.

People from different communities in the villages inform such tasks only to these individuals. These responsible and earmarked Mayana Vettiyans have to decide how many have to attend, how to attend and what could be done. Twenty years back number of activities have been carried out by the Vettiyans from the day of burning to the 16th day of burning rituals. They had been carried out by the Vettiyans on consent as observed by the participants. No doubt they have faced volley of problems in performing these functions. But they never feel that they have to give it up. They feel that they are also doing a function as Brahmins do it in the temples. But now they have started realizing the problems they faced are imposed by the traditions of the communities. Yet, they have not prepared for resisting it or to abandon it. Now they compare themselves with Brahmins. Why Brahmins are respected why the Vettiyans are not respected? Why people pay what Brahmins demand? Why Vettiyans have to accept what the community gives for the job they do? are the questions now they raise among themselves.

They perform variety of responsibilities related to death and death related events. They carry out both burials and burning the dead bodies. To perform the above activities, and for which there is no fixed amount earmarked either by the community or the Vettiyans. When death occurs in the affluent families they get more wages than their average wage they earn per day. They cannot expect much money from the poor families to perform the same works. Depending on the requirements, workers are being mobilized and for which Vettiyan is responsible. Vettiyan is being contacted if any death happens. It is his responsibility to mobilize workers to perform either burial or burning the dead bodies in the villages. The work starts from informing their relatives about the death of a person, drum beating, preparing the burial ground or burning ground for burial or burning. From information given to the relatives of the deceased to burning the dead bodies, all the activities are to be performed by the Vettiyans. There is no fixed cost for each of the work. The expenditure and wages are highly arbitrary and the Vettiyans have no say and they cannot demand. At present barring burial and burning all other activities are being carried out by many. Technology has come to the rescue of the dalits who have been involved in this burial and burning work. Technology has come to all other activities barring burning and burial in the rural areas. If it is burial, it is only an hour work. If it is burning, it is almost twelve hours work after laying the body on the burning place. Mostly that work is carried out during the night. On an average one individual can get Rs. 500 per night and Rs. 350 for assisting the person who is involved in burning the dead bodies.

They never take any safety measures while performing their job of burning the bodies. Even they never cover their legs by using shoes. With only a knife and a small stick they manage the work. Before they start the work, they take alcohol. They perform the task in the influence of alcohol. Bodies are of different types. No one inform them about the cause of death and with great risk they do the work. Only during the burning they understand the nature of the body. Mostly they will be in a drunken mood. They will be in the job to complete the target. It will take seven to twelve hours. Till the process of burning is completed the Vettiyans have to be in the place in the midst of fumes. Each community has its own place either for burial or for burning. In the rural areas, the burial and burning ground has been used by the public for open air defecation. So cleaning the place is the difficult task. It is just like a manual scavenger, Vettiyan has to clean the place. Once the burning is completed, it is to be informed in the respective families.

After burning the body, they have to keep the burnt body in such a way that the family members have to easily trace the skull, leg and hands for the ceremony they do in the next day. While burning the bodies, they notice changes and by noticing it they have to procure fuel and add it in the fire to complete the burning quickly. Some of the bodies produce intolerable foul smell and the Vettiyans have to tolerate the smell till the job is over. Till the burning is over the Vettiyans will be inside the smoke. Dead bodies are different types. Suicide committed bodies and HIV infected bodies are also burnt by them. The Vettiyans do not know the details of the death or causes for the death but they have to carry out the job as per the decision of the community. Some of the intricacies of the death of some individuals came to light only through opinion makers in the village. The Vettiyans can guess from their body reactions while in burning about the nature of death.

Sometimes bodies come due to suicides, and in such occasion, the bodies have to be burnt quickly. During that time heavy fuel has to be added. Normally white sugar used to be poured on the body. Fumes come out of body while burning it. They cannot move out from the fumes. They smell it and it is a difficult process. The odour of the fumes vary from body to body. They cannot move away from the site. They have to enable the body to burn properly. Hence, they will be very closer to the site. Only instrument they use during the burning process is a long wooden stick with one lengthy knife. In normal condition, they cannot tolerate the smell of the fumes and that is why they consume alcohol. Everyone knows that the people involved in burning dead bodies consume alcohol. They reported that for consume alcohol, they liberally get money from the community. After burning dead bodies, they cannot do any work for two or three days. They will be so tired or sometime they are not in any mood to work. So the next two or three days they cannot earn anything. But it is not compensated, they reported. In many of the occasions, they fell ill due to unknown reason. They have to spend money for the treatment. No one is giving money for the treatment. Though women are involved in this task[8], in East Tanjure district women are not involved in this work.

Women involved in this job are not new. It is in practice in other states also[9].

There is yet another job the Vettiyan has to do. Removing dead animals, mostly dead cows and bulls. Vettiyan receive information about the death of animals in the farmer's house. Community gives the information to the Vettiyan through some one about the death of cows or bulls. It is the role of Vettiyans to remove the dead animals. Vettiyan has to organise four members to carry the dead animals to their habitat. They have a specific place to remove the fur from the animal. After removing the skin, the animals have to be buried in a safe place. The whole process takes minimum of four to five hours time. During summer burying the dead animal is a difficult one as taking pit for burial will take longer time. For the whole process nothing is paid. There are some individuals having realized the labour lost in this process, they give money. Others feel that it is the duty of Vettiyan to remove the dead animals and hence they will not give money. The skin of the animal can be sold. But the cost of the skin will not meet the cost of labour involved in disposing of the dead animals. At present, this problem has been reduced as animal population is dwindling down and drastically reduced. Further, the farmers feel by burying the dead animals in their plantation will become good manure to the plants. Hence, they bury the dead animals in their plantation itself.

After the present generation, there will not be anyone willingly to do the work anymore. This Vettiyan groups have internalized this work as their duty and commitment to the community and hence they are doing it. The sons and daughters are in the schools and they do not like this job to be carried out by their fathers. Hence, there is no guarantee that their wards will continue this practice in these villages after their death. By going through the nature of the task, the Vettiyans can be paid more. But normally it does not take place. Almost all of them had the feeling that they are not paid well. Yet they felt that they should not bargain with the community since it is related to death. They feel that it is beneath their dignity. The community has to realize that they are paying less to Vettiyans for the work done by them. Previously, there was a practice that Vettiyans have to collect paddy during harvest seasons by visiting paddy field. By collecting paddy, every household of Vettiyans would collect paddy to the requirements for the family for a year. Now for the past two years, there is no cultivation of paddy during farming seasons. While interacting with Vettiyans one will find their generosity. They stated that it is unfair to bargain on the dead bodies. But it is the responsibility of the community to look at the wage part of it. The same Vettiyans said that they are fighting for their wages when they involved in agriculture work.

In the event of Vettiyan sick for a particular day, he has to nominate a person among his community to perform the functions. Even during sickness, they are discharging their duties. But nobody to bother about their health. While interacting with them, on their health conditions, many indicated that they have multiple health problems. One will find many scars in their body. When they are asked about it, they informed that they got several wounds during the process of burning the bodies. Many have problems in their eyes. They have several ailments and for which they get treatments in the hospitals. They consume medicine worth about Rs. 1000 per month. Lot of money has been spent on health. Most of the occasions, they borrow money for interest not in the bank but from the moneylenders. Of them no one has got bank account and no one has got savings. No one expressed hope that their life can be changed or transformed. Their life is to earn for their food and other daily requirements. They are always in debt. Savings is to repay the loan which they borrow for their family needs. They have no answer to the question, why they are not refusing to do the obnoxious works? They feel that it is the work imposed on them and yet they feel that they have to do the work as it is destined.

There is an organisation working for this category of people. It is called "Mayana Vettiyan Sangam"[10]. It was established in the year 2007 by the Tamil Nadu Labour Union at Madurai. It wanted to bring all the Vettiyans all over the state under one fold. After the enrolment of the member, the organization conducted a conference on 7th January, 2008 at Madurai. When they organized the conference a Minister Mrs. Tamilarasi Ravikumar for Adi Dravidar Welfare, Government of Tamil Nadu participated. The organization has put up several demands to the Government of Tamil Nadu. They are: creation of separate board for them; minimum salary for them, old age pension, maternity benefits for the women workers; rest rooms and toilet facilities in burning ground. These are all the major demands projected by them and handed over to the Minister. They continuously organized some rallies to press their demands subsequently. But the association seems to be a closed chapter as it could not mobilize Vettiyans to build a movement. No civil society is engaged in mobilizing them. But the respondents are not aware of the association and its activities. Everyone wants assistance to protect their health. They want a specific scheme to ensure their livelihood and help to protect their health.

Box—I: Vettiyan becomes the President of Gram Panchayat

Koduvilarpatti Gram Panchayat president post has been reserved for SC and hence Mr. Chinnavaradhan has been asked to file his nomination. He is a Vettiyan performing his traditional role of burning and burying the dead bodies. He promised the people even after the election he will continue the work of burning and burying the dead bodies. He won the election and continued the traditional duties and responsibilities. Many persuaded him to do the Vettiyan work. But he did the job as promised to the people. He mentioned that he need not explain the problems of Vettiyan as everyone knows. What he informed is that he brought several facilities to graveyard. No one has taken such steps to beautify the graveyard. It is a neglected place. Everyone comes to graveyard but their stay is for a few minutes. Hence, it is not registering in their minds. But I stay here for the whole night when I burn dead bodies. Hence, the condition of the graveyard is in my memory. When I got an opportunity I have started providing all the facilities. Water facilities, shed for burning dead bodies, planting of trees, approach road to graveyard have been provided. He also said that he maintained cleanliness in the graveyard. A compound has been constructed for the graveyard. He said that he performed his task as president of the Gram Panchayat along with his traditional role.

—*Dinamalar*, 4.7.2017

Box–II: Women in Graveyard

Even men dare to visit graveyard during the time of burning the dead bodies. But Ms. Vairamani is performing the role of a Vettiyan in Chokkampudur graveyard in Coimbatore district, Tamil Nadu. She performs her duty mostly in night without having any support of man. It was the duty of her father to perform burning and burying dead bodies as per the practice of the community. She got married and has three children. She married at the young age as it was decided by her father. Husband could not take care of her family through his earning. At this juncture, her father died and nobody to take responsibility to perform her father's role. Hence, she has decided to take up this job as she can earn through this work. Since she helped her father to perform this job, she has no fear. She considered it as a divine place. She fixes Rs. 2000 per body either for burial or for burning. She keeps one assistant to do the job. She gets this amount after a tough bargaining. Many of the occasions, dead bodies are brought to burial ground without relatives. During those occasions she cannot ask for labour charge. Her children are studying in the schools. Normally, six to seven hours the dead bodies will take to be consigned. The work is tiresome and it has to be performed in smoke. Dead bodies are brought to the graveyard but no one inform the cause of the death. Only during the time of burning the dead bodies, one can guess the reasons for the death. It is not a healthy job and she had no other option, she had decided to do.

—*Dinamalar*, 9th June, 2013.

Box–III: Mayana Vettiyan's Green Route

Everyone sympathize with graveyard workers when one visits graveyard and forget about them after the departure from the graveyard. Their conditions are deplorable. They work in hazardous conditions by risking his life. Everyone knows yet no help from anyone. Ministers, people representatives, business man, intellectuals, officials are visiting graveyard and they will be there briefly but no one take any step either in cleaning and beautifying the graveyard as in the west or rehabilitating the graveyard worker. But Mr. Hari, a graveyard worker in the graveyard at Thathaneri cremation ground in Madurai has done a yeoman service to the society. Apart from burying and cremating the dead bodies, he planted saplings in the cremation yard and watering them continuously for the plants to make it a green cover. No one gives money to buy saplings. He pays from his pocket. When he was asked, he said that he has a concern for the people who visit graveyard along with dead bodies as they are in scorching sun or in rain without having any shade in the graveyard when they come along with dead bodies. "They are not bothered about me or themselves. But I have a concern for them" he said while interacting. He further lamented that people spent much money for temples but they are not interested in keeping the cremation ground clean, neat and green. Sympathy, empathy, concern and compassion are with the poorest of the poor not with elites and educated.

—*The New Indian Express*, 24th September, 2014

Conclusion

Vettiyans have to be relieved from such hazardous works and they have to be rehabilitated. The Government Order passed by the Government of Tamil Nadu has to be implemented in letter and spirit. Till government finds alternative to this practice of burning and burying the dead bodies, the grievances of the Vettiyans have to be redressed. Protective measures have to be taken by giving instruments and safety equipment for the works they do. The wage has to be hiked by doubling the wage of unskilled workers. Minimum wage has to be fixed for the work and that can be done by the government. Burial and burning ground should have some basic facilities and the place should be maintained as clean as the divine place. An electric light provision has to be made in the burning ground. Water and toilet facilities have to be created there. Shade giving trees have to be planted in the premises of the burial and burning ground. The graveyard has to be maintained neat and clean. Compound walls have to be constructed. All the above facilities have to be created by the Gram Panchayat. Professional training has to be conducted for them to perform the task more scientifically. There are modern cemeteries constructed by various civil society organisations. These cemeteries never use firewood to burn the bodies. After performing the religious rites, the dead bodies will be inserted into the cemetery. The body will be burnt in the natural heat generated in the cemetery. Government of Tamil Nadu can think of alternative mode of disposal of dead bodies as devised by civil society organisations. Considering the quantum of firewood used for this purpose, an alternative mode can be thought of. Thus for every five panchayats one cemetery could be created and they can be managed professionally by the local bodies. User fee can be levied from the users. Cost of maintenance can be met from the user fee collected from the users. Thus, this Vettiyans can be liberated from this unscientific task and modernize the very process of burning the dead bodies.

NOTES

1. Vidya Venkat, (2008). "They deal with death every day at work," *The Hindu*, 24th August.
2. Bhasha Singh, (2014); *Unseen: The truth about Indian's Manual Scavengers.* New Delhi: Penguin Books; B.N. Srivastava, (1997). *Manual Scavenging in India: A Disgrace to the Country.* New Delhi: Concept Publishing Company.
3. Grenville Austin, (2012). *Working a Democratic Constitution: A History of the Indian Experience*, New Delhi: Oxford University Press.
4. D. Senthil Natarajan (2016). "Two women oversee burial ground work", *Deccan Chronicle*, 25th August.
5. Kathy Charmaz (1983). "The Grounded Theory Method: An Explication and Interpretation", In *Contemporary Field Research* (eds.) R.M. Emerson. Boston: Little Brown.
6. U. Flick, (1998). *An Introduction to Qualitative Research,* London: Sage Publications.
7. "Burning the body in the night by women Vettiyan" (in Tamil), *Dinamalar* Tamil Daily, 9th June, 2013.
8. B. Madhu Gopal, (2014). "Women caretaker at burial ground", *The Hindu*, 19th March.
9. Tamil Nadu Mayana Vettiyan Sangam, *Epic Age to the Present: The Life of the Mayana Vettiyans A Report*, Madurai: Tamil Nadu Labour Union, 2009.
10. Gokul Vannan, (2014). "Grave Digger Takes Green Route to Mark Amavasya at Madurai Cremation Ground", *The New Indian Express* 24th September.
11. "A Woman in Challenging task at Graveyard", *Social,* 8th March, 2017.

11

Critical Analysis of the Functioning of Ombudsman in Tamil Nadu

G. Palanithurai

Introduction

Societies in the world are changing fastly and moving towards democracy. Nearly 80 per cent of the people in the world are in a democratic governance arrangement. As a result, people's expectations from the democratic governments are increasing. Commensurate with the increasing expectations, process of governance and administration are also undergoing unexpected changes.[1] Increasing aspirations of the people have increased the workload of the governments and their administration[2]. Several new initiatives have been taken to reform governance and administration. Serious questions have been raised as to what extent the changes brought in governance and administration has enabled the poor to have their entitlements and to have access to justice. Of the innovations ombudsman creation is one and significant which is aimed at easing out the frustration of the public over public institutions by redressing the grievances of the people. It is a global phenomenon in strengthening public administration[3]. It was being innovated to redress the complaints and grievances of the public over the conduct of bureaucrats. Most of the countries in the world have created this mechanism to keep up the credibility of the public administration. Though it originated in the beginning of the 19th century in Sweden, it spread across the world and sharpened in the later part of the 20th century. It has reached its sophistication in the beginning of 21st century.[4] In India, it came in the public discourse during the later part of 1960s as the first Administrative Reform Commission recommended for the creation of ombudsman both at the Centre and the States[5]. In India, it is popularly called Lokpal at the Centre and Lokayukta at the States[6]. It should be headed by a retired Judge of the Courts. So far 17 states have set up Lokayuktas headed by retired judges. But down below the state, it was the Kerala government which created ombudsman first in the country in 2001.[7] Now the Tamil Nadu government has also set up the local body ombudsman for the same purpose. How it functions now is the question investigated in this chapter.

Ombudsman: Theory and Practice

Basically it is an institutional mechanism to redress the grievances of the people. Though it originated for public institutions, it has expanded to both public and private institutions and organisations. It is an alternate dispute settlement mechanism. It has to enable the poor to get their grievances redressed without much complication and expenses[8]. It should have simplified procedures and access to the institutions to get their grievances to be redressed. Generally ombudsman in public sector institutions has to supervise the administrative activities of the executive branch. The ombudsman has to receive complaints from the public and investigate the same and resolve the problem. Mostly it is related to conduct of government administration.[9] Essentially the basic objective is to enhance efficiency of public administration and effectiveness of service delivery to the public. It has to ensure government accountability to the public. It has to enhance the transparency of governance and administration. In a democracy governance institutions have to instill confidence among the citizens. There should not be trust deficit. In order to enhance the trust of the people over public institutions efficiency and effectiveness of service delivery has to be monitored and supervised. Basically it is a democratic deepening process.[10] All investigations will exclude judiciary and legislative bodies. Its jurisdiction covers mostly the government departments and other public agencies. It has got powers to make recommendations to bring change in the laws of the country. Basically the framework of ombudsman relies on its autonomy, adequate powers, adequate institutional facilities, easy procedures, access to public, cost effective, timely delivery, and impartial conduct[11]. The ombudsman should be established through law and it should be made independent. It should have needed autonomy. It should have needed powers to investigate the grievances. It should handle cases with all fairness and sense of justice. Ombudsman should have balance and equipoise to deliver decisions fairly. Hence, it is neither anti-state and anti-people or citizen. Basically the ombudsman should have power to act and independent from the government. The institutional framework, powers and process of investigation vary from country to country in context. Now, it has to work for the poor as judiciary works above their level of reach as they do not have adequate resources to go to judicial system. Further, basic services are being provided by the local institutions. When the services are not reaching the poor, poor have to have an institutional mechanism to sort out their grievance within their resource capacity. For this purpose even the rich countries have created such mechanism and it also vary from country to country. In India, at present a governance mechanism has been created at the grassroots level constitutionally and the same institutions are delivering basic services to the communities. There is a provision in the institutional arrangement to have a redressal of mechanism through the participation of people in the meetings of Gram Sabha. Apart from the above, there is yet another arrangement created called ombudsman for local bodies. Against this background, the ombudsman created for local bodies in Tamil Nadu is being investigated.

A Note on the Methodology

To examine the activities of the ombudsman crated in Tamil Nadu, the author relied on the documents supplied by the Office of the Ombudsman, Chennai and interacted with the officials of the Ombudsman including the Chief of the Ombudsman. The interactions on wide range of subjects and for most of the issues, the Chief responded as he is the person to set up the entire office from scratch. Officials have supplied the documents.

A Brief Note on the Creation of Ombudsman

The whole exercise started from the recommendations of the Thirteenth Finance Commission itself. It recommends that the state government must put in place a system of independent local body ombudsman to inquire into the complaints of corruption and maladministration against the functionaries of the local bodies and the elected representatives. Government of Tamil Nadu is always in the forefront in complying with the mandates of the statutory bodies and the provisions of the Constitution of India. Hence, the state government has decided to create an independent ombudsman for local bodies. First an ordinance was promulgated and subsequently it brought legislation in the Tamil Nadu

Legislative Assembly in the year 2014. It is established with an objective of conducting inquiry on the allegations against the elected members of the local bodies and the officials of the local bodies in the state of Tamil Nadu. As per the Tamil Nadu Local Bodies Ombudsman Act, 2014, there shall be an authority for the local bodies at state level to be known as "Ombudsman" for making enquiries in respect of charges on any action involving corruption or maladministration or irregularities in the discharge of administrative functions in accordance with the provisions of the relevant law, by the elected members of the local bodies, the officers and employers working under the local bodies and for the disposal of such complaints. Thus, an institutional mechanism came into existence on 15th December, 2014.[12]

Powers and Functions of the Tamil Nadu Local Bodies Ombudsman

It is an independent institutional mechanism with quasi-judicial powers. The ombudsman shall not be removed from his office, except by order of the Governor based on the resolution of Legislative Assembly of the state supported by majority of the members of Legislative Assembly present and voting for such removal on the ground of proved misbehaviour or incapacity. The following local body institutions are coming under the purview of the Tamil Nadu Ombudsman:

A. All the Municipal Corporations of Tamil Nadu (12 Municipal Corporations);
B. All the Municipalities (124);
C. All the Town Panchayats (528 Town Panchayats); and
D. All the District Panchayats (31 District Panchayats).

All the Gram Panchayats and Panchayat Unions are not under the purview of this Ombudsman as they are under the purview of inspectors of panchayats (District Collector).[13]

Procedure to be Followed

Following are the procedures to be followed:

Each complaint shall be in writing in Form I with supporting documents, if any, and shall be filed either in person before the Secretary to the Ombudsman or sent to him by registered post. The Complainant shall affix Court Fees Stamp to the value of Rs. 10 on each complaint towards fee but no fees shall be paid if a complaint is filed on behalf of the Government by a person authorized by the Government. Complaints in conformity with the provisions of the Act and Rules shall be numbered serially and the details of the compliant shall be entered in the Complaint Register as prescribed in Form-II. On registration, an acknowledgement as prescribed in Form-III shall be issued to the complainant. After examining the complaint, if the Ombudsman is satisfied that there is a prima facie case, he shall issue a notice as prescribed in Form-IV to the respondent(s) to file a written statement of defence with connected documents within fifteen days from the date of receipt of the notice. The Ombudsman shall use either Tamil or English during his enquiry, proceedings and passing of orders as he may deem fit. All the parties to the complaint and other persons to whom a direction is issued by Ombudsman in his order are liable to implement the order of the Ombudsman. In case of non-implementation, severe action shall be taken by the competent authorities against those who fail to implement the orders of the Ombudsman on a reference made by the Ombudsman. In case there is no specific provision in those rules regarding the procedure to be followed in any contingency in the disposal of the complaints, the Ombudsman may follow any appropriate procedure as he thinks fit.

Administrative Structure

The Municipal Administration and Water Supply Department is the nodal department for the authority of the Tamil Nadu Local Bodies Ombudsman. As per the provisions of sub-section (1) of section 6 of the said Act, the Ombudsman shall have a Secretary and such other officers and employees as the Government may determine in consultation with the Ombudsman to assist the Ombudsman in exercise of his powers and discharge of his functions under the said Act. Accordingly, in G.O. (MS) No. 14, Municipal Administration and Water Supply (Election) Department, dated 28-01-2016, the Government, in consultation with the Ombudsman, have accorded sanction for creation of the following posts to this office:

Sl. No.	*Name of the Post Sanctioned*	*No. of Posts*	*Scale of Pay*
I.	**Personal Staff of the Ombudsman**		
1.	Private Secretary	1	15,600—39,100 + 5,400
2.	Personal Assistant	1	9,300—34,800 + 4,600
3.	Driver	1	5,200—20,200 + 2,400
4.	Office Assistant	4	4,800—10,000 + 1,300
	Total	**7**	

(*Contd.*)

Sl. No.	Name of the Post Sanctioned	No. of Posts	Scale of Pay
II.	**Office**		
1.	Secretary–DRO cadre	1	15,600—39,100 + 7,600
2.	Legal Adviser (Deputy Secretary–Law)	1	15,600—39,100 + 7,600
3.	Assistant Registrar (Under Secretary)	1	15,600—39,100 + 6,600
4.	Section Officers	3	15,600—39,100 + 5,400
5.	Assistant Section Officer	6	9,300—34,800 + 4,600
6.	Personal Clerk	3	5,200—20,200 + 2,800
7.	Typist	3	5,200—20,200 + 2,400
8.	Office Assistant	5	4,800—10,000 + 1,300
9.	Driver	2	5,200—20,200 + 2,400
10.	Record Clerk	1	4,800—10,000 + 1,400
11.	Watchman	1	4,800—10,000 + 1,300
12.	Sweeper	2	4,800—10,000 + 1,300
	Total	**29**	

Annual Budget

During the financial year 2015-16, a budgetary provision of Rs. 83,50,000 (Rupees Eighty Lakh and Fifty Thousand only) was made to the Tamil Nadu Local Bodies Ombudsman in Demand No. 34 Municipal Administration and Water Supply Department. During the financial year 2016-17, a budgetary provision of Rs. 1,77,99,000 (Rupees One Crore Seventy Seven Lakh and Ninety Nine Thousand only) was made to the Tamil Nadu Local Bodies Ombudsman in Demand No. 34 Municipal Administration and Water Supply Department.

Assigned Activities

According to the provisions of section 7 of the said Act, the Ombudsman shall perform all or any of the following functions, namely:

(i) Enquire into any written complaint from the Government or that has come to the notice of the Ombudsman in which corruption or maladministration of a public servant or a local body is alleged;

(ii) Pass an order on the proved allegation in the following manner, namely:

(a) Where the irregularity involves a criminal offence committed by a public servant, the matter shall be referred to the appropriate investigating agency for necessary action;

(b) Where the irregularity involves loss of the fund of the local body, order for the recovery of such loss from those who are responsible for such irregularity;

(c) Where the irregularity is due to wilful negligence or dereliction of duty of any officer or employee of the local body, recommend for departmental action by the appropriate authority under the relevant rules.

As per the provisions of sub-section (1) of section 8 of the Tamil Nadu Local Bodies Ombudsman Act, 2014, the Ombudsman shall, for the purpose of any enquiry, have all the powers of a civil court trying a suit under the Code of Civil Procedure, 908 (Central Act V of 1908) and, in particular, in respect of the following matters, namely:

(a) summoning and enforcing the attendance of complainant or witnesses and examining him/her on oath;

(b) requiring the discovery and production of any relevant and necessary document;

(c) receiving evidence on affidavits;

(d) requisitioning any public record, or copy thereof from any court or office;

(e) issuing commission for the examination of witness and documents; and

(f) any other matter which may be prescribed.

Sub-section (2) of section 8 of the said Act, empowers the Ombudsman to pass direction to the complainant to pay to the opposite party an amount by way of cost, if he finds, after enquiry that the allegation contained in a complaint is without any substance. Further as per the provisions of sub-sections (3) and (4) of the said section 8, where the allegation contained in a written complaint is about the loss of fund of the local body, the Ombudsman may, during enquiry, collect evidence, determine the loss and direct in his order, the amount to be realised from the person responsible and if the amount payable as per the order is not paid within the specified period, the same shall be recovered as if it were an arrear of land revenue under the Tamil Nadu Revenue Recovery Act, 1864 (Tamil Nadu Act II of 1864).

Performance

The Ombudsman has enquired various kinds of complaints and suitable orders were issued by the Ombudsman. Some of the important cases are illustrated below:

(i) On enquiry of complaints against the grant of licence for the buildings at unapproved lay-outs and irregularity caused in the work of erection of bore-well by the functionaries of the Town Panchayat concerned, it was found that the lay-outs in question were not approved by the DTCP, but the local body concerned had granted licence to the buildings at the said unapproved lay-outs without levying any development charges and without obtaining 10 per cent of land reserved for public purpose. In that case, based on the report of the local fund audit and the local inspection report of the Directorate of the Town Panchayats, the said irregularities were confirmed and it was concluded that the said irregularities had caused monetary loss to the local body concerned to the tune of Rs. 37,41,366 and hence it was ordered to recover the said loss from the officers concerned, who were responsible for the said irregularities and also ordered to recover all other losses as per the audit report.

(ii) On enquiry of a complaint against the encroachment by constructing a compound wall by a third person, it was found that the public pathway was encroached by such an act. Hence orders were passed by the Ombudsman by which the encroachment was removed by the Municipality concerned. In that case, action taken report of the Municipality concerned was also received stating that the said encroachment to the extent of 1581 square metres with a guideline value of Rs. 2,04,26,520 was removed.

(iii) The enquiry of a complaint against a Town Panchayat causing delay of the refund of deposit amount even after the completion of the work and audit, by the Ombudsman facilitated the complainant to receive his deposit amount of Rs. 4,58,246.

(iv) Likewise, on enquiry conducted by the Ombudsman on a complaint of one lady Doctor against Vellore Corporation for non-transfer of the pension contribution even after two years of her transfer, the pension contribution of Rs. 2,23,979 was transferred to the account of the Chennai Corporation and the amount of Rs. 1,01,634 which was recovered in excess was also duly refunded, based on the enquiry and orders of the Ombudsman.

(v) On enquiry of a complaint against irregularity in the purchase of one computer and two printers by the officials of a Municipality, it was concluded that the expenditure on the said purchase was not in accordance with the norms and rules and hence treating such an irregular expenditure as loss, it was ordered to recover the said loss from the officials responsible for the said irregularity.

Suo Motu Complaints

Apart from the complaints filed by the individuals before the Ombudsman, various news items published in the newspapers relating to the activities of the local bodies which may be construed as maladministration or corruption in the local body, have also been suo motu entertained as complaints under section 7 of the Tamil Nadu Local Bodies Ombudsman Act, 2014, enquired and suitable orders have been issued obtaining reports and conducting enquiry with the officials concerned. Some of such suo motu complaints are illustrated below:

A news item published in a Daily Newspaper dated 2.9.2015, regarding the encroachment of lake in Madipakkam, was taken on file as a complaint and enquired. In that case, the Commissioner concerned submitted his report that in the Sarkar Poramboke Lands, only the construction works of Water Tank and Home for Urban Homeless were undertaken under the Drinking Water Supply Improvement Scheme and National Urban Livelihood Mission.

Similarly, a news item published in a Tamil Daily Newspaper dated 18.1.2016 regarding damage of the Madhiravedu bridge connecting Thiruverkadu and Poonamalle, was taken on file as a complaint and enquired obtaining the report of the Commissioner concerned and suitable orders were issued to the Municipality concerned to complete the work soon.

The authority of the Tamil Nadu Local Bodies has had major and constructive impacts on the functioning of the local bodies, as the elected members and officials of the local bodies have now realized that all their activities involving corruption and maladministration are monitored and reviewed by the Ombudsman. The Tamil Nadu Local Bodies Ombudsman has now been identified as an important mechanism for enhancing accountability of the local bodies. The public have also realized that there is an easily accessible statutory redressal forum to address their complaints and grievances against the local bodies. The enquiry and orders of the Ombudsman has brought wide-ranging value-added benefits to both the local bodies and the public at large. Some of such benefits are reducing maladministration and supporting good governance given below:

1. Encroachment Removal and Regain Amount

Sl. No.	*Petition No/Final order no with dates*	*Details of the local bodies involved*	*Details of the property recovered with the actual value*
1	31/2017 M (119/17dt.20th may, 2017	Encroachment removal in Salem Corporation in play ground	Rs. 50,00,000.00
2	25/2017. M (81/17 dated. 27/4/17)	Encroachment removal ordered for Avadi Municipality road (100 sq.ft)	Rs. 40,000.00
3	3/2017 (86/17 dated. 4/5/17)	Encroachment removal order for Mettur municipality road 976.51 sq.ft	Rs. 3,92,550.00
4	517/2016 (96/17 dated. 4/5/17 Dinamalar 3/6/17)	Encroachment removal ordered for Chennai Metropolitans, Zone 13, ward 175, public ground (15 grounds)	Rs. 60.00 cr
5	72/2017 M (132/17 dt. 22/5/17 Dinamalar 11/4/17)	Encroachment removal ordered for removing of Chennai Metropolitan road and platforms (840 sq.ft)	Rs. 6.30 cr
6	221/2017 M (262/17 dated. 21/11/17	Encroachment removal ordered for cleaning Chennai Metropolitan's zone 11, area covered in Valasaravakkam and Ramapuram 1.75 sq.ft	Rs. 45.00 cr
7	26/2017 (270/17 dt. 23.11.17)	Removal of encroachment ordered for Mangadu Town Panchayat 10 ft road (1050 ft)	Rs. 11,25,600.00
8	46/2017 (237/17 dated 20.09.2017)	Removal of encroachment ordered at Thoothukudi district Nasareth Town Panchayat, Government lands (18 Sq.ft)	Rs. 1950.00

(*Contd.*)

Sl. No.	*Petition No/Final order no with dates*	*Details of the local bodies involved*	*Details of the property recovered with the actual value*
9	52/2016 (284/17 date 18.12.2017) (Dinamalar 22.11.2016	Removal of Encroachment of water bodies order at Chennai Metropolitan Zone 15, Thuraip-pakam (Thuraippakam water bodies)	Rs. 10.00 cr
10	123/17 N	Removal of encroachment ordered for Thiruvallur Munici-pality to remove encroachment at 15 parks which belongs to the above municipality	Rs. 200.00 cr
11	53/15/001/16 dated 04.01.2016	Removal of encroachment ordered to Devakottail Municipality Individual Encroachment of public road	Rs. 2,24,26,520.00
12	169/2015/170/16 dated 22.1.2016	Encroachment removal ordered to Chennai Metropoli-tan Zone 11 to clear the encroachment at Ramapuram Rayala Nagar public utilization land (4584.52 sq.ft)	Rs. 30.00 cr
		Total	**Rs. 354.20 cr**

2. Recovery of Financial Loss to Local Bodies

Sl. No.	*Petition No/Order No with date*	*Local Bodies Involved*	*Reason*	*Amount Recovered*
1.	321/2015/85/17 dated. 3.5.17	Vellalur Town Panchayat	Approval given to construct houses in the unapproved lands–getting of reservation for public utility	Compensation Amount Rs. 81,80,220.00
2.	56/2016/111/17 dated 12.5.17	Seththur Town Panchayat	Seeking permission for utility land	Rs. 1,33,43,932
3.	6/2017 M 139/17 dated 07.06.17	Chennai Corporation (Madavaram Zone)	Seeking approval for roads and public utility lands (24.000 Sq.ft)	Rs. 25.00 cr

(Contd.)

Sl. No.	*Petition No/Order No with date*	*Local Bodies Involved*	*Reason*	*Amount Recovered*
4.	129/2015/71/16 dated. 15.4.2016	Modakkuruchi Town Panchayat	The guidelines amount for 10% land which should need to reserve for public utiity as prescribed % not received Compensation in case of borewell	Rs. 37,41,366
5.	348/2015/186/16 dated 3.12.2016	Commissioner and officer of Kayalpattinam Municipality	Misappropriation in purchasing of computers and printers	Rs. 63,000
6.	461/2016/53/17 dated 31.03.2017	Chennai Metropolitan	In order to, charge to usage of building and refix the property taxes	Rs. 10.00 cr
7.	1150/2016/131/17 dated 5.10.17	Arcot Municipality	The order for collecting the fees for extension of housing plots from the housing plan organizer	Rs. 96.46 lakhs
8.	080/2017/160/17 dated 19.06.17	Kallakuruchi Municipality	The order to collect commercial tax for Thirumana Mahal from 2015-16	Rs. 11,015
	Total			**Rs. 37.79 Cr**

3. Disciplinary Action Initiated Against Officials Based on the Complaints

Sl. No.	*Complaints/ Order No. with date*	*Local bodies involved*	*Reason*
1	1179/2016/50/2017 dated 25.03.2017 (Dinamalar New 23.11.2016	Thiruvallur Municipality Commissioner and officials	Misappropriation and permission for drinking water connections
2	175/2015 order 65/2017 dated 13.4.2017	Thirumurugan Poondi Secretary	Tax levied for misappropriated and constructed buildings

(*Contd.*)

Sl. No.	*Complaints/ Order No. with date*	*Local bodies involved*	*Reason*
3	562/2016/85/2017 dated 3.5.2017	Bhuvanagiri, Town Panchayat secretary	Loss, because of tendering of ponds for fish catching
4	321/2015/TPT 88/2017 dated 3.5.2017	Vellalur Town Panchayat 3 secretaries	Misappropriation in the construction work
5	539/2016/102/2017 dated 8.5.2017	Thirubuvanam Town Panchayat Secretary	Malpractice in appointment order on agreement
6	56/2016/TPT/111/17 dated 12.5.2017	Sethur town Panchayat Secretary	Given permission to construct houses in the unapproved housing plots
7	666/2016/116/2017 dated 20.5.2017	Palanichettipatti Secretary	Loss accrued to town panchayat due to construction of buildings beyond rules and regulation
8	803/2016/117/2017 dated 20.5.2017	Illayangudi Town Panchayat Secretary	Levied property tax to the building which are constructed without proper rules and regulation
9	15/2017 M/126/2017 dated 20.5.17 (25.1.2017 Dinamalar)	Thiruthani Municipality Commissioner	Non-tendering of the shops which belong to the municipality in time
10	1042/2016/157/2017 dated 19.6.2017	Pennadam Town Panchayat Secretary and officials	Negligence to take action against the building which was constructed without proper rules and regulations
11	80/2017/160/2017 dated 19.6.2017	Kallakuruchi Municipality Commissioner along with officials	Negligence to take action against the building which was constructed without proper rules
12	1322/2016/161/2017 dated 19.6.2017	Thenkasi Municipality officials	Malpractice on works under construction recommended to anti-corruption department

(Contd.)

Sl. No.	Complaints/ Order No. with date	Local bodies involved	Reason
13	034/2015/M/812016 dated 26.4.2016	Pollachi Municipality officials	Malpractice in tendering
14	129/2015/71/2016 dated 15.4.2016	Modakuruchi town Panchayat Secretary along with officials	Failed to receive the land for public utility under deed of settlement on donation. Mud road received under deed on settlement on donation for but extension fee failed to be received. Given permission to construct building in the unapproved plots
15	348/2015/186/2016 dated 3.12.2016	Kayalpattinam Municipality Commissioner along with officials	i) Misappropriation in purchase of computers and printers Rs. 63,000 ii) the high power committee was set up for inspection to unsanctioned works without permission of the municipality
16	290/2016/210/2017 dated 22.8.17	Adigareddy Town Panchayat secretary along with officials	Change of name without proper gazette order, misappropriation in allocation of property tax, given permission to building without proper rules and regulations
17	335/2016/286/2017 dated 29.11.2017	Omalur Town Panchayat, secretary	Not collected the tendering amount and made delay in tendering
18	385/2016/150/2016 dated 16.9.2016	Killiyur Town Panchayat secretary	Levied tax for the building which are constructed without proper permission

(*Contd.*)

Sl. No.	*Complaints/ Order No. with date*	*Local bodies involved*	*Reason*
19	162/2017/M/252/2017 dated 2.11.2017	Sivaganga Municipality Commissioner along with officials	Made correction in service register
20	189/201/46/2016 dated 30.3.2016	Modakuruchi town Panchayat secretary	Malpractice in tendering
21	1020/2016/227/2017 dated 12.9.2017	Balugal town Panchayat secretary	Malpractice in work under contraction
22	1217/2016/231/2017 dated 14.9.2017	Ettayapuram town panchayat secretary	Malpractice in utilization of town panchayat fund
23	35/2017/216/2017 dated 29.8.2017	Nagapattinam Municipality Commissioner along with officials	Negligence of noticed the building which are constructed without proper rules
24	528/2016/42/2018 dated 2.3.2018	Palakkode town Panchayat secretary	Malpractice in shop tenders
25	173/2015/76/2017 dated 26.4.2017	Thiruvaigundam town Panchayat, Electric Board Engineer	Tamilselvan, constructed house without permission
26	175/2015/65/2017 dated 13.4.2017	Thirumurugan Poondi town Panchayat secretary	Not getting of public utility place and also not received the amount as per the guidelines value for that public utility place
27	121/2016/55/2017 dated 27.3.2017	Ramanathapuram Municipality, Commissioner along with officials	Malpractice in auction activity
28	495/2016/36/2017 dated 24.3.2017	Karaikudi Municipality, Revenue Inspector and Revenue Assistant	Corruption and violation of rules

(*Contd.*)

Sl. No.	*Complaints/ Order No. with date*	*Local bodies involved*	*Reason*
29	928/2016/188/2016 dated 19.7.2017	Alarvaimozhi town Panchayat secretary along with officials	Malpractice in the sanitation work order
30	935/2016/34/2017 dated 24.3.2017	Ammapettai town Panchayat secretary	Negligence of taking action against the housing plots for approval
31	938/2016/44/2017 dated 27.3.2017	Verkilambi town Panchayat secretary	Given permission to the blue print for constructing a building without proper rules and regulation
32	952/968/2016/19/2017 07.2.2017	Melur Municipality, Commissioner along with officials	Malpractice in fishing tender
33	1010/2016/172/2017 dated 27.6.2017	Chidambaram Municipality Commissioner along with officials	Not taking action against the construction of the Thirumana Mahal in the area which was approved for housing plots
34	1028/2016/190/2017 dated 27.4.2017	Ayakudi town Panchayat secretary	Malpractice in the name change in drinking water connection
35	1150/2016/131/2017 dated 5.10.2017	Arcot Muicipality, the Engineer along with other officials	The extension of roads have not been done as per the value
36	1179/2016/50/17/dated 25.3.2017	Thiruvallur Municipality the Engineer along with other officials	Given connections for drinking water without proper permission
37	027/2017/170/2017 dated 22.6.2017	Karaikudi Municipality, Revenue Assistant along with other officials	Levied in appropriate taxes

(*Contd.*)

Sl. No.	*Complaints/ Order No. with date*	*Local bodies involved*	*Reason*
38	056/2017/167/2017 dated 21.6.2017	Nagapattinam Municipality Housing Board Inspector along with officials	Negligence of duty on taking action against the building which are constructed without proper permission
39	122/2017/307/2017 dated 29.12.2017	Pallikonda Town Panchayat Document writer	Malpractice in purchasing of properties
40	0085/2016 dated 12.12017	Virudhunagar Municipality, Municipality officials	Malpractice in selection of beneficiaries under IH SDP Scheme
41	183/2016/275/2017 dated 14.12.2017	Modakuruchi Town Panchayat secretary	Missed to get the public utility place
42	57/2015/117/2016 dated 4.7.2016	Idaikkuzhinadu, Kanchipuram District former secretaries (2 Members)	Without proper rules and regulation spent Rs. 12.5 Lakhs

4. Action against ER.LB

Sl. No.	*Petition/Order No.*	*Local Bodies Details*	*Reason*
1.	603/2016/TPT/78/2017 dated. 27.04.2017	Achcharapakkam Town Panchayat, Chairman, Town Panchayat	Giving certificate to misappropriated housing plots, and for that it was recommended to take criminal action
2.	935/2016/34/2017 dated 24.03.2017	Ammapettai Town Panchayat, Chairman Town Panchayat	It was ordered to take criminal action for acting against law, rules and regulation, purchasing of properties beyond the income limit
3.	0019/2015/18/2016 dated 15.03.2016	Pattukkottai Town Panchayat K.V. Iravi, Counselor	Irresponsibility towards the interim period given by the Ombudsman and threatening the officials, and for that it was fined Rs. 5000

(*Contd.*)

Sl. No.	Petition/Order No.	Local Bodies Details	Reason
4.	666/2016 TPT.116/2017 Dated 20.05.2017	Palanichettipatti Town Panchayat, Former Chairman Thiru. Balasubramaniam	Action against constructing building without following prescribed rules
5.	666/2016 TPT.116/2017 Dated 20.05.2017	Palanichettipatti Town Panchayat, Former Chairman Thiru. Balasubramaniam	Regarding the Ombudsman Interim order the former Vice Chairman appealed at High Court Madurai bench, the court ordered to seal the building.
6.	1118/2016/TPT.1118/2016 dated 28.9.2017	Kutralam Town Panchayat, Former Town Panchayat Chairman	Regarding different complaints on corruption, it was ordered to make investigation by anti-corruption and vigilance department.

An Assessment

It is an instrument and mechanism to facilitate the poor to get their grievances redressed in public administration. Procedures have been evolved in such a way that even a poorest person can approach the Ombudsman by giving a petition by affixing a stamp worth about Rs. 10. Since it is in a nascent stage, all the hearings are taking place only at the headquarters of the office at Chennai. During 2015-16, there were 122 sittings held and during 2016-17, there were about 322 sittings conducted. As such the Ombudsman has received 215 complaints in the year 2015-16, 357 complaints have been received in the year 2016-17. Within a short span of time, it has done a tremendous work to reduce corruption. Annually, government spends around one crore rupees for the functioning of the Ombudsman. But by its function Ombudsman retrieve property worth about several crores from encroachment. In the same way, it recovers the loss incurred by the government due to wrong approvals and orders to the tone of several lakhs. It is in a nascent stage functioning well. But, its visibility is very limited. In Kerala, all the local body institutions are brought under the fold of ombudsman. But in Tamil Nadu both Gram Panchayat and Block Panchayats have been excluded from the ombudsman. There is an ombudsman for these local bodies. The inspector of Panchayati Raj is performing the task. But nobody knows that inspector of Panchayati Raj is ombudsman.

Conclusion

Ombudsman for local bodies in Tamil Nadu is new and it is in a nascent stage. For any objective evaluation of the performance of any institution that too on governance, administration and service delivery it requires at least a minimum of five years. Officially, it came into being only on 14th December, 2014. Primarily it is an investigating agency to inquire into the allegations against the elected representatives, officers and employees of local bodies of Tamil Nadu. Still, it is in the process of establishing itself as a vibrant functional unit to discharge the assigned responsibilities. It is a known fact that Tamil Nadu is always a state prompt in adhering to the mandates of the Constitution. It is not lacking behind any state in compliance with the mandates of the Constitution of India. Whether the state is performing all the activities in line with the spirit of the Constitution of India is a debatable question. It is also a reality in Tamil Nadu many of the institutions have excelled in performance only because of the efficient leadership of the institutions. Thus, leadership plays a crucial role in determining the quality of performance. Against this background, a cursory assessment is undertaken to understand the functioning of the ombudsman in Tamil Nadu. For many of the aspects in local bodies, generally opinion makers used to quote the experience of the Kerala state as it is a pioneering state in establishing a vibrant local buy system in Kerala. Though, it wanted to follow the state of Kerala, Tamil Nadu has not fully followed the state of Kerala. The Gram panchayats and the block panchayats have not included in the ombudsman jurisdiction and they are under the jurisdiction of the inspector of panchayats (District Collector). Many do not know the role of inspector of panchayats. Many are not aware of the ombudsman role of the inspector of panchayats.

Within the short span of time, an establishment has been created and started its ombudsman function. It started receiving complaints and they are being investigated. In the first year, the ombudsman received 215 complaints and the second year it received 357 complaints from the public. With the limited infrastructure and the staff the Tamil Nadu ombudsman has conducted 122 sittings to hear the complaints in the first year and 322 sittings have been conducted in the second year. In the short span of time, ombudsman has saved commons worth about several crores from the encroachment. Corrupt officials have been punished. Appropriate directions have been given to the officials for their functioning. There is no investigative agency available at the disposal of ombudsman. There is no adequate advertisement for the mechanism. It is high time to make recommendation for the inclusion of Gram panchayat and block panchayats in the ombudsman system as more of violations and deviations are happened in such lower level institutions in the New Panchayati Raj system. The ombudsman has to move from state headquarters to district headquarters and conduct inquires on the allegations against the officials and the elected representatives. By doing so, it can bring visibility. Within the short span of time, because of the leadership, huge commons worth about several crores have been saved. For the functioning of the ombudsman, Government of Tamil Nadu spends only one to two crore rupees. But through its functioning it had saved huge money through unearthing the violations of procedures and rules to favour private individuals. Thus, the ombudsman has demonstrated that it will be helpful to reduce corruption at the grassroots.

NOTES

1. Bidyut Chakrabarty and Mohit Bhattacharya (eds.), (2005). *Administrative Change and Innovation: A Reader*, New Delhi: Oxford University Press.
2. Bidyut Chakrabarty and Mohit Bhattacharya (eds.) (2008). *The Governance Discourse: A Reader*, New Delhi: Oxford University Press.
3. L.C. Reif (ed.) (1999). *The International Ombudsman Anthology: Selected Writings from the International Ombudsman Institute*. The Haque: Kluwer Law International.
4. R. Gregory and P. Giddings (eds.) (2000). *Righting Wrongs: The Ombudsman in Six Continents*. Amsterdam: IOS Press.
5. Norman Lewis and S.S. Singh (eds.) (1995). *Ombudsman: India and the World Community*. New Delhi: Indian Institute of Public Administration.
6. Subhas Chandra Gupta (1995). *Ombudsman: An Indian Perspective*. New Delhi: Monak Publications.
7. Joshna, J.M. Stark. *The Kerala Ombudsman*. New Delhi: Accountability Initiative.
8. L.C. Reif (ed.) (1995). *The Ombudsman Concept*. Edmonton: International Ombudsman Institute.
9. Bidyut Chakrabarty and Mohit Bhattacharya (eds.), (2003). *Public Administration: A Reader*, New Delhi: Oxford University Press.
10. Paul Gimsborg, (2009). *Democracy: Crisis and Renewal*, London: Profile Books.

11. D.C. Rowat. (1985). *The Ombudsman Plan: The Worldwide Spread of an Idea*. Lanham, Md: University Press of America.
12. Government of Tamil Nadu, *Tamil Nadu Local Bodies Ombudsman Act–2014* (Tamil Nadu Act 27.04.2017).
13. G. Palanithurai, (2002). *Inspector of Panchayats*. Gandhigram: The Rajiv Gandhi Chair for Panchayati Raj Studies.

12

Effective Implementation of the Corporate Social Responsibility

A Study on the Role of Local Self Governments in Kerala

Afseer, K.P., Sonny Jose and *Gopakumar, K.*

Introduction

The concept of Corporate Social Responsibility (henceforth 'CSR') is a company's sense of responsibility towards the community and environment in which it operates. It is concerned with treating the stakeholders of a company or institution ethically or in a responsible manner (Hopkins, 2012). The concept has its roots in the ancient India where religious charity and philanthropy were practised by the kings and noblemen. The last decade of the twentieth century witnessed a swing away from charity and traditional philanthropy towards more direct engagement of business in mainstream development and concern for disadvantaged groups in the society (Mohan, 2001).

The current perception of business has grown to acknowledge that the companies achieving good performance in their social, ethical and environmental fields will also perform well in their financial matters (Solomon, 2007). Nowadays, a business firm regards CSR as an important part of the business, and not a sideline activity. In India, the business associations and forums such as FICCI and CII have been generally advocating for CSR is to be considered as an obligation rather than an option among the business firms.

The mounting interest in Corporate Social Responsibility over the recent decades is an indication of the companies' obligation to go beyond the short-term goal of profit maximisation to broader goals such as concerns—economic, social and environmental—of the local society, and even the nations at large. In this very competitive business world, firms are becoming increasingly conscious of sustainability aspects (Jyothi, 2011).

All this lead the Indian Parliament to incorporate a specific provision in the Companies Act, 2013 to impose responsibility upon the certain category of companies to implement CSR. Section 135 of the Companies Act, 2013 deals with CSR. Those companies having a net worth of rupees five hundred crores or more, or turnover of rupees one thousand crores or The Companies Act, 2013 passed by the Ministry of Law and Justice in parliament. The law mandates companies to spend at least two percentage of profit after all taxes (PAT) of preceding three years on CSR activities. Section 135 of the Companies Act suggests that every company more or a net profit of rupees five crores or more during any financial year shall constitute a Corporate Social Responsibility Committee or the Board consisting of three or more directors, one of whom shall be an independent director. The Act also envisages forming a committee to look after the CSR initiatives undertaken by the company (The Companies Act, 2013).

Corporate Social Responsibility

The concept of CSR is used synonymic to the concepts like Corporate Citizenship, Corporate Conscience and Business Responsibility. The definitions of CSR are generally fallen into two schools of thoughts. One is those that argue that business is obligated only to maximise profits within the boundaries of the law and minimal ethical constraints and those that have suggested a broader range of obligations towards society (Carroll, et al., 2010). A popular definition for CSR given by World Business Council for Sustainable Development (WBCSD, 2002) explains it as an ongoing commitment or duty or obligation by business organisations to behave ethically and contributing to sustainable economic development by bringing together all stakeholders from an employee to large society. The highlight of the definition is CSR is considered as the obligation of business as part of the ethical behaviour and for social development.

According to the United Nations and European Commission, Corporate Social Responsibility leads to the Tipple Bottom Line concept, environmental protection and fight for social justice. It is expected that civil society activists groups, government and business should work together to create appropriate means of avenues of outcasts and bring them to the ordinary courts. It is important that the business sector identifies, promote and implement effective policies and practices to achieve triple bottom line. At one end of the spectrum, CSR may be considered simply as a set of civic activities incurred by various agencies. At the other extreme, it can be a way of doing business has a significant impact on society.

The vast majority of India's poorest people live in villages and these villages are in a state of neglect underdeveloped with impoverished people. The problem of hunger, ignorance and ill health, high mortality and illiteracy are most acute in rural areas. It is not only because of a shortage of materials but also because of defects in the planning process and investment pattern. India has the potential to meet the challenges in rural areas. However, the efforts of government may not be adequate to provide basic services to its citizens. It is being increasingly recognised that progress and welfare of the state are not only responsibility of the government alone, but many more stakeholders need to be involved in attaining the developmental goals.

Research Question

Although many companies do have CSR projects, the successful accomplishment of each project depends on the identification of real problem, i.e. felt-need. However, serious efforts are seldom taken by the companies to identify the felt need. This dilemma can be rectified to a great extent with the support of local governing institutions working in the lower strata of society (Jane, 2007). In certain previous research works, the researcher has noticed that there are companies such as ACC Ltd., Larsen and Toubro Ltd., GMR Infrastructure Ltd., have associated with the local government institutions in planning and executing CSR programmes which have given commendable results. The uniqueness of such projects was a better reach to the public in general and specific target groups in particular.

In such instances, the effectiveness of CSR programmes can be improved if the stakeholders of the project are actively involved in the various stages of a CSR project's life cycle. It is well established in the theory of Freeman on Stakeholder Management (1983). Local Self Government Institutions can be considered as one of the key stakeholders as per this interpretation of the theory.

The relationship between a corporate firm and the concerned LSG institutions usually starts from the inception visits, followed by licensing for the functioning of business, annual compliance reporting for various licences renewal is also performed under concerned LSG institution of the business enterprises. The role of LSGs is not only limited to licensing and permission, it continues in several areas like infrastructural development and supply of necessary resources such as water and power. The provision of various facilities available for employment and utilisation of natural resources is also monitored by the concerned LSGs for a great extent. So there is a possibility for having concurrent interaction, relationship and for some extent of influence for LSGs in corporate matters in this per se.

The potential knowledge and service reach of the LSGs in their respective areas and the awareness level of the needs, as well as resources availability, can be utilised very well if the CSR programmes are planned along with LSGs support. The concept of felt-need can be easily traced out from the involvement of different level of local representatives in their respective areas.

Considering all these aspects and having CSR projects with the support of LSGs can be effective by involving the local body representatives in various stages from planning to assure the reach and analyse progress periodically based on the above-mentioned arguments. So making an analysis on the role of LSGs in CSR will bring more insights into the aspects of scope and strategic matters in relation to the matter of LSGs involvement in CSR.

Objectives

1. To analyse the current perception about CSR projects and practices undertaking in India among the respondents.
2. To highlight the expectations of the respondents about effective CSR and to find out their opinion about areas to be focused while selecting CSR projects in the given context.
3. To discuss what are the policy level suggestions recommended for effective implementation of CSR with support of LSGs—role analysis, implementation pattern, policy level expectations for effective implementation, partnership-PPP, financial model.

CSR and Social Development

Gigantic investments of corporates bring huge changes in any geographical location effecting on lifestyle, culture, thinking process, economy and so on. But they remain away from taking the responsibility of the changes which bring several disturbances in the environment, micro to the macro economy; culture, poverty reasons, unhealthy and unknown effects on life and vegetation. The speed with which the corporate grow never matches with the growth or changes of people displaced, affected and live in close vicinity of industry or mines. People suffer a lot because the changes caused by the giant profit making units and sacrifice their peace and healthy life. We people in the corporate claim that there is a positive economic change across the industrial area. It is true that corporate try to build up huge infrastructures, physical facilities and bring many other people benefiting programmes. The underneath aim is to keep people silent over the large scale changes they make while operating on the forest, agriculture land, streams, rivers which are mostly revered as, Mother nature-natural resources. With those, the culture and emotion of local people are attached. Their livelihood, lifestyle, food, traditional knowledge, medicines, religion, language and thinking process are inter-winged. Neither any progressive Government nor any profit making business house can value it. Because the priority and mission motive is to move forward to make physical infrastructure, profit and facilities as the urban facility are a single point focus for them (Mohanty, 2012).

Organizations careful about the ethical expenditures of the CSR fund are also careful about the sustainability of the programmes, projects and effects of events they organize. Their events always satisfy and linked to the vision, mission and sustainability reasons. When they fail to identify the reasons of sustainability in the programme, projects or events, mostly local people's unrest occur in the area. Today CSR is looked as a strategic approach to manage the risks from local people's resentment and superficially meet the commitment to government. When there is a resentment of people in government, media and politics get aware of the troubled relationship between people and corporate house. Before that, they remain silent. Thus another pressure and a conflicting situation arise. To meet these situations and pacify people's outcry against the negligence of corporate usually a collaborating effort of liaison department, PR department, corporate communication and CSR Department come together. All of them in collaborative coordination try to meet the situations and solve through different means and methods. In these problem-solving approaches, two major approaches are usually observed. One is to calm down the reactions of government and media by applying legal and illegal means. Another one is fulfilling the demands of people through negotiation and some kind of philanthropic approaches.

Methodology

The study is an enquiry to seek the role of LSGs in CSR projects for effective implementation. The methodology followed in the study is a case study in which interview with experts in the domain as considered as the major technique to get different perspectives in on the research question. A descriptive analysis has conducted based on the interviews conducted with experts. To get specific aspects and questions to discuss with experts, a detailed literature survey was conducted to understand the current status and role perceived by Local Self Government Institutions in Kerala about CSR. The experts are interviewed based on a previously prepared interview schedules for each category.

A series of expert consultations has been conducted with a different section of respondents representing all core areas related to CSR projects and LSG institutions. The list of experts includes represents from the following five major areas such as a policy maker, an NGO professional, LSGD official, academicians and corporate delegate to provide their own perspectives.

A criterion is set for selection of respondents to get reliable and valid reflections about the phenomenon. Respondents are selected among the target people who are having a minimum of five years of direct experience in their respective area of expertise. All respondents are selected from Kerala to get strategic opinions and suggestions from the similar environment.

Perception About Current CSR Practice

There are different opinions collected from the discussions with experts related to LSGs and CSR and there are some specific points are mentioned here on the aspect of CSR. The major points are the following. The statement by John C.P. said that the broad objective of CSR is to bring positive change in mindset of people associating in corporate sector towards their living society.

The point about the ethical aspect of business by a public policy specialist that 'all companies cannot undertake dedicated CSR activities even though there is a mandatory provision for that due to their internal policies and strategies.' The only companies running ethically in their whole business process can only target wider social stakeholders of any such initiatives. The parent company must have an eye on the ethical functioning of all subsidiaries. The unfair trade practices undertaken by subsidiaries are also to be considered very seriously to enhance loyalty and brand value of the company. The ethical treatment of employees is an important aspect, in which the practice of casual labour and contract labour engagement for a long time has to be avoided. The benefits provided by the company to those kinds of labours to be enhanced rather than doing some dedicated activity with a wide area focus in the name of CSR. Other areas of ethical treatment expected from corporates are avoidance of child labour, fair wage and environmental friendliness in the business processing according to respondent in this study. For example, Tea estate labours issues on the fair wage in Munnar in Kerala from Kanan Deven as a subsidiary of TATA Global Beverages Company.

According to LSG official, the Ministry of Corporate Affairs have the responsibility to give right orientation to the companies from the very developing stage itself. Continuous and systematic programmes for awareness generation and capacity building are important. As of now, even before mandating CSR by law, some companies are doing very well with utmost dedication as opinion shared by an LSG official. The corporate representative's opinion is that, since it is mandated by law, CSR becoming more effective and proper in planning and guidelines are in developing stage according to a corporate CSR department head in a premier company. In some cases CSR is limited in just distributing some material support rather than an integrated development approach, so an effective CSR project must be sustainable and accountability has to assured at the project level. And there are some corporates, who expect more visibility and public reach through their CSR programmes in collaboration with LSGs according to the view shared by NGO professional.

There are incidents that in some companies employee welfare programmes were reported as CSR in their annual mandatory reports, so there should be specific instructions to companies on the concept of ideal CSR.

Perception about Current Status of Social Development Programmes

There are two major opinions regarding the perceived social development process in the state. The first one was regarding the social development policy and efficiency in its implementation. 'Even though there are a lot of policies in discussion and programmes in functioning, many of the social development areas, the benefits of these programmes are not properly reaching to all people in an effective manner as perceived. The functioning mechanism of social development-oriented projects has to be improved and delivery system has to be enriched to reach up to the last person, according to the opinion of the corporate respondent in the study.

Another major concern raised by a few respondents is regarding the professional competency in different development projects associated personnel. The opinion is that the 'social development programmes' were organising all over the world since long back. The way in which implement it in different parts of the world and their socio-cultural as well demographic situation makes difference in its effectiveness. Those countries employing trained professionals are achieving their goals perfectly to a great extent. So the country has to be more organised with involving more professional expertise to achieve the targeted goals in a better manner. In the current Kerala scenario, it's really high time to ensure the social scientist's expertise in the development process to ensure the optimum input-output process and the result.

Areas Suggested for CSR Projects

The scope for CSR in India is really enormous in the current socio-development context, as a developing country with potential human capital which is largely represented by young population will enrich the new investments in the field of social development as part of CSR. Nowadays it is shown to the world that corporate houses took up sustainable development as their core agenda in which CSR is a major area they focus on addressing many socio-economic and environmental issues and concerns.

India has several developmental concerns and requirements. The concerns and requirements are not constant and similar at every place. It purely depends upon the nature of the location and their socio-economic characteristics.

The requirements are broadly classified into several areas such as agro-production—food security, food processing, equal distribution and sharing of common properties resources, land management, soil conservation, education/human resources development, groundwater management, human trafficking, child labour, begging on street, people with disabilities (PWD), women and children concerns, elderly people and poor people having low access to quality health services, loss of biodiversity, industrial pollution, climate change, digital divide, health and food concern of livestocks, transport, communication, research and analysis and popularisation of appropriate technology, legal awareness, employment/self-employment concerns and so on. It is expected to initiate various projects in the above-said issues.

Schedule VII of the Companies Act recommends few areas-initiatives for eradicating extreme hunger and poverty; promotion of education; promoting gender equality and empowering women; reducing child mortality and improving maternal health; combating HIV/AIDS, malaria and other diseases—to corporates with regard to CSR activities. The Act also recommends that companies concentrate on initiatives for environmental sustainability; programmes for employment enhancing vocational skills development and to invest in social entrepreneurship (The Companies Act, 2013).

In India, there are studies given a specific recommendation to corporates, to invest in few areas based the need and current situation of the country. The specific recommendations include the delivery of basic services such as Education, Health and Infrastructure, and make the growth more inclusive with sustainability as a focus. In these suggested area companies has to focus in these fields with proactive concern (Hucche Gowda, 2014).

Hucche Gowda's recommendations to corporates include the following specific instructions:

- Companies should extend their CSR activities in less privileged states rather than concentrate in resource-rich states;
- It will give better results if activities are based on more participatory approach and touch the grassroots level;
- There is also need for public-private partnership well-defined controls and process for the best use of resources for social change;
- Special training needs to be given to business managers in working with social problems;
- Participation of small and medium business in CSR has to be encouraged.

There are suggestions regarding the areas to be focused while undertaking or developing CSR projects in support of LSGs especially in the state of Kerala. There is a high priority required areas such as adoption of backwards institutions or villages or panchayat as such and focus and integrated development, skill development of the personnel, infrastructure support in various institutions and public utility spaces, building for public toilets and shelters.

The suggestion from NGO representative is on to focus on skill training for the less educated youth and for industry linkage. There are high need more finishing schools for the young professionals. In development sector to ensure a sustainable life, there is need to invest in renewable energy sector. Another respondent has shared the opinion that there is a huge investment requirement in drinking water quality enhancement in the state. Even if the state has a rich water belt, the problem of non-availability of sufficient water in remote areas still very prominent. It has to be addressed with the support of corporates and LSGs mutual along with Jalanidhi project. There is some focus required in social engineering, in which the functioning of some social system has to be taken for improvement.

There is massive scope in the state for school adoption and related activities, in which the quality of system service can be assured. For example, Nadakkavu High School in Kozhikode district as promoted to model school standard with better infrastructure and system practice.

Models Suggested

There are suggestions regarding the model in which how effectively corporates can undertake projects in their CSR. The built and transfer (BoT) model development support for infrastructural development projects and Public Private Partnership (PPP) model can be initiated by corporates from their CSR funding. Further maintenance and all are to rest with concerned LSG authority.

List of examples suggested by the experts in the study.

- The CSR project 'Twenty-20' undertaken by Kitex Limited at Kizahakkambalam Panchayat of the Ernakulam district in Kerala.
- The Subiksha model project initiatives by Perambra Block Panchayat of the Kozhikode district in Kerala. In which 1400 women are trained and started their own micro enterprises independently.
- The CSR initiatives by Pankajakasthoori Herbals and projects undertaken by Mitra Niketan NGO, Trivandrum.
- Total village adoption programme like India's former Cricket player Sachin Tendulkar adopted a few villages completely in Andhra Pradesh and Maharashtra as part of Sansad Adarsh Gram Yojana scheme.

- Shobha City's CSR project 'Kurumba Foundation' in Kizhakkancheri and Vadakkancheri panchayats in Trichur district of Kerala.

Strategic Recommendations for LSGs Partnership in CSR

There are some recommendations regarding the process and as some guidelines for implementing CSR projects in support of LSGs. Most important is that the projects are to be developed based on the concerned authority's recommendation and followed by scientific need analysis by involving professional with field expertise especially experienced hands in project management. The financial support for the total project and practical sponsorship model are workable based on the nature and requirement of the project when they associating with LSGs according to one senior LSG state level respondent.

The LSG official also recommends to initiate one-time investment oriented projects has to be promoted especially in the areas of infrastructural development. It says that CSR projects must concentrate on the projects which have less recurring expense after build-up and in maintenance. The initiatives must focus beyond plant located city in which the reach should be ensured beyond the periphery of the primary business areas of rural and suburban areas.

The CSR initiatives must be religiously neutral according to the policymaker respondent in the study. And it should always try to focus the smaller part of the target audience or a few numbers of populations and concentrate on holistic development-focus development initiatives. The best thing would be rather than setting up new systems, CSR initiatives can concentrate to improve the efficiency of existing systems and practices such as drinking water quality, efficiency improvement in educational system followed are few examples.

According to an LSG official, CSR initiative or project has to be considered as a separate entity in which the functioning can be smooth and fast. A separate **administrative** team has to be formed for ensuring an effective functioning of projects beyond daily routine monitoring from the part of the company.

The administrative cost for establishment of the system has to be kept minimum from the total project's budget. The salary and other benefits payment of the staff who are undertaking CSR from the part of the company should be paid by the company directly and it should not deduct from the total budget. All administrative cost has to be limited to 15-20 per cent and utilisation of rest should focus primary stakeholders according to the viewpoint of an Academician in this study.

There must be professionally trained social workers and administrators to enhance the quality of delivery of CSR in all companies, where section 135 of the Act is applicable. Lack of experienced and professionally qualified personnel in the CSR wing of many companies may create a layman approach in the CSR activities and it may deteriorate the quality of activities and attainment of objectives according to NGO professional.

In connection with the areas of **partnership** and mutual projects with LSGs, there some specific strategic suggestions are raised by the respondents in the study. The Panchayat **manual** should contain very specific and clear-cut working and partnership instructions to undertake CSR project and partnerships with corporates. It should include in the NITI Ayog's guidelines for LSGs according to LSG official. New policy specification has to be brought out in the next panchayat guideline in which corporate funding and CSR project management has to be mentioned in detail. As of now, there are a very few panchayat institutions only utilising the CSR funds widely, since the awareness programmes have to be conducted to ensure the effective utilisation according to the policy-makers response in the study.

In making an analysis of Kerala states situation, there is a hesitation from corporates that on the **political** dynamics of the state. One responded that at present very limited scope due to the highly political situation in LSGs. Once a ruling party opts for one company's CSR project for partnership mode of implementation, the opposition party at the local level may make unwanted propaganda that LSG or ruling governing body has selected the project with a vested interest according to a respondent in the study. So there is a need for a very concrete policy regarding the association between an LSG institute and a corporate concern. And the authority, responsibility and financial model are also to be defined clearly to avoid these kinds of future uncertainties in this regard.

Local bodies have wide **community reach** and systems for implementations in their respective area of functioning. So there is a wider scope for ensuring CSR project's benefits to all people if they intended to do so. One of the respondents shared the opinion that the objective of participative project implementation can be easily achieved if a CSR project implemented along with the support of LSGs. Larger community participation is very well required for the success of CSR projects in almost all projects, but there are some areas in which it is necessary for the areas of projects in public health promotion and women empowerment.

The LSG official shared the point that the possibility for easy **networking** and speedy communication is likely to be with institutions such as schools and ICDS centres in the purview of LSGs. In general, LSGs are performing their active roles efficiently in most of the areas with limited resources and network were people's presence is highly required to serve the developmental programmes. And most importantly the aspects of post project follow-up of the initiatives are likely to be achieved by LSGs officers and sustainability of the programme can be ensured to a great extent.

While implementing CSR projects at several locations of the corporate organisation, institutional partnerships and proper **communication** systems are highly required. And it is very much possible with the support of young officers and elected representatives and counsellors according to the opinion of one of the corporate respondent in this study. The same aspect of efficient communication and project management and networking are to be in the hands of young people according to the LSG official also.

Another respondent has given a strong suggestion that a crowd fund for local institutions like panchayat can be formed in the name of 'Social Responsibility Fund' or the possibility of adding it to panchayat president's development fund. So far no any CDS agency has utilised the amount of any companies CSR fund, even if there is a provision for that.

Summary and Conclusion

The concept of Corporate Social Responsibility is a company's sense of responsibility towards the community and environment in which it operates. The current perception has grown to acknowledge that the companies achieving good performance in their social, ethical and environmental fields will also perform well in their financial matters. The enactment of New Companies Act in 2013 has mandated CSR in India, and this has led to a very strong discussion on CSR in the country last decade.

Here CSR is defined as a principle stating that corporations should be accountable for the effects of any of their actions on their community and environment. Which intend the need of having a healthy relationship for corporates with other social stakeholders of the business organisation. The study is based on the assumption of having a better relationship and involvement for LSGs with corporates, local community and society at large to understand as well as to design an effective solution for the problems, i.e. for felt-needs and problems.

The study is based on the Freemans Stakeholder Management theory in which the role and expectation of different social and non-social stakeholders in the contexts of CSR have very well explained. The methodology followed is case study design in which expert discussions are very well applied.

The expert discussion with a various segment of people includes academician, policy-maker, NGO professional, LSG official and corporate representative has given a cross-sectional dimensions on perceived role of LSGs in CSR. The areas suggested for CSR projects in the context of state has been classified under 10 heads, which all are cross verified the important to suggest in the socio-cultural and business contexts.

The major concerns highlighted by many experts are on the inclusion of very specific guidelines on CSR projects undertaking model in the upcoming Panchayat Manual of the state. Also, recommends taking up effective measures and training sessions for LSG officials to increase the awareness level of CSR and future possibilities.

REFERENCES

Carroll, A.B., Karrem, Shabana (2010). "The Business Case for Corporate Social Responsibility: A Review of Concepts, Research and Practice, British Academy of Management", *International Journal of Management Reviews.*

CSR Policy, ACC Limited (2013), accessed from www.acclimited.com, on June 6, 2014.

Friedman, M. (1970). "The social responsibility of business is to increase its profits", New York, *Times Magazine*, September, 13.

Government Vision on CSR, Dutch Government Publications, 2007.

Gowda, H., (2014). *CSR in Rural Development Sector in India*, pp. 25-36, Corporate Social Responsibility, APH Publishing Corporation, New Delhi.

Hopkins, M. (2012). Definition of Corporate Social Responsibility, accessed from www.mhcinternational.com on March 27, 2016.

Jane, N. (2008). CSR and Public policy: New forms of engagement between business and government, Working paper No. 45, May 2008, John F. Kennedy School of Government, Harvard University.

Jyothi, M. and Mathiraj, S.P. (2011). "The strategic role of HRM in Corporate Social Responsibility Practices: An overview", *HRM Review*, Vol. No. XI, 9/11, ICFAI University Press, Delhi.

Mohan, A. (2001), "Corporate citizenship: perspectives from India", *Journal of Corporate Citizenship*, Vol. 12.

Mohanty, B.P. (2012), Sustainable Development *Vis-a-Vis* Actual Corporate Social Responsibility, India CSR, accessed from www.indiacsr.in, on 10.10.2015.

Solomon, J. (2007). *Corporate Governance and Accountability*; Wiley.

The Companies Act, 2013, Government of India.

The WBCSD's Journey, (2002). Corporate Social Responsibility, World Business Council for Sustainable Development.

13

Legal Configuration of GST in the Indian E-Commerce Industry

M. Sarngadharan

Introduction

There is every possibility that the ongoing digital transformation in India, created by Flipkart, Amazon India and Paytm Mall would be instrumental to elaborating the internet user base from 445.96 million in 2017 to 829 million by 2021. It is estimated that India's internet economy would surge from US$ 125 billion of 2017 to US$ 250 billion by 2020 and a dollop of this accounts for e-commerce transactions. In tune with this, the total revenue of Indian E-commerce industry is envisaged to go up from US$ 39 billion in 2017 to US$ 120 billion in 2020, pinpointing an annual rate growth of 51 per cent, probably, the highest in the world. During 2018, electronics is currently the biggest contributor to online retail sales in India with a share of 48 per cent, followed closely by apparel at 29 per cent. Initiatives taken by the Government of India like, Digital India, Make in India, Start-ups India, Skill India and Innovation Fund would support the growth of Indian e-commerce industry considerably. Besides, there are specific measures from the part of government to promote e-commerce sector across the nation. They include breakthrough in the limit of foreign direct investment (FDI) in the Business-to-Business (B2B) deals of e-commerce marketplace model up to 100 per cent. The government has allocated Rs. 8,000 crore (US$ 1.24 billion) to BharatNet Project, to provide broadband services to 150,000 rural local bodies in the Union Budget of 2018-19. It is likely that by 2020, about 55 per cent of online sales would be steered by cashless transactions.

It is in this background that an attempt is made in this paper to assess: (a) the structure of e-commerce industry in India; (b) the salient provisions of the GST Act, 2017 pertaining to the e-commerce industry; and (c) apparent after-effect of the unraveled by GST rules on the e-commerce industry. Secondary data available in research reports and periodicals were collected and used for the work.

Structure of e-Commerce Industry

E-commerce is a broad term that evinces the exchange of services and products online, inclusive of services of all kinds as well as affiliate, physical, and digital products that involve an exchange of funds online. The CGST Act, 2017 defines Electronic Commerce as the supply of goods or services or both, including digital products over digital or electronic network. A person, who owns, operates or manages digital or electronic facility or platform for electronic commerce is known as Electronic Commerce operator [Section 2(45)].

Models of e-Commerce Deals

There are various models of e-commerce deals, such as Business-to-Business (B2B); Business-to-Consumer (B2C); Consumer-to-Consumer (C2C); Consumer-to-Business (C2B); Business-to-Administration (B2A); and Consumer-to-Administration (C2A). B2B e-commerce model focuses on providing products from one business to another, whereas B2C e-commerce model is one in which a business sells to individuals and the deal is conducted online. However, the idea of C2C is different, as it allows trading, buying, and selling items between customers, usually second-hand or used items. C2B e-commerce is online deal, in which the consumer sells goods or services to business houses. E-commerce implicates government/public administration co-acting ecommerce transactions with businesses or consumers and these e-commerce models are referred to as B2G (also called B2A) and C2G (also called C2A) respectively.

Models Based on the Mode of Sales

There is yet another categorization for e-commerce models based on the mode of sales. The most popular models under this category are: 'Sale of Goods/Services–Online Shop–Traditional Model' and 'Sale of Goods–

Market Place–The aggregator model'. In the former model, the platform is owned by the supplier whereas the inventory of goods/services offered is either owned or controlled by him. Under the Sale of Goods–Market Place–The aggregator model, the platform is owned by one person and the goods or services are administered on such platform by another person. The buyers/client visits the site where he can catch the appropriate goods or services. The payment is made to the site owner although the specified product or service is directly handed over to the buyer/client by the seller or service provider. The site owner settles the payment with the seller or service provider after deducting his margin/commission. Apart from the aforesaid service providers, there are other support functions that coexist in the e-commerce community, such as payment gateways, e-wallets, internet services providers and so on.

E-Commerce Revenue Models

Depending on the system design by which a business devises its solutions, products, and services e-commerce revenue model becomes apparent. In essence, it is the business plan for an enterprise to make money as it elucidates how a business induces revenue streams from the value created for customers. There are multifarious types of revenue models and an innovative company originates its own unique revenue model well suited to it. A robust and state-of-the-art revenue model is imperative for early stage startups as their investors are mostly cognizant of monetization and return on their investment (ROI). Existing businesses revamp their revenue models to cope with the new generation of customers and competitors. Prominent Business Revenue Models are Drop Shipping; Wholesaling and Warehousing; Private Labeling and Manufacturing; and White Labeling.

Prospects of e-Commerce

The Indian e-commerce industry has been rolling through an extensive revamping and this has transfigured the composition of business activities in the country. Umpteen constituents, such as intensified penetration of internet and mobiles, online payments and contributive demographics have reconstructed the business-customer relationship drastically. The practice prevalent at present in the e-commerce world is to focus much on to reach the customers through mobile apps for proliferation of enhanced volume of sales. In short, the prospects of e-commerce in India looks luminous in the days to come and this would nourish mobile platforms, personalization, social media analytics, omni-channel service and sharing economy business models to mature in a strong tone.

With the execution of GST laws, it is hopeful that many problems such as tax issues and problems with supply chain management will be resolved. This will enable faster shipping and reduce paperwork formalities. GST has brought about greater compliances for e-commerce players, along with this comes significant benefits. The removal of restrictions on cross-utilization of credits will show a significant gain in the e-commerce sector. At present, the credit of service tax paid on input services such as warehousing, logistics and commission of marketplace has been denied by the traders, simultaneously the claim credit of VAT paid on goods that are used for providing output services has not been allowed by the service providers. The cascading effect results in a significant blocked unit tax cost for this sector due to the fact that VAT is applicable on the output side, while most input costs are services. But flipping the coin, this will surely result in the reduction of cascading effect of taxes. In the present scenario, there are differential rates of VAT in different states even for the same products along with the further fragmenting of VAT Rate as well. However, the rates at Central and State Level are expected to be uniform that would ultimately reduce the disputes. It is the expectation of the people of India that GST would be a win-win proposition for all sectors of the economy in spite of its not being a perfect one because of certain constraints of a joint venture between Centre and thirty one States ruled by different political parties. In the midst of the high expectation, a discordant note is being heard from one particular sector, that is, the e-commerce sector. This sector has raised many concerns, particularly on the issue of tax collection at source (TCS) by the e-commerce operators from their vendors and depositing it with the tax authorities (Section 52).

This being the situation, it would be pertinent to get familiarized with the other intrusive provisions of the GST Act, 2017 pertaining to the e-commerce industry in a separate section.

Goods and Services Tax and Indian e-Commerce Industry

The Goods and Services Tax (GST), as cited earlier, has subsumed various taxes, like Service Tax, VAT, Excise Duty and so on, since its introduction in the commencement of July 2017. This has fortified the indirect tax mechanism of both Central and State governments in simplifying the taxation system in India with the displacement of multiple taxes. GST is also productive in discharging the legal disputes in respect of double taxation wherein excise duty was being levied first and subsequently VAT on the same item. The Invoice Matching Concept underlying in GST gauges the revenue leakages and helps the business houses to deposit the legal and principled tax with the Government. In this context, it is pertinent to learn the methodology adopted by business houses to evade indirect taxes in the system existing hitherto and how such evasions could be prevented in the GST system.

Legal Disposition

It is mandatory for e-commerce operator to obtain registration under section 24(x) of the CGST Act, irrespective of the value of supply made by him. However, a person supplying services, other than supplier of services under section 9(5) of the CGST Act, 2017, through an e-commerce platform are exempted from obtaining compulsory registration provided their aggregate turnover does not exceed INR 20 lakh (or INR 10 lakh in case of specified special category States) in a financial year. As per the existent law, registration for TCS would be required in each State/UT as the obligation for collecting TCS would be there for every intra-State or inter-State supply in order to facilitate the obtaining of registration in each State/UT, for obtaining registration in that State/UT where it does not have physical presence. Foreign e-commerce operators do not have place of business in India since they operate from outside. Where registered supplier is supplying goods or services through a foreign e-commerce operator to a customer in India, such foreign e-commerce operator would be liable to collect TCS on such supply and would be required to obtain registration in each State/UT. If the foreign e-commerce operator does not have physical presence in a particular State/UT, he may appoint an agent on his behalf. E-Commerce operator has to obtain separate registration for TCS irrespective of the fact whether e-Commerce operator is already registered under GST as a supplier or otherwise and has GSTIN.

In the earlier system of indirect taxation let us assume that X has availed services worth Rs. 10 lakh from Y. Service Tax @ 15 per cent i.e. Rs. 1.5 lakh was required to be paid by X to Y. The system insisted Y to deposit this amount of Rs. 1.5 lakh with the Government. As a result, X was able to avail the benefit of Input Tax Credit worth Rs. 1.5 lakh. Suppose Y, for personal reasons, didn't deposit this amount of Service Tax, either partially or in full with the Government. In this case, let us assume, that in his Service Tax return, he states that Service Tax of Rs. 50,000 was paid to A and Service Tax of Rs. 50,000 to B and thus, claims the benefit of input tax credit of such amount paid. The balance Rs. 50,000 was deposited with the Government. Actually, the amount paid to A was a genuine claim, whereas the amount paid to B was a bogus claim. It is in this frame of reference that GST is regarded as a major reform the economy in respect of indirect taxation. It aids to preclude tax evasion through input tax credit (ITC); a massive IT backbone called GSTN; and e-way bill, a tool that monitors the movement of goods.

Legal Composition

Every registered taxable person shall, subject to such conditions and restrictions as may be stated and within the time and manner specified in section 35, be entitled to take credit of input tax (ITC) admissible to him and the said amount shall be credited to the electronic credit ledger of such person (Section 16). In order to claim ITC, the registered person needs to follow some conditions and restriction as specified in section 35. Section 35 says that credit of IGST shall be first utilized for payment of IGST then for CGST and last for SGST. On filing of Return by the seller, ITC shall be credited to buyer E-Ledger, which may be seen after login to site. The GSTN or Goods and Service Tax Network, a tax registration number under the new tax structure, manages the entire IT system of the GST portal. This platform is be used by the government to track financial transaction and other tax details. Each taxpayer is allotted a state-wise PAN-based 15-digit GSTIN, in which the first two digits of the number represents the state code as per Indian Census 2011. E-Way Bill is generated with a unique Number (EBN) and is made available to the supplier, recipient and the transporter. The e-Way Bill replaces the Way Bill, which was a physical document and existed during the VAT regime for the movement of goods. E-waybill travels with the shipment, identifies its consignor, consignee, origin and destination, describes the goods, and shows their weight and freight. It is neither a contract of carriage nor a negotiable instrument.

Suppose A buys a bottle of a product, manufactured by Nestle, from Z and sold it first to a regional distributor X. Then, X sold it to Y, a wholesaler and he supplied it to Z, a retailer. When A buys it from Z, the retailer, let us assume two situations–one he pays tax and the other, he doesn't pay the tax. If he doesn't pay the tax, there is no easy way for the government to know about it. In this condition Z, the shopkeeper cheerfully holds the amount in his possession. Strictly speaking this amount should have gone to the exchequer. In the GST regime, the government grabs each transaction registered through its GSTN portal and administers incentive for the major companies to follow the rules over the ITC. In this alternated system, the government is equipped to ascertain both the buyer and seller. The ITC allows them to drawback the taxes they have to pay from the taxes they have already paid while procuring the raw materials. This induces the huge business houses to follow the rule and anyone who picks up goods from them is also triggered to follow the rule as the GSTN would record both purchase and sale.

Again coming back to the immediately preceding illustration of the above mentioned product, it can be noted that the government would know what Nestle is shipping and there would be a tax levied on that. Nestle can adjust this tax against the raw materials like cocoa and so on, they have paid for. The distributor who gets the package containing the Boost has to now bill his vendor properly, in the absence of which he cannot claim his input tax credit. The vendor now has to bill his retailer, failing which he cannot demand his tax credit. By the time, it reaches the retailer most of the tax is already paid. In this stage, the government is also aware of the absolute number of bottles procured and possessed by the retailer. Now it is mandatory on the part of the retailer to bill the customer and then demand an Input Tax Credit. Sales executed by the retailer without billing would put him into a loss since the tax was already paid for the main segments aforetime product reached him and he must have realized the tax from the customer through proper billing. This conglomeration of taxes and the sequential recording of it online is the innovative articulation of the system.

E-Commerce Operator

The e-commerce operator, not being an agent, is required to collect an amount calculated at the rate not exceeding one per cent, as notified by the Government on the recommendations of the Council, of the net value of taxable supplies made through it, where the consideration with respect to such supplies is to be collected by such operator (Section 52). The amount so collected is called as Tax Collection at Source (TCS). TCS is to be collected once supply has been made through the e-commerce operator and where the business model is that the consideration is to be collected by the e-commerce operator irrespective of the actual collection of the consideration. For example, if the supply has taken place through the e-commerce operator on 30th October, 2018, but the consideration for the same has been collected in the month of November, 2018, then TCS for such supply has to be collected and reported in the statement for the month of October, 2018. However, TCS is not required to be collected on exempt supplies. So also, TCS is not required to be collected on supplies on which the recipient is required to pay tax on reverse charge basis. A composition taxpayer cannot make supplies through e-commerce operator and hence question of collecting TCS in respect of supplies made by the composition taxpayer does not arise. Import of goods would fall within the domain of the Customs Act, 1962.

The amount collected towards TCS by the operator is to be paid to appropriate government within 10 days after the end of the month in which the said amount was so collected. The amount of TCS deposited by the operator with the appropriate Government will be reflected in the electronic cash ledger of the actual registered. The said credit can be used at the time of discharge of tax liability by the actual supplier. TCS collected is to be deposited by the e-commerce operator separately under the respective tax head (i.e. Central tax/State tax/Union territory tax/ Integrated tax). Based on the statement filed by the e-commerce operator, the same would be credited to the electronic cash ledger of the actual supplier in the respective tax head. If the supplier is not able to use the amount lying in the said cash ledger, the actual supplier may claim refund of the excess balance lying in his electronic cash ledger in accordance with the provisions contained in section 54(1) of the CGST Act.

Apparent After-Effects of Legal Configuration

The introduction of GST has facilitated single tax rule and this makes it far rockier to evade the single authority. GST system is unique in more aspects. The system prevailed earlier grouped the services and products separately. The products were taxed by the state governments and the services by the Central Government. The problem endured previously to differentiate between a product and a service has been faded away now. By integrating the product and service, the system makes it easier to levy tax since the lone authority would tax them and that too, at the same rate.

There were unjust taxes and more number of taxes in the erstwhile system. Along with this, there existed a tendency among the producers as well as traders, in the economy as a whole, to evade taxes to the maximum extent possible. In this backdrop, GST arose as a decisive reform in preventing tax evasion through Input Tax Credit (ITC), GSTN and a system to monitor the movement of goods-E-way bill (Section 16). There are millions of small business houses (mostly traders) and each such business unit makes a profit of at least Rupees 5 to 10 lakh per annum but these traders were filing tax returns be it commercial taxes or income tax. In any local wholesale market in the major cities selling items ranging from footwear to textiles, hardware to electrical items, food products to industrial chemicals and agricultural inputs, the practice prevalent was that buyer was able to avail himself of two options for each business deal. The first option was to secure the bill for every wholesale purchase and the other one was to make purchases without a proper bill. Under the GST Rule, details in respect of all invoices are to be mentioned in the GST Return. The rationale behind insisting this is that by doing so, the government is able to track, whether the required taxes are paid. As a result, it is possible to ensure that the gain under input tax credit is not misused.

Marketplace

The marketplace is an e-commerce platform owned by the E-commerce Operator such as Flipkart, Snapdeal, Amazon and so on. It empowers third-party sellers to register and sell online on their respective platform. Based on sale value, marketplace charges the subscription fees/ commission from listed sellers. Third-party sellers under this model build-up access to a larger customer base, registered with the marketplace. Under this footing, customers get more passages for contacting multiple sellers and availing gains of competitive prices for the desired products. Items purchased on such marketplaces are either shipped by Merchant/ Third-party seller directly or through the fulfillment centre managed by the Marketplace Operator. The Union Government has conceded of Foreign Direct Investments under this model to stimulate e-commerce marketplace business model in the economy. In conjunction with the expansion in the number of vendors and the assurgent size of business the GST regime has taken up marketplaces and has brought out unequivocal rules and regulations for this segment.

Marketplace Operator

Under the GST regime, marketplace operators are obligatory that a required percentage amount is deducted towards the GST liability of seller and the sum deposited with the government, under the mechanism designated as

Tax Collection at Source (TCS). Ultimately, the marketplace seller has to file monthly return under GST to demand the credit of TCS collected by the marketplace operator. The impact of this adjustment is that it would shake the liquidity and cash flow of the sellers involved in the deals. Despite the fact that the marketplace operators have already completed the introductory level analysis of impact of GST on their operations, marketplace sellers are to get well acquainted with these criteria underlying in GST rules. It is imperative that marketplace sellers have to keep themselves well aware of the changes that are going to come and they must start A high level impact analysis of GST on Online Marketplace India's e-commerce market has come out with the results that the online retail revenue would generate $100 billion by 2020.

Some of the features of a marketplace model are unique in nature. Marketplace enables third-party sellers to register and sell online on their platform. It charges a subscription fees/commission on sale value from listed sellers. Third-party sellers under this model gain access to a larger customer base, registered with marketplace. Customer on the other hand gains access to multiple sellers and competitive prices for desired products. Items purchased on such marketplaces are either shipped by Merchant/ Third-party seller directly or through the fulfillment centre managed by Marketplace Operator. The Government has also allowed Foreign Direct Investments under such model to promote e-commerce marketplace business model in India. Marketplaces have provided retailers with additional channel of sales and reach which was unimaginable for an offline seller. Major marketplaces claim to have numerous sellers affiliated with their platform with millions of SKUs. While the number of sellers and their quantum of business have increased significantly, GST has specifically taken up marketplaces and has come out with rules and regulations specific to this segment.

Broadly, impact of GST on all e-commerce companies would be massive. This is mostly on account of the fact that e-commerce companies market the products and services all over the nation. GST, being a consumer based taxation regime, is to be paid in the State where the goods or services are consumed. It is a widely known fact that many e-commerce houses were, prior to introduction of GST avoiding indirect taxes such as, VAT/CST/Excise/Service Tax/TDS levied on offline business houses. In the broadening tax base of GST, and naturally the burden of tax for e-commerce business is on the increasing side. This being the case, with the growing e-commerce market, there is every possibility that the government would be forced to grant some incentives/exemptions for austerity faced on the regulatory front by such business units.

Dichotomy of Goods and Services

Involvement of logistics/reverse logistics, advertising and promotion services, goods like software, music, and e-books made it hard earlier to differentiate goods and services component of each transaction. The prevalence of statutory forms/e-way bills and the like made it complex to do interstate transactions. Market places also needed to comply with requirements of registrations and declaration of turnover to multiple state tax departments. Under GST, India has become a common market and drive uniformity, reduce compliance costs. Due to restrictions on cross utilization of input of central taxes against state taxes there occurred price escalation due to taxes sticking to products sold. Under GST both e-commerce companies and their sellers have to simultaneously register the warehouses as principal and additional place of business, respectively. This would be challenging as these warehouses do not have dealer-wise physically separated or denominated areas within the warehouse.

Conjointly, the treatment of stock transfer from seller to the warehouse under GST would be different as any 'supply' is taxable. This might lead to cascading of taxes as typically sellers do not 'sell' stock to e-commerce companies. However, on the positive side the 'Fulfilled by Amazon', 'Flipkart Advantage' or 'Snapdeal Plus' model wherein dealers store their products at warehouse is currently forbidden in States like Karnataka has been revived. Right away, registration of market place warehouse as additional place of business is repudiated and under GST regime this may change. Market places also have to take registration in each of the States (optional) and Union Territories.

Treatment of Gifts/Discounts

Gifts/Discounts are to be distinctly quoted in the invoice to arrive at transaction value on which GST is applicable. It is significant to note that post-sale discount of any nature attracts GST. While determining place of supply of goods to customers is easy to determine, the place of supply of services by E-commerce firms to the sellers may be little difficult. Under the erstwhile tax laws, sellers on e-commerce platforms were compelled to deduct tax at source (TDS) on the commission they paid to the platform. They had to deposit the TDS, obtain Form 16 submit to the e-commerce player and get refund. The entire process has been blockheaded in GST, wherein the marketplace would deduct its commission as well as TDS and file TDS return. The TDS deducted would appear automatically as credit in the electronic credit ledger of seller which he can use to discharge his tax liability. The impact is subdued when sales returns occur and the deducted TDS has to be reversed. It is customary that E-commerce encounters with 10-20 per cent returns based on the products dealt with. Both the e-commerce player and the seller have to upload invoice-wise details of supplies in their respective returns and the GST system would match them. In case of any supply reported by the respective platform and not reported by marketplace unless reconciled, is added to the liability of the seller.

GST would lead a more transparent and neutral manner to raise revenue. Simplified and cost saving system as procedural cost reduces due to uniform accounting for all types of taxes–maintaining only three accounts, namely, CGST, SGST, and IGST. GST is structured in such a way as a long term strategy leading to a higher output, more employment opportunities, and economic boom. GST is beneficial for both economy and corporations. The reduced tax burden.

Limitations

Although GST is being referred as a single taxation system but in reality it is a dual tax in which state and centre both collects separate tax on a single transaction of sale and service. In previous system, the main Indirect tax of Central Government was central excise. All the goods and commodities were not covered by the central excise and further there was an exemption limit of Rs. 1.50 crore in the central excise and further traders were not liable to pay central excise. The central excise was payable up to the stage of manufacturing but now GST is payable up to the stage of sale. Prior to the introduction of GST, majority of the dealers were not covered with the central excise but were only paying VAT in the state. This situation has changed disturbingly that all the VAT dealers are required to pay Central Goods and Service Tax.

The Revenue Neutral Rate is the rate at which the amount of taxes currently collected by the government and the amount expected to be collected after GST remains the same. As a result, there would be change in the volume of revenue coming into the exchequer. This means GST proposal is revenue neutral ensuring neither increases nor decreases in tax revenues when compared to existing law. RNR calculation has to include the cascading effect on certain goods having no excise or sales tax implications. Thus, focus under GST is to arrive at such rates which would not decrease the current revenue generation by Central and State Governments.

However, in practice, calculation of RNR (Revenue Neutral Rate) is very difficult since government wants to enhance its revenue. This rate is higher, in comparison with the fact that small and medium industries were not covered by the central excise and most of the goods such as agricultural products were out of the purview of the central excise. Improvement in the manufacturing and distribution of goods and service, increase in exports, various reforms, check on corruption, less government control were some of the factors that hindered the economic growth of the country. Such being the situation it is doubtful whether GST is able to bring forward significant and revolutionary modulation in the economy.

Conclusion

It may be concluded that with the inclusion of retail entrepreneurs in the ambit of GST and the introduction of specific provisions for e-commerce companies, certain areas of GST will impact the e-commerce sector. Every company in India, be it a multinational company or a small/medium enterprise, is gearing up for the implementation of GST. The e-commerce sector would follow suit in its preparation by focusing on provisions specific to this sector in the GST law. The success of the e-commerce sector is largely a dependent on the increasing number of retail entrepreneurs, who fall in the unorganized retail sector category. The government has included such players in the ambit of GST with an intention of broadening the tax base and has introduced specific provisions for the e-commerce companies.

REFERENCES

Government of India: Ministry of Law and (Legislative Department), The Central Goods and Services Tax Act, 2017 (No. 12 of 2017), The Gazette of India, New Delhi, April, 12, 2017.

Pooja H. Ramchandani, (2016). Growth of e-commerce in India and its impact on Indian economy, Abhinav International monthly referred in Journal of Research in Management and Technology, Vol. 5, Issue 8, August.

https://www.forbes.com/sites/krnkashyap/2017/07/20/how-goods-and-service-tax-gstimpacts-these-five-sectors-of-indiaseconomy/

https://www.gstindia.com/e-commerce-to-benefit-from-faster-delivery-and-transparency/

https://www.gstindia.com/how-large-consumer-goods-companies-benefitted-due-to-gst-e-commerce-in-2018

https://www.profitbooks.net/gst-impact-on-ecommerce-business

14

M-Commerce and Its Influence on the Consumer's Perceptions

Shahir Bhatt and *Amola Bhatt*

Introduction

Mobile is becoming the dominant means for accessing communications primarily because deploying mobile network is not only more cost-efficient but also mobile provides greater flexibility and convenience to its subscribers than landline telephone (Sanjay, 2007). Mobile Commerce is the subset of e-commerce, which includes all e-commerce transactions, carried out using a mobile (hand held) device (Sharma, 2009). Mobile commerce, which is commonly referred to as m-commerce, has become an important concept in today's business environment (Rottenberg et al., 2002).

According to *Oxford Dictionary*, M-Commerce means commercial transactions conducted electronically by mobiles. Investopedia defines Mobile Commerce as the use of information technologies and communication technologies for the purpose of mobile integration of different value chains and business processes, and for the purpose of management of business relationships. Over the last few decades, mobile applications have been evolving in India, with a wide variety now in use. Applications have been developed for existing mobile platforms including smart-phones, laptop PCs, PDAs, tablets and specialty pagers.

The explosive growth of penetration and usage of mobile devices is frequently noted in research studies (Barnes and Scornavacca, 2004; Dholakia et al., 2004; Massoud and Gupta, 2003). In 2011, twenty one million smart-phones were sold in India. This went to grow to thirty two million in 2012, and it will eventually reach hundred million smart-phones by 2015 (TRAI, 2012). M-commerce is adding significant value to the businesses in India. Key drivers of M-commerce include widespread adoption of mobile phones and smart-phones and rising affluent middle class consumers. These factors have increased the appetite for M-Commerce in India. It has led to newer opportunities for the businesses to grow and for the M-consumers to obtain benefits in terms of convenience, freedom and speed of work. Inclusive growth means ensuring that India's economic development lifts all boats; which is a critical national priority. One key focus has been on the role of Indian companies in enabling inclusive growth. Mobile commerce can be used to tackle the issues of productivity and sustainability.

Literature Review

To date, major e-commerce journals and some business journals have published special editions on m-commerce topic: the first was in Electronic Markets in 2002, followed by *International Journal of Electronic Commerce, Decision Support Systems* and *Journal of Business Research*, amongst others. The focus of the journals varied, from technical to managerial topics, and exemplified the complex nature of m-commerce components. A series of papers by Barnes [2002a, 2002b] were among the pioneering efforts in mobile research in general. He proposed preliminary frameworks for value-chain creation and wireless advertising, respectively.

Feng, Hoegler, and Stucky (2006) suggested that m-commerce is more than e-commerce due to its different interaction style, usage pattern and value chain. Feng *et al.* (2006) stated that m-commerce is a new and innovative business opportunity with its own unique characteristics and functions, such as mobility and broad reach ability. Harris, Rettie and Chak Kwan (2008) reported that there are significant differences between the UK and Hong Kong in usage of and attitudes to m-commerce services. The literature suggests that individual differences play an important role in how technology is used and perceived by consumers (Agarwal and Prasad, 1999; Kwon and Chidambaram, 2000; Venkatesh and Davis, 2000). Mobile users' perceptions and intention to use m-commerce will be differentiated by variability of the users' demographics, shopping motivations, and media dependency.

Several factors are driving the growth of mobile commerce (m-commerce hereafter). First, access to the mobile Internet has become easier and cheaper. Mobile devices such as smart phones and tablet PCs, which are designed to increase usability of the mobile Internet, have gained widespread popularity. Statistics show that smart phone adoption grew by 50 per cent during each of the past two years (*eMarketer*, 2011). Mobile Internet prices across various wireless Internet technologies are falling, and this trend is expected to continue (Harbor Research, 2010). Mobile Internet traffic worldwide, accordingly, rose to 5.02 per cent in June 2011, up from 1.82 per cent in March 2010 and has doubled within the past year (Sullivan, 2011). Second, companies and retailers are increasingly considering m-commerce as a new venue for future growth; thus, their corresponding efforts are also lifting m-commerce. As web traffic via the mobile Internet accounts for over 10 per cent of the traffic, more retailers are creating mobile sites enabled for m-commerce (Patel, 2011).

Consumer experiences evoked with mobile phones may differ by shopping motivations, as m-commerce can provide both hedonic (entertainment) and utilitarian (efficiency and time-critical) features (Anckar and D'Incau, 2002). According to Babin, Darden, and Griffin (1994), consumers with a hedonic shopping motivation seek experiential value (i.e., fun, arousal, or leisure), whereas consumers with a utilitarian shopping motivation seek instrumental value (such as saving time or effort, or completing tasks). Hedonic shoppers may want to use the entertainment, music services, and innovative services by m-commerce, as they enjoy the stimulation offered by product newness and the exploration of new and interesting shopping experiences (Gehrt and Carter, 1992). On the other hand, utilitarian shoppers may prefer to use services that are timely, decisive, and task-oriented (e.g. payment services, location-based) via m-commerce, as they attempt to minimize time and effort, and maximize convenience (Bellenger and Korgaonkar, 1980).

Dholakia (2004) stated that M-commerce has opened up opportunities for reaching customers at multiple (targeted) locations, for configuring services and offerings in novel (pinpointed) ways, and enabling new types of shopping and service consumption experiences. Bhatti (2007) explored the factors influencing M-commerce adoption. These included subjective norms, perceived usefulness, perceived ease of use and behavioural control. Shimul and Hossain (2013) concluded that university students have a positive perception towards M-Commerce and has a high usage rate of the products and services offered by M-Commerce. Batra and Juneja (2013) also reflected that M-commerce is adding significant value to the businesses in India. This chapter tries to explore the awareness level, usage pattern, factors to be considered for adopting M-commerce and ultimately segments the shoppers.

Research Objectives

- To study the factors influencing the Usage of M-Commerce.
- To segment the mobile users on the basis of the factors brought out from the study.

Research Methodology

The research design for the study is descriptive in nature and the sampling unit consists consumers who are aware of M-commerce. The questionnaire constructed for the study included several questions which were continuous and categorical in nature. A scale was constructed with five point Likert type statements in which respondents were asked to indicate their level of agreement (1 = strongly disagree to 5 = strongly agree). For this study, the scale constructed by Bhatti (2007) was used which comprised 20 Likert scale statements. The final study involved a survey conducted in Ahmedabad between January and February 2014. The sampling technique used for the study was convenient sampling. Reponses were obtained from 179 respondents. SPSS 19 was used to analyze the data. Factor Analysis along with Cluster Analysis was used to analyze the data collected.

Sample Characteristics

See Table 14.1.

Factors Influencing the Usage of M-Commerce

The Principal Component Factor Analysis (PCA) with varimax rotation was performed for the 20 items exploring the factors influencing the consumer usage intention of m-commerce. The result indicated that the Bartlett's Test of Sphericity (Bartlett, 1954) was significant (Chi-Square 1580.036, p-value < 0.0001). The Kaiser-Mayer-Olkin (KMO) measure of sampling adequacy was high at 0.845. This KMO value of 0.845 is excellent since it exceeded the recommended value of 0.6 (Kaiser, 1974). The above results suggest that the data is appropriate to proceed with the factor analysis procedure (Malhotra, 2010).

Exploratory Factor Analysis (EFA) was performed and only those factors were retained which had an eigen value more than 1 since they were considered significant. An eigen value represents the amount of

Table 14.1: Demographic Characteristics

		Frequency	*Percentage*
Gender	Male	99	55.3
	Female	80	44.7
Age	less than 20 years	57	31.8
	Equal or More than 20 years	122	68.2
Education	SSC	3	1.7
	HSC	10	5.6
	Bachelor's Degree	83	46.4
	Master's Degree	83	46.4
Occupation	Self Employed	7	3.9
	Homemaker/Housewife	8	4.5
	Student	98	54.7
	Business	19	10.6
	Job/Service	47	26.3
Monthly Income	Less than 25000	154	86.0
	Equal or More than 25000	25	14.0

variance associated with the factor. The result was that there were a total of 5 factors which influenced the usage of m-commerce, which explained for 63.896 per cent of the total variance. The inter-item correlation and inter-item consistency of each Factor was also measured by calculating each Factor's Cronbach's alpha (Cronbach, 1951) (Table 14.2).

Factor 1 is loaded on 6 variables. This can be labeled as "**Attitude towards M-commerce**", as these 6 variables revealed the attitude of consumers towards M-commerce. This included the individual's likeability to take chances, social influence, and faith and belief towards m-commerce. The items received a mean of 3.56 on a scale of 1 to 5 where majority of them agreed that individual's attitude is an influential factor for the m-commerce transactions. Identical study by Bhatti, (2007) also considered behavioural intention as one of the important factors influencing M-commerce usage.

Factor 2 is loaded on 5 variables. This can be termed as "**Perceived Benefits**", as this variable describes about the advantages of using

Table 14.2: Factors Influencing Usage of M-commerce

	Component					
	1	*2*	*3*	*4*	*5*	*Relia-bility*
Factor 1: Attitude towards M-commerce						.817
S15: I like to take chances	0.783					
S17: People important to me think I should use M-commerce	0.748					
S19: People whom I look up, expect that I use M-commerce	0.648					
S13: It is easy to make M-commerce do what I want it to	0.664					
S7: I like to experiment the new ways of doing things	0.591					
S9: M-commerce would not lead to an invasion of personal privacy	0.572					
Factor 2: Perceived Benefits						.848
S1: M-commerce helps me save time		0.818				
S2: I have necessary means and resources to use m-commerce		0.767				
S3: My interaction with m-commerce is clear and understandable		0.693				
S5: M-commerce contributes to the betterment of life		0.658				
S11: Learning to use M-commerce is easy for me		0.601				
Factor 3: Adventure						.628
S16: I am very curious about how things work			0.803			
S14: I often seek out info about new products			0.629			
S4: I like to be around unconventional people who dare to try new things			0.380			
Factor 4: Perceived Risk						.640
S18: I feel free to use the kind of M-commerce transaction I like to				0.683		
S6: It is safe to purchase using m-commerce				0.644		
S20: M-commerce functions are entirely within my control				0.519		

(*Contd.*)

	Component					
	1	*2*	*3*	*4*	*5*	*Relia-bility*
Factor 5: Idea						.618
S8: It is fashionable and trendy to use m-commerce					0.751	
S10: M-commerce is compatible with the existing technology					0.535	
S12: It is expected that people like me make use of M-commerce					0.458	

m-commerce. This includes user-friendliness, convenience, time-saving and betterment of life. Mean obtained for this factor was 3.71 on the scale of 1 to 5, which was the highest received, from which it can be said that majority of the respondents believed that Perceived Benefits influenced their intention to use m-commerce. Perceived ease of use is an individual's assessment of the extent to which interaction with a specific information system or technology is free of mental effort (Davis, 1989). The perceived ease of use for a system is defined as the degree to which an individual believes that using a particular technology will be free of effort. The results of many of the prior empirical studies have demonstrated that perceived ease of use has a positive correlation with behavioural intention, both directly (Davis, 1989; Gefen and Straub, 1997, 2000; Venkatesh, 2000; Venkatesh and Davis, 2000; Gefen, 2003) and indirectly.

Factor 3 includes variables related to thrill and excitement in individuals on using m-commerce, learning new things and exploring innovative products and services. This factor can be described as "**Adventure**". Mean obtained for this factor was 3.51 on the scale of 1 to 5, from which it can be said that majority of the respondents believed that Innovativeness influenced their intention to use m-commerce. It has been recognized that highly innovative individuals are active information seekers about new ideas. Drawing upon Rogers' theory of the diffusion of innovations, Agarwal and Prasad (1998) described personal innovativeness as symbolizing the risk-taking propensity that exists in certain individuals and not in others. They are able to cope with high levels of uncertainty and develop more positive intentions toward acceptance (Rogers, 1983; 1995). Citrin *et al.* (2000) study also found that personal innovativeness predicts consumer adoption of internet shopping.

Factor 4 is loaded on 3 variables. This factor includes variables like safety, customization and control. So this factor might be labeled as

"**Perceived Risk**". Mean obtained for this factor was 3.54 on the scale of 1 to 5, from which it can be said that majority of the respondents agreed that Perceived Risk influences their intention to use m-commerce. Lee (2007) also pointed risk aversion as one of the factors influencing m-commerce usage.

Factor 5 is loaded on 3 variables. This can be referred as "**Idea**". This is because it is believed that smart shoppers believe that it is fashionable and trendy to use m-commerce. Mean obtained for this factor was 3.592 on the scale of 1 to 5, from which it can be said that majority of the respondents believed that the idea about m-commerce being trendy and compatible with existing technology influenced their intention to use m-commerce.

Segmenting the Shoppers

Cluster analysis is a statistical procedure for grouping observations with shared characteristics. A combination approach using a hierarchical clustering method followed by a non-hierarchical method is often advisable. First step was hierarchical clustering using squared Euclidean distance, between-group linkage (average linkage) clustering method and Ward clustering method, was conducted to select the number of clusters and cluster centres that serve as initial cluster seeds in the following non-hierarchical procedure. The non-hierarchical method, k-means method, then clusters all observations using the seed points to provide more accurate cluster memberships.

According to distance coefficients we can say that a three-cluster solution was found to be most appropriate. ANOVA test indicated that all five factors contributed to differentiating the three clusters ($p<0.001$). Tables 14.3 to 14.5 present results of cluster analysis for the three clusters.

Interpretation

Cluster 1: Reserved Shoppers

It is the smallest cluster comprising of 9.49 per cent of shoppers. It has moderate mean score of 3 for two factors namely attitude towards m-commerce and perceived risk. Additionally below average mean scores are also found for perceived benefits, adventure and idea. The shoppers in the cluster are very passive and conventional in nature. Frequency of mobile commerce transaction is less and majority of them seek information while using m-commerce.

Table 14.3: Final Cluster Centres

	Cluster		
	Reserved Shoppers (n = 17)	*Utilitarian Shoppers (n = 58)*	*Assured Shoppers (n = 104)*
Attitude towards M-Commerce	3	3	4
Perceived Benefits	2	4	4
Adventure	2	3	4
Perceived Risk	3	3	4
Idea	**2**	**3**	**4**

Note: Mean values were computed on the basis of 5-point scale 1-Strongly Disagree, 5-Strongly Agree.

Table 14.4: ANOVA

	Cluster		*Error*		*F*	*Sig.*
	Mean Square	df	*Mean Square*	*df*		
Attitude towards M-Commerce	12.314	2	0.167	176	73.776	0
Perceived Benefits	17.576	2	0.223	176	78.97	0
Adventure	22.107	2	0.254	176	86.964	0
Perceived Risk	21.925	2	0.129	176	170.261	0
Idea	20.022	2	0.19	176	105.307	0

Cluster 2: Utilitarian Shoppers

It comprises 32.4 per cent of shoppers. It has high mean score for one factor i.e. Perceived Benefits. It appears that the shoppers have high expectations from m-commerce transactions. They look for several advantages like user-friendliness, convenience, time-saving and betterment of life. Mean scores are moderate for all other factors. Majority of them (75.8%) are above the age of 20 years, they (88.8%) are either graduates or post graduates; majority of them (51%) frequently opt for mobile commerce transactions (more than 10 times a year) and majority ([illegible]8.9%) seek information while using m-commerce.

Cluster 3: Assured Shoppers

The cluster comprises 58.1 per cent of shoppers, representing the largest group of respondents. It was found to have high mean scores for all five factors. They are very confident about m-commerce and frequently use

Table 14.5: Demographic Characteristics/Usage Patterns of Cluster Groups

		Reserved Shoppers (n=17)	*Utilitarian Shoppers (n=58)*	*Assured Shoppers (n=104)*
Respondent's Gender	Male	7	37	55
	Female	10	21	49
Respondent's Age	Less than 20 years	3	14	40
	Equal or More than 20 years	14	44	64
Respondent's Education	SSC	0	2	1
	HSC	0	5	5
	Bachelor's Degree	8	23	52
	Master's Degree	9	28	46
Respondent's Occupation	Self-employed	1	1	5
	Homemaker/Housewife	2	0	6
	Student	9	33	56
	Business	3	5	11
	Job/Service	2	19	26
Respondent's Monthly Income	Less than 25000	14	49	91
	Equal or More than 25000	3	9	13
Name of the mobile phone company primarily used	Samsung	10	25	40
	NOKIA	3	14	16
	Micromax	3	8	11
	HTC	1	5	8
	Others	0	6	29
Name of the service provider primarily used	Vodafone	8	17	50
	Airtel	0	9	14
	Docomo	2	7	9
	Idea	4	10	16
	BSNL	2	11	9
	Reliance	0	3	4
	Uninor	1	1	2
Frequency of Mobile Commerce Transactions in last 12 months	Once or twice	5	15	1
	3-5 times	8	6	2
	6-10 times	1	7	8
	more than 10 times	3	30	93
Services that would interest the most to use m-commerce	Information	7	40	67
	Financial	1	2	1
	Purchasing	4	7	4
	Location based	1	0	3
	Advertising	1	0	1
	Entertainment	3	9	28

m-commerce. Majority of them use Vodafone (48.07%) for m-commerce transactions. They usually seek information or entertainment via m-commerce.

Conclusion

The prolific usage of mobile devices and the growth in the mobile sales has opened an array of opportunities as far as payment and settlements are concerned. Following e-commerce and its success story, m-commerce has also paved its way to success. Hence, the current study investigates the factors which influence people in resorting to m-commerce transactions and further also segregates the consumers according to their characteristics.

The factors which erupted from the study which influence the usage of M-commerce were Attitude towards M-commerce, Perceived Benefits, Adventure, Perceived Risk and Idea. Further, three segments of M-commerce users were brought out from the study, which included Reserved Shoppers, Utilitarian Shoppers, and Assured Shoppers. Assured shoppers were the ones who were already using m-commerce and were contented with the same, utilitarian shoppers used m-commerce when they perceived it to be beneficial while reserved shoppers showed inhibitions in resorting to m-commerce.

All said and done, with the growth in smart phones and other mobile devices, the future of m-commerce is bright, provided the service providers convince the users that it is a safe, handy and cost-effective way of transacting in the modern era.

REFERENCES

Agarwal, R. and Prasad, J. (1998). "A conceptual and operational definition of personal innovativeness in the domain of information technology", *Information Systems Research*, 9(2): 204-15.

Altuna, O.K. and Konuk, F.A. (2009). "Understanding Consumer Attitudes Toward Mobile Advertising and Its Impact on Consumers' Behavioural Intentions: A Cross-Market Comparison of United States and Turkish Consumers", *International Journal of Mobile Marketing*, 4(2): 43-51.

Barnes, S.J. and Scornavacca, E. (2004). "Mobile Marketing: The Role of Permission and Acceptance", *International Journal of Mobile Communication*, 2(2):128-139.

Batra, Sunil (Dr.) and Dr. Neenu Juneja, (2013). "M-Commerce in India: Emerging Issues", *International Journal of Advanced Researching IT and Engineering*.

Bhatti, T. (2007). "Exploring Factors Influencing the Adoption of Mobile Commerce", *Journal of Internet Banking and Commerce*, Vol. 12, No. 3.

Chari, S., P. Kermani, S. Smith and L. Tassiulas, "Security Issues in M-Commerce: A usage-Based Taxonomy," In *E-Commerce Agents, Marketplace Solutions, Security Issues, and Supply and Demand*. London: Springer-Verlag, 2001, pp. 264-282.

Chen, Z., Lee, M. and Cheung, C. (2001). A Framework for Mobile Commerce. Proceedings of 7th Americas Conference on Information Systems conference (AMCIS), Boston, USA.

Clarke, I. (2001). "Emerging Value Propositions for M-Commerce". *Journal of Business Strategies*, 18(2): 133-149.

Dahlberg, T. et al., (2007). "Past, present and future of mobile payments research: A literature review", *Electronic Commerce Research* and *Applications* doi: 10.1016/j.elerap.2007.02.001

Dai, H., Palvia, P.C., (2009), "Mobile Commerce Adoption in China and the United States: A Cross-Cultural Study", *The DATA BASE for Advances in Information Systems*, 40(4): pp. 43-61.

Dholakia, N., Dholakia, R.R., Lehrer, M. and Kshetri, N. (2009). *Global Heterogeneity in the Emerging M-commerce Landscape*, University of Rhode Island, Kingston, RI.

Feng, H., Hoegler, T. and Stucky, W. (2006). Exploring the Critical Success Factors for Mobile Commerce. Paper presented at the International Conference on Mobile Business (ICMB'06), IEEE Computer Society.

Fraunholz, B. and Unnithan, C. (2004). "Critical Success Factors in Mobile Communications: A comparative roadmap for Germany and India", *International Journal of Mobile Communication*, 2(1): 87-101.

Friedrich, R., Grone, F., Holbling, K. and Peterson, M. (2009). "The March of Mobile Marketing: New Chances for Consumer Companies, New opportunities for Mobile operators", *Journal of Advertising Research*, 49(1), 54-61.

Gupta, Avdhesh, C.K. Jha, Arvind Shukla, (2012). "Impact of Trust towards M-commerce Service," *IOSR Journal,* Vol. 3, Issue 5.

ITU (1997). "World Telecommunication Development Report 1996-97: Trade in Telecommunications, International Telecommunications union, http://www.itu.int/plwebcgi/fastweb?getdoc+view1+www+27994+7++waiting%20time%20and%20teleph one.

Jahanshahi, A.A., Mirzaie, A., Asadollahi, A. (2011). "Mobile Commerce Beyond Electronic Commerce: Issue and Challenges", *Asian Journal of Business and Management Sciences*, 1(2): 119-129.

Jayawardhena, C. and Foley, P. (2000). Changes in the banking sector—the case of Internet banking in the UK. *Internet Research*, 10(1): 19-31.

Jih, W.J.K., S.F. Lee (2003). "An exploratory analysis of relationships between cellular phone uses' shopping motivators and life-style indicators", *Journal of Computer Information Systems* 44(2): 65–73.

Kungpisdan, S., B. Srinivasan and P.D. Le, "A secure account based mobile payment protocol," presented at Information Technology: Coding and Computing, 2004. Proceedings. ITCC 2004. International Conference on Volume: 1, April 5-7, 2004

Lee, Hyun-Hwa and Seung-Eun Lee, (May 2007), "Mobile Commerce: An Analysis of Key Success Factors". *Journal of Shopping Centre Research.*

Lewis, W., Agrawal, R. and Sambamurthy, V. (2003). "Sources of influence on beliefs about information technology use: An empirical study of knowledge workers", *MIS Quarterly*. 27(4): 657-679.

Mahatanankoon, P. and Vila-Ruiz, J. (2007). "Why Won't Consumers Adopt M Commerce? An Exploratory Study", *Journal of Internet Commerce*, Vol. 6(4).

Mahatanankoon, Pruthikrai, JoaquinVila-Ruiz (2007). "Why Won't Consumers Adopt M-Commerce? An Exploratory Study", *Journal of Internet Commerce*, Vol. 6(4).

Malloy, A.D., U. Varshney and A.P. Snow (2002). "Supporting mobile commerce applications using dependable wireless networks", *Mobile Networks and Applications* 7(3): 225–234.

Massoud, S. (2011). "M-Commerce: Any Time, Any Place, Any Where", *The Review of Business Information Systems*, Vol. 7, No. 3.

Massoud, S.L. and Gupta, O. (2003). "Consumer Perception and Attitude Toward Mobile Communications". Fort H Coming, *International Journal of Mobile Communications (IJMC)*.

Murphy, Samantha (2012, March 7). *Why Mobile Commerce Is on the Rise.* Retrieved from http://mashable.com/2012/03/07/mobile-Commerce outlook/

Okazaki, Shintaro, (2005), "New Perspectives on M-Commerce Research", *Journal of Electronic Commerce Research*, Vol. 6, No. 3.

Plavini, P. and Durgesh, P. (2011). Attitude towards Mobile Advertising: A Study of Indian consumers. Paper presented at the International Conference on Management, Economics and Social Sciences, (ICMESS'2011) Bangkok December, 2011.

Rettie, Ruth (2008). "Mobile phones as network capital: facilitating connections", *Mobilities*, 3(2): 291-311.

Sanjay, K.S. (2007). *The diffusion of mobile commerce in India*, Department of Humanities and Social Sciences, Indian Institute of Technology, Kanpur.

Sharma, D. (2009). *Government Policies and Regulations: Impact on Mobile Commerce in Indian Context*, Indian Broadcasting (Engineering) Services, Government of India.

Singh, Kanwalvir and Himanshu Aggarwal, (2013). "Critical Factors in Consumers Perception towards Mobile Commerce in E-Governance Implementation: An Indian Perspective", *International Journal of Engineering and Advanced Technology* (IJEAT).

Stafford, T. and Gillenson, M. (2009). "Mobile Commerce: What It Is and What It Could Be, "*Communications of the ACM*, December, 46(12): 33-34.

Summer University on IT in Agriculture and Rural Development–2007 Recen, Hungary, Adam Pentek-University of Debrecen "Payment methods in e commerce".

15

Reproduction of Marginality through Developmentalism

The Case of Tribal Population in Attappadi, Kerala

Nishamol, M. and *Rajesh, K.*

Introduction

Since 1950, Kerala has been passing through many radical changes as the reforms in education and land, universalization of public distribution system, enactment of minimum wages, expansion of public health system to all villages etc. The remarkable achievement of Human Development in the State is observed as the outcome of these reforms which have been implemented in the various stages of the evolution of Kerala State (Kannan in KDR, 2008). Notwithstanding the higher human development achievements of the general population, the indigenous communities such as Scheduled Caste, Scheduled Tribes and Fisher Folks are living under higher level of deprivation (Kerala Development Report 2008; Census 2011). This indicates the actual benefits of these changes have not been percolated to the marginalized population of the State. The Human Development Indicators of these groups are far lower than the average of mainstream communities in Kerala. Among these three groups, Scheduled Tribes are most vulnerable and facing extreme forms of deprivation.

In general, the term 'Poor' means that the people having income below the poverty line. But, a single dimensional parameter like income cannot be able to describe the intensity of poverty of a family. Poverty is closely linked with multi-dimensional parameters as poor health status, lack of sanitation, drinking water facilities, lack of education and lack of shelter (Sen, 1995). When we link poverty with indigeneity of tribal population, it can be seen that though the term 'tribe' is a common nomenclature, the deprivation rate among the tribal communities are different. In Kerala, tribal population have been facing various forms of deprivation as geographical deprivation, economic deprivation, social and cultural deprivation. These have been directly or indirectly affecting the capability formation of tribal communities in wealth distribution, employability and income generation.

The Central and State Ministries have been trying to reduce the deprivation rate among the tribal communities by executing various developmental and welfare schemes since 1974 under Tribal Sub Plan, for providing basic need and infrastructure facilities, capability formation through education and health support, implementing various projects and programmes for income generation through the expansion of livelihood activities in the tribal areas all over Kerala. Moreover, for the promotion of household or community-based tribal development programmes in the tribal concentrated areas, the Integrated Tribal Development Project (ITDP) was started in the state during the period 1974-83 (KSPB, 2012). Among seven ITDPs in Kerala, only Attappady ITDP in Palakkad district was formulated by the Central Government in 1976. Most of the tribal communities in the Palakkad district are generally considered as disadvantaged categories, especially, the tribal groups in Attappady. So, as the objective of sustainable development among the tribal communities or area development in Attappady, both governments implemented various projects as Attappady Valley Irrigation Projects, Attappady Farming Society, Attappady Goat Farm, Western Ghats Development Project and Attappady Wasteland Comprehensive Environmental Conservation Project (AWCECP) etc. (Annamalai, 2006). However, despite the large expenditure of governments on development projects, these could not make significant effect in the progress of socio-economic lives of tribes in Attappady. This might be happening due to the negligence of understanding the need of traditional societies in the project landmark and the imperfections in project planning, implementation and monitoring process. As an unintended consequence, many of these developmental programmes have created new social, cultural, economic and traditional issues in the tribal areas such as transition of tribal cultivators to wage labours, intrusion of settlers, alienation of tribal land etc. (KFRI, 1991). Along with this, it should be noticed the miserable condition of the health of the tribal people in Attappady. Despite the government has started a tribal hospital in Attappady, they have been facing lot of health issues as severe malnutrition, high infant mortality rate, underweight of children and paucity of basic health infrastructure facilities etc. (Suchithra, 2013).

In several projects in Attappady Block, AWCECP was one of the major government interventions among them, implemented by Attappady Hills Area Development Society (AHADS) in 1996. It was designed as a participatory development programme. The one of the major objectives were eco-restoration and sustainable livelihood development of tribal communities through the promotion of both agricultural and afforestation activities in the affected areas (KSPB, 2010). Nonetheless, they did not give much emphasis to the agricultural activities whereas more focus has been given on eco-restoration and afforestation activities. Their negligence in the area of agricultural sector made unintended impact on the sustainable livelihood activities of the tribal population. On the light of experience of AHADS, this paper argues that a celebrated project that used the language of participatory development will also lead to the deeper marginality of already marginalized group due to the erosion of their participation in real decision making at policy level. Based on certain questions we are trying to find out the effects of developmental initiatives of AHADS in Attappady.

1. To what extent AHADS supported the enhancement of socio-economic conditions of tribal communities in Attappady?
2. Did the tribal communities get real benefit from the livelihood activities of AHADS?
3. Had any trouble lie in between service delivery, planning and administration systems in the project areas?

Attappady Block: A Brief Description

Attappady is an extensive east slopping mountain valley on Western Ghat, about 745 sq. km. in area. It is located in the north of Palakkad district and adjoining with Coimbatore and Nilgiri districts of Tamil Nadu. Attappady Tribal Block was formed in 1962 under Mannarkad Taluk in Palakkad District. This block comprises three Panchayaths viz. Agali, Pudur and Sholayur. Bhavani and Siruvani rivers flow through the valley, irrigating the whole area. The climate of the Attappady is entirely different from other part of Palakkad, even it is varied from Agali to Sholayoor Panchayath (Annamalai, 2006; KFRI, 1991; Sanathanan, 2004). In 1975, as per the directions from the State Planning Board, the Central Government considered Attappady for starting Integrated Tribal Development Project (ITDP) due to the assessment of most vulnerable tribal block in Kerala. During the period 1930-1940, Attappady was 100 per cent tribal area. But, from the starting of 1950, the massive in-migration of people from the plains of western regions of Kerala and eastern low-lying part of Tamil Nadu has made drastic changes in the population dynamics of this area. Initially, the migration was provisional with the objective of work, business and commercial purposes and subsequently, migration became permanent and regular phenomenon (KFRI, 1991; Mathur, 1977; SPB, 2010).

Tribal Communities in Attappady

The tribal population in Attappady belongs to Irular, Mudugar and Kurumbar who are the broad categories of Dravidian tribes. These communities have been staying 192 tribal hamlets in Agali (73), Pudur (67) and Sholayoor (52) Gram Panchayaths (STDD, 2013). In accordance with the data of ITDP Attappady (2018), the total number of tribal families in the block is 11,016 which consists of Irular (9370), Mudugar (980) and Kurumbar (666). The total tribal population is 32,956 which includes Irular (26,908), Mudugar (3,497) and Kurumbar (2,551). The average family size of the total tribal population in Attappady is 2.9. Among them, Kurumbar shows highest family size as 3.83 and after that Mudugar (3.5) and Irular (2.87). The average literacy rate of the tribal population in Attappady is 62 per cent. Kurumbar community is showing highest literacy rate as 69.92 per cent and then followed by Irular (60 per cent) and Mudugar (56.36 per cent) communities. The decadal population rate of Attappady is given in Table 15.1.

Table 15.1: Population Growth in Attappady During the Period 1951-2011

Year	*Total Population*	*Tribal Population*	*Non-tribal Population*	*Percentage of Tribes*	*Percentage of non-tribes*
1951	11,300	10,200	1,100	90.27	9.73
1961	21,461	12,972	8,489	60.45	39.55
1971	39,183	16,536	22,647	42.21	57.79
1981	62,246	20,659	41,587	33.00	67.00
1991	62,033	24,228	37,745	39.15	60.85
2001	66,171	27,121	39,050	41.00	59.00
2011	64,318	27,627	36,691	42.95	57.05

Sources: Report from Kerala Forest Research Institute, Peechi (1991); Census of India 1981 to 2011.

Irular are dominant tribal population in Attappady who migrated from Coimbatore of Tamil Nadu state at the end of 16th century or the beginning of 17th century. They are patrilineal and patriarchal society, speaking the mixture of Tamil, Kannada and Malayalam languages. The name Irular derived from their pitch-black complexion. Traditionally, they are shifting cultivators and also engaged in hunting and gathering of non-timber forest produces. But, due to the overwhelming of land alienation, majority of the workforce in Irular community have been engaging in the agriculture labouring of settlers' land. Mudugas are the second largest tribal community in Attappady, migrated from Coimbatore. The name is originated from the primitive nature of carrying the children on their back (Muthuk). Historically, there was a relationship between Mudugar and Kurumbar communities. But later, Mudugas separated from Kurumbas and started to live as a separate clan. In earlier period, Mudugar engaged with shifting cultivation and collection of non-timber forest produces. But, nowadays, majority of them are agriculture labours of settled cultivators. Some of them are engaged in agriculture and allied activities. Kurumbar belongs to Primitive Tribal Group, the earliest inhabitants of Attappady, mainly constituted in Puthoor Panchayath. They have been living in Reserve and Vested forest lands. So, the land encroachment of migrants did not seriously affect the lives of Kurumbar families. Traditionally, Mudugar are shifting cultivators. Moreover, they experts in cattle rearing and collection of non-timber forest produces. They are speaking the mixture of Malayalam and Tamil. According to Mathur, Kurumbas were totally illiterate. But the recent reports show that the younger generation of Kurumbar community is most enthusiastic in organizing themselves and getting education (ITDP, 2019; Mathur, 1977; Sanathanan, 2004; STDD, 2013).

Relation between Land, Forest and Tribes in Attappady

Historically and genetically, there is a strong relationship between tribes and land as well as tribes and forest. It is mainly associated with their rituals and festivals, birth and death, livelihood activities, food gathering etc. Moreover, the ownership of sizable amount of land is the symbol their cultural identity and socio-economic status, especially the ownership of traditional land. Hence, the displacement or alienation of hereditary land will destroy their culture, lives and existence (Mathur, 1977; Therakam, 2010). Several studies show that there was huge amount of tribal land alienated in all over the state. According to Kerala Development Report 2008, 4219.85 acres of lands were alienated from the tribal community in the state during the period 1962-82 and the alienated land under dispute as on 30.6.1996 was 17971.12 acres in all over the state.

After 1950, as a consequence of the implementation of developmental projects without rationality and uncontrollable immigration of non-tribes to the tribal lands and their unscientific cultivation pattern in the valley of Attappady, the deforestation of forest land had been multiplied. Due to rampant deforestation, the natural mechanism of rain water conservation became failure, subsequently, the extension of soil erosion was highly increased in the hilly regions. Thus, soil erosion and the low after carrying capacity of the hills led to the drying of local streams. This seriously affected the agriculture-based economy of the tribes and settlers in Attappady (Annamalai, 2006). Though land degradation and marginalization are technically two different phenomena which are highly interlinked in the case of communities who depend on land for their livelihood. Deforestation, high influx of settlers to tribal lands and their unsuitable agricultural practices negatively affected the natural ecosystem of land use in Attappady which led to land degradation and marginalization of tribal communities in this region. (KFRI, 2010).

Tribal communities have their own social and economic practices which is entirely different from mainstream communities. The uncontrollable inland migration to the tribal land and the alienation of land negatively affected the socio-economic and cultural lives of tribal populations in Attappady. Several studies indicate lot of agriculture land of tribal communities were alienated due to rampant migration from Tamil Nadu and Travancore-Cochin to Attappady and their intrusion to land of aboriginals. Majority of the tribal families lost their cultivation because of land encroachment of immigrants. Gradually, they became wage labours of migrant cultivators and contractors of various developmental projects at cheap wage rates. Moreover, the influence of immigrants the traditional cultivation pattern in Attappady was totally changed and started cash crop cultivation without considering the geographical specialties of valley. This harmfully affected the structure of soil and also the nature of local economy in the block. Because of the intensive involvement of migrants, the peripheral economy has moved to cash economy. Moreover, they forcefully turned the tribal communities to the part of modern economy instead of their tribal economy. Subsequently, the lives of tribes became more miserable due to low wage rate, lack of livelihood activities and employment, degrading in social status, depletion of forest land etc. As a result, once self-sufficient tribal population, are now struggling for survival and depending the government authorities for the attainment of basic needs.

Attappady Hills Area Development Society (AHADS)

Attappady Wasteland Comprehensive Environmental Conservation Project (AWCECP) was one of the major projects executed in Attappady Block with the financial aid from the Japan Bank for International Co-operation (JBIC), renamed as Japan International Co-operation Agency (JICA). The project was started by the recommendation of National Wasteland Development Board (NWDB), because of Attappady having highest proportion of wasteland in Kerala when compared to other places. Due to the dwindling of forest areas, rampant degradation of natural resources and acute poverty among the tribal population, in 1993 the Government of Kerala decided to formulate an integrated sustainable eco-restoration project for the reclamation of 507 sq. km. wasteland in Attappady and also provide livelihood facilities to the local people especially to the tribal communities through participatory management of resources. The framework of the project was prepared by the Centre for Water Resources Development and Management (CWRDM) by getting the instruction from Kerala State Rural Development Department. The Project was submitted to the Department of Economic Affairs (DEA), Government of India with a request for loan assistance from the Overseas Economic Co-operation Fund (OECF), later renamed as Japan Bank for International Co-operation, now changed the name as Japan International Co-operation Agency (JICA). Actually, it was a bilateral agreement between JICA and Government of India. In January 1995, DEA short listed the Project for posing it to the OECF and making discussion with Central and State ministries. Subsequently, in October, 1995, the Government of Kerala took a decision to handover the project to an autonomous institution under the control of Local Self Government Department, naming Attappady Hills Area Development Society (AHADS), registered on 31st October 1995, under the Charitable Societies Registration Act, 1860. The project implementation process was started since 26th March, 1996 at the headquarters in Agali. Initially, the project was named as Integrated and Sustainable Eco-Development of Attappady Wastelands, later renamed as Attappady Wasteland Comprehensive Environmental Conservation

Project. The major objective of the project was "*Ecological restoration of degraded wasteland in Attappady and development of replicable models of participative eco-restoration, so as to prevent further degradation and to promote sustainable method of livelihood to the local people (with special emphasis of tribal population) in harmony with resource base*" (Annamalai, 2006; AHADS, 2008; KSPB, 2010).

In 2002, AHADS was restructured the objectives of AWCECP project after conducting a field survey, for the purpose of assessing the effectiveness of the entire developmental activities in Attappady. As the outcomes of field survey, they realized the attainment of the objective of participatory eco-restoration would not be possible without considering the basic issues of tribal population which is related to their poverty alleviation, livelihood activities, backwardness in education and health etc.

Strategies and Approaches in AWCECP of AHADS: A Review

For the effective implementation of AWCECP project, AHADS divided the 745 square km area of Attappady into 146 micro-watersheds. Among them, only 93 water sheds have the habitations and hence 93 Users' Association formulated in a democratic way based on 93 micro-watersheds. Subsequently, they started Ooru Vikasana Samithi for monitoring the developmental activities in the hamlets. Moreover, five Multi-disciplinary team constituted for the formulation and implementation of eco-restoration activities in a timely manner. Each team included the experts of various subjects like forestry, soil conservation, civil engineering, agriculture etc. Ecological Restoration, Soil and Water Conservation and Total Hamlet Development Programmes were the major activities implemented by AHADS with the support of community participation.

- AHADS implemented watershed based natural resource management system which includes soil and moisture conservation, gully plugging, planting and fencing etc. for the ecological restoration of Attappady. The expansion of tree plantation resulted to reduce the over flow of surface water, improved the quantity of subsurface water, rejuvenated the streams and rivulets etc. These also promoted the agriculture activities in the project areas. See Table 15.2.
- Soil and water conservation activities given re-birth to gullies

and rivulets in Attappady. The main purpose of the programme was to ensure the water availability in a sustained manner through the protection of existing water resources. It includes development of water resources, ground water recharging systems and irrigation systems etc.

- The rich people were major beneficiaries of the land developmental activities like water and soil conservation or afforestation, and at the same time, the tribes who were already expelled from their best lands, they could not be able to derive the benefits getting from the programmes undertaken through the Users' Association. For avoiding these issues, AHADS designed a new strategy for tribes as the part of their project, named as Total Hamlet Development Programme (THDP). In this programme, AHADS gave more priority to attain the basic needs and wants of the tribal communities through the construction of living space based on the family size, cost effective water supply and sanitation systems. In addition, they gave more emphasis on the facilities for the promotion of education, recreation and cultural activities. The main purpose of the programme was the empowerment of tribal communities in Attappady. But, based on the deprivation rate of the tribal families, they implemented this programme only in 54 tribal hamlets out of 192.

Table 15.2: Land Use Changes in Attappady from 2001-2005

Major Land Uses	*Land Use (Km^2)*		*Percentage Change in Land Use*
	2001	*2005*	
Forest land	386.84	401.32	+3.74
Agriculture land	119.55	164.04	+37.21
Degraded land	238.18	180.24	-24.33

Source: Kerala State Planning Board Report (2010).

People's Institution (PIs) is one of the methods for the innovative practices of transparent governance through grassroots level. This mainly focuses the area of assessment, planning, implementation and monitoring the developmental activities in a locality for its sustainable livelihood achievement and environmental protection. Local participation is essential for the protection and regeneration of natural resources (KSPB, 2010). In Attappady, AHADS started the project in the name of participatory programme and followed People Institution's strategy for their project implementation process. They constituted a range of organizations of the local people for executing various activities of the project for the successful attainment of its objectives. The organizations are, User's Association (UA) as the workforce under AHADS for doing contract works, focusing the expansion of basic need and infrastructure facilities etc.; Ooru Vikasana Samithi (OVS) formed for the prevention of land alienation, monitoring of developmental activities in the hamlets etc.; Joint Forest Management Committees (JFMC) established for the protection of forest land and prevention of land degradation and alienation; Income Generation Activity Groups (IGAG) under UAs framed for the promotion of income generated livelihood activities in the project area through micro credit system; finally, Thaikula Sangams (TKSs) formed for the empowerment of women among the downtrodden families through the intensive intervention of fight against alcoholism, drugs and atrocities against women, education and health assistance etc. AHADS made new rules and regulations for the effective functions and controlling of these groups and they also provided financial assistance and technical guidelines for the proper functioning of these associations as a part of project objectives.

The Attappady Wasteland Comprehensive Environmental Conservation project mainly focused area-based development programmes than the community development programmes. So, the entire population in the project area was engaged in the developmental activities. The objectives and initiatives of AWCECP project was attractive and at a limit they successfully implemented the project plans and programmes. However, AHADS could not success in the reduction of poverty among the deprived communities in Attappady because of the negligence in the forecasting of long-term sustainability of project outcomes, failure in policy frame work and execution of programmes and lack of initiative for finding permanent solution for livelihood issues of tribal population. Moreover, AHADS failed to find out the ways for the long-term existence of the several collectives of people started at the time of project period. During the running period of project, people get the regular income from the labouring work of AHADS and the local economy was aroused. But everything was collapsed after closing the project of AHADS, especially, the lives of tribal families who were working as labourers in the project for livelihood, became more miserable. Here, we attempt to explore the reasons behind the reproduction of marginality among the tribal population in Attappady after winding up of AHADS.

Discourses on Development

The word 'development' is an ever-contested nomenclature which is used in different dimensions. There are two major approaches on development. One follows the Top to Bottom process of development and the other is from Bottom to Top. The Centralized Planning is another term for Top to Bottom approach, which is largely the replication of Soviet Model of Development. Jawaharlal Nehru, the ardent follower of socialist planning in Soviet Union, introduced this system in India. In this model, the decisions on development policies, programmes and schemes are framed by Top Level Authority (policy-makers) and implemented through the hierarchical bureaucratic system. In this approach, people, the real beneficiaries of developmental programmes are not getting the chance for expressing their ideas, telling about their actual needs or wants and also to participate in the decision-making process (Isaac and Franke, 2000). The other one is Bottom to Top approach, which largely follows the path of participatory development. Here, the developmental goals and programmes are decided by the people themselves and they would have larger participation in implementing these programmes (Parameswaran, 1999). Even in the case of decentralized mode of development planning, there are different approaches used by different development agencies i.e. devolution, delegation and de-concentration (Gurukkal, 2001).

De-concentration refers to transfer the administrative responsibility for specified functions to the lower levels of Central Government bureaucracy based on certain positions in general (Ferguson and Chandrasekharan, 2011). It does not allow the autonomy of local people in the framing of programmes at bottom level. Here, the major decisions are taken at the Central Level and delegate the power to Bottom level only for the implementation of programmes rather than the decision making. Participatory bodies are framed at lower levels which are considered as a tool of programme implementation (Heller, 2001). In the case of **delegation**, Central Level authority delegates certain responsibilities to the lower level for the effective implementation of programmes. Supremacy of authority may not co-exist with the delegation of powers and resources, which are the indispensable factors for effective development process. The third way of decentralization is **devolution**. In this method powers, responsibilities, and resources are devolved to the lower level which provides higher level of autonomy to the lowest tiers for planning and implementation of programmes. This recognises the concept of autonomy and provides prominent space to the local people and communities in the planning process of developmental activities (Isaac and Franke, 2000). Development process is also equated with Freedom in the literature authored by Amartya Sen. He explained development as the process of improving the capabilities of individuals and communities (Sen, 1995).

The AHADS project in Attappady largely followed the path of de-concentration method in the process of planning of developmental activities. Because of the objectives and activities were pre-designed by the international consultants and higher-level officials without making any discussion with the beneficiaries and considering the actual situation and demand of the local areas. The public got a participatory role in the designing of certain programme at local level under User's Association, Ooru Vikasana Samithi (Hamlet Development Committee) and Joint Forest Management Committees; but actually, they performed the major roles in the implementation process as supervisors, wage labourers etc. This indicates the good instances that how a project can alienate the local people from its process through instrumental approach even though it uses the language of participation. In the case of regions like Attappady where the tribal concentration is high, the development approach of devolution is more significant. This approach can provide more administrative power to the local people on decision making and implementation and can avail more control on assets and right on resource that can ensure more autonomy to the local people for the implementation of programmes based on their requirements. This kind of an approach of devolution and autonomy was missing in AHADS project.

Lacunae in AWCECP of AHADS

Unlike the other tribal areas in Kerala, majority of the tribes in Attappady holds their own agriculture land in a reasonable size, even though lot of tribal land has been encroached by immigrants. But, AHADS did not promote the agricultural activities in the tribal land and their negligence in the area of the agricultural activities made unintended impact on the sustainable livelihood of the tribal population. Correspondingly, they largely used tribal population only as labour force for the implementation of their projects; particularly afforestation and construction activities. Because of the continuous availability of wage labouring, tribes lost their interest in agricultural activities and finally their lands became barren in nature. And also, the shifting of job pattern from cultivator to labourer also affected their food culture and nutritional intake. The tribal people in Attappady who had a good cattle population sold most of them because of the wage labour culture inculcated among them. AHADS authorities also promoted tribes in selling cattle in the name of destruction of saplings planted as the part of afforestation activities. Agriculture destruction along with the loss of cattle population seriously affected their nutritional intake.

Majority of the productive land of tribal families in irrigated areas such as riverside have been occupied by the settlers in 1960s and 70s. They got the ownership over this land from tribes through various forms of exploitations such as preparation of pseudo-documents, paying nominal price, providing liquor to the tribal leaders etc. And also, most of their remaining agriculture land situates in the hilltops whereas irrigation facilities not available. It was negatively affected their farming culture and socio-economic status. This has created the necessity of good lift irrigation schemes to provide irrigation to the tribal land, whereas such efforts were missing in the AHADS project. There was no focus from the AHADS project to provide institutional support for undertaking agriculture activities such as distribution of seeds and seed links, organizing institutional credit, and making facilitations for the agricultural activities. Since agriculture and animal husbandry were the major livelihood sources of the tribal communities in the region, neglect of AHADS project in supporting these activities in long-term perspective contributed to the decline of their self-reliant livelihood sources. The limitations of the AHADS project in the agricultural and land development activities in the land of tribal people acted as a hurdle in bringing the investments for the expansion of irrigation and soil conservation activities in tribal land. This has indirectly made advantages to the settlers to take the tribal lands on lease and to do their own agricultural activities.

AHADS has mentioned in their document that the major objective of the AWCECP project was only eco-restoration through afforestation and soil conservation, not the agricultural development with livelihood focus. This shows the fault in the project design itself. While the objective of the AHADS projects has been formulated, the actual livelihood situation of the tribal people and their historical modes of livelihood have not been taken in to consideration. Thus, it has led to the formation of a project with eco-restoration as a major objective in an area where the primary livelihood of the people derives out of agriculture and animal husbandry. Instead of this project, the eco restoration could be done through the agricultural rejuvenation was the real need and suitable approach to this region.

The above lacunae underscore the bureaucratic centred approach in the evolution of this project even though it adopts participatory practices at the time of implementation. Unlike the other government project AHADS projects largely relied on people's organizations for its implementation, whereas the formulation of the project objectives was centrally decided by the funding agencies and higher officials. The basic fault occurred in the designing of the project in accordance with the real need of the tribal people made unintended impacts in the life of the tribal people even after its implementation. The withdrawal of the project literally affected the income source of the tribes, whereas they could not go back to the own production system from which they have been alienated for more than a decade. This could be taken as an interesting example that how a development project can uproot the people from their self-reliant livelihood pattern to a highly dependent community on wage labour offered by the development.

This could be seen as a replication of a colonial development strategy which alienates the colonialized people from their self-reliant living processes in order to create a colonial mind among them. Alienation from agricultural activity and own food production system which was largely depended on cereals and pulses, has badly affected the food intake and nutritional status of the tribal people. In a way, this also has contributed to the higher rate of malnutrition, particularly, among women and children who have intensively faced the contemporary phenomena of infant deaths in tribal colonies. AWCECP indicates that a project need not be participatory in its origin and process, even though it uses the language of participation and it has been implemented through participatory institutions and structures. A participatory project will also be a failure, in addressing felt need of the people unless and until its objectives are set through participatory exercises.

In 2010, the project was closed and which negatively affected the lives of tribes who were totally depended on the works of AHADS as a community who lost self-reliant culture through the continuous offering of wage labour for years. Their socio-economic pattern has been totally changed even their purchasing power moved downward and the financial conditions of the families directly influence the food intake. All these factors lead to the reduction of self-reliance of tribal community and make their situation more deprived. Thus, the Aboriginal people lost the dominance they had in their local economy. While we analyzing the experience of AHADS project, it is worth mentioning that they did not have a well-designed exit policy which could have ensured the sustainable livelihood of the tribes who engaged in the project activities. This in turn could also have contributed to the increase in the deprivation rate among the tribal labours in AHADS. Even though AHADS project is not the sole reason for the continuing tribal deprivation in Attappady it has directly and indirectly contributed to the stagnation of the social mobility of the tribal population in the region.

Conclusion

In records, Attappady is a tribal block and the only one ITDP in the state established by the Central Ministry. After the implementation of Tribal Sub Plan in 1974, the Central and State Ministries have been introduced various tribal development activities in all over the tribal regions in India. As the part of those developmental programmes, various government institutions have implemented many projects in Attappady. But, the performance of some projects was totally disappointed due to the failure of attaining the real goal of the tasks. The evaluation studies of various projects indicating that the presence of nepotism and mismanagement in the fund allocation and project implementation processes; the execution of projects and programmes are not based on the necessity of ground reality; lack of monitoring and social auditing process in the project areas; centralized decision-makers are not considering the actual needs and demands of local communities when they are constructing the policy framework of projects; and formation of the nexus of vested interest groups i.e. officials, political parties, contractors and powerful immigrants etc. The major reasons for the formation of nexus are the information asymmetry among tribes, lack of awareness about the tribal development programmes and their rights, socio-economic and educational backwardness, lack of negotiation potential and the exploitation of settlers etc. Some of these reasons might be influenced the government for receding the interventions without achieving the genuine objectives of tribal developmental activities in Attappady.

Participatory approach of AHADS was successful in the areas of avoiding the nexus between vested interest groups and delivering manual works to the people with reasonable wage rate. Within that project period, the lifestyle of the people changed a lot and they purchased furniture and electronic items to the home, preferred hotel foods and increasing their social involvement and knowledge regarding various developmental activities etc. While we use the analytical framework of capability, it could be noted that the AHADS project assisted the tribal population to develop their capabilities in terms of engaging and negotiating with public. At the same time, to an extent it has failed in developing the sustainable livelihood and capability formation of tribal communities in terms of income generation.

After the completion of the project duration, the means of livelihood of tribal population have ceased and then the people became unemployed and their agriculture land became barren. Their cattle had already been forfeited to work at AHADS. Subsequently, they moved to unabatable deprivation. The major drawbacks of AHADS project implementation process are; the participatory forums of tribes were framed by AHADS only for manual works and not for the decision-making process of the activities in tribal hamlets through that they avoided grassroots problems, in this case they followed de-concentration approach; and also they could not focus the long-term livelihood activities and sustainable development of the vulnerable communities in Attappady. It emphasises that most of the projects funded by the international agencies in the third world countries are implemented with the prefixed objectives without considering the ground reality or neglecting the real need of the people.

REFERENCES

Annamalai, V. (2005). *Restoration of commons through Peoples Institutions: Study on the process and impact of the Attappady Wasteland Comprehensive Environmental Conservation project in Kerala*, India. Centre for Water and Land Management (CWLM). Retrieved from https://dlc.dlib.indiana.edu/dlc/bitstream/handle/10535/2304/Annamalai_ V.pdf?sequence=1

Attappady Hills Area Development Society (2008). Status report on *Attappady Wasteland Comprehensive Environmental Conservation Project, Attappady, Palakkad District*. Kerala, India: AHADS. Retrieved from http://www.globalrestorationnetwork.org/uploads/files/CaseStudy Attachments/249_attappady3.pdf.

Ferguson, I. and Chandrasekharan, C. (October 2011). Paths and Pitfalls of Decentralisation for sustainable Forest Management: Experiences of Asia-Pacific Region. *Conference Paper*, International Tropical Timber Organisation. Retrieved from https://www.researchgate.net/publication/241752581

Government of India, Planning Commission (Niti Aayog). (2008). *Kerala Development Report*.

Government of India, Census of India. (1981-2011). *Census Reports 1981-2011*.

Government of Kerala, State Planning Board. (October 2010). *A Report on Socio-economic Impacts of AHADS in Attappady: A Quick Evaluation Study*. https://www.scribd.com/document/237257046/GOK-Socio-Economic-Impact-of-AHADS-in-Attappady-A-Quick-Evaluation-Study-2010.

Government of Kerala, Directorate of Scheduled Tribe Development Departments.

(November 2013). *Report on the socio-economic status of scheduled tribes in Kerala.* http://www.stdd.kerala.gov.in/sites/default/files/inline-files/surveyd_2008.pdf

Government of Kerala, State Planning Board. (August 2012). *Working Group Report on Scheduled Tribe Development (XII Five Year Plan).*

Government of Kerala, Kerala Forest Research Institute. (March 1991). *Studies on Human Ecology and Eco-Restoration of Attappady Valley.*

Government of Kerala, Integrated Tribal Development Project, Attappady. (March 2018). *Statistical Data on Tribal Communities in Attappady.* Retrieved from https://itdpattappady.kerala.gov.in/2018/03/21/attapady-profile/

Gurukkal, R. (2001). "When coalition of conflicting interests decentralizes: A theoretical critique of decentralization politics in Kerala", *Social Scientist,* 29(9): 8-47.

Heller, P. (2001). Moving the state: The politics of democratic decentralization in Kerala, South Africa and Porto Alegra. *Politics and Society*, 29(1): 31-163.

Isaac, T.M.T. and Franke, R.W. (2002). *Local Democracy and Development: The Kerala People's Campaign for Decentralized Planning*. Lanham, Maryland, USA: Rowman & Littlefield.

Mathur, P.R.G. (1977). *Tribal Situation in Kerala* (1st ed.). Thiruvananthapuram, Kerala, India: Kerala Historical Society.

Parameswaran, M.P. (1999). *Vikendreekritha Janadhipathyam Keralathil: 1958–98* [*Democratic decentralization in Kerala: 1958-98: Malayalam*]. Kozhikkod, Kerala, India: Kerala Sasthra Sahithya Parishath.

Sen, A. (1995). *Inequality Re-examined* (13th ed.). New Delhi, India: Oxford.

Suchithra, M. (2015, July 4). Criminal neglect takes toll on Attappady tribes, studies find. *Down To Earth*. Retrieved from https://www.down-toearth.org.in/news/criminal-neglect-takes-toll-on-attappady-tribes-41569

Therakam, T.J. (2010). Adivasi Rights Violations. *Conference Papers of Paniya Sadas,* 27-45.

Velluva, S. (2004). *Developmental effects on Livelihood Strategies of Tribal people in Attappady, Kerala*. Centre for Development Studies. Thiruvananthapuram, Kerala, India: Kerala Research Programme on Local Level Development.

16

Location of Democracy and Governance in India with Special Reference to Participation among the Tribals in the Plain Areas of West Bengal

Case Studies of Kanksa and Jamalpur Blocks in the District of Burdwan, West Bengal

Ayub Mallik

Democracy is a balance between consent and control, a crystal of rules and laws binding on all. It is the on-going responsiveness on the part of the Government to the choices of its citizens politically equal. Considered as political equals they have to formulate choices, to signify them in terms of individual and collective actions and to take into action their choices weighted equally by the government. Vernon Bogdanor (1985) points out four main roles of the parliamentarians: constituency role, partisan role, role as protector of interests and scrutiniser of legislation (Bogdanor 1985, p. 5). In democracy the party which wins the electoral battle rules the territory, i.e. the majority rules over the minority. Mill propounded the thesis that the minority should be represented by a minority. 'Therefore, the logic of Mill's democratic principle of minority representation by the minority would take us to the position where they should be encouraged to form political parties or political pressure groups in a system of competitive politics' (Chaudhury 1985, p. 959). So, the democratic political process and liberal political structure should not be suffered from narrow and unqualified equilibrium of dominant interest groups saturated in sectarian politics. In plural society the general tendency of the majority community is to denigrate and suppress the interests of the minority community. So, an open system with proper and adequate minority representation in the legislative assembly, political and other rights, a system of rule of law and actual voices and choices of the minority, and democracy rather than party-cracy--all are necessary equipment and technologies of parliamentary democratic set-up to be meaningful. In democracy people and all parties concerned have to be operated for the well-being of the public. 'Democracy would be endangered if people concerned are not careful in this regard' (Prakasa 1957, p. 17). Electoral mechanisms are the necessary ways and means through which consent and representation can be translated into reality (Bogdanor and Butler 1983, p. 1).

Democracy needs competitive polity, where each party contests for political power and conflict between various interests are institutionalized, as Dahrendorf has said, through 'imperatively co-ordinated association' (Dahrendorf 1959, p. 242) and various groups suggest alternative policy approach and mobilize public support for their own positions. Myron Weiner an Joseph La Palombara in this connection point out that partics in a democracy are organizations involved in both the expression and the management of conflict (La Plombara and Weiner 1966, p. 399). In response to the demands for greater participation government or so to say party government may follow either repression measures or accommodation measures: mobilization, limited admission, full admission etc. Therefore,

(a) threat to elite dominance and elite's interests and values repression to demands for greater participation;
(b) conflict between elite values and interests *vis-à-vis* values and interests made by other groups demanding greater participation = repression;
(c) reluctance on the part of the party government to share power with other groups = repression.

If this happens, then party government becomes un-parliamentary and prejudiced to dictatorship. When the party government institutionalizes the alienation of the groups demanding greater participation, but gives certain rights to organize public opinion, then there is no attachment to democratic principles. The party government may allow full admission into the party system when they are either ideologically oriented or electorally motivated and there is attachment to democracy and legitimacy.

In competitive party system, the parties in competition have rested largely on democratic values: one man, one vote and one value, freedom and equality and the principles: from governing to criticism and from criticism to governing that may strengthen national integration by holding national and common interests instead of parochial and segmental one. In competitive parliamentary system 'one way of coping with social diversity is to use forceful means to suppress and eradicate it, another is to search out institutional arrangement that will encourage dialogue, unblock communication channels, keep political and government leaders on their toes, facilitate the articulation and aggregation of conflicting interests and in these ways create a sense of political efficacy while building national unity out of ethnic diversity' (La Palombara and Weiner 1966, p. 418). Hence, parties are instruments of political development when speaking about the impact of parties on greater participation, legitimacy and national integration.

The system of interaction between party and parliamentarism or so to say the system of parliamentary democracy is an open one under continuous changes in the input of matter and output of energy (Fig. 16.1). Unlike the equilibrium state in a closed system, an open system may reach a time-independent steady state in which all macroscopic quantities, for example, socio-economic infrastructure may remain unchanged and all microscopic processes of input of voting and power transmission from one party to another, diffusion and operation and output of institutions and operations of parliamentary government, rights and freedom of the individuals and organizations go on continuously. In such a time-independent steady state the actual concentration of power in an interpenetrative system of party and parliamentarism is equal to zero, *i.e.* not changing in condition and quantity, when and where $\frac{dQi}{dt} = 0$, t (time) $\neq 0$, Q_i = a characteristic (actual power concentration) of element I of the interpenetrative system. As society is an organism and organisms are open systems, then they are capable of performing work for long time even in a steady state under continuous inflow of political socialization and recruitment, interest articulation and aggregation and political communication, and outflow of rule-making, rule-application and rule-adjudication. In such a system a steady state may remain under continuous inflow of matters, i.e. input variables and output of energy, *i.e.* output variables (Fig. 16.1). But, during the process of change from inflow to outflow and from outflow to inflow through feedback, $\frac{dQi}{dt} \neq 0$, t (time) $\neq 0$. Party system in parliamentary democracy in relation with parliamentarism is an open system, where input variables, output variables, variables of infrastructural positions and conditions and values are in constant interaction with each of the variables causing transmission and appearance of power. Here,

1. input variables, for example, are political socialization and recruitment, interest articulation, interest aggregation and political communication;
2. output variables, for example, are rule making, rule application and rule adjudication;
3. infrastructural variables, for example, are economic development, urbanization, spread of education, capitalist economy, open class system, equalitarian value system, participation in voluntary organizations etc.; and
4. values, for example, are representation, participation, consent ad control, rights and freedom, equality and justice.

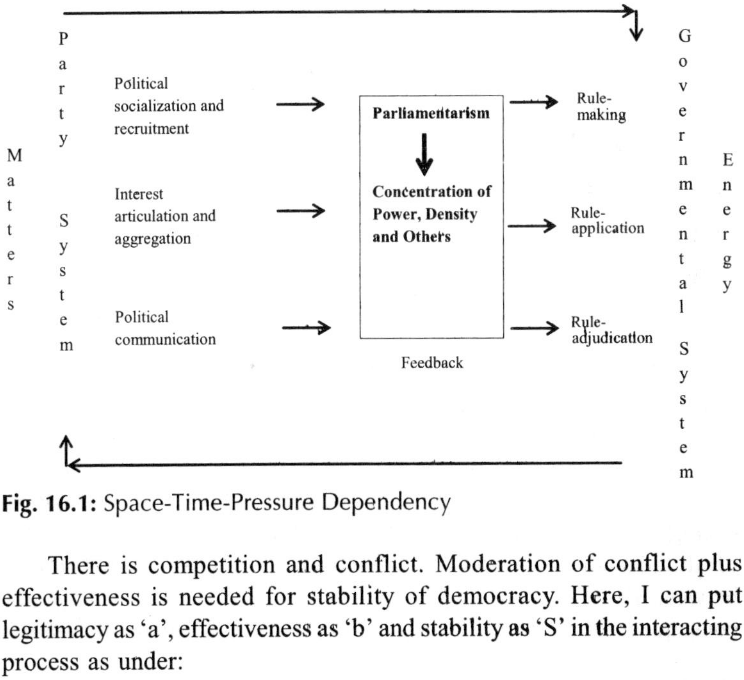

Fig. 16.1: Space-Time-Pressure Dependency

There is competition and conflict. Moderation of conflict plus effectiveness is needed for stability of democracy. Here, I can put legitimacy as ‘a’, effectiveness as ‘b’ and stability as ‘S’ in the interacting process as under:

$$
\begin{aligned}
(+a)+(+b) &= 2S = \text{Highly democratic}\\
(+a)+(-b) &= S = \text{Democratic}\\
(-a)+(+b) &= \text{Reasonably effective, but not democratic}\\
(-a)+(-b) &= \text{Undemocratic}
\end{aligned}
$$

Therefore, parliamentarism is best suited in the first category of highly democratic state with stability and to some extent to the second category as per with the rule that a highly effective but illegitimate government is more unstable than a regime having relatively low effectiveness, but ranging high in legitimacy. The process of democratic stability is continuous, i.e. variables are related with their immediate predecessors, for example, party system, electoral system, representation, responsiveness, legitimacy and effectiveness. They are related with each other. The democratic process is continuous. Here, I can generalize the process of democratic stability as such–

$$DS = P\{(L_n+E_n)\text{£}S_n\}, [L_1, L_2, \ldots L_n; E_1, E_2, \ldots E_n; S_1, S_2, \ldots S_n] \ldots \quad (1)$$

$$DC = P\{(L_n+E_n)\text{£}C_n\}, [L_1, L_2, \ldots L_n; E_1, E_2, \ldots E_n; S_1, S_2, \ldots S_n] \ldots \quad (2)$$

$$D = P(DS+DC) \quad \ldots(3)$$

Here, DS = Total process of democratic stability with regard to significance.

P = Probability of happenings
L_n = nth index of legitimacy
E_n = nth index of effectiveness
S = Total democratic process with regard to significance
S_n = nth index of democratic process with regard to significance
C = Total democratic process with regard to significance
C_n = nth index of democratic process with regard to significance.

A party system with left-right division may go through radical changes, progress and stability if there is composition and decomposition of attitudes and behaviour of individual party units, interpenetration between party and parliamentarism, probability of social change and consequent relative equilibrium position. Then, the system remains in a steady state, when $\frac{dQi}{dt} = 0$, t (time) $\neq 0$. If L is a set of leftism and R becomes a set of rightism, and X is equal to relative equilibrium position when L intersects R, then

$$L \cap R, X \in L, X \in R$$

Here, progress (P), stability (S) and social change (C) are mutually exclusive, exhaustive and equally likely and depend upon the composition and disposition and relative prevalence (abcd) of four dispositions: liberalism (A), conservatism (B), reactionism (C) and radicalism (D).

Democracy is a form of government, a set of values and a system of attitudes and interests of both the people in general and parties or groups in particular. Joseph Schumpeter in his book, *Capitalism, Socialism and Democracy* has said that democracy is a procedural system, an institutional arrangement for arriving at political decisions in which individuals acquire the power to decide by mean of a competitive struggle for the people's vote which may or may not produce social or economic justice. The competitive character of democracy makes democracy meaningful (Lenthold, 1968, p. 1). Political campaign is the mechanism or process of using political resources, such as power and securing of votes, party leadership and organization, the issues and money by which attitudes of the public and various groups, such as labour unions, farmer's union, business groups are moulded. In fact, 'it will be a mistake to think that election campaigns have suddenly taken a market character only in recent years. Campaigning has always had a marketing character' (Sarwate 1990, p. 11). Political marketing is a process of management involving analysis of marketing chances and opportunities (political and economic), planning of political or marketing resources, implementation of decisions or marketing policies, identifying and converting people's needs and desires, i.e. target markets and control over marketing or political performance by securing highest votes against the competitors. Therefore, the success or failure of a candidate depends upon the ability of the parties to mobilize the voters, who prefer one issue or other within the n-dimensional policy boundary, where $n \geq 2$. After winning the election and forming government, majority should respect minority opinion, minority interests should not be immersed thoroughly into the majority community's interests causing laboured breathing and fixed into a wooden framework of immolation leaving only a sacrificial death. The representative should at after the desires and interests of effective majority of his constituency and desires and interests of the nation of 'on effective majority of it' (Pickles, 1970, p. 118). In fact, representation of interests is an agglomeration of both majority and minority interests. The sweep of social change has produced a resultant impatient body structure in a party system which needs patience (Rubin 1976, p. 181). If it is difficult for political elites to cope with the growing new demands (inputs) of various social groups and high expectations of outputs, then democracy will suffer from difficulties and instabilities and succumb to disaggregating pressures. Several conditions to be fulfilled to become democratic–the structure and functioning of political institution and system, their capacity to response to the changing conditions of time and needs and solve overwhelming social problems, the nature of interests represented or unrepresented and conciliation of conflicting interests, nature of distribution of benefit and influence among them, and lastly, the stability of regime with high in legitimacy and effectiveness, or at least highly legitimate and less effective regime.

Political parties must educate the people about the rules and norms without which the system just cannot function, and the need to abide by these. Party or parties formulate policies, mobilize public support in favour of their policy opinions, motivate their interests and 'ask them to vote their nominees who seek entry into the portals of legislature some as winners and others as runners…' (Mital 1972, p. 80). In essence, 'Everyone has to abide by some rules… . The rules and institutions by which a democratic society has to abide are not the ones which will guarantee that a particular individual will always get what he deserves or even needs; they are rules as Professor Hayek would say, which when generally obeyed will enable all members of the group to more effectively strive to attain their changing goals' (Shourie, 1990, p. 21).

The constitutionalization of politics is most important for a democratic society. It depends upon two inversely related conditions: responsible opposition, proliferation of parties and party inducements plus institutionalization. Therefore, $C = (R \times P_n) + I$, where C refers to constitutionalization, R refers to responsibility of party or parties. 'A fundamental condition for the existence of "polity" is the existence of conflicts; a fundamental condition for the stability of such regimes is the legitimization of conflict (usually, but not always, in the form of party competition); and a useful and common device for this legitimization (common but by no means universal) is the institutionalizing within the parliament or assembly of public opposition to the government of the day' (Dahl, 1971, p. 8). In fact, the essentials of a parliamentary democracy are institutionalization of conflicts or conflicting interests, expression of those interests for orderly management of society, constructive criticism over the policies and programmes of the government, improvement of the performance of the government by criticism over omissions and commissions, and injustices of the past performances of government and enlightenment of the public through widespread publicity and demonstration in a disciplined manner. 'The democratic approach is persuasion, argument, debate and collective decisions' (Bhardwaj, 1983, p. 29).

Democracy equates development, economic growth, human freedom and desired goals. Democracy is also equated with capital accumulation and industrialization. '...it is a multifaceted process embracing industrialization, equitable distribution of societal goods, and democracy...there is no freedom without democracy. At a minimum, democracy consists in the accountability of the governing authority to the people at large; in a more substantive vein, it includes the right of participation in the making of decisions that are authoritatively binding on collectivity. Capitalism can in principle be compatible with both industrialization and democracy. To be sure, capitalist democracy fails fully to guarantee freedom; for, in defining as non-political key structures and institutions of economic power, it places them arbitrarily beyond the reach of democratic norms and, thereby, enables them to go on functioning as mechanisms of domination, exploitation, and accumulation of class privilege. Nevertheless, late-capitalist democracy provides institutionally for some political control of economic life; the right of political association, meanwhile, allows elements of the subordinate classes to acquire autochthonously a capacity for self-definition and pursuit of their class interests' (Becker, 1984, pp. 411-413). Late capitalist democracy (1) provides institutionally some political control of economic life, (2) provides the right of political participation and association, (3) allows the subordinate classes to acquire capacity or capacities for self-definition and pursuit of class interests, (4) allows distributional equity in order to gain social peace and stability, and (5) accommodates most urgent demands of the lower classes, but not all the demands put forwarded. Figure 16.2 explains the processes of democracy and development.

. Democratic Scenario in India: An Overview

In a party-democratic society like India organizational decline within the Congress party (the so-called democratic nation builder) and the so many power disputed within that have much more contributed to the de-stabilization of the established pattern of local authority in association

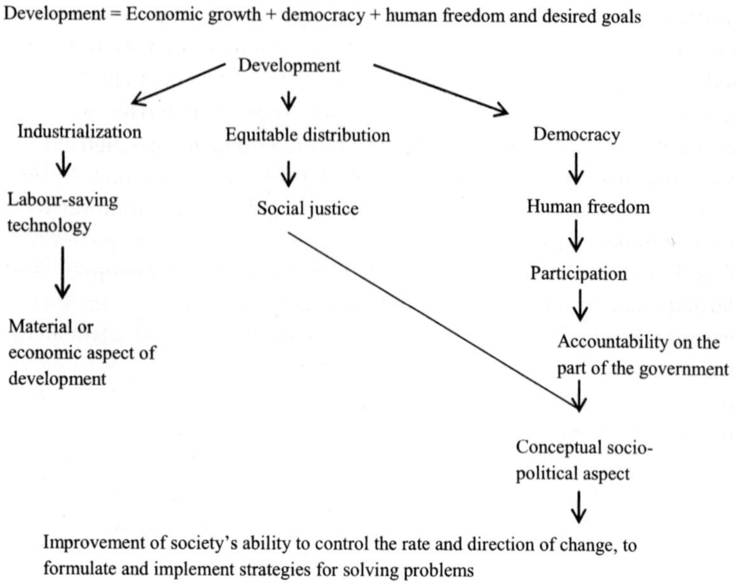

Fig. 16.2

with the local level governance of democracy. The spirit here is participatory democracy. 'The institutional vacuum in the periphery vacuum in the periphery, in turn, helps explain a number of political trends, including coalitional instability and substantial fluctuations in the "political mood" and thus in electoral outcomes, ineffective local government, and the emergence of personal rule, often with ruffians as de facto local leaders' (Kohli 1992, p. 15). The fluctuation in the political moods of the leaders, the so-called elites help to intensify democratic coalition, participatory governance, proliferation of personal rule, local leaders' rough and tough methods of mobilization and promotion of personal local parallel administration. This is not suited to our democratic spirit in the preamble of our Constitution–secular, socialist, democratic and republic. Institutionalization, following Huntington (1968) refers to the process by which organizations and procedures acquire value and stability within the levels of adaptability, complexity, autonomy and coherence. Four interrelated factors contributing to the decline of institutionalization, democracy and governability are: the changing role of political elite, weak and ineffective political organizations, mobilization of previously passive groups for electoral competition and growing conflict between contending social groups, such as haves and have-nots, privileged and under-privileged. Deinstitutionalization, centralization and personalization of power have contributed significantly to the growing problems of governability during the Congress era. Secularism, socialism and democracy lost credibility. During 1980s, Hindu majoritarian politics was great regional challenge to the Central Congress regime. Central Congress regime became implicit to religiously based majoritarianism to party regional threats. In 1991 Congress government came to power with New Economic Policy under the leadership of P.V. Narasimha Rao. Participatory development lost its importance. Democracy also lost its ground. The institutions of democracy and development failed under the pressure of de-institutionalization. 'The political cost of pursuing a lopsided reform process, which contributed to the defeat of the Congress in the 1996 elections, appear to be enabling the long forgotten intrinsic values of development to re-enter the discourse' (Bose and Jalal, 1998, p. 229). The intrinsic values of development have been cited in Figure 16.2 in the first part. Amartya Sen and Jean Dreze have made a powerful case for Indian development debate beyond liberalization to focus on expanding social and economic opportunities. 'But the failed institutions of state have yet to be imaginatively fashioned. On the one hand the privileged but besieged defenders of the centralized monolith have resorted to the dangerous course of a bigoted religious majoritarianism propagated by the Bharatiya Janata Party and its allies and followers. On the other, the new populism of the first 1996 United Front government in New Delhi led by H.D. Deve Gowda and then by I.K. Gujral, of which several regional and left-wing parties are members, has displayed deep taints of localism and agrarianism with a rich-farmer bias while proclaiming solidarity with the poor and disadvantaged majority. The successful realization of the idioms of equitable development requires the appropriate instruments, both economic and political, which are yet to be carefully crafted' (Bose and Jalal, 1998, pp. 229-230). India's formally democratic spoils system coupled with bureaucratic corruption and inefficiency may have hampered the prospects of economic development.

Indian State has given power to the state machineries to restrict fundamental rights to achieve the aims of modernization, industrialization, democracy, secularism and socialism etc. New instrumentalities were created to plan, review, and monitor programmes for the disadvantaged–the Scheduled Castes and the Scheduled Tribes. The planning process is an imperative to maintain the soul of Directive Principle of State Policy in disguise and to present these principles as veritable dustbin of sentiment that listed certain priorities–'national ownership of all resources, a uniform civil code to replace existing personal laws, the creation of new but indigenous based forms of dispute settlement and a new economic policy for a living wage for low…The parallel political declaration of creating a mixed economy with State Socialist and capitalist components set the stage for adjustments, compromises, entropy, and corruption' (Galanter 1992, p. xxii). In India, planning for the disadvantaged and planned industrialization are parts of the process of 'passive revolution of capital' (Chatterjee, 1997, pp. 271-297). According to Gramsci, passive revolution is a reformist method, where the new claimants of power opt for a path of reformism in a tactical manner or under the pressure or overload of capitalist accumulation. Mention here may be made that accumulation is necessary for development. They opt for this new path only to make the demands of a new society satisfied by small dosages in a reformist manner. It may be equated with Gandhian tactics: pressure ® compromise ® pressure. Here, the emphasis is based on 'commodity' and 'accumulation', produce two implications: planning is a way to avoid the 'unnecessary rigours' of an industrial transition and planning is a positive instrument for resolving conflict in a large and heterogeneous society. Accumulation under capitalist production proper could be made legitimate by equal right to property and universal freedom of contract on the basis of property rights over commodities. The 'necessary rigours' are the necessary policies of the state with accumulation plus legitimization. It is the process of development with democracy and social justice; but original accumulation separates direct producer from the means of production. Therefore,

> Original accumulation = forms of expropriation of subsistence producers that could not be legitimized through the representative processes of politics = 'unnecessary rigours' of an industrial transition

In India, 'passive revolution' is the process of political-ideological programme of forming politically independent nation-state. The essential aspect of post-colonial hegemonic democratic construction is combining accumulation with legitimation while 'unnecessary rigours' of social conflict. Ambiguities of legitimacy are exposed in the well-known forms of interest groups and the competing demands may be voiced not only on the basis of permanent 'interest group' organizations but also as mobilizations building upon pre-existing cultural solidarities such as locality, caste, tribe, religious community and ethnic identity. The state can manipulate modern forms of relations between the community and the state, the civil society and the political society to secure legitimacy. The state, therefore, shifts from community development to poverty alleviation programmes. In fact, 'rational' planning and 'irrational' politics are inseparable parts of the very logic of this state conducting the passive revolution. Planning is a rational instrument for resolving conflict, and political process uses this instrument for producing consent for capital's passive revolution (Chatterjee, 1997).

But, there is a gap between the promises on the part of the party-state and performances on the part of the state machinery. Politicians make promises and change these promises by maintaining the gaps to prevent their fulfillment. 'Gap theory is really a political ploy to persuade the disadvantaged that the programmes which were designed for their benefit had, somehow, accidently, rather than deliberately, misfired... At the level of instrumentalities, new laws had to be designed which had to be fitted into the legal framework of the Constitution and guided by a socio-political understanding of the uses and abuses which any such programme would both engender and encounter. New regulatory organizations and bureaucracies had to be entrusted with powers to match the gigantic responsibilities ascribed to these agencies. These instrumentalities had to be created by a democratic legislature and implemented by a politically accountable executive' (Galanter, 1992, pp. xxii-xxiii).

Justice A.N. Ray in the *State of Kerala v. N.M. Thomas* (1976)[1] has observed that equality of opportunity for the unequal can only mean aggravation of inequality and equality of opportunity admits discrimination with reason. Can the classical liberal principles concerning individual rights be reconciled with group preference policies, which some refer to as affirmative action others as reverse discrimination? International Convention on the Elimination of All Forms of Racial Discrimination (1969) on the elimination of racial discrimination has categorically specified that special measures for purpose of securing adequate advancement of certain racial or ethnic groups or individuals requiring such protection may be necessary to ensure such groups or individuals equal enjoyment of human rights. Market discrimination and culture-based discrimination are not mutually exclusive. We know that the pattern of distribution of rewards in a given society is determined by the character and values of the dominant cultural group. This discrimination has to be rectified and stopped through preferential policies. Are these policies necessary and justifiable to end discrimination and inequality? Affirmative actions are related to compensation for handicaps on account of ethnicity and cultural backwardness. In fact, disparities and deprivations related to ethnicity and culture are distinct from those related to class.

Any democratic society faces the challenge of harmonizing two essentially contradictory political concepts—one, equality before the law irrespective of religion, caste, creed, race, and gender, and the other, social justice at the cost of the same commitment for equality before the law. Even a developed democracy like the United States is no exception to the rule and has taken recourse to affirmative action to ensure justice for the less privileged sections of the society at the cost of individual merit and equality of all citizens before the law. In India large numbers of people have experienced social discrimination through centuries on account of its peculiar institution called the caste system, efforts have been made to provide redress for these underprivileged sections, through the policy of reservations or quotas for them in jobs, seats in educational institutions and legislatures, and in governmental aid, loans and other developmental assistance. To ensure social justice positive discrimination is needed. The disadvantaged minority groups need and deserve protective discriminatory measures or affirmative actions. Minority rights do not conflict with citizenship rights. Civility and civic identities are legitimate attempts on the part of the minority groups (Kymlicka and Norman, 2000). It is self-respect or recognition based on the principle of autonomy is of particular relevance to minority rights. Communitarians claim for the safeguard and preservation of minority cultures by the state on a long-term basis. The communitarians challenge to the liberal arguments of procedural justice of John Rawls (1971) along with the Habermasian (1984) force of ideal speech situation, better argument and rational action. The need is the recognition of differences and to acknowledge the 'fact and fluidity of difference', the 'ineliminability of difference' and 'a recognition that specific differences may change from time to time and from place to place, and… human rights as regulatory devices for the accommodation of difference, not justifications for the assertion of similarity' (Mendus 1995, p. 23 in Beetham, 1995). Democratization of politics permits the play of identity politics and the recognition of differences. 'Whereas democracy has been used to defend the right of property in the name of freedom, it has been equally used to critique the institution of private property from the standpoint of equality…. Democracy has been interpreted as elitist or as pluralist democracy, participative, institutional or substantive democracy, or as egalitarian democracy' (Chandhoke, 1999, p. 123). In democracy there is the possibility of self-regulating communities in civil society instead of oppressive state apparatus. Foucault also permits that there are the multiple centres of power in post-modern society, where power is not concentrated into a single whole. Power is dispersed. But the communities in civil society should not be community-in-itself like that of state-in-itself instead of the cultural homogeneity, concreteness and boundedness of the communities. These communities should also take their responsibility or responsibilities not only to their own, but also to the others in a broader sense. Extreme group one-sidedness is not accountable to us. Group consideration along with greater community consciousness is our consideration. Group identity or community identity should be preserved but not at the expense of the other or others. '... defense of extreme group relativism is actually undertaken in the name of wanting to secure a truer democracy... Legislating independently on family and other matters the community need not give reasons to outsiders. But to be tolerant it must give reasons to itself through some public and representative process, i.e. be accountable to its own constituency. However, the mechanisms of accountability here would seem to be no different from those operative elsewhere.... Antipathy to the overbearness of state forms has only resulted in the endorsement here of the overbearness of a community from itself perceived in much the same way as a state-in-itself' (Vanaik, 1997, p. 191).

The state should try to protect the interests of the groups and resolve group disputes within the periphery of the state. Gutmann and Thomson (1996) regard that the principle of reciprocity should be directed against the all odds of liberal democracy, against all forms of fundamentalism, but not against religions and cultures as such. This principle should be directed exclusively and explicitly against the principle of neutrality of liberal democracy. 'The case for reciprocity, and more generally for the deliberative perspective, must be defended on substantive moral grounds, and there is no reason to expect that such a defense would have the same (positive or negative) implications for all moral positions. But the value of public reason expressed by the deliberative perspective is not just another morality. It is offered as the morally optimal basis on which citizens, who disagree about moralities and religions, can act collectively to make educational policy. The principle of reciprocity is not privileged in the sense that it needs no moral defense' (Gutmann and Thompson, 1996, p. 67). The inevitable non-neutrality of the liberal state and of morality should act as inevitable secularity of the state. Gutmann (1994) regards that 'recognizing and treating members of some groups as equals now seems to require public institutions to acknowledge rather than ignore cultural particularities, at least for those people whose self-understanding depends on the vitality of their culture. This requirement of political recognition of cultural particularity–extended to all groups–is compatible with a form of universalism that counts the culture and cultural context valued by individuals as among their basic interests' (Gutmann, 1994, p. 3). The need is accommodation of cultural diversity and inter-cultural dialogue, where diverse and sovereign cultural groups and citizens negotiate with each other in accordance with the three conventions of mutual recognition, consent and cultural continuity (Tully, 1995). The language of constitutionalism is taken into account where the demands are taken up and adjudicated. Cultures are interdependent, interactive and negotiable. Cultures are differentiated, contested, imagined and re-imagined, and negotiated and transformed.

Identity is about how individuals or groups see and define themselves, and how other individuals or groups see and define them. Identity is formed through the socialization process and the influence of social institutions like the family, the education system and the mass media. The concept of identity is an important one, as it is only through establishing our own identities and learning about the identities of other individuals and groups that we come to know what makes us similar to some people and different from others, and therefore form social connections with them. How you see yourself will influence the friends you have, who you will marry or live with, and the communities and groups to which you relate and belong. If people did not have an identity, they would lack the means of identifying with or relating to their peer group, to their neighbours, to the communities in which they lived or to the people they came across in their everyday lives. Identity, therefore, 'fits' individuals into the society in which they live. The identity of individuals and groups involves both elements of personal choice and the responses and attitudes of others. Individuals are not free to adopt any identity they like, and factors like their social class, their ethnic group and their sex are likely to influence how others see them. The identity that an individual wants to assert and which they may wish others to see them having may not be the one that others accept or recognize. Identities may also change over time. Difference, Norris (1982) remarks that it 'remains suspended between the two French verbs "to differ" and "to defer" (postpone), both of which contribute to its textual force but neither of which can fully capture its meaning. Language depends on difference, as Saussure showed... the structure of distinctive propositions which make up its basic economy. Where Derrida breaks new ground... is in the extent to which "differ" shades into "defer"... the idea that meaning is always deferred, perhaps to this point of an endless supplementarity, by the play of signification' (Norris, 1982, p. 32).

The Constitution of independent India which largely followed the pattern of the Government of India Act, 1935, made provisions for positive discrimination in favour of the Scheduled Castes and Scheduled Tribes (SCs & STs) which constituted about 23 per cent of the divided India's population. Protective discrimination is expressed in Article 46 of the Indian Constitution. It states that '... State shall promote with special care the educational and economic interests of the weaker sections of the people, and, in particular, of the Scheduled Castes and the Scheduled Tribes, and shall protect them from social injustice and all forms of exploitation.' Two types of preferential policies are prevalent in India– one type is affirmative action, analogous to the American type, where the beneficiary target groups are at the bottom of the birth-determined stratified system, and another type is 'sons-of-the-soil' policy, analogous to the Malaysian 'Bhumiputra', where the beneficiary target groups are disadvantaged local ethnic groups, irrespective of caste and tribal affiliation. In this respect the 'congruities of blood, speech and custom and so on are seen to have an infallible and, at times, overpowering coerciveness in and of themselves. One is bound to one's kinsmen, one's neighbour, and one's fellow-believer; *ipso facto*, as the result not merely of personal affection, practical necessity, common interest or incurred obligations, but at least in great part by virtue of some unaccountable absolute import attributed to the very tie itself. The general strength of such primordial bonds, and the types of them that are important, differ from person to person, from society to society, and from time to time. But, for virtually every person, in every society, and almost at all times, some attachments seem to flow from a sense of natural, some would say spiritual, affinity than from social interaction' (Geertz, 1963, pp. 109-110). Indian preferential policies are based on four principles of compensation for injustices, protection of the weaker sections under Article 46 of the Constitution, proportional equality and social justice incorporating distributive justice and social welfare. Besides reserving parliamentary seats for them they were given advantages in terms of admission to schools and colleges, jobs in the public sector, various pecuniary benefits for their overall development, and so on. The Constitution indeed guarantees the fundamental right of equality of all citizens before the law, but it also categorically lies down that nothing in the constitution "shall prevent the State from making any special provision for the advancement of any socially and educationally backward classes of citizens or for the

Scheduled Castes and the Scheduled Tribes." The Constitution of India has provided, among other various protections and safeguards, safeguards for Public employment to the persons belonging to the Scheduled Castes and Scheduled Tribes, keeping in view the discrimination and disabilities suffered by these classes to catch up and compete successfully with the more fortunate ones in the matter of securing public employment. Specific provisions for reservations in services in favour of the members of Scheduled Castes and Scheduled Tribes have been made as follows in the Constitution of India:

> Article 16(1): There shall be equality of opportunity for all citizens in matters relating to employment or appointment to any office under the State. Article 16(4): Article 16 provides for equality of opportunity for all citizens in matters relating to employment or appointment to any office under the State, Nevertheless, "nothing in this Article shall prevent the State from making any provision for the reservation of appointments or posts in favour of any backward class of citizens which, in the opinion of the State, is not adequately represented in the services under the State." There have been two Constitution Amendments incorporated in Article 16(4), they are: Article 16 (4-A): Nothing in this article shall prevent the state from making any provision for reservation in matters of promotions, with consequential seniority, to any class or classes of posts in services under the adequately represented in the services under the state. The 77th Amendment to the Constitution has been brought into effect permitting reservation in promotion to the Scheduled Castes and Scheduled Tribes. Some of the constitutional provisions which aimed at positive discrimination are: Article 17: abolition of "untouchability" and making its practice in any form a punishable offence, Article 46: promotion of educational and economic interests, Articles 16 and 335: preferential treatment in matters of employment in public services, Articles 330 and 332: reservation of seats in the Lok Sabha and State Assemblies.

The Constitution (Eighty-First Amendment) Act, 2000 has added Article 16(4B) to the Constitution. The Amendment envisages that the unfilled reserved vacancies are to be carried forward to the subsequent years and these vacancies are to be treated as distinct and separate from the current vacancies during any year. The rule of 50 per cent reservation laid down by the Supreme Court is to be applied only to normal vacancies. This means that the unfilled reserved vacancies can be carried forward from year to year without any limit, and are to be filled separately from the normal vacancies. This Amendment also modifies the proposition laid down by the Supreme Court in Indira Sawhney. In *Indira Sawhney and Ors.* v. *Union of India and Ors.*[2], the Court observed that the meaning of the expression "backward classes of citizens" is not qualified or restricted by saying that it means those other backward classes who are situated similarly to Scheduled Caste and/or Scheduled Tribes. Backwardness being a relative term must in the context be judged by the general level of advancement of the entire population of the country or the State, as the case may be. Article 335 provides that "the claims of the members of the SCs and STs shall be taken into consideration, consistently with the maintenance of efficiency of administration in the making of appointments in services and posts in connection with the affairs of the Union or of a State."

Any determination of backwardness is neither a subjective exercise nor a matter of subjective satisfaction. The exercise is an objective one. Certain objective social and other criteria have to be satisfied before any group or class of citizens could be treated as backward. If the executive includes, for collateral reasons, groups or classes not satisfying the relevant criteria, it would be a clear case of fraud on power. 'Caste' neither can be the sole criterion nor can it be equated with 'class' for the purpose of Article 16 (4) for ascertaining the social and educational backwardness of any section or group of people so as to bring them within the wider connotation of 'backward class'. Nevertheless 'caste' in Hindu society becomes a dominant factor or primary criterion in determining the backwardness of a class of citizens. Unless 'caste' satisfies the primary test of social backwardness as well as the educational and economic backwardness which are the established and accepted criteria to identify the 'backward class', a caste per se without satisfying the agreed formulae generally cannot fall within the meaning of 'backward class of citizens' under Article 16 (4), save in given exceptional circumstances such as the caste itself being identifiable with the traditional occupation of the lower strata—indicating the social backwardness. And 'Class' has occupation and caste nexus; it is homogeneous and is determined by birth. It further approved Chitralekha case[3]. Further in case of *Jagdish Negi* v. *State of U.P.*[4] Court held that backwardness is not a static phenomenon. It cannot continue indefinitely and the State is entitled to review the situation from time to time.

II. Political and Developmental Participation among the Tribals

I have selected two blocks, Kanksa and Jamalpur of Burdwan district from West Bengal as the two plain areas, where the former is the ITDP block and another the Scheduled area. These two blocks are less developed or underdeveloped blocks in the district of Burdwan. The district of Burdwan, one of the western districts of Burdwan Division, is situated between 22°56′ north latitude and between 86°48′ and 88°25′ east longitude. The district lies mainly between the Ajay, the Bhagirathi or Hooghly and the Damodar rivers. Kanksa is one of the underdeveloped blocks in the district of Burdwan, situated in the *Pargana* of *Senapahari*. The most important river in this area is no doubt the *Damodar* with which the Santhal legend is deeply connected. It touches upon the Bankura district just after it has received the waters of the Barakar, and flowing in a south-easterly direction for about forty-five miles, enters Burdwan near Silampur village. Jamalpur block is one of the agricultural blocks in the district of Burdwan. The population in this block is mixed in character, including pure Hindu castes, semi-aboriginals recently admitted in the pale of Hinduism and pure aboriginal tribes. Most of them work as agricultural labourers than as cultivators. The rainfall being often deficient in total amount or irregular in distribution, artificial irrigation is necessary for almost all important crops. There is only protective irrigation work, the Eden Canal, an irrigational channel 22 miles in length from Kanchannagar to Jamalpur. In this area, *aus, aman* and *boro* rice are sown. Cultivation of potato, onion, sugarcane, vegetables and other valuable crops are made in this area. There are four main tribes in area, for example Santal, Kora, Oraon, Bhumij, Mahali and Malpahari etc. Santal is the most important tribe in these two areas. Comparatively, Jamalpur block is much more developed in terms of irrigation than that of Kanksa.

The study is based on intensive fieldwork. For empirical work survey method has been adopted. Questions asked to the tribals were informal, unstructured and open-ended. The survey was conducted by the researcher himself. The work is mainly qualitative. In few cases qualitative method has been supplemented by quantitative method of observation. Attempt has been made mainly to elicit information through what Galtung had characterized as dialogical method in the interview process. Primary sources of this study are sample survey, informal interviews, focused interviews etc. Books, journals etc. have been used as secondary sources.

In these two areas tribal people live in smaller communities, but at present they are in constant interaction with the mainstream system and the non-tribal people who mainly supply local political leadership and man highly specialized institutions like bureaucracy. The introduction of money economy has introduced changes in the economic life and drawn the tribal people very close to the non-tribal people. Due to incessant interaction with the neighbouring non-tribal communities they could form a new social order with a good deal of integration with local community culture, forming a balanced synthesis of tribal-non-tribal way of life, particularly in economic and political spheres.

Field Results from Kanksa

Majority of the tribal people in my study area is landless agricultural labourers. Few are owner cultivators. Out of 175 tribal respondents 109 work as agricultural labourers in the lands of neighbouring caste peasants, 59 earn their livelihood as share-croppers in the fields of non-tribal peasants and remaining 7 in non-agricultural fields.

Tribals' participation includes voting, canvassing, discussing political matters, attending meetings, contributing to election fund etc. Several factors that contributed to this type of political behaviour may be stated as decay of their traditional panchayats, growing importance of traditional panchayats, industrialization, growth of market economy and the community development programmes and their various schemes etc. The tribals have now imbibed new influences, values, attitudes and beliefs. The tribals now take part in politics and modern political process for pursuing economic need, social needs, and establishing particular values. Political participation and political awareness each influences one another and makes room for others. It is a fact that because of the lack of education and of socio-economic and political backwardness, the tribal people are not full politically aware. Their level of awareness is low and their voting behaviour is influenced by money, mobilization activities of the political parties, friends and neighbours. 'Panchayati Raj has introduced the politics of opportunity and participation into the Indian village and in this respect has opened the way for significant change' (Madan, 1977, p. 62). They are hard-working and freedom-loving. They are easily mobilized and have become dedicated workers for the party. Election provides the opportunity for participation and signifies their urge for social mobility. They have come to realize the significance of election. It is a fact that 'the tribal people exercised hardly any political power, but after the introduction of adult franchise they are courted by political parties from all directions, particularly when the time election comes. The result has been that this new factor has begun to play a fairly important part in the changes to which tribes are being subjected todays' (Bose, 1977, p. 57). Political parties mobilize them for electoral ends primarily. The vast mass of the tribals could not avail of the benefits of the development programmes undertaken by the government. The fruits of development programmes are pocketed by the well-off section of the tribal communities, a small elite class created by the government and the party for their own interests. The well-off privileged minority utilizes the benefits bestowed on the tribals in the form of special concessions in their game for power (Desai, 1977). They perform the role as spectators, i.e. they show sticker or batch, attempt to influence the voters, join political discussion, voting etc. They maintain a low profile in participatory activities mainly due to low levels of education, occupational status and income. Sometimes, they feel deprived, but this lack of feeling of belonging to a national political community does not preclude their participation in political life. The mass participate in electoral activities like canvassing, postering, attending meetings, voting etc. without appearing to possess sentiments of belonging and national integration.

The tribals take part in elections because they do not want to alienate themselves from the mainstream politics. They have adapted themselves to the regime values and norms. Their attitudes towards political order and attitudes towards mobilization do not differ basically from that of the general mass of the population, though their culture of participation is not participatory in real sense of the term. With regard to attitudes political order there appears to be an agreement 'on what procedures shall be considered legitimate for purposes of obtaining and exercising governmental power regularizes political conflict and supports political order by making violent techniques exceptional rather than ordinary' (Willhoites, 1963, p. 303). The tribal people are adaptive to and prone to compromise with the prevailing attitudes towards socio-political conditions. They cast votes, discuss political matters with their leaders, friends and neighbours and also attend political meetings. Though they are not aware of various political issues they participate in elections as a social duty. Though a significant number of tribal voters turn out to the polling booths, most of them do not know the significance of voting, their rights and duties and their role in the political system. They elect the candidates, whom they support without keeping in mind the socio-economic background of the candidates, their leadership qualities and without being aware of the principles and policies of their party. Though take part in political discussions casually they show their keen interest in elections and politics. It is seen that on the basis of meetings and discussions attended, it may be held that interest in politics is greater among the people of lower category, illiterates and agricultural labourers than in that of medium and high categories, literate people having formal education and share-croppers (Table 16.1). From the survey it seems clear that illiterates take interest in politics, take part in political discussion and cast their votes with percentage varying from 52 per cent to 45.14 per cent in spite of their lack of political consciousness. Illiterates do attend meeting less, and therefore, have less control over policy-decisions and less contact with party-panchayat leaders. Conscience, knowledge and wisdom; political competence, interest and responsibility; self-confidence, dominance and articulateness do not direct their political attitudes. The formally educated people attend meeting than ill-educated or illiterates. With regard to occupation the agricultural labourers (64%) and sharecroppers (35%) do take much more interest in politics, in attending meetings and casting their votes. 59.43 per cent and 31.43 per cent take part in political discussion, 64 per cent and 33.71 per cent take interest in politics, 64 per cent and 35 per cent cast their votes, but only 40.57 per cent and 14.28 per cent attend meetings. The tribal people are less interested in attending meetings and taking part in decision-making process. Due to lack of education they are not fully exposed to wider political information. Though they are aware of political happenings, they cast their votes, attend meetings, take part in political discussion and take interest in political matters more in a routine manner than in any active conscious manner. '...educational attainment appears to have the most important demographic effect on political attitudes. Among the demographic variables usually investigated none compares with the educational variable in the extent to which it seems to determine political attitudes. The uneducated man or man with limited education is a different political actor from the man who has achieved a higher level of education' (Almond and Verba, 1963, p. 379). Talking about politics is a time pass business to them in leisure time. Due to lack of education they are not fully exposed to wider political information through mass media, and therefore, they lack political competence, wider access to information about political issues and analysis of issues etc. 'Democratic competence is closely related to having valid information about political issues and processes and to the ability to use information in the analysis of issues and the devising of influence strategies' (Almond and Verba, 1963, p. 95). They receive political

Table 16.1: Socio-economic Indicators and Political Prticipation of the Tribals

Parameters	*Total no. of respondents*	*Votes cast*		*Political discussion*		*Attending meetings*		*Interest in politics*		*Percentage*
	No.	*Percentage*	*No.*	*Percentage*	*No.*	*Percentage*	*No.*	*Percentage*	*No.*	
Economics										
Low	143	82.00	143	82.00	135	77.14	65	37.14	143	82.00
Medium	30	16.89	30	16.89	22	12.57	16	9.14	24	13.71
High	2	1.11	2	1.11	1	0.57	2	1.11	2	1.11
Education										
Illiterate	91	52.00	91	52.00	79	45.14	41	23.42	91	52.00
Literate	68	39.00	68	39.00	61	34.86	33	18.86	65	37.14
Class I-IV	8	4.11	8	4.11	8	4.11	3	1.71	5	2.89
Class IV-X	5	2.89	5	2.89	5	2.89	5	2.89	4	2.29
Class X-XII	3	2.00	3	2.00	3	2.00	2	1.14	3	2.00
Occupation										
Agricultural Labourer	112	64.00	112	64.00	98	59.43	71	40.57	112	64.00
Sharecroppers	61	35.00	61	35.00	55	31.43	25	14.28	59	33.71
Business	2	1.00	2	1.00	...	...	...	...	...	...
Others	...	...	...	...	...	...	...	...	...	...

Source: Field Survey.

information from their leaders and are politicized by party-Panchayat leaders.

It is to be noted here that tribals' sustainable development depends upon a system of self-development based on their own creative force and corporate productive resources. The plan for tribal development must take forest and land resources as the base. Tribals should become co-sharers in the creation of wealth and take active part in its management. To ensure man-nature-society symbiotic relationship without generating conflicts between them, emphasis should be laid on maximization of creative participation and minimization of socio-economic disorder. The tribal people should be properly organized and politicized, imbued with a sense of co-operative participation among them in view of the productive resources, productive relations, manpower position and socio-economic orientation. In fact, development centres round a high rate of economic growth with social justice, priority investment, political decentralization and moulding of tradition with modernization. Popular participation should be treated as the basic policy in national development. Active participation of all individuals in the development process is the *sine qua non* of development. Participation provides the beneficiaries of development an opportunity for opinion building, helps the planners in setting goals and objectives, formulating policies, implementing plans and programmes, organizing and evaluating the target community, the less privileged. The problems of the tribals, the rural down-trodden germinate from structural condition and not the functional ones. Participation makes the people aware of their problems relating to development and empowerment and the root causes behind it. Tables 16.2 to 16.8 explain that 38.75 per cent respondents were regular in attending *gram sansad* meetings, 42.00 per cent and 46.00 per cent were non-participatory when needed and occasionally. Only 1 per cent was never non-participatory. Participation of the tribals in the development programmes was mainly through labour, moral support and benefits sharing, but very poor through decision-making process, which remained only within 6.24 per cent while 93.76 per cent of the tribal people did not participate in the making of decision at all as to who would get the benefits, how the benefits should be provided, and how much the beneficiary would get. The respondents who were mainly from the age groups of 21-30 and 31-50 years with a socio-economic background: mostly illiterate, agricultural labourers and sharecroppers in the low to medium category having a minimum portion of land in their ownership, except share-cropping reported that participation in the decision-making was not their task. The leaders themselves made

Table 16.2: Frequency of Respondents' Attendance to Gram Sansad Meetings

Frequency	*Number and percentages of respondents*		
	Participation	*Casual*	*Non-participatory*
Regular	68 (38.75%)	74 (42.00%)	17 (10.00%)
When needed	27 (15.25%)	10 (6.00%)	75 (43.00%)
Occasionally	71 (41.00%)	71 (41.00%)	80 (46.00%)
Never	9 (5.00%)	20 (11.00%)	3 (1.00%)
Total	**175 (100.00%)**	**175 (100.00%)**	**175 (100.00%)**

Source: Field Survey.

Table 16.3: Participation of Tribal People in Development Programmes

Parameter	*Partici-pation/ Non-partici-pation*	*Number*	*%*
Contribution through labour	Yes	168	95.78
	No	7	4.22
Contribution through money	Yes	10	5.56
	No	165	94.44
Contribution through moral support and benefit sharing	Yes	157	90.00
	No	18	10.00
Participation through decision-making	Yes	11	6.24
	No	164	93.76

Source: Field Survey.

Table 16.4: Perception about Objectives of IRDP, TSP, JRY, STAD etc.

Parameter	*Number*	*Percentage*
Do not know	105	59.75
For self-employment	44	25.00
To get rid of poverty	21	12.25
No response	5	3.00

Source: Field Survey.

decisions, took the decisions and justified the decisions. Most of the respondents who were from the lower to middle category did not know the objectives of various development programmes. 3 per cent of the total was silent. 25 per cent answered in favour of self-employment and 12.25 per cent for poverty alleviation. 72 per cent respondents said that

Table 16.5: Awareness of the Guidelines about IRDP, TSP, JRY etc.

Parameter	*Number*	*Percentage*
Do not know	126	72.00
Know	49	28.00
Sources of information:		
Panchayat Samity	3	2.00
Gram Panchayats	18	10.00
Party-panchayat leaders	21	12.00
Peer groups	5	3.00
Voluntary organization	2	1.00

Source: Field Survey.

Table 16.6: Respondents' Answer to the Desired Effective Implementation

Parameter	*Number*	*Percentage*
They can buy more	37	21.14
They will live with certainty	19	11.00
They will cultivate their lands without the help of the landowners or even money-lenders	21	12.00
Not getting adequate benefits and more facilities should be provided	27	15.34
Good for employment opportunities	23	13.24
Effective implementation will bring changes in their social outlook	10	6.00
Funds are not properly utilized	35	20.00
Banks should be liberal in terms of loans	3	1.28

Source: Field Survey.

Table 16.7: Kinds of Help Provided to the Beneficiaries

Parameter	*Number*	*Percentage*
Help in form of loan and subsidy	52	30.00
Technical know-how	2	1.00
Employment and daily labour	112	64.00
Social forestry	9	5.00

Source: Field Survey.

they did not know the guidelines required for IRDP, TSP, JRY and the like. They took money as governmental help and for self-employment and poverty alleviation. Only 28 per cent of the respondents knew about the guidelines. They received information from gram panchayat offices and party-panchayat leaders of their locality. It is to be noted that ignorance has made them more oriented to consumption pattern rather than

Table 16.8: Mode of Selection of Beneficiaries through IRDP, TSP, IAY etc.

Parameter	*Number*	*Percentage*
PROCEDURE:		
Selection from depressed and poor families	44	25.00
Selection by the Beneficiary Committee	95	55.00
Selection through meeting	35	20.00
SATISFACTORY/NON-SATISFACTORY:		
Selection procedure satisfactory	116	66.44
Selection procedure not satisfactory	59	33.56

Sources: Field Survey.

investment. Among the respondents only 12 per cent were interested in investment. 1.28 per cent said that banks should be liberal in terms of loan. An environment of investment has not been created among the tribals. Most of the beneficiaries were not satisfied with the selection of beneficiaries. They said that the depressed and poor families were least benefited. Selection of beneficiaries was based on good understanding with the party-panchayat leaders and members of the Beneficiary Committee than on economic background. The former scored 75 per cent and the latter 2 per cent only.

The problem of non-participation of should be dealt with in the following way: people should prepare their own development programmes and the government should participate in these programmes by ways of financial, legal and technical assistance. The area under study lacks the conscious participation of the tribals. Participatory culture is absent in real sense. However, participation has to be institutionalized to ensure involvement of people in all stages of development: societal and extra-societal environment research, planning and programme design, implementation and management of programmes. For sustainable development capital formation and output raising capacity should have to be developed, and if growth process is sustained, 'trickle-down effect' would ensure better living standard for the tribal. Sustainable resource utilization, appropriate technology intervention for resource conservation and regeneration, gradual empowerment of the socially disadvantaged group–all these can be ensured through the participation of the people. People would participate in the development process if the expected benefits exceed the expected costs of participation, if they are empowered to do so, if they have the ability to organize and motivate the co-villagers, if the local leadership provides opportunities to them to participate in various development programmes, and if the government provides sizeable amount of financial and technical assistance in mobilizing people's resources and developing appropriate infrastructural facilities. From Table 16.9 it seems to me that the parameters of participation are at a low level and not properly maintained or utilized so as to induce high level of participation among the tribes. They in a passive mood get or receive or

Table 16.9: 'Respondents' Answers to Participation in the Development Programmes

Parameter	*Answer*	*Number*	*Percentage*
Cost-benefit analysis	What would be the result? Nothing	103	58.56
	Beneficiaries are selected before Gram Sansad meetings	56	32.00
	We follow our leaders, we participate	16	9.14
Empowerment to the people	People having close relation with party-panchayats have the power to decide	68	38.85
	Programmes are selected at the top level through panchayats	89	50.86
	We receive loans and benefits and do not take part in decision-making	10	5.72
	We take part in decision and discuss matters with others	8	4.75
People's ability to organize and motivate co-villagers	We themselves cannot do it, we are poor and illiterate	163	93.14
	Party leaders can do it	13	93.14
	Do not say anything	12	6.86
Local leadership	Local leadership controls all	173	99.15
	General people participate in decision-making	2	0.85
Financial and technical help from government	Meagre	94	53.71
	Meagre and not properly utilized	42	24.00
	Not conducive to our requirements	39	22.29

Source: Field Survey.

share the benefits. Most of the beneficiaries said that financial and technical help from the government were meagre. Funds were not properly utilized. They did not know the actualities of non-utilization did not try to find out the causes behind it nor assess the actual requirements to make a sustained development of their own. The extent of their perception is not clear. The tempo of literacy campaign through outside intervention may have to be developed and sustained by making local leadership responsive and improving the capacity of the people, in creating awareness of the importance of environment, natural resources and educational competence for building up their knowledge, skill and required attitude to effectively participate in the management of common property resources and the overall development process. The major problem with governmental programme is that these have not been involved with the people. People are alienated from the natural resources as a result of increasing takeover by the State of the natural resources in the name of conservation and development. Lack of management abilities on the part of the tribals has led to the failure in agriculture, poultry farming, DWCRA group formation and management of natural resources. The tribal people do not enthusiastically come forward to receive the development assistance. The higher groups are able to retain their socio-economic power. They do not know all the pros and cons of assistance, hence, need help from village level leaders and are guided by them. The elite do not want the rural poor to come into contact with government officials.

Field Results from Jamalpur

Tribal development in *Jamalpur* block of Burdwan district can be realized from 1991 Census report, where 50.83 per cent tribal people are engaged in primary sector, 46.17 per cent are agricultural labourers, 0.26 per cent are in manufacturing and processing other than household industry, 0.15 per cent are in trade and commerce, 0.25 per cent are in services other than transport, storage and communication. Out of 16.52 per cent literate to the total tribal population only 3.56 per cent females are literate in comparison to the district figures of 20.58 per cent ad 5.76 per cent. The block is mainly agricultural. The tribals themselves are not so conscious or aware to develop their own as per the requirements of integration with national mainstream. In this area, the sampling size and interview techniques are like: sampling size: 245, type of sample: quota sampling, type of observation: both participant and non-participant, units of observation: individuals and institutions, distribution of questionnaire:

socio-economic and political data, approximate number of questions asked: ten, approximate time for interview: ten minutes, interviews conducted: free associational and focused, particular characteristics of interviews: short and precise, indicative and projective.

The extent of participation of the tribal people in the formulation and decision-making process of the development programmes in this block is an important indicator of development paradigm. To this end I surveyed *Jamalpur* block. In fact, development is associated with democracy. People 'feel that even the limited power at the disposal of the Left Front Government has not been properly used. It will not be an exaggeration to say that procrastination and misuse in the administration are on increase. In areas like education, health, transport, irrigation works, labour, electricity, local self-government... which are closely connected with the people, the role of the government has no impact on the masses. Even progressive measures like taking over the vested land and cancellation of illegal *pattas*, *barga* recording... all undertaken for the good of the people have not been properly implemented' (Burdwan District Committee, CPI-M. 1985, pp. 26-27). The destitution of most of the tribal people does not end with the implementation of the development programmes. They are dissociated from the control of the resources, from decision-making in resource utilization pattern and development programmes. From the field survey it becomes clear that 59.75 per cent respondents regularly did not attend *gram sansad* meetings, 40.25 per cent respondents were regular in attending *gram sansad* meetings, 43 per cent were regularly casual, 16.35 per cent 40 per cent were non-participatory when needed and occasionally. Henceforth, 40.25 per cent were never non-participatory (Table 16.10). On an average, the *gram sansad* meetings were casual and occasionally participatory (Table 16.11). Therefore, the tribal people regularly participated less in the formulation of development programmes, i.e. who will take the benefits, how the benefits will be percolated down and the overall decision-making process. Understanding from the views of the respondents it is evident that party-panchayat leaders, *gram sansad* members and *pradhans* combined a trio, contributed 95.11 per cent in their control over decision-making process–benefits–who gets what, when and how? As decision-making agents general tribal people contribute only 1.63 per cent, which is just double than that of the Panchayat Samity. The influential personalities, who were influential during 1950s and 1960s, contribute only 2.45 per cent now and in a subtle way form a covert alliance with the newly dominant party—panchayat leaders-*gram sansad* members-*pradhan* trio. In the development programmes 75.92 per cent

Table 16.10: Formulation Process: Attendance to *Gram Sansad* Meetings

	Number of respondents		
Frequency	*Participatory*	*Casual*	*Non-participatory*
Regular	99 (40.25%)	105 (43.00%)	8 (3.40%)
When needed	40 (16.35%)	14 (5.85%)	40 (16.35%)
Occasionally	98 (40.00%)	94 (38.15%)	98 (40.00%)
Never	8 (3.40%)	32 (13.00%)	99 (40.25%)
Total	**245 (100%)**	**245 (100%)**	**245 (100%)**

Source: Field Survey.

Table 16.11: Formulation Process: Perception about *Gram Sansad* Meetings

	Number of respondents				
Frequency	*Regular*	*When needed*	*Occasionally*	*Never*	*Total*
Participatory	99 (40.25%)	40 (16.35%)	98 (40.00%)	8 (3.40%)	245 (100%)
Casual	105 (43.00%)	14 (5.85%)	9 (38.16%)	32 (13.00%)	245 (100%)
Non-participatory	8 (3.40%)	40 (16.35%)	98 (40.00%)	99 (40.25%)	245 (100%)

Source: Field Survey.

tribal people participated as daily labour. This participation through daily labour is significantly supported by moral enthusiasm and benefit sharing of only 18.37 per cent and 75.50 per cent of participation through discussion. The poles apart diversification of tribal participation in the development programmes: participation through decision-making and participation through discussion, and participation through money and participation through labour is ridicule, believes to be an unexpected phenomenon (Table 16.12 and Fig. 16.3). These large-scale deviations of diversification of participation need to be shortened. It seems clear that participation of the tribals in the development programme was mainly through labour, moral support and benefit sharing, but very poor through decision-making. The deviation above 70 per cent is not conducive to the requirements of rural development in association with tribal development. It has been observed from the field study that majority of the respondents expressed that active participation and involvement of the tribal people or the rural populace is essential for the success of the development programmes. 94.28 per cent respondents expressed deep sorrows about

Table 16.12: Formulation and Implementation Processes: Perception about Decision-making Agents and Participation in the Development Programmes

Formulation process			*Implementation process*		
Decision-making Agents			*Participation in development programmes*		
Parameter	*Control/De-control*	*Number (%)*	*Parameter*	*Participation/Non-participation*	*Number (%)*
Panchayat Samity	Control De-control	2 (0.81) 243 (99.19)	Through labour	Yes No	186 (75.92) 59 (24.08)
Influential leaders or individuals	Control De-control	6 (2.45) 239 (99.19)	Through moral support and benefit sharing	Yes No	45 (18.37) 200 (81.63)
Party and panchayat leaders	Control De-control	55 (22.45) 190 (77.55)	Through money	Yes No	10 (4.08) 235 (95.92)
Gram Sansad members	Control De-control	60 (24.50) 185 (75.50)	Through decision-making	Yes No	4 (1.63) 241 (98.37)
Pradhan	Control De-control	118 (48.16) 127 (51.84)	Through discussion	Yes No	185 (75.50) 60 (24.50)
General people	Control De-control	4 (1.63) 241 (98.37)	....	....	....

Source: Field Survey.

their non-involvement and non-participation in multiple development programmes, were taken for their development. Regarding the choice of the scheme in majority of cases it was found that the beneficiaries were not allowed to select their own scheme, rather it was imposed on them. The awareness of the tribals about various development schemes is about 61.63 per cent. Despite the awareness, they only heard about decisions and participated in the *gram sansad* meetings only to raise hands and voices in favour of decisions, but did not say anything that counteract the decisions and muddle the decision-making process. 24.08 per cent of the respondents received benefits in terms of loans and subsidy, 2.45 per cent in the form of technical know-how. A negligible 0.82 per cent was in social forestry, when a larger share of 72.65 per cent in wage employment produced a negative tendency to tribal development. They received

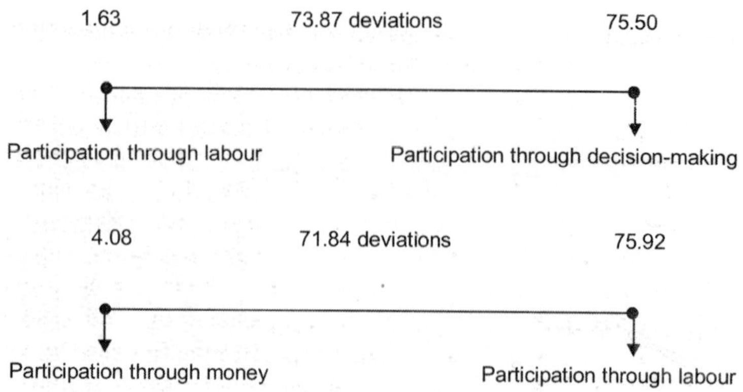

Fig. 16.3

information about development schemes from Panchayat members (7.34 per cent contribution as source of information), local party leaders (38.78 per cent contribution as source of information) and *gram sansad* members (40 per cent contribution as source of information) out of total 86.12 per cent. Though only 13.88 per cent respondents did not receive information or were not interested to get information, the level of information or the quality of information, which the remaining portion received from the probable sources was at the low ebb, had retarded confidence building among them–this is my perception (Field Survey). The backdrops produced out of poverty illiteracy have resulted in ignorance produced out of low qualities of perception, information and awareness among them–this is also my perception about my field area (Field Survey and Fig. 16.4). Low qualities of information produce ignorance directly and indirectly (diagonally) through poverty, illiteracy and backdrops, and reduces confidence indirectly through the same. Ignorance has made them oriented more towards consumption rather than investment. With regard to the desired effects of effective plan implementation 10.20 per cent respondents expressed their favour to increase in income, savings and investment and depending less on landowners or moneylenders. An environment of investment has not been created among the tribals. Only 1.23 per cent said that banks should be liberal in providing loans. 45.30 per cent of the respondents expressed most lamentably that they were not getting adequate benefits and more facilities should be provided to them for buying more foods and consumer durables (24.50 per cent), living lives with more certainty and for getting more employment opportunities (2.86 per cent). The 3.26 per cent respondents also criticised

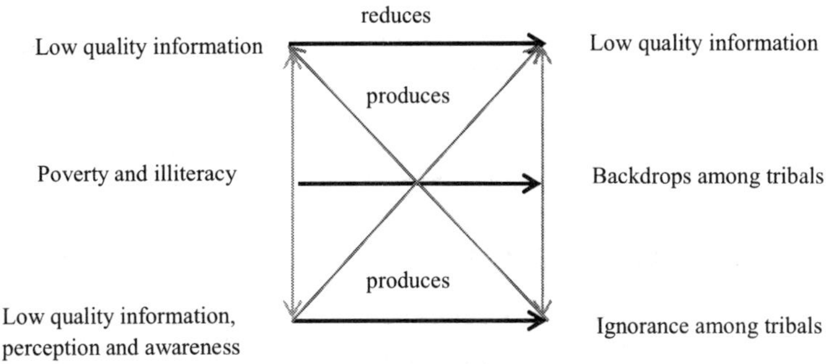

Fig. 16.4

the functioning of Panchayat authorities for non-utilization of funds properly. 53.47 per cent of the respondents were not satisfied with the selection of beneficiaries. Selection through Beneficiary Committee and *gram sansad* meetings was not proper. Schemes were superimposed on the beneficiaries. Out of total respondents 27.35 per cent received loans, technical know-how and help for social forestry. Most of the beneficiaries (79.10 per cent) are from lower economic category. Only 11.43 per cent expressed that the loans sanctioned for various development schemes were properly utilized and the remaining 88.57 per cent were in the category of non-repayment. Due to superimposition of projects the spontaneous involvement of the tribal people in the development programmes becomes absent. Panchayats' demand for people's participation in development programmes was more casual than participatory, but more participatory (57.55 per cent) than non-participatory (42.45 per cent) (Table 16.13).

The respondents who were mainly from the age group of 21-30 years (67.35 per cent) and 31-50 years (20 per cent) with a socio-economic background: mostly illiterate (37.14 per cent) and literate (37.14 per cent), agricultural labourers (59.18 per cent) and share-croppers (34.69 per cent) in low to medium category having a minimum portion of land in their ownership, except share-cropping and *patta* lands reported that participation in the decision-making was not their task. The leaders took decisions and did the task of decision-making. I have categorized the socio-economic status of the respondents into high (70>), medium (35-69) and low (up to 35) on the basis of points scored by the respondents. I have ranked them on the basis of living standard of the respondents, their daily food habits, socio-economic outlook, creativity and sources of information, recreational implements, and their greater political access (Table 16.14). The respondents of lower category form 67.76 per cent,

Table 16.13: Awareness and Participation of the Tribals

Parameter	*Number*	*Percentage*
Awareness of the tribals about various development programmes	Yes 151 No 94	61.63 38.37
Active involvement and participation is essential for the success of various schemes and improvement of the tribals	Yes 231 No 14	94.28 5.72
What type of loans received:		
Help in the form of loan and subsidy	59	24.08
Help in the form of technical know-how	6	2.45
Help in the form of employment and daily labour	178	72.65
Help in the form of social forestry	2	0.82
Selection from depressed and poor families	Yes 123 No 122	50.20 49.80
Desired effects of effective programme implementation:		
Buying more foods and consumer durables	60	24.50
Living lives with more certainty	22	8.98
Increase in income and depending lesson landowners or moneylenders	25	10.20
Not getting adequate benefits and more facilities should be provided	111	45.30
Good for employment opportunities	7	2.86
Effective implementation will bring about changes in their social outlook	9	3.67
Funds not properly utilized	8	3.26
Banks should be liberal in terms of loans	3	1.23
Selection of beneficiaries not satisfactory	131	53.47
Receiving information about development programmes	Yes 211 No 34	86.12 13.88
Sources of information:		
Panchayat members	18	7.34
Local party leaders	95	38.78
Gram Sansad members	98	40.00
Panchayat members demand for people's participation	Yes 141 No 104	57.55 42.45
Banks interested to provide loan	Yes 21 No 224	8.57 91.43
Loans properly utilized	Yes 28 No 217	11.43 88.57

Source: Field Survey.

who participate less in the decision-making. The beneficiaries in the forms of loans and subsidy, technical knowhow and social forestry were only 27.35 per cent, i.e. 57 in number. Out of these, 54.39 per cent, 24.57 per cent, 21.04 per cent and 14.93 per cent respondents gave their first, second, third and negative preferences to their environment with Panchayat members *vis-à-vis* 8.96 per cent, 5.97 per cent, 11.94 per cent and 73.13 per cent to their involvement with Government functionaries. Most of these beneficiaries were from the age group of 21-30 years (76.12 per cent), low economy (79.10 per cent), illiterate group (62.69 per cent and agricultural labourers (67.16 per cent) (Table 16.15). Landless agricultural labourer and landless share-croppers also represented these groups of beneficiaries. Out of total respondents (245), 80.82 per cent tribals were landless and 11.02 per cent were of having lands <1 acre. Very few (6.94 per cent and 1.22 per cent) reported to have 1-3 acre and 3>acres (Table 16.14). The down-trodden people are far away from acting as decision-making agents. Distribution of *patta* lands and *barga* operation were acts of dictated mobilization by political parties and political leaders.

Table 16.14: Respondents' Socio-Economic Profiles

Parameter	*Classification*	*Number*	*Percentage*
Age	21-30 years	165	67.35
	31-50 years	49	20.00
	51-60 years	31	12.65
Education	Illiterate	91	37.14
	Literate	89	36.33
	Class I-IV	51	20.82
	Class IV-X	12	4.90
	Class X-XII	2	0.81
Occupation	Agricultural labourers	145	59.18
	Share-croppers	85	34.69
	Business	2	0.81
	Others	13	5.31
Landholding	Ownership (including patta and barga lands):		
	Landless	198	80.82
	Less than 1 acre	27	11.02
	1-3 acres	17	6.94
	3 acres >	3	1.22
	Share-cropping (90 respondents out of 245 have no barga land):		
	Less than 1 acre	65	41.93
	1-3 acres	72	46.45
	3 acres >	18	11.61
Socio-economic status	High (70)	30	1224
	Medium (35-69)	49	20.00
	Low (up to 35)	166	67.76

Source: Field Survey.

Table 16.15: Socio-economic Background of the Beneficiaries (Direct Beneficiary in the Forms of Loans and Subsidy, Technical Know-How and Social Forestry)

Parameter	Number	Percentage
Economy:		
Low	53	79.10
Medium	14	20.90
High	...	...
Education:		
Illiterate	42	62.69
Literate	17	25.37
Class I-IV	8	11.94
Class IVX	...	...
Class X-XII	...	...
Occupation:		
Agricultural labourer	45	67.16
Share-cropper	22	32.48
Business	...	...
Others	...	...
Age:		
21-30 years	51	76.12
31-50 years	12	17.91
51-60 years	4	5.97
Socio-political relations:		
Involvement with panchayat members	Yes 57	85.07
	First preference 31	54.39
	Second preference 14	24.57
	Third preference 12	21.04
	No 10	14.93
Involvement with government functionaries	Yes 18	26.87
	First preference 6	8.96
	Second preference 4	5.97
	Third preference 8	11.94
	No 49	73.13

Source: Field Survey

Decisions were not taken by tribals themselves, rather motivated by the party-panchayat leaders in this regard. Non-distribution of *khas* lands, non-recording of *patta* lands and non-distribution of *patta* papers have produced non-participation among the tribal people in this area, when and where they act after the dictates of political leaders. This directed mobilization is mostly unsuited to their participatory development. Participatory culture is absent in real sense. Participation has to be institutionalized to ensure involvement of the people at all stages of development: societal and extra-societal environmental research, planning and programme design, implementation and management of programmes. Sustainable resource utilization, appropriate technology intervention for resource conservation and regeneration, gradual empowerment of the socially disadvantaged group—all these efforts can be ensured through the participation of the people. People would participate in the development process if the expected benefits exceed the expected costs of participation, if they are empowered to do so, if they have the ability to organize and motivate the co-villagers, if local leadership provides opportunities to participate in various development programmes, and if the government provides sizeable amount of financial technical assistance in mobilizing people's resources and appropriate infrastructural facilities. The parameters of participation are at the low level. In 'cost-benefit analysis' parameter 55.92 per cent accepted the fact that receiving of benefits from development schemes would not improve their life pattern in real sense, in 'cmpowerment to the people' parameter they (38 77 per cent and 4572 per cent respondents) expressed their deep concern and insincere attitude to the power to decide and selection of programmes, in 'people's ability to organize and motivate the co-villagers' parameter 72.65 per cent affirmed that party leaders were able to organize and motivate the villagers, in 'local leadership' parameter 98.37 per cent respondents agreed with the decision-making power of local leadership and in 'financial and technical help from the government' parameter 87.75 per cent said that government help in terms of loans, subsidy and technical assistance were meagre and not properly utilized (Table 16.16). My perception here is that they did not know the actualities of non-utilization, try to find out the causes behind it and the actual requirements to make sustained development of their own (Field Survey). The domain of their perception is not clear.

The institutionalization of Panchayats through the mobilization of the poor has not been possible, rather mobilization of the middle class intellectuals and concentration and consolidation of party politics have become the reality of the hour. In *Jamalpur* Panchayat Samity only 16.66 per cent tribal members are represented during the year 1998-2003. Only 15.67 per cent tribal members represented the Gram Panchayat scene on an average. Popular participation in the panchayat is quite encouraging. The participatory orientation of the tribals in different elections is high. Most of the respondents expressed their views that they cast their votes in almost all elections; they faced (Table 16.17). The tribal people are adaptive to and compromising with the prevailing attitudes towards socio-

Table 16.16: Respondents' Answers to Participation in Development Programmes

Parameter	*Respondents' answers*	*Number*	*Percentage*
Cost-benefit analysis	(a) After receiving benefits from development schemes, what would be the result? Nothing	137	55.92
	(b) Beneficiaries are selected before *Gram Sansad* meetings	65	26.53
	(c) We follow our leaders, we participate	43	17.55
Empowerment to the people	(a) People having close relation with party-panchayat leaders have the power to decide	95	38.77
	(b) Programmes are selected at the top level through Panchayats	112	45.72
	(c) We receive loans and benefits, but do not take part in decision-making	28	1.43
	(d) We take part in decision-making and discuss matters with others	10	4.08
People's ability to organize and motivate the co-villagers	(a) Party leaders can do it	178	72.65
	(b) We themselves cannot do it, we are poor and illiterate	53	21.63
	(c) Do not say anything	14	5.72
Local leadership	(a) Local leadership controls	241	98.37
	(b) General people participate in decision-making	4	1.63
Financial and technical help from government	(a) Meagre	109	44.49
	(b) Meagre and not properly utilized	106	4.26
	(c) Not conducive to our requirements	30	12.25

Source: Field Survey.

economic conditions. They cast their votes, discuss political matters with their leaders, friends and neighbours, and also attend political meetings. Most of the respondents are not aware of various political issues, but they participate in elections for expressive purposes. Though the number of voting turn-out is significant, most of them do not know the significance of voting, their rights and duties and their role in the political system. 37.14 per cent and 62.86 per cent respondents expressed

Table 16.17: Factors of Tribal Political Participation

Parameter	*Age*	*Total respon-dents*	*Distribution of respon-dents*	*Casting of votes in tie*	*Percentage*
No. of time votes cast	21-30	165	7	2 to 3	4.24
			16	4 to 5	9.70
			133	6 to 7	80.61
			9	8 to 9	5.45
			...	10 to 11	...
			...	12 to 13	...
	31-50	49	5	14 to 15	10.21
			16	16 to 17	32.65
			28	18 to 19	57.14
	51-60	31	...	20 to 21	...
			18	22 to 23	58.06
			13	24 to 25	41.94
			...	26 to 27	...
Motivation behind voting	21-60	245	...	...	100
A. Electing the candidate	...	91	...	...	37.14
B. If elected, he will provide help to us	...	154	...	...	62.86
Motivating agents	21-60	245	...	...	100
A. Socio-economic back ground of the candidate	...	...	23	...	9.39
B. Political leaders	...	...	105	...	42.86
C. Friends and relatives	...	...	17	...	6.94
D. Allurements like wage increase, land distribution etc.	...	...	100	...	40.81
Discussion of political issues	21-60	245	...	...	100
A. Casually	...	...	138	...	56.33
B. Regularly	...	...	85	...	34.69
C. No	...	...	22	...	8.98
Discussion with	21-60	245	...	...	100
A. Political leaders	...	...	168	...	75.34
B. Friends and relatives	...	...	30	...	13.45
C. Family members	...	...	25	...	11.21
Information gathered through	21-60	245	...	...	100
A. Radio/TV	...	...	45	...	18.37
B. Political leaders	...	...	142	...	58.00
C. Election agents	...	...	58	...	23.63
Political awareness	21-60	245	...	...	100
No. of political parties					
Yes	...	...	167	...	68.16
No	...	...	78	...	31.84
Election manifestoes and programmes					
Yes	...	...	32	...	13.06
No	...	...	213	...	86.94

Source: Field Survey.

that they cast their votes with a view to elect their candidate only and to elect the same as he would provide goods and services after being elected, respectively. Being allured by wage increase, *patta* lands distribution and operation *barga* (40.8 per cent as motivating agent), motivated by political leaders (42.86 per cent as motivating agent) and inspired and encouraged by friends and relatives (6.94 per cent as motivating agent), they cast their votes without exactly knowing or without going to know or to understand what they are doing and why they are doing. They elect the candidate, which they support without keeping in mind the socio-economic background of the candidates, their leadership qualities and without being aware of the principles of their party. Though they took part in political discussion casually (56.33 per cent), however, they showed their keen interest in elections and politics. The number of tribal people interested in politics does take part in political discussion, but the same percentage of people does not attend meetings (Table 16.18). The difference may be cited as–

Difference (D) = Attending meetings – Political discussion or Interest n politics
Low = 0.82 < Medium = 2.04 > High = - 2.04
Illiterate = 1.22 > Literate = – 0.82 < Cass I-IV = – 0.40 > Class IV-X = – 1.63 < Class X-XII = 0
Agricultural labourer = 0.8 = Share-cropper = 0.81
Business = 0 > Others = 0 – 0.81

III. Conclusion

The success of parliamentary democracy depends upon willingness of the minority to accept the majority rule, agreement on fundamental rules of the game and eternal vigilance of the public (Bhardwaj, 1980, p. 30). Otherwise, it will weaken democracy, what Norberto Bobbio (1987) calls 'broken promises' of democracy (Bobbio, 1987, p. 8). Bobbio warns about the defects in inherence that without proper application and operation democracy might result in discordance, irregularities, disorder and instability. So, due respect to the rules of the game, both constitutive and regulatory should there be. The simple fact of the matter is that the world has never built a multi-ethnic democracy in which no particular ethnic group is in majority and where political equality, social equality and economies that empower all have been achieved. Representation is public, therefore, no secret session, secret agreements be committed to ensure democracy educative, creative, logical and comprehensive, in essence, harmless and idyllic. Today's parliamentary democracy drifts away from its purposes and goals abolishing separation of powers between executive, legislature and judiciary, freedom of the individuals and parliamentary privileges and immunities, thereby public suffers from terrible disillusionment about parties and parliaments as of close-door politics of party coteries and formality politics of parliamentarians (Schmitt, 1985, pp. 49-50). Therefore, openness and discussion are two main pillars of parliamentarism, i.e. truth and justice. Here, participation in politics and participation in the development process are also important.

There are four measures of protecting democracy, namely following the rules of the game of democracy, giving the opportunity and legitimacy to political opponents or opposition parties, toleration of political violence and giving the political opponents to flourish to take part in socio-political dialogue.

NOTES

1. AIR 1964 SC 1823.
2. AIR 1976 SC 490.
3. AIR 1993 SC 477.
4. AIR 1997 SC 3505.

REFERENCES

Almond, G.A. and Verba, S. (1963). *The Civic Culture*, New Jersey, Princeton University Press.

Becker, David G. (1984). "Development, Democracy and Dependency in Latin America: A Post-Imperialist View", *Third World Quarterly*, Vol. 6, No. 2.

Beetham, David (Ed.) (1995). *Politics and Human Rights*, London, Blackwell.

Bhardwaj, R.K. (1983). *Parliamentary Democracy and Legislators*, New Delhi, National Publishing House.

Bobbio, Norberto (1987). *The Future of Democracy,* London, Polity Press.

Bogdanor, Vernon (1985). *Representatives of the People?: Parliamentarians and Constituents in Western Democracies*, England, Gower Publishing Company.

Bogdanor, Vernon and Butler, David (1983). *Democracy and Elections: Electoral Systems and their Political Consequences*, New York, Cambridge University Press.

Bose, Nirmal (1977). "India's Eastern Tribes", In Romesh Thapar (Ed.), *Tribe, Caste and Religion in India*, Meerut, Macmillan.

Bose, Sugata and Jalal, Ayesha (1998). *Modern South Asia*, New Delhi: Oxford

University Press.

Burdwan District Committee, CPI (M) (1985). *Shamiksha: Ashtam Lok Sabha Nirbachan*, February 28.

Chandhoke, Neera (1999). "A Nation Searching for a Narrative in terms of Globalization", *Economic and Political Weekly*, Vol. XXXIV, No. 18.

Chatterjee, Partha (1997). "Development Planning and the Indian State", In Partha Chatterjee (Ed.), *State and Politics in India*, New Delhi, Oxford University Press.

Chaudhury, Mrinal Datta (1985). "On the Political Structure of a Liberal Democracy", *Economic and Political Weekly*, June 1.

Dahl, Robert A. (1971), *Polyarchy: Participation and Opposition*, New Haven, Yale University Press.

Dahrendorf, R. (1959). *Class and Class Conflict in Industrial Society*, London, Routledge and Kegan Paul. (Like that of the 'industrial enterprise', I propose that modern parliament and state legislatures are imperatively co-ordinated associations which institutionalize various conflicts within the structure of liberal parliamentary setup).

Desai, A.R. (1977). "Tribes in Transition", In Romesh Thapar (Ed.), *Tribe, Caste and Religion in India*, Meerut, Macmillan.

Galanter, Marc (1992). *Law and Society in Modern India,* New Delhi, Oxford University Press.

Geertz, C. (1963). "The Integrative Revolution", In Geertz (Ed.), *Old Societies and New States*, New York, The Free Press of Glencoe.

Gutmann, A. (1994). *Multiculturalism: Examining the Politics of Recognition*, Princeton, Princeton University Press.

Gutmann, A. and Thompson, D. (1996). *Democracy and Disagreement*, Masachussetts, Harvard University Press.

Habermas, J. (1984). *A Theory of Communicative Action*, London, Beacon Press.

Huntington, S.P. (1968). *Political Order in Changing Societies*, New York, Yale University Press.

Karnath, G.K. (1996). "Caste in Contemporary Rural India", In M.N. Srinivas (Ed.), *Caste–Its Twentieth Century Avatar*, New Delhi, Viking Penguin India.

Kohli, Atul (1992). *Democracy and Discontent*, New York, Cambridge University Press.

Kymlicka, W. and Norman, W. (2000), "Introduction", In Kymlicka and Norman (Eds.), *Citizenship in Diverse Societies*, Oxford, Oxford University Press.

La Palombara, Joseph and Weiner, Myron (1966). *Political Parties and Political Development*, Princeton, Princeton University Press.

Lenthold, David A. (1968). *Electioneering in a Democracy*, London, John Wiley and Sons.

Madan, T.N. (1977). "Indian Society: The Rural Context", In S.C. Dube (Ed.), *India since Independence*, New Delhi, Vikas.

Mital, Nemi Sharan (1972). "Crisis of Political Parties in India", In *Indian Parties and Politics* (Ed.), Simla, The Institute of Constitutional and Parliamentary Studies.

Norris, Christopher (1982). *Deconstruction: Theory and Practice*, London.

Pickles, Dorothy (1970). *Democracy*, London, Methuen and Co. Ltd.

Prakasa, H.E. Shri (1957). *Democracy and Parliamentary Government*, Ahmedabad, Harold Laski Institute of Political Science.

Rawls, John (1971). *A Theory of Justice*, Harvard, Harvard University Press.

Rubin, Richard L. (1976). *Party Dynamics: The Democratic Coalition and the Politics of Change*, New York, Oxford University Press.

Sarwate, Dilip M. (1990). *Political Marketing*, New Delhi, Tata McGraw-Hill Publishing Co.

Schmitt, Carl (1985). *The Crisis of Parliamentary Democracy*, Massachusetts, MIT Press.

Shourie, Arun (1990). *Individuals, Institutions, Processes*, New Delhi, Viking.

Tully, James (1995). *Strange Multiplicity: Constitutionalism in an Age of Diversity*, Cambridge, Cambridge University Press.

Vanaik, Achin (1997). *Communalism Contested: Religion, Modernity and Secularization*, New Delhi, Vistaar Publications.

Willhoites, Fred H. (1963). "Political Order and Consensus: A Continuing Problem", *The Western Political Quarterly*, Vol. XXVI, June.

Williams, R.M. (1964). *Strangers Next Door*, Englewood Cliffs, Prentice-Hall.

17

Village Adoption: Transforming Rural World

A Case of Jorandajhariya

S.N. Rao

> "Village adoption means not only building the infrastructure but focusing on social indicators like education, nutrition, health and also bringing a change in attitude of the people towards development."
> —*Dr. W.R. Reddy*

India is largely rural and a country of villages. According to Census 2011, there are 6,49,481 villages representing rural India. The village economy is the soul of Indian economy and provides food security to the country. If the villages fail to produce foodgrains, the country starves. Culturally, the villages are full of traditions and family values continue. It is a tradition of joint family and the human relations were unbroken. The human feelings and emotions expressed in villages are still a happy family. The rural India (villages) is vibrant with 68.84 per cent of human resources, fascinating culture and ethnic values but, often unemployed and underutilised.

The rural India suffers from innumerable problems. The widespread poverty, growing inequalities, rapid population growth, rising unemployment (65% of youth are in the age group of working) in rural areas is a concern. The problems of hunger, ignorance, ill health and high mortality are most acute. The villages also face natural calamities like droughts, floods. Therefore, there is a dire necessity to develop the infrastructure and also to improve the quality of life in rural areas.

The rural India suffers from innumerable problems. The widespread poverty, growing inequalities, rapid population growth, rising unemployment (65% of youth are in the age group of working) in rural areas is a concern. The problems of hunger, ignorance, ill health and high mortality are most acute. No schools. If the school exists, the teacher will not be available or one teacher headed schools and the buildings of the government schools are in dilapidated condition. The sanitation conditions in Government Schools are worst. The girls are afraid to attend the schools due to bad sanitation conditions in the schools.

In the villages, there is no infrastructure, like roads and drinking water. 67 per cent of villages do not have water for irrigation, depends upon the vagaries of monsoon. Liquor is the main enemy of the villagers and it is available and destroying the families. But for some bad elements it is a livelihood and profit making activity. Conflicts in the village have become common as politics divide the people. As a result many families were disturbed. Corruption has become a common feature affecting the poorest of the poor. Many people has lost livelihoods in rural areas and migrated to urban areas. The villages also face natural calamities like droughts, floods. Therefore, there is a dire necessity to develop the infrastructure and also to improve the quality of life in rural areas. The Government is initiating many schemes to develop the rural India.

The development process of rural India has witnessed several changes and achieved a new dimension. The people have become the 'centre-stage' in the process of participatory development. The journey of rural development has started from food security to Rural Livelihoods. In fact 'three' -pronged strategy was adopted to alleviate poverty in rural areas. The first strategy is creation of employment and infrastructure through major schemes like MGNREGA, NRLM, DDU-GKY etc. The second strategy is area development through different schemes like PMKSY, MGNREGA etc. The third strategy is social security measures, i.e. special assistance to the differently disabled, under NSAP. Besides these strategies, there are many schemes which also target different individuals. Ministry of the Rural Development (MoRD) with the outlay of more than Rs. 1,15,000 crore carries out various programmes of Rural Development like MGNREGS, NRLM, DDU GKY, PMGSY, NSAP, PMAY(R) etc.

The new initiative of the Government of India is Village Adoption by the Members of Parliament, i.e. Sansad Adarsh Gram Yojana (SAGY).[1] The Prime Minister Shri Narendra Modi has launched the SAGY (SAANJHI) on 11th October, 2014, i.e. on the birth anniversary of Shri Lok Nayak Jai Prakash Narayan. The aim of SAGY is to providing access to basic amenities and opportunities to enable the villagers to shape their own destiny. The SAGY is an innovative approach to create a 'Model Village/Adarsh Village'. Under this scheme, each Member of Parliament has to choose one village from the constituency that they represent, except their own village or their in-laws village and fix parameters and make it a model village by 2016. Under the SAGY, the Cricketer Shri Sachin Tendulkar has adopted Puttamraju Kandriga village in Nellore district of Andhra Pradesh and transformed it into a modern village with the infrastructure, the villagers never dreamed of these facilities. Prime Minister Shri Narendra Modi has adopted Jayapur in Varanasi. The present case study focuses on Jorandajharia village adopted by the Hon'ble Member of Parliament Shri Nanda Kumar Sai.

The model village concept has 'two' aspects: i) Development of infrastructure and livelihoods and ii) Inculcating moral values. In development aspect the SAGY aims provision of basic amenities like education, health, sanitation, agriculture, livelihoods and infrastructure like roads. The moral values are people's participation, Antyodaya, gender equality, dignity of women, social justice, spirit of community service, cleanliness, eco-friendliness, maintaining ecological balance, peace and harmony, mutual cooperation, self-reliance, local self-government, transparency and accountability in public life etc.

Concept of Development of Model Village

The concept of 'model village' encompasses 'four' elements in development process:

1. **Personality Development:** The personality development focuses on behavioural changes of the villagers. The behavioural changes are attitude of trust and belongingness, liquor free, open defecation free (ODF), internal dispute mechanism and development of village.
2. **Human Development:** The human development focuses on Education (Children and Adult), Health, Nutrition, Institutional Delivery, social security measures like old age pension and widow pension.
3. **Economic Development:** The Economic Development focuses on Livelihood and skill development, financial inclusion, SHG formation, providing micro-credit to the groups for entrepreneurial activities and providing basic minimum services.

4. **Social Development:** The social development focuses on voluntarism, i.e. shramadaan to achieve ODF, to built the roads and houses, water harvesting structure for all pucca buildings, ponds cleaning, overall cleanliness of the village, soak pit construction near all hand pumps and buildings social values like peaceful coexistence. In sports, frequent inter-school competitions, self-defence training for girls. Good governance like responsibility and transparent administration.

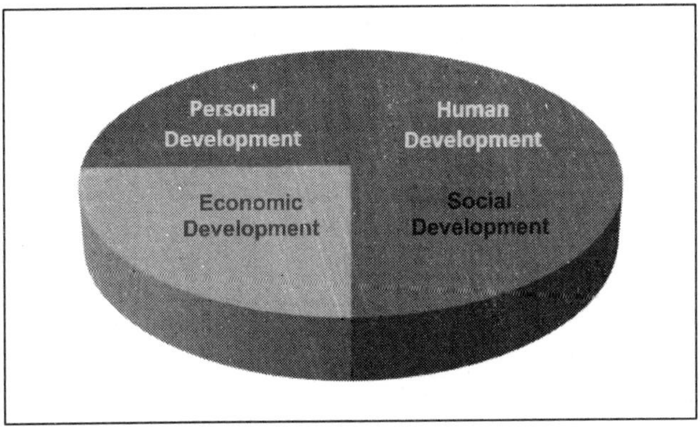

Concept of Development of Model Village

Fundings

Funds for 'Model Village' are from the following sources:

1. Funds from central RD schemes, such as the Mahatma Gandhi National Rural Employment Guarantee Scheme, Indira Awas Yojana, Pradhan Mantri Gram Sadak Yojana, and Backward Regions Grant Fund and other state government schemes,
2. The Member of Parliament Local Area Development Scheme (MPLADS),
3. The gram panchayat's own revenue,
4. Central and State Finance Commission Grants, and
5. Corporate Social Responsibility funds.

Strategy

The following strategy was adopted to make the village as a model village:

1. Entry point activities to energize and mobilize the community towards positive common action.
2. Participatory planning exercise for identifying people's needs and priorities in an integrated manner.
3. Converging Centrally Sponsored Schemes and other State schemes.
4. Repairing and renovating existing infrastructure.
5. Strengthening the Gram Panchayats, people's institutions and promoting transparency and accountability.

A Case of Jorandajharia

Jorandajhariya is a small tiny Gram Panchayat in Farsabahar block of Jashpur district of Chhattisgarh state. The majority of the population belongs to the tribes, i.e. Oraon/Kurukh, Baiga and Munda. The GP is situated 25 km away from block headquarters of Farsabahar and 107 km away from district headquarters Jashpur. Jorandajhariya Gram Panchayat has a population of 1451 and 285 households. The GP falls under the Schedule V of the Indian Constitution where PESA (Panchayat Extension in Scheduled Areas) is implemented. The Act provides special powers to the Gram Sabha to "safeguard and preserve the traditions and customs of people, their cultural identity, community resources and the customary mode of dispute resolution." The tribal community have strong unity and ethnic binding. The Jashpur district is a left wing extremist (LWE) infested district bordering Jharkhand and Odisha and Jorandjharia was a movement corridor of Naxalites.

The Hon'ble MP from Rajya Sabha Shri Nand Kumar Sai adopted Jorandajharia Gram Panchayat from Jashpur district in Chhattisgarh under Phase I of SAGY. This village is a remote location and have innumerable problems and a challenge development. It is a Naxalite corridor, elephant corridor, snake corridor and have evils like liquor consumption and internal quarrel. The literacy rate was low. The Hon'ble MP, Shri Nand Kumar Sai and Charge Officer, Shri Deepak Soni has taken as a challenge to develop the village.

To initiate the process, the Hon'ble MP conducted a meeting with the district officers and the villagers in the village itself. The Hon'ble MP informed that to develop the village as Adarsh Village, the people should become Adarsh. The strategy to initiate various developmental activities was based on the axiom that "any change, for it to be long lasting, has to be from within the community with active participation from all." The meetings used to be regular with the people and the officers. As a result, the administration has built a rapport with the villagers and confidence of the locals has increased.

Through regular interaction with people the confidence was built among the people. The administration would facilitate any good initiative that the people took towards development and behavioural change. In a span of one and a half years, the panchayat has many achievements to its credit and the village was transformed into model village.

Problems in Jorandajharia

Naxalite Corridor: The Jashpur is a Left Wing Extremist (LWE) infested district bordering Jharkhand and Odisha. The Jorandajharia is a border village of three states, namely, Chhattisgarh, Jharkhand and Odisha. In a thick forest, the village under the cloud of Naxalite corridor. After 5 pm the people used to afraid to come out of the village, due to naxalite passage through this village. If they give shelter to the naxalites, the police harass them. To avoid the problems, the people used to stay in the houses. Due to naxalite passage, the police used to visit the village frequently and harass the people whom they suspect of being naxalite sympathiser. The people were always sufferers in this passage and lived with the fear.

Elephant Corridor: Elephant corridors are narrow strips of land that allow elephants to move from one habitat patch to another. There are 88 identified elephant corridors in India. 12 are in North-western India, 20 in Central India, 14 in Northern West Bengal, 22 in North-eastern India and 20 in Southern India. Of the total, 77.3 per cent of the corridors are being regularly used by elephants[2]. Jorandjharia falls in East and Central India. In a thick cover of forest, the elephants used to visit the village in day time and also in nights. Whenever the elephants visit the village, the people used to hide in their houses, fields and wherever they find a place to hide. The elephants used to destroy the crops and also houses. The peoples used to afraid of the elephants and will be vigilant about their visit to the village. The people were not able to control the menace of the elephants as it is a natural passage of the elephants. The people of the village are always afraid of elephant passage. Sometimes, the elephants become violent. This will threaten the fields and their lives are in jeopardy.

Snake Corridor: At the village entrance, the Health and Family Welfare Department has displayed big flexi board about the famous poisonous snakes are moving in the village. The village is a part of Tapkara Region which is having a large variety of snakes. This region is referred as a Naglok (kingdom of snakes) due to the number of snakes that are moving in this region. The varieties of snakes are Indian Cobra, Common Krait and Common Cobra. Different poisonous snakes will be moving in day time and night time. In, all the houses, the people use to keep anti-venom medicine. Sometimes the people carry anti-venom medicine in their pockets. But still, every year 4 to 5 people die of snake bite.

Liquor Consumption: Most of the people in the village belonged to tribes. As a part of the tribal culture, the people consume local liquor (rice beer). It is a custom to consume the liquor. But it has become an addiction and women also used to consume the liquor. As a result the people suffered with poverty, the break of families and internal quarrels were common. The liquor has destroyed the people's income, livelihoods and health. Sometimes, the people quarrel. As a result, the people go to the police station. It affects family life and children education.

Jorandajharia-Transformation Towards Model Village

The concept of SAGY (Model Village) has Hon'ble Member of Parliament (MP) and in-charge officer to oversee the development process of village.

Aadarsh MP: Hon'ble MP Shri **Nand Kumar Sai,** MP, from Rajya Sabha adopted the village Jorandajharia. He was 'thrice' elected as Member of Legislative Assembly (MLA) and twice as Member of Parliament (Lok Sabha) (MP) and twice he has become a Rajya Sabha MP. This shows that his commitment towards development. Jorandajharia, a village neighbour to his native village and have innumerable problems. The officers expressed aghast about selection of this village. They asked him, Sir, Why you select this village. This village is having full of problems'. Liquor consumption is high. Even the women used to consume liquor regularly. The naxalites are very active in this village. The officers dare not to visit this village after 5 pm. Conflicts are common. But the Hon'ble MP took as a challenge to this village.

Charge Officer: The adopted village facilitated by the officer, called as charge officer. Mr. Deepak Soni, a young civil servant, (2011-batch) was Chief Executive Officer, Zilla Parishaed, Jashpur district and Charge Officer of Jorandajharia. He is a mentor who made a Jorandajharia as Adarsh Village. In a brief stint, he worked in Narayapur district of Bastar region, a Naxalite Corridor. He made his mark and got awarded for successful implementation of MGNREGA in Naxalite region. After that he was posted to urban areas, i.e. Raipur (state headquarters). He was disappointed with the urban posting, that to state headquarters, he went to the Chief Secretary and requested him for posting in tribal and remote part of the region. The Chief Secretary was aghast about his desire to post in remote and tribal areas, because most of the officers request him for urban posting, mainly state headquarters. But, Mr. Deepak Soni has requested the Chief Secretary to post him in remote and tribal areas. He says that "I don't want urban posting. I want work in remote and tribal areas. He further says that "If I want, I should have become a Software Engineer and should have gone to USA. But I choose this career to help the poor tribals." The Chief Secretary was aghast but posted him to Jashpur district, i.e. tribal and Naxalite area.

Initially, the people have not cooperated with him, because, the village falls under the Naxalite corridor and after 5 pm the Naxalites will be moving in this area. The people felt that there is a risk in talking to him. But he keeps on visiting this area, and used to stay up to 8 pm talking to the people. He gradually reduced the gap between the people and the administration. Slowly, the people weaned from Naxalites. He used to respond to phone calls and to SMS even in midnight. This made the people to accept him as good administrator. He used to solve their problems immediately.

After acceptance by the people, he started his work of changing the attitude of the villagers. In one of the meeting with the people he said that "I can make all roads as cement roads. I can make all houses pucca houses, construct more anganwadi centres and additional rooms for the school. But you should change your attitude towards development. He put few principles to the people:

1. Stop taking liquor.
2. Entire village should be ODF.
3. Stopping conflicts.
4. To become a literate.

The people trusted and promised him to make their village as a 'model village'.

Transforming Jorandajharia

The most prominent issue to transform the village is to change the attitude of people towards development. The first challenge is to make the village as a 'Liquor free Village'. The liquor consumption is a tradition of the tribals and it is a part of their culture. The women are also used to consume the liquor. It has become a challenge to the administration.

1. Liquor Free Village: To make the village as liquor free, a movement was created by involving the people. From each tribe, the leaders were selected and were made as the torchbearers of the movement. The tribals have a tradition of unity and listening to their leaders. The harm of the consumption of liquor was printed on flexi boards and pasted on different places in the villages. The flexi boards clearly described the wife beating, children suffering of denial of education due to financial loss, internal quarrels and loss of health. At the same time, the benefits of not consuming liquor also depicted on flexi boards like the concept of happy family, children going to schools, financial improvement and construction of new houses and buying new vehicle and travel by the entire family on the vehicle. Besides, putting flexi boards, street plays were enacted about the bad and good about the stopping of liquor consumption. The women were told not to allow the drunken husbands inside of the house. The SHG women have taken as a challenge to stop the liquor consumption.

The first step was a resolution passed by the gram sabha in which people unanimously decided:

- Not to make any liquor in homes.
- Stored liquor bottles may be destroyed in public view.
- No. to buy or sell liquor in panchayat area (special powers under PESA).
- Not to engage in drinking of liquor in, around and outside of the Panchayat.

Soon the people have formed 'Nasha Mukti Samiti', which included Self-Help Group (SHG) members in majority, with the objective to oversee the implementation of above passed resolution. Children added to the momentum by requesting their family members to continue abstinence and formed their own drama society, teachers scripted plays for the society to present to the people. In successive gram sabhas people reviewed the situation, the liquor quitters were honoured and the defaulters were publically admonished. In one sabha, the natives decided for the provision of penalty, with a fine of Rs. 1000 being imposed for every defaulting act and the informer to be rewarded with 50 per cent of the amount so collected. This led to collection of Rs. 3000. The people slowly stopped weaning away from the liquor.

In one of the meeting, the Hon'ble MP Shri Nanda Kumar Sai was addressing the awareness meeting about the hazardous impact of liquor consumption. One drunkard put a question to Hon'ble MP saying that

"Liquor is like a salt. Without that we cannot live. If you stop taking salt, we will stop liquor consumption." The Hon'ble MP declared in public meeting saying that **"I will not take salt in rest of my life".** He has kept his promise and he stopped taking salt. This convinced the villagers and slowly the villagers gave up liquor consumption. This is a biggest achievement of MP to make the village as Aadarsh village.

Today, Jorandajharia is a total addiction free panchayat with people taking pride in their achievement. They are now engaging themselves in spreading the message of de-addiction in the neighbouring panchayats. On Independence Day the people of the village vowed to inspire 15 other villages to become liquor addiction free villages by the next 15th August 2019.

2. People's Participation: Participation is an essential element of human development. Participation refers to "taking part or sharing". Participation means involvement of people in the economic, social, cultural and political processes that affect their lives. People may, in some cases, have complete and direct control over these processes. In other cases, the control may be partial or indirect. One important aspect of participation is that the people should have constant access to decision-making and power.

The concept of participation is understood differently in different contests. Stan Burkey (1993) defines participation as "an essential part of human initiative, creativity, responsibility, pride and cooperation." Burkey understands that "participation as a process by which people learn to take charge of their own lives and find solutions to their own problems." People's participation is central to development in democratic systems. The operation of democracy results in innovations and provides opportunity for citizens to participate in the activities of democratic functioning and developing themselves.

People's participation is a hall mark in development of Jorandajharia. The motivation of Deepak Soni, Charge Officer and Hon'ble MP created a sense of unity and participation in development works. The people's participation has started with shramadan to construct toilets to make the village as an ODF.

3. Women's Participation: 'Women hold up half the sky'—Mao Zedong[3]. Development surrounds the women. Women's participation is essential to the success of development and plays a catalytic role towards achievement of transformational economic, environmental and social changes required for sustainable development.

The women are near equal to men in numbers (49.55%), but there exists a gender gap in access to education and finances. In India, the women were less literate compared to men. The women are 65.46 per cent literate and whereas the men are 82.14 per cent literate (Census–2011). The women have limited access to credit, health care and education. These are further aggravated by the global food and economic crises and climate change. Empowering them is essential, not only for the well-being of individuals, families and rural communities, but also for overall economic productivity, given women's large presence in the agricultural workforce worldwide.[4] Empowering women with finances, education and they will change the society towards development.

The success of Jorandajharia is women's participation. To initiate the process, the women formed as Self-Help Groups. This unity has strengthened them and made frontrunners in all the movements. The women are the most sufferers due to liquor consumption by the men. Open defecation is hazardous, as they go out for defecation, particularly in the nights they face problems with the scorpions, snakes. The women are in forefront in Nasha bandh (Liquor stopping) and united to stop the preparation and consumption of liquor. They are in forefront in making the village as open defecation free (ODF), achieving the literacy and children's education. They have formed different committees like education committee to achieve 100 per cent literacy and to take care of children's education. The women participated in construction of toilets and made the men to participate in construction of toilets. To make the success of Joradhjharia, as a model village the women played a crucial role.

4. Open Defecation Free (ODF): Swachh Village: "Let us build a clean India, Country can do it", the Prime Minister Narendra Modi's clarion call to make the India as a 'Clean India'. The Prime Minister has launched 'Clean India Mission' on 145th birth anniversary of Mahatma Gandhi on 2nd October in 2014. Clean India Mission or Swachh Bharat Mission is a major policy of Prime Minister Narendra Modi to make the country as a clean India by 2nd October, 2019, by 150th birth anniversary of Mahatma Gandhi. This is to fulfil the dream of Mahatma Gandhi towards Swachh India.

The mission is a massive mass movement to initiate the theme of cleanliness all through the India. The mission aims to cover all the rural and urban areas to make India as an ideal country before the world. The target of the mission is to eliminate open defecation, converting insanitary toilets into pour flush toilets, eradicating manual scavenging, complete disposal and reuse of solid and liquid wastes. The mission also aims to bring behavioural changes of people to practice health practices, spreading cleanliness among the people.

"Sanitation is more important than Independence" Mahatma Gandhi said before declaring India Independence. He emphasised cleanliness and sanitation in daily lives of the people. But the campaign has failed because of lack of people's participation. After 68 years of Independence, the most effective campaign was launched, requesting all sections of the people to participate in this mission and to make India as the clean India[5].

Swachh Bharat Mission aims to achieve an Open-Defecation Free (ODF) India by 2 October, 2019, the 150th anniversary of the birth of Mahatma Gandhi by constructing 90 million toilets in rural India.[6] The mission also aims to establish an accountable mechanism of monitoring of toilet use. It also contributes to India reaching Sustainable Development Goal No. 6 (SDG-6).

Building a toilet at home and using it regularly is a healthy habit and should be practised by everyone irrespective of their age and gender[7]. To initiate the process, swachh committees were formed. Slogans were written as "Swachhta by the people and for the people". The swachhta rally was conducted; the street plays were enacted to harm and the benefits of household toilets. The members of the swachh committees are students, teachers, SHG members, village elders and Panchayat Members. These committee members used to get up early in the morning and go to different directions where the villagers go for open defecation. Anyone is found; they will blow a vigil and instruct him to go back his/her house for defecation. This vigilance made them to construct the household toilets. The Gram Sabha has decided that all the villagers should voluntarily contribute shramadan (Voluntary labour) to construct the toilets.

The charge officer, Deepak Soni, has utilised all the problems into positive aspects. In Gram Sabha, he has asked all the villagers, 'Would you like to suffer with scorpion bite or die with the snake bite or trample by the elephant by going out for defecation.' So his slogan was "construct toilet and live long". Most of the villagers suffered scorpion bite and also snake bite. Few people died because of snake bite. This village is a passage for elephants, the elephants used to pass at any time. The villagers have to run to their houses, as soon as they see elephant and run for lives. As the village is a snake corridor, elephant corridor, they preferred the choice to live. All the villages agreed to construct the household toilets and community toilets at the anganwadis and at schools. The people contributed voluntary labour and the funds were taken from the MGNREGA and Swachh Bharat Mission. In the village all the households have toilets and they are utilising the toilets. Each household is supplied with the torchlight, to identify the snake/scorpion in the toilets. Jorandjharia achieved the status of ODF. But it has struggle a lot to achieve ODF status.

5. Swachh Village: The Jorandajharia is a clean village. The streets are very clean and the houses are clean and hygienic. The schools, anganwadis are hygienic. The pictures on the walls are expresses not only hygiene but expresses the objectivity of the schools and anganwadi. The Gram Panchayat assured that each street is clean and each house is clean. The tribals may be poor economically, but rich in hygiene. The houses are very clean. Everyday the wet waste and dry waste is separated. The Panchayat staff will come and pick up the waste and put in dumping yard.

6. Livelihoods Creation. First and foremost in Sustainable Development Goals is "End poverty in all its forms everywhere". According to 'World Poverty Clock', 8 per cent of the world population live in extreme poverty[8]. According to official estimates in India (2012) 22 per cent of its population is below poverty. It is said that in the country 190.7 million people in India will sleep hungry every night.[9] Although, the extreme poverty is decreasing, the poverty in the country is a grave concern. In India, 25.70 per cent of rural population is below poverty line and 13.70 per cent is below poverty line in urban areas.

The first priority of governance is to eradicate poverty. The livelihoods promotion is a vital concept of Model Village. Livelihood is a "means of economic activity to secure basic amenities such as—food, water, shelter, clothing, education and health of life". It provides the dignity of life and protects the culture of the community. To initiate the process the women have started organised as SHG groups. Each group was allowed to select the economic activity depending upon the interest. Young girls choose tailoring and computer education. The women choose lac cultivation, which is suitable to that area. The Charge Officer Mr. Deepak Soni facilitated the marketing of goods. The young boys choose bike repairs and service and computer skills. The youth of village got employed in nearby town, after acquiring skills. The Charge Officer, Deepak Soni took a special care of the youth not to join in naxalite movement, which was very active in the region.

7. Children's Education

"Let us pick up our books and pencils. They are our most powerful weapons"—Malala Yousafzai[10]. "The children are the future of the country. Education enables them to acquire skills, knowledge, values and attitudes necessary to become responsible and active citizens of India"[11]. Right to Education Act (RTE) was enacted on 4 August, 2009 by the Parliament of India. The Act makes education as a fundamental right. It emphasizes free and compulsory education for children between the ages of 6 to 14 years in India under the Article 21-A of the Indian Constitution. After passing the Act, India became one of 135 countries to make free and compulsory education to the children between the ages of 6 to 14 years. 'Compulsory education' is an obligation of the Government and local authorities to provide and ensure admission, attendance and completion of elementary education by all children in the 6-14 age groups.

Education is very important tool for everyone to succeed in life. It helps in lessening the challenges of difficult life. Knowledge gained through the education enables every individual confident about their life[12]. **Education** is the key to success in personal and professional life. It provides us various types of knowledge and skills. Education is continuous process of entire life[13]. Education brings success and confidence in everyone's life.

The children are the future of the globe. The children should be nurtured in mind in body. The education and school environment play a vital role in maturity of the mind and body of the children. The Model Village concept focuses on making the village as cent percent literate. Initially the literacy level of Jorandhjharia was very low. The initiatives of Hon'ble MP made success of cent-per-cent literate. To initiate the process, education committees were formed. The teacher heads the committees. The members are youth and students. The committees visit different wards and take the special class in their houses. The SHG Members facilitated the process of evening classes and monitored the learning process. Students were instructed to make literate their parents.

The village is having high school and elementary school. The education committee assures 100 per cent attendance of children. The parent teacher committee reviews the progress of the children. If any children's progress is slow, special classes will be arranged in the evening to improve their performances. Deepak Soni, Special Officer to the village visits the school often, at least twice in a week. He assures the children's as well as teacher's attendance. He sometimes takes special classes in English, maths and equips them with the current affairs.

The researcher visited the school along with Mr. Deepak Soni and interacted with the students on current affairs. They are well versed with the geography of the states, capitals, countries. On political current affairs, they are up-to-date. On being asked the question, what you would like to be in the future, most of the students replied that they have answered that they would like to be the teachers and quite few of them has said that they would like to be police. The teacher is a role model, as everyday they interact with the teachers. As the village is a Naxal corridor, the police used to move in the village. They have said that they would like to become a police. It is surprised that no one would like to be Deepak Soni, who is an IAS Officer. The IAS is beyond their grasp. They also do not like to be a Politician, as Hon'ble MP visits the school often. The dream of the students is not big, as they are surrounded with the environment of teachers and police. They feel that they should become either teacher or police.

8. Zero Malnourishment: Malnutrition is complex aspect. It is defined as a lack of proper nutrition, caused by not having enough to eat, or not eating enough right kind of food to eat. There are various forms of nutrition deficient–stunted, (low height for age) wasted (low weight for height), anaemic (deficiency of haemoglobin in blood) and underweight (low weight for age). The joint study of Assocham-EY (2017) says that 'India is home to the largest number of malnourished children in the world and 50 per cent children in India are undernourished.'[14]

Although, there has been an overall reduction in the infant mortality rates and under-five mortality rate the country is having about 50 per cent of undernourished children of the world.[15] The study reveals that end of 2015, an about 40 per cent of the children were undernourished, about 37 per cent of under-five children are underweight, 39 per cent are stunted, 21 per cent are wasted and 8 per cent are severely acutely malnourished.

The prevalence of underweight children was higher (38%) in rural areas compared to urban cities (29%). Only about 10 per cent children under the age 6-23 months were reported to receive an adequate diet. Various forms of undernutrition are predominant in rural India. According to National Family Health Survey (NFHS)–4 (2015-16) to the Global Nutrition Report 2016 and the Global Hunger Index (GHI) 2017, ranks India at 100 out of 119 countries.[16] According to GHI and NFHS reports, in India, less than 25 per cent children, less than 5 age are still malnourished.[17] Among the children less than 5 years, wasting (low weight for height), is 20 per cent in 1992 and 21 per cent in the 2017. There has been a reduction in stunting (height for age) from 61.9 per cent in 1992 to 38.4 per cent in 2017. Mortality among children less than 5 years old has declined to around 5 per cent from 11 per cent during the same period.[18]

The Government is trying with utmost care to bring down the mal nourishment. Integrated Child Development Service (ICDS) with strong network of 1.4 million Anganwadi centres are reaching almost 100 million beneficiaries who include pregnant and nursing children in schools, and the Public Distribution System (PDS) reaching over 800 million people. The National Nutrition Strategy (NNS) has set very ambitious targets for 2022 and the Poshan Abhiyaan has also specified three-year targets to reduce stunting, undernutrition and low birth weight by 25 each year, and to reduce anaemia by 3 per cent each year. Besides, the government efforts, multiple sustained interventions like increased availability and accessibility of nutritious food, potable water, hygiene and sanitation, primary health care will help in reduce of malnourishment. The charge officer Mr. Deepak Soni took care of nourishing the children. He visited regularly Anganwadi centres to make sure that nutritious food is provided to the children. Sudden visits were made to Anganwadi centres and he used to take the lunch along with the children. This assured the each and every child fit mentally and physically. The undernourished children were given a special attention and provided the nutritious food until they grow as a normal child.

9. Self-Defence Skills for Girls

"India is the most dangerous nation for women", says Thomson Reuters Foundation[19] poll. The government have a greater focus on women's safety after the gang rape of Ms. Jyoti Singh Pandey, Physiotherapist on December 16, December 2012 in a private bus. This didn't deter the perpetrators. In 2016 nearly 40,000 rapes were reported[20]. India's capital New Delhi is dubbed as an "India's rape capital". The official data says nearly 40 crimes against women takes place every hour[21]. Women in India– from executives to women in middle-class homes, in factories or farms– face the dangers of sexual violence and harassment. According to World Bank data (2005) at least 20 million women have left the workforce due to their poor treatment and at present only 27 per cent work.

Thomson Reuters Foundation's poll of 548 experts on women's issues, found that 'India was the most dangerous country for women in terms of human trafficking including sex slavery and domestic servitude'. The Government passed "Nirbhaya Act' on April 3, 2013, i.e. new anti-rape law to deal with sec crimes against women. The Act prescribes life imprisonment as the maximum sentences for rape and death penalty for repeat offenders. Insulting modesty of women, by uttering any word or gesture shall be punished with jail up to three years.

The recent incident of Kathua rape case[22] (abduction, rape, and murder of an 8-year-old girl, Asifa Bano, in Rasana village near Kathua in the Indian state of Jammu and Kashmir in January 2018) and Unnao rape case, i.e. rape of a 17 year old girl on 4 June, 2017 has brought a crime on women particularly, girl children are vulnerable to the rape and killings.[23] In India it was recorded that 106 rapes per day and four out of ten victims are minors.[24]

The National Crime Records Bureau (NCRB)'s "Crime in India 2016" report reveals that in 94.6 per cent cases, the perpetrators were none other than the victim's relatives including brothers, fathers, grandfathers or acquaintances. The report showed that in the year 2016, a total of 38,947 cases of rape were registered in the country under Protection of Children from Sexual Offences Act (POCSO) as well as Section 376 and other related sections of the Indian Penal Code. Among these 38,947 cases, in 36,859 matters, accused are related to the victims, it said. The conviction rate is very low. The conviction rate is very low compared to all congnisable crimes. India's conviction rate for rape is at 25.5 per cent, remains low compared to all cognisable crimes–those that do not require a magistrate's permission to investigate–under the Indian Penal Code (46.9% in 2015). In 2016, only one in four rape cases in India ended in conviction–the lowest since 2012–according to national crime data.

The girls are insecure in the house and outside of the house. To travel to the town/city, the companion is necessary. In order to protect themselves from the perpetrators, the girls and women were taught self-defence skills to combat in any untoward incident. The girls were given training in karate and Kung Fu to defend themselves. The self-defence skills gave self-confidence, courage to meet any challenge in the life. Now the girls can go to towns/cities on their own without accompanier. Interacting with the girls in the school, they explained that initially they had a fear to talk to men mainly strangers. Now they don't fear any one as they know how to defend themselves in any toward incident.

Conclusion

Jorandajhazia was a backward and underdeveloped village. After, its adoption by the Hon'ble MP Nand Kumar Sai and Charge Officer Mr. Deepak Soni took the charge of development of the village. The Charge Officer, Shri Deepak Soni has owned this village and put his efforts to make Jorandajharia as one of the model village and can be replicated to this development model. The villagers painted the houses, buildings with pink colour and they call it as **'Pink Joranda'.** According to their culture the pink stands for unity, happiness, prosperity and development. In terms of community led social development, Pink Joranda has become a true Model Village for others to emulate. As per the concept of village the best infrastructure was provided and moral values were incorporated among the villagers. The people of Jorandajharia have volunteered to become make other villages as a model villages like Jorandajharia.

The main weakness in the process of Model Village was failure to develop the leadership in the village. After the MP and Charge Officer withdrawal from the development process, the development may be weakened in the village and the village may go back to the underdeveloped stage. In any adopted village, developing leadership is essential to sustain the development process.

NOTES

1. Wikipedia (2018). "Sansad Adarsh Gram Yojana", https://em.wikipedia.org/wiki/Sansad_Adarsh_Gram_Yojana#cite, note-5
2. Buch, Nirmala (2003). Panchayats in India–Forum for Citizens Participation in Local Governance: Representation and participation of Rural Women–Experience and Challenges, http://www.ciff.on.ca/Reference/documents/MX-36_1_files/Papers/Buch.htm, 1/9/03, p. 1.
3. United Nations Development Programme (1993). *Human Development Report,* New York, p. 1.
4. Stan, Burkey (1993). *People First: A Guide to Self-Reliant Participatory Rural Development*, Zed Books, London and New York.
5. Prachett, Lawrence (1999). "New Fashions in Public Participation: Towards Greater Democracy", *Parliamentary Affairs*, Vol. 52, No. 4, October. New Delhi.
6. Beetham, D. (1994). "Key Principles and Indices for a Democratic Audit", In Beetham, D. (ed.). *Defining and Measuring Democracy*, Sage Publications, New Delhi, p. 1.
7. Mao Zedong also known as Chairman Mao. Mao was a Chinese communist revolutionary. Founding father of the People's Republic of China. Mao ruled China as the Chairman of the Communist Party of China from 1949 until his death in 1976.
8. Rural–Women-food-poverty (2018). http://www.unwomen.org/en/news/in-focus/rural-women-food-poverty, 8-08-2018.
9. Swachh Bharat Abhiyan (2018) https://www.indiacelebrating.com/essay/swachh-bharat-abhiyan-essay/13-08-2018

10. Wikipedia (2018) https://en.wikipedia.org/wiki/swachh_bharat_Misssion# cite, note-bs-1
11. SBM (2018) #SBM pic.twitter.com/DbefYVM…13-08-2018
12. World Poverty (2018) https://worldpoverty.io/index.html, 21-08-2018
13. Vinita Bhali (2018). "No Child Left Behind", *The Hindu*, August 18, p. 10.
14. Malala Yousafzai is a Pakistani activist for female education and the youngest Nobel Peace Prize laureate in 2014.
15. Press Information Bureau (2010). Prime Minister's Address to the Nation on the Fundamental Right of Children on Elementary Education" pib.nic.in, 1-9-2010.
16. Malnourished Children (2018), https://www.livemint.com/Politics/16-08-2018.
17. *Ibid.*
18. Vinita Bhali (2018). "No Child Left Behind", *The Hindu*, August 18, p. 10.
19. *Ibid.*
20. *Ibid.*
21. Thomson Reuters Foundation is the London-based charitable arm of Thomson Reuters, a Canadian global information and news network. The Foundation is a registered charity in the United States and United Kingdom and is headquartered in Canary Wharf.
22. Wikipedia (2018) https://en.wikipedia.org/wiki/Kathua_rape_case and https://en.wikipedia.org/wiki/Unnao_rape_case: 27-08-2018
23. Indian Express (2018) https://indianexpress.com/article/india/executives-to-maids-women-across-india-face-the-dangers-of-sexual-violence-and-harassment-5233583/27-09-2018
24. *Ibid.*

18

Marketing Methods Preferred for Women Enterprises in Kerala Owned and Managed by Scheduled Castes

Swapna Aji

Introduction

Growth and development of entrepreneurship is considered to be indispensible in any economy since it determines innovation, marketing, employment opportunities, income generation, and distribution of available resources equitably for enhancing per capita income. Gross National Product gets increased together with the growth of enterprises ensuring reasonable standard of living and quality of life of the people. Entrepreneurship is a purposeful activity that covers all activities like production, distribution and marketing of goods and services for gaining surplus and this would be reflected in all domains of the society. Almost all developed countries have realized, it seems, the significance of entrepreneurship and implemented appropriate policies and programmes for the development of entrepreneurship years back eliminating gender discrimination. Nations such as US, Japan, and United Kingdom had opened up their markets globally with active involvement of women entrepreneurs. This has widened opportunity to market their products and services in the international market. This has been instrumental in expanding the economic activities altogether inducting professionalism. Many closed economies have now become open economies as a result of globalization with the participation of women entrepreneurs.

However, women in the field of entrepreneurship has been a recent phenomenon in developing nations. In developing economies, like India, it is yet to explore the skills and talents of womenfolk in entrepreneurship to the maximum extent for exploiting the wide potential of global market. From ancient years onwards, Indian economy was remaining a closed economy and a lot of gender discriminations existed in the society, hindering women to enter the field of entrepreneurship.

Scheduled Caste Women Enterprises in Kerala

For attaining gender equality and the empowerment of women in economic, social, political, cultural and legal areas, especially those belonging to weaker sections of the society is the need of the hour for Indian economy. Womenfolk from oppressed and downtrodden sections in the society belonging to the scheduled castes should be uplifted by joint efforts of the society and the government. They remain backward owing to social customs imposed upon them by a small sections in the society who dominated in exercising power for controlling the people as a whole. Despite several incentives and support provided by the government, the number of women entrepreneurs from scheduled castes remains lesser compared to other sections in the economy. This group of women entrepreneurs have been confronted with many challenges in agricultural, manufacturing, and service sectors although in theory they are considered as vital economic players for the advancement of the economy. Entrepreneurship would definitely help the scheduled caste women to secure equality and fair treatment in the society as a vital tool of women empowerment. As a result of support from family members, friends and execution of required support from the part of government, the fact that the economy has witnessed the emergence of scheduled caste women as entrepreneurs cannot be totally ignored. Special as well as specific entrepreneurship development programmes organised by the government agencies at national level and state level motivate the scheduled caste women entrepreneurs to emanate successful entrepreneurs. The scheduled caste women entrepreneurs in the state possess higher literacy rates as compared to other states in India and this has been helping them to gain theoretical as well practical knowledge for effectively running the enterprises.

Marketing of Products and Services

In general, there exists a sensation for all the small and medium enterprises

(SMEs) in the State for marketing their product and services even in local and domestic markets. Marketing, it is observed by social scientists, acts as a serious bane for the growth and development of SMEs. This has been on account of the domination gained by multi-national companies in the rural-urban markets of Kerala with the modern marketing methods and techniques highlighting the high quality, long span of life and lower price of their products. At the same time entrepreneurs in general and women entrepreneurs in specific from Kerala have chosen conservative methods for their products and services even in the globalised era. It is to be noted in this context that marketing in the modern management world is not simply an act of advertising or selling a product. It circumscribes several components involved in developing and managing a product meant for providing satisfaction to the needs of customers. It anchors on making the product available at right place, at right time and a price, acceptable to customers. In short, marketing deals with product development pricing, determination of distribution channel, advertising, sales promotion and after-sale services. Sheth and Sisodia (1999) observed that marketing is context dependent, and that when changes occur in the contextual elements surrounding it, the discipline may find much of its toolkit and conceptual inventory becoming obsolete. Zeithaml and Zeithaml (1984) claims that the fundamental responsibility of the marketing function is to effect and manage change in the external environment.

It is in this context that the present study was undertaken with the following objectives:

Objectives

1. To examine the methods adopted by scheduled caste women enterprises in marketing their products and services; and
2. To identify the hindrances faced by the scheduled caste women entrepreneurs in marketing and pricing of their products.

Methodology

The data for the study was drawn from both primary and secondary sources. Primary data were collected from 420 scheduled caste women enterprises registered as per MSME Act in the District Industries Centres in the State, using a structured questionnaire. The scheduled caste business enterprises covered under the sample were grouped into nine categories based on the nature of business norms adopted by the government as food processing units, readymade and garments units, software and IETs, manufacturing units, trading enterprises, traditional industries, agricultural and allied industrial units, poultry and dairy product units for analysis and interpretation of data. The findings of the analysis are given below:

Location of the Units

Location is considered as a vital factor having a greater influence on the well-being of the business. Of the total business enterprises covered under the sample for the study, 162 enterprises were located in municipal area, 139 business enterprises in village panchayath area and 119 business enterprises in Municipal Corporation areas.

Methods of Marketing

Availability of raw materials, availability of labour, infrastructural facilities, adequate information technology networks and many other supporting factors are the major determinants for the marketing of products and services in local market. Hunt (1976) provided a theoretical outline to characterize and guide the scientific development of marketing. Identifying the market for the products manufactured by the scheduled caste entrepreneurs is challenging and based on the products manufactured the scheduled caste women have to choose the most appropriate marketing opportunity to sell their products.

Table 18.1: Method of Marketing

Location of market	*Percentage of marketing*	*Number of sample*
Local market	66.06	418
Within the district	29.17	353
Within state	4.67	133
Within country	0.10	4
Export	0.00	0

Source: Field Survey.

Various methods of marketing include marketing the goods in local market, within the district, within the state, within the country and export. Marketing methods of scheduled caste women entrepreneurs shown in Table 18.1 reveals that 418 respondents (66.06%) sold their goods in local market, 353 respondents (29.17%) sold within the district, and 4.67 per cent and 0.10 per cent of the respondents sold their products within the state and country respectively. As these women belonged to scheduled caste category they lack opportunities in the market and hence majority of women depended on local market for selling their goods and services. Due to the constraints faced by the respondents, only a small portion of the respondents could expand their market within country and it was observed that the scheduled caste women entrepreneurs were not exporting their products to the international markets.

Marketing Channels

A market is a place where the original ownership of goods is transferred from producers to consumers. The enterprise should have adequate and up-to-date knowledge about the current market scenario for identifying available marketing channels. Selection of the marketing channel suited to the organisation is important as the physical movement of goods and services take place through this marketing channel and hence it is felt proper to have a detailed analysis of different marketing channels started by these scheduled caste entrepreneurs covered under the study for marketing their products and services.

Table 18.2: Marketing Channels

Channels	*Mean*	*SD*
Direct sales	33.60	24.00
Friends and relatives	16.90	10.50
Dealers	16.70	9.50
Agents	16.00	8.30
Bulk supply	11.00	9.70
Through sales representatives	4.60	7.00
Government supply	0.10	1.60
Exports	0.00	0.50
Others	1.10	6.10

Source: Field Survey.

The data contained in Table 18.2 reveal that majority of the respondents remained with a mean score of 33.60 and depended on the direct selling of their products as this method is beneficial to them. It involves the direct contact with the end users/customers. They also sold their products to the friends, well-wishers and relatives with a mean score of 16.90, dealers with a mean score of 16.70 and also to agents with a mean score of 16. The least accepted marketing channel by the respondents was marketing the products through government supply with a mean score of 0.10.

Hindrances in Marketing

Tactical decisions reduce the challenges involved in marketing of products and decision on this aspect should be taken at the right time for a business enterprise. A profound evaluation of marketing strategies is to be carried out giving due consideration to the strength, weakness, opportunity and threat existing in the market; analyzing different trade strategies adopted by the competitors; and evaluating the existing market share of each such competitor. The prominent barriers fixed for the present study are presented in Table 18.3. They are competition in local markets, competition from large/multinational companies, lack of adequate marketing strategies, shrinkage in the marketing and distribution networks/channels, lack of marketing skills, inadequate market share for the finished products, inadequacy of professional competency, inadequacy of Research and Development, inadequate sales promotion measures. In order to ascertain the most prominent hindrances faced by the scheduled caste women entrepreneurs in marketing their products, they were asked to mark five major factors in the order of their preference from among the nine alternatives stated above. The responses were scored at five-point scale assigning the weights five points to the first preference, four points to the second preference, three points to the third preference, two points to the fourth preference and one point to the fifth preference. The data indicated that most prominent hindrance faced by the respondents in marketing was the competition they are confronted in local market with a weighted score of 890.

Criteria for Selecting the Location of Enterprise

Apt location helps an entrepreneur to market the products easily, to overcome the difficulties related to business and to organize various factors of production. Selecting a location for the business is a major challenge for the scheduled caste women entrepreneur as it depends on many internal and external factors. Before selecting location for the business, entrepreneur should take into consideration the availability of raw materials, transportation cost, availability of skilled and unskilled labour, availability of finance and also the availability of other infrastructural facilities. For identifying different criteria for selecting the

Table 18.3: Hindrances in Marketing

	Competition in local market	Competition from large/multinational companies	Lack of adequate marketing strategies	Shrinkage in the marketing and distribution networks/channels	Lack of marketing skills	Inadequate market share for finished products	Inadequacy of professional competency	Inadequate Research and Development	Inadequate sales promotion measures	Total
Proprietary	585	309	454	419	430	547	453	442	426	4065
Self Help Group	229	136	154	188	169	206	183	195	190	1650
Cooperatives	52	23	45	67	59	47	66	57	49	465
Public Ltd. Company	18	4	11	7	0	4	20	8	3	75
Private Ltd Company	6	5	5	5	5	4	7	3	5	45
Total	**890**	**477**	**669**	**686**	**663**	**808**	**729**	**705**	**673**	**6300**

Source: Field Survey.

present location they are classified into different heads like easy availability of land, regular supply of raw materials, availability of raw materials, availability of markets, lesser competition, native place, local demand for products and services, lesser cost of production and support received from family members. The respondents were asked to select three factors in the order of preference in order to identify the most prominent factor which pulls an entrepreneur in selecting the location for their business. The table points out that the most prominent reason for selecting the location of business was the support they received from the family members with a mean score of 1.20 followed by native place with a mean score of 0.93 and local demand for products and services with a mean score of .80. The least preferred criteria for selecting the present location for business is the easy availability of land with a mean score of 0.25.

Table 18.4: Criteria for Selecting the Present Location

	Mean	*SD*	*Rank*
Easy availability of land	0.25	0.73	8
Regular supply of raw materials	0.69	1.06	6
Availability of market	0.78	1.06	4
Lesser competition	0.73	1.08	5
Native place	0.93	1.18	2
Local demand for product and services	0.80	1.07	3
Lesser cost of production	0.61	0.97	7
Support of family members	1.20	1.26	1
Others (Specify)	0.00	0.00	9

Source: Field Survey.

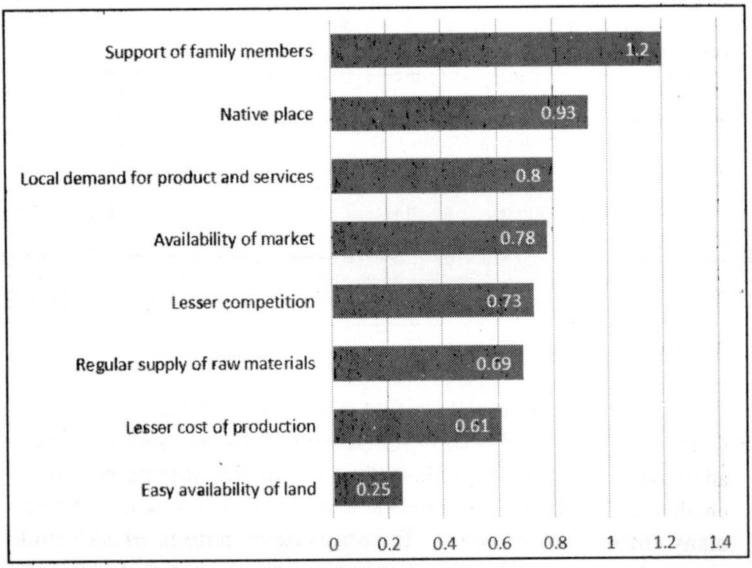

Source: Field Survey.

Sales Promotion Measures

Sales promotion is needed to enhance the sales of the product by adopting different methods such as discounts, coupons, gifts, bestowing sample, conducting contests and providing trade discounts. Sales promotion measures are strategic rather than tactical and they should be framed in such a way that they should attract the customers and thereby ensure support for increasing the volume of sales of the enterprise. The major sales promotion measures adopted by the units were categorized for the present study as: providing trade discount, providing gifts, providing additional quantity and distribution of coupons. The study identified that the respondents were using more than one sales promotion techniques for marketing the products and services. Out of the 420 respondents, 360 respondents were marketing the products at discounted rates for bulk purchases and the results on this facet are presented in Table 18.5. The widely accepted sales promotion technique followed by the respondents was selling the products by providing attractive trade discount, followed by providing additional quantity (20.42 per cent) in case of bulk purchases to regular customers and the least followed sales promotion technique was marketing by providing coupons (10.99 per cent).

Table 18.5: Sales Promotion

Sl. No.	*Method*	*n*	*%*
1.	By Trade discount	360	94.24
2.	By providing gifts	65	17.02
3.	By additional quantity	78	20.42
4.	By Coupon	42	10.99
	Multiple Response		

Source: Field Survey.

Pricing of Products

For fixing the price, there are many methods available in the business world like cost plus pricing, competitive pricing, and government administered pricing. Selection of an appropriate pricing method is a challenge before the entrepreneur as pricing decisions depend on so many internal and external factors. The responses of the women entrepreneurs covered in the present study are presented in Table 18.6.

Table 18.6: Pricing Methods for Products

Method	*n*	*%*
Cost plus method	303	72.14
Competitive price method	185	44.05
Government Administered Price	21	5.00
Others (specify)	10	2.38
Multiple Response		

Source: Field Survey.

The data shown in Table 18.6 indicate that 303 respondents (72.14%) used cost plus method for pricing their products, 185 respondents (44.05%) followed competitive pricing method, 21 respondents (5%) Government Administered Pricing and 10 respondents (2.38%) other pricing methods. In the present study the respondents were using more than one method for pricing their products based on the existing market situations. Majority of the respondents were arrogated with cost plus method as it is one of the traditional methods of pricing. Under this method, the price is fixed by adding a certain amount as margin to the total cost of production and this method can be adopted in a normal market situation where there is low competition.

Difficulties in Pricing

Price fixation is a more complicated phase in marketing of the products. Price is fixed based on the existing market situation like demand, price of complimentary products, and elasticity of demand and supply conditions in the market and so on. For the purpose of analysing the hindrances experienced in pricing of products the present study, the major difficulties in pricing were grouped into five major heads, i.e. price of complimentary goods, existing demand for the product, lack of feedback from the customers, identifying the magnitude of competition in the market and analysing customers' behaviour. For the purpose of analysis of the present situation, the respondents were asked to select major difficulties that they are facing in fixing the price in the order of preference and also analysis is carried out to identify the difficulty level based on the nature of business organization. For this purpose, the business organisations were classified into proprietary concerns, self-help groups, co-operatives, public limited companies and private limited companies. The results in Table 18.7 evinced that in respect of proprietary concerns the major difficulty for price fixation was the price of complimentary goods with a weighted score of 369 followed by existing demand for the product with a weighted score of 334. In case of self-help group the most prominent challenge in fixing the price is the existing demand for the product with a weighted score of 140 followed by the price of complimentary products with a score of 137. In case of cooperatives, public limited company and private limited company the major difficulty in price fixation was identifying the magnitude of competition in the market, lack of feedback from customers and price of complimentary products respectively.

Table 18.7: Difficulties in Pricing Decisions

Category	*Price of complimentary goods*	*Existing demand for the product*	*Lack of feedback from the custommers*	*Identifying the magnitude of competition in the market*	*Analysing customers behaviour*	*Total*
Proprietary	369	334	285	347	291	1626
Self Help Group	137	140	135	123	125	660
Cooperatives	30	38	41	42	35	186
Public Ltd. Company	5	6	9	2	8	30
Private Ltd. Company	8	2	4	4	0	18
Total	**549**	**520**	**474**	**518**	**459**	**2520**

Source: Field Survey.

Package of Products

Physical appearance of the product is significant and hence the packaging. Neatly packed products attracted customers and buyers prefer to purchase such products. Package protects the goods from physical damage during transportation; it attracts and appeals the customer attention and easy identification of the product. As the package has direct bearing on the sales of the products, it is considered suitable to study this aspect.

Table 18.8: Package of Products

	n	*%*	*Mean*	*SD*	*t*	*Sig.*
Less Accepted	189	45.00	1.66	0.67	10.464	0.000
Accepted	185	44.00				
Highly Accepted	46	11.00				
Total	**420**	**100.00**				

ource: Field Survey.

The data collected from 420 respondents shown in Table 18.8 reveal that 189 respondents (45%) feel that their packaging of the product was less accepted by the customers, 185 respondents (44%) respond that their package was accepted and 46 respondents (11%) told that their package is highly accepted and appreciated by the customers. The present study identifies that more than 50 per cent of the respondents believed that the package of the product provided satisfaction to the customers and t-test also confirmed that the package was accepted by the customers as the result is significant at 5 per cent level.

Conclusion

The results of the study prompt to draw the conclusion that women belonging to scheduled caste category were in shortage of wide opportunities in the market and as such majority of them depended on local market for disposing of their goods and services. Owing to the constraints faced by the respondents only an insignificant section of this category of enterprises could expand the market throughout the nation. It is surprising that this category of enterprises are yet to explore marketing benefits of international scenario. It is high time for the policy-makers the government agencies concerned to take steps for motivating and support to this category of entrepreneurs and uplifting them to the mainstream of the society.

REFERENCES

Hunt, S.D. (1976). "The Nature and Scope of Marketing," *Journal of Marketing*, 40(3): 17-28.

Sheth, J.N., R.S. Sisodia and A. Sharma (2000). "The Antecedents and Consequences of Customer-centric Marketing", *Journal of the Academy of Marketing Science*, 28(1): 55-66.

Zeithaml, C. and Zeithaml, V. (1984). "Environmental Management: Revising the Marketing Perspective," *Journal of Marketing*, 48 (Spring), 46-53.

19

Economic Status of Denotified Tribes

A Case Study of Domban Community in Palakkad District, Kerala

Akhil, K.O.

Introduction

In 1871, the British Indian government declared certain Tribal, Nomadic, Semi-nomadic groups as 'Born Criminals' by the fleeting of the Criminal Tribes Act, 1871 (CTA)[1]. In reality, they were nomadic wandering communities. In pursuit of their traditional occupations and activities some lived in the forests and according to the British-raj, only criminals would do so and therefore brought them under CTA, 1871. Actually, this act was a result of British crooked mentality. In contrast, there were some communities engaged in petty crimes, but based on this bringing all pastoral and nomadic communities into the fold of the CTA was a major fault in the Act (D'Souza, 1999). The majority of these groups was kept in British-run and monitored camps for decades in the name of reforming and emancipating them from their criminal behaviour. This has negatively impacted their behaviour and haunting them even after the British left India (Bokil, Raghavan, 2016). But in actuality, they all were brainwashed and tortured to accept that they are born criminals. In 1952, the act was repealed by the Government of India[2], and the communities were 'Denotified'[3], hence the name (Japhet, Balgurumurthy, G., and Sabharwal, 2015; Ministry of Social Justice and Empowerment, 2008). Officially 'Denotified' them from CTA but renamed the old Act with the new Act 'Habitual Offender's Act, 1952'[4] and passed without much changes to it. The new Act was not very different from the 'Criminal Tribes Act, 1871'.

Further, this amended Act in the post-independent India made no provisions for their livelihood. De-notified tribes have continued to face historical dislocation, dishonour, social neglect, discrimination as ex-criminals and dacoits (Dandekar, 2009; Kapadia, 1952).

The question many scholars posed was as to how a community could be considered and treated as criminals by birth. They noted that there may be a few individuals who commit unlawful acts, but the community as a whole cannot be born as criminals. This is nothing but an absurd idea which advocates a clear agenda to isolate, contain a large number of nomadic communities and exterminate some of the small princely groups from power, sovereignty, freedom, etc. It was also argued in the literature that these groups were working as informants to the freedom fighters, providing them with food, money, and ammunition and fighting along with them in the freedom struggle. Some groups who had princely background with small kingdoms were thrown out of power and listed them in CTA so as to deprive them of ruling powers and lose their identity for ever (Dandekar, 2009; Radhakrishna, 2000).

As a result of rapid industrialization and advent of railways, roads, and technology that was taking place in India, many of the wandering communities have gradually lost their livelihood and outsiders entering in their domain of activities. Other groups were gradually alienated from land holdings by local dominant communities and forced to live in poor conditions. This situation prevailed after the De-notification of these communities. As a result, they were systematically marginalised to the lowest rung of the society. Today, the survival of the De-notified communities is a question mark. Some others eke out living on petty trading, entertainers etc. They possess no/little land, lack proper housing, no fixed assets and therefore wander from one place to another in search of means of survival. Urban ghettos, isolated open arena and dilapidated areas are their usual habitats. They living in a vulnerable physical condition (Radhakrishana, 2009). They are isolated and excluded from mainstream development processes. Human rights violations against them are common and frequent and the reality with which they are living today. The British regime filled with such cruel tactics was proved fatal to every life and livelihood of those tribal people whose identity is prima facie is 'Denotified or Vimuktha Jathi' rather than Indian. Among Indian states, Kerala is well acclaimed nationally and internationally for the kind of social, economic and political development that it has achieved. In Kerala, there is one Denotified community lives with SC status and there are no studies dealing with the community. In this study researcher wish to investigate about the social positioning and economic well-being of the so called Denotified tribes in Kerala state.

1. Background of the Study

The actual goal of the Criminal Tribes Act is to use the general tactics of identification and registration to control deviant behaviour. Furthermore, the Criminal Tribes Act relies on the assumptions and understanding of caste in order to identify and police behaviour, and consequently, caste characteristics and criminality act in simultaneously explaining each. Many nomadic and semi-nomadic communities participated in the freedom movement of 1857, which was also a cause of worry for the administrator it did not want to it to snowball into a national movement. British believed that the nomads helped the freedom fighters through passing messages between them. Against this backdrop British declared all Nomadic and Semi-Nomadic communities as criminal tribes. British consider this as the best way to control the mass (Ministry of Social Justice and Empowerment, 2008). After repealing the Act in 1952, our society's perception about this community remains unchanged they carry the criminal stigma from the past. These communities neither have any SC nor ST status. These people's living condition is very poor. These people are spread all over India. In south India their presence is very high. In Kerala there is one Denotified community lived called Domban.

2. Statement of the Problem

Among Indian states, Kerala is well acclaimed nationally and internationally for the kind of social, economic and political development that it has achieved. But Kerala Model of Development suffers criticisms because of the anomalies and the kind of lag associated with development and progress of the downtrodden sections such as SCs and STs. Among the marginalised they are further alienated that is marginalised among them. This is so inferred because even the apex bodies associated with SCs and STs are stuck with the availability of information regarding them. In such a backdrop the Domban group remain as a paradox to the so-called celebrated Kerala Development Paradigm.

3. Objectives

1. To analyse the economic wellbeing and social position of Domban community.

4. Research Methodology

The study is based on primary data collected from Palakkad district. The researcher used snowball sampling which is one of the non-probability sampling technique for selecting the sample. There is no proper record available for the settlement of the community. Majority of the Domban community people live in Palakkad District. Apart from that, for availing qualitative data for supplementing quantitative data, information related to social stigma and discrimination is collected by discussions and interviews with the elderly people in the community and also made discussions with other people outside the colony. For analyzing the socio-economic status of the community, the researcher carried out household survey focusing on their living condition, employment, educational status and details about the formalization of citizenship[5].

5. Economic Well-being and Social Positioning of Domban Community

This deals with the economic well-being and social positioning of Domban community, i.e. income, consumption expenditure, debt position health status.

5.1 Monthly Income distribution of the Sample Population

Income is an important means which increases the range of consumption options, especially when our economy and all around the world have become more and more monetized. Earning help the people to buy different nutritious food instead of eating their own crops, and the remaining help them to pay for their children's education and healthcare. The increasing dependence on private income means that even a slight change in income has a major influence on changes in consumption. For most of the population when income increases, their consumption also increases and vice versa. Table 19.1 shows the monthly income distribution of the sample population.

The study results that, median income of the respondent is Rs. 7,668 with high Standard Deviation Rs. 5,062. 50 per cent of the households have income between Rs. 5,202 and 16,298. Majority of the people engaged as casual workers. Casual work is characterised by unorganized sector and low remuneration. Due to this, they receive a low wage which reduces their income. Few among the Domban community people earn a regular

Table 19.1: Monthly Income Distribution of the Sample Population

*Income**	*Frequency*	*Per cent*
<= 5201	2	9.1
5202-16298	11	50.0
16299-27394	6	27.3
27395+	3	13.6
Total	**22**	**100.0**

Source: Primary Data.

* Data cut points have done through visual binning (a data analysis option is SPSS)

salary from the government (state and central) and their income is much better than others. Low income leads to low consumption, which in turn affect the productivity of the people.

5.2 Consumption Expenditure of the Sample Population

The consumption expenditure along with income is an important factor which helps us to understand the economic situation of the people. According to NSS 68th round consumer expenditure survey report, the precipitate household consumption expenditure was Rs. 1,430 for rural areas and Rs. 2,629.7 for urban areas during 2011-12 (selected statistics). (*Source:* National Sample Survey Office (NSSO), *Note:* the results are based on thin samples).

The household expenditure data of Domban people was collected through a detailed survey from the households. To understand the standard of living of the household, the consumption pattern and quality of consumption budget of the people indicate the standard of living of the households. The human existence and prosperity of his life ultimately depends upon consumption. Consumption clearly contributes to human development when it enlarges the capabilities and enriches the living of people without adversely affecting the well-being of the others. Just like environmental, socio-economic and cultural differences, variation existing in different societies this study shows difference in consumption also. Table 19.2 shows the monthly consumption expenditure of the sample population.

The study reveals the fact that, millions of people do not have a good range of consumption options which prevent the chance of enlarging their capabilities. A lot of things are responsible for this, income is an important factor among them.

Table 19.2: Monthly Consumption Expenditure of the Sample Population

*Amount of expenditure**	*Frequency*	*Percent*
<= 4809	5	22.7
4810-8107	6	27.3
8108-11404	8	36.4
11405+	3	13.6
Total	**22**	**100.0**

Source: Primary Data.

* Data cut pints have done through visual binning (a data analysis option is SPSS).

The minimum consumption expenditure for Domban is Rs. 3,000 per month and maximum Rs.14,360 per month. Per capita consumption expenditure of the Domban is Rs. 1,942 which is far below than that of the national average (Urban area).

5.3 Debt Position of the Sample Households

When one's income is not adequate to meet his consumption needs he/she is compelled to borrow money from others (may be individual or institutions). The lion's share of the Domban community people have debt.

An investigation into the debt position of sample household reveals that, about 86 per cent (19 households) of the households have debt.

5.3.1 Source of Debt for the Sample Households

Today various financial and non-financial institutions are providing loans to the people. Moneylenders are playing a crucial role in this respect. Table 19.3 shows the various sources from which the sample households borrowed money.

Table 19.3: Source of debt for the Sample Households

Source of Debt	*Frequency*	*Per cent*
Commercial Bank	7	36.8
Co-operative bank	1	5.3
NBFC (Manappuram, Muthut, Bajaj Fin cop.)	1	5.3
Moneylender	5	26.3
Neighbour/Relatives	1	5.3
SHG	2	10.5
Others (Specify)	2	10.5

Source: Primary Data.

A close examination in this regard shows that, majority among the sample households have borrowed money from Commercial Banks and moneylenders. They borrowed money from various sources to meet their emergency needs. Many microfinance offices that have come to give a small amount of loan to the common man and the poor and now those microfinance company's looting the wealth of the people in terms of high-interest payment. And the majority of the household borrowed money from the commercial bank (36.8%) and 26 per cent of the households borrowed money from the moneylender. He charges a high-interest rate, but these people prefer him due to the fact that it is very easy to avail loan. In banks, they need so many documentation and which consume time and they need security for availing the loan they prefer commercial bank.

5.3.2 Purpose of debt of Sample Households

An investigation into the reason for debt reveals that majority of them have taken the debt for construction of the houses, which is considered as a basic human need. Even though the government is providing them funds for house construction through various schemes, it is not enough to complete the construction so they are depending on other sources of debt. The details about the debt position of samples are given in the Table 19.4. From the results, it gives a clear picture that those who constructed house is now falling into serious indebtedness.

Table 19.4: Purpose of Debt of Sample Households

Purpose of Debt	*Frequency*	*Per cent*
Business	1	5.3
Marriage	2	10.5
Housing	15	78.9
Others	1	5.3

Source: Primary Data.

About 78 per cent of the people borrowed money for completing their house construction. In the present market situation the price for building materials are high, so the cost of building a house is very high. The amount provided by the government is not enough to cover the cost of production. They were compelled to borrow money from the commercial bank and in some situation, they need to borrow money from money lenders and NBFC at a high-interest rate.

5.3.3 Amount of Debt by the Sample Households

Here Table 19.5 deals with the amount of debt of these people towards various institutions.

Table 19.5: Amount of Debt of the Sample Households

*Amount of Debt**	*Frequency debt*	*Per cent*
9702-78737	13	68.4
78738-147773	1	5.3
147774+	5	26.3

Source: Primary Data.

* Data cut pints have done through visual binning (a data analysis option is SPSS).

An examination about the total amount of debt made by the sample households shows that, total debt of 19 families is about Rs. 14,96,000 with minimum debt of Rs. 15,000 and maximum debt of Rs. 2,00,000. People borrowed money from various sources. Once these people borrowed money from NBFC, they promote and compel these people to borrow money from their institution. Moreover, these institutions provide loans to female members of the family as they are more responsible for repaying the debt than males in the family.

5.4 Land Owned by the Sample Households

Our own land sometimes gives as empowerment (only a hunch of the researcher). Person with and without land is different. If a person owns land, which makes him capable to assert his rights. The sample households owned only 3 or 4 cent land only. These people did not receive any agricultural land from the government. Table 19.6 deals with the way of owning land by the sample households.

Table 19.6: Way of Owning the Land by the Sample Households

	Frequency	*Per cent*
Government provided	15	68.2
Inherited	1	4.5
Bought	6	27.3

Source: Primary Data.

The study results show that, 68.2 per cent of the households received land from the government. Most of the landholders received small pieces of land from the government. According to Shyjan & Sunitha (2009), the factors such as land reforms, educational attainments have little influence on marginalized communities of Kerala, their study raises a need for second generation land reforms which should be benefitted for the true deprived people in the society.

5.5 Educational Qualification of the Sampled Households

Education remains the most crucial requirement for the sustained growth of the developing society. In all India level, the literacy rate of ST inclusive of DNTs (Whoever Applicable) was 8.5 per cent in 1901 Census and has steadily increased to reach 58.9 in 2011 Census. Yet it is far below the overall national literacy rate.

In order to understand the educational status of the members of the Domban community, researcher dealt with their current educational status, dropout ratio, never enrolled to school details and so on. Table 19.7 shows the educational profile of the sample households. From the study results, it is evident that educational status of the Domban community is very bad. Majority of the adults in the Domban community are illiterate. But everyone in the new generation of the community has a better educational level. This section deal with factors which contribute to the poor position in education among the sample population.

Table 19.7: Educational Qualification of the Sample Households

	Frequency	*Per cent*
Illiterate	18	21.4
Literate without schooling	2	2.4
LP	10	11.9
UP	10	11.9
High school	14	16.7
SSLC	20	23.8
Plus two	9	10.7
Degree	1	1.2

Source: Primary Data.

An examination into the educational status of sample population reveals that majority of the people do not have higher education. Most of them studied up to SSLC. Only one person from this community completed graduation. The educational status of tribes in Kerala is not very good, especially in the case of women and the retention rate is very low among the scheduled tribes in Kerala, which in turn shows the prevalence of high dropout rates among the scheduled tribes and also there exist a gap in literacy rate among ST people and general population (Shyjan & Sunitha, 2009), while there are a lot of studies about educational status of the marginalized communities in India and Kerala, these studies never touch the status of education among Domban or even it does not mention about the broader social category of Denotified tribes in Kerala. So we can say that there are no studies which have not come up yet. Renke Commission Report (2008).

In the study results show, there are 21 school-going children (age group 5-19). Table 8 shows the gender-wise enrolment status of the students.

Table 19.8: Gender-wise Enrolment Status of the Students

Enrolment status	*Male*	*Female*	*Total*
Currently Enrolled	10	11	21
Never Enrolled	0	0	0
Drop-out	0	0	0
Illiterate	7	11	18

Source: Primary Data.

The study results show, dropout rate and never enrolled rate is zero among the community. Overall, the educational status among the Domban is better than the other DNT community. In national level 42 per cent of the Denotified communities report that children in their community attend school regularly (Ministry of Social Justice & Empowerment, 2008). Domban people enjoy legally secure housing colony and accessibility to government schools. One girl scored nearly 90 per cent in plus two in 2018. She is from Melarkod Panchayath. She scored high marks by studying without the accessibility of electricity in her home.

Another reason for dropout of the students is the failure in examinations. The failed students face disrespect from their friends and teachers. So the examination results coupled with poverty and family problem alienate students from schooling (Korra, 2017b).

Overall, the study found that educational status of Domban is dismal as compared to the general population of Kerala. Domban families stayed in Chittoor Municipality and Melarkode Panchayath have accessibility to government schools near their settlement, so people in this area enjoyed a better education environment. In spite of these students from Domban community often do not go for higher studies after SSLC and Plus Two. There are so many factors that cause the break in the studies.

5.5.1 Factors Contributing to the Poor Educational Attainment of the Sample Population

Poor housing condition. The process of educational attainment is not better among the Domban. Their housing condition is very poor that students have no facilities for better study and reading. The rooms in the house are not conducive for providing a good environment for studies and the houses lack basic furniture. Due to these factors, their academic performance in schools is very poor. The poor condition of the house also leads to the inability to access the basic stationaries related to study.

Parental motivation. Parent's care in studies of children is an important motive for the students. Their mental and moral support is necessary for the children for building a better career. The Domban community does not give much importance to their children's study. They do not recognize the importance of education in the modern era. Because education needs more time to get a good job and for earning this it requires a long gestation period. Some parents are even skeptic about the positive impact of education. The worst thing is that parents do not care about the attendance of their children in schools.

School environment. In Kerala Model of Development, Keralites are well educated but still, our education system is not free from some kind of discrimination. During the survey, students from Domban community shared their experience of being the victims of discrimination in schools by their peer group. They tease them due to their SC status. But these students have a good opinion about teachers. Teachers give full support to students in their studies and motivate them for studying

Child marriage. Child marriage is one of the reason for the poor educational status of the community. Majority of the girl children got married before reaching the prescribed legal age of marriage. In spite of this, no dropout and 100 per cent enrolment rate is good for educational progress. Drop out ratio is reduced due to the fact that students from this community discontinue their studies after completing SSLC or Plus Two because of the poor family income. They want to help their parents and they find their earnings inevitable to lead a standard life. Not only the traditional practices but also poor economic situation lead the parents to prefer early marriage. Early marriage of the children shows the poor educational indicators and the early entry into the labour force also a reason for the same.

Child labour. Irregular schooling led to lower marks in examinations which demotivate the students from studying. In the self-employed family, the children usually help their parents by selling cloth. These activities increase the family income and eat their time and enthusiasm for schooling.

5.6 Health Position of Sample Households

A healthy body provides healthy mind which directs to good thoughts. So health is very important for human being. Sanitation also is of the same importance. So here the researcher discusses some points related to this.

As per Census of India, if a household has access to drinking water supplied from a tap or a hand pump/tube well situated within or outside the premises, it is considered as having access to safe drinking water. (National Human Development Report, 2001).

Drinking water is an essential thing that is not separable from one's life. One can live for a day or two days without a meal, but he cannot stand for a long time without water. The public in Kerala is dependent on various sources for drinking water. The lack of drinking water creates a variety of health issues.

According to Census 2011, in all-India level, 46.6 per cent households have availability of drinking water within the premises, 35.8 per cent away from the premises. In rural areas, 77.9 per cent households have availability of drinking water either within the premises or near the premises whereas, in urban areas, 91.9 per cent household have availability of drinking water either within the premises or near the premises.

5.6.1 Source of Water for Drinking

In all India level, the major source of drinking water both in rural and urban is Tap water followed by a hand pump in (2011 population census). Table 19.9 shows the details about the source of water for drinking used by the sample households.

Table 19.9: Source of Water for Drinking

Source of water for drinking	*Frequency*	*Per cent*
Public tap	14	63.6
Public supply of water	8	36.4

Source: Primary Data.

The study reveals that even in the backward communities like SC & ST, families don't depend on the unprotected source of drinking water. Even in the rural area 100 per cent of the households have access to protected source of drinking water. But during the survey, researcher could find out a water-related issue in Chittoor Municipality, that is, the authorities are supplying water to the colony from a river that is near to their village, but recently the people noticed that the river is polluted. Because of this, people in the area afraid of health issues, and started protesting against this. According to (NFHS 5 2015-16), 93.4 per cent of the households have improved drinking water source available in Palakkad District.

5.6.2 Type of Latrine Used by the Sample Households

The advertisement related to Swatchch Bharath programme focuses to curtail open defecation in India. The lack of better latrine facility creates so many health problems among people. Kerala today stands at first place among the Indian states in terms HDI which is par with some developed countries. So no one will believe the presence of open defecation in Kerala.

About half of the Indian households (48%) use improved toilet facilities, which are not shared. This will prevent people from coming into contact with human waste can reduce the transmission of diseases. From the study results, it is clear that about 39 per cent of households do not use any toilet facility, i.e. they prefer open defecation which is shown in the Figure 19.1.

The study reveals that 23 per cent of the households do not use any toilet facilities. Only one household use a shared toilet because these two families are relatives.

Sanitation and quality of drinking water are related. Poor sanitation will pollute water sources in turn causes health problems like vomiting, diarrhoea among the people, which is caused mainly due to contaminated water.

Sanitation coverage in Kerala is 94.40 per cent (Census 2011). According to NSSO (2008) sanitation coverage in Kerala is about 94.70 per cent, i.e. rank one among the Indian States.

5.6.3 Beneficiary of ICDS Among the Sample Households

The ICDS scheme launched in 1975 is being addressed for children,

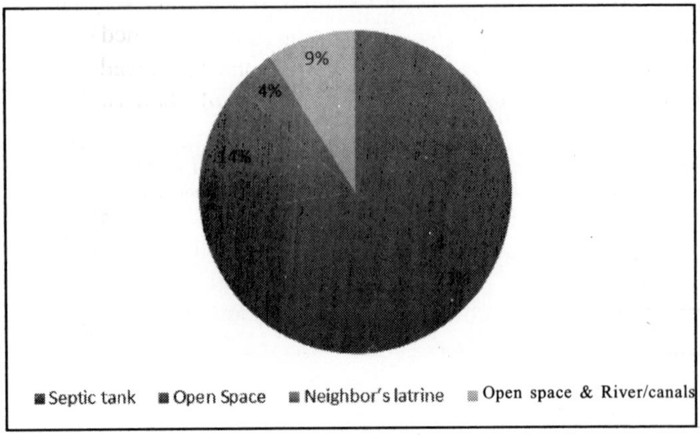

Fig. 19.1: Type of Latrine Used by the Sample Households

Source: Primary Data.

pregnant women, nursing mothers and adolescent girls in close combination with the health services for the improvement of health status and overall development of children and other beneficiaries. The SC and ST are two socio-economically backward and less privileged sections of the Indian society. They are far behind the mainstream people in these two underprivileged sections, the status of children and women is more pathetic. Table 19.10 shows the beneficiary of ICDS among the sample households.

Table 10: Beneficiary of ICDS Among the Sample Households

	Frequency	*Per cent*
Yes	14	63.6
No	8	36.4

Source: Primary Data.

The study results show that 36 per cent of the households do not receive any benefit from ICDS. It is a serious issue because ICDS services are carried out by Anganwadis. The poor performance of ICDS service will lead to malnourishment and nutrition problem among children.

5.6.4 Use of ASHA Service by the Sampled Households

One of the key strategies under the NRHM is a community health worker called ASHA (Accredited Social Health Activists) for every village at a norm of 1000 population. They have various duties assigned by the health department to serve the people. Asha workers and Anganwadi are working with the same coordination. The details in this regards shown in Table 19.11.

Table 19.11: Use of ASHA Service by the Sample Households

	Frequency	*Per cent*
Yes	7	33.3
No	14	66.7
Total	**21**	**100**

Source: Primary Data.

The study results shows that, about 66.6 per cent of the people do not get the services of ASHA in the study area and some of them have not even heard of ASHA workers. This locality is not a remote area, it is within the 5 km from the main town. This area lacked the services of ASHA workers. So we can imagine the status of their services in the remote area.

5.6.5 Health Institutions Preferred by the Sample Population

In the survey area, more than 3/4th of the people prefer government hospitals for availing medical facilities. Table 19.12 deals with such kind of information.

Table 19.12: Health Institutions Preferred by the Sample Population

Type of hospital	*Frequency*	*Per cent*
Primary Health Centre	17	42.5
Community Health Centre	13	32.5
Government District College	2	5
Government Medical College	1	2.5
Private Hospitals	6	15
Others	1	2.5

Source: Primary Data.

From the study results, it is evident that in Kerala, the services provided by the government hospitals are much better than that of any other states in India. So not only the SC people, the general population also prefer government hospitals. All sorts of treatments and diagnosis are available in the government hospitals today (this is shared by one of the sample during the survey).

5.7 Details about the Sample Population Being Faced Discrimination

In order to understand the extent of discrimination, researcher included some questions related to it. Most of the elderly people reported that till the date they did not face any discrimination from the society. But contrary to this, students of the community shared the experience of discrimination from their peer groups in schools. This kind of information are discussing in Table 19.13.

An investigation into the discrimination and social stigma attached to Domban reveals that in the modern economic world, people belong to these communities are not free from social stigma and discrimination. Even today, the young generation from this community experienced caste discrimination during their schooling. Their peer groups tease them by calling their caste name (experience shared by a girl respondent, she is just completed her SSLC in this year). During the survey, the researcher understood that except a few students, other adolescents do not face any discrimination from the society where they live. So today they have a better status in the society. The reason behind this is the marvellous educational attainment of the society.

Table 19.13: Details about the Sample Population Being Faced Discrimination

Type of Discrimination	*Frequency*	*Per cent*
No Discrimination	18	85.7
Being called by caste name	2	9.5
Being addressed as uncultured	1	4.8

Source: Primary Data.

The study results show that 86 per cent of the households do not face any discrimination from the society. But the students from this community in schools are the victims of discrimination from the peer group.

Where do They Stand?: It was understood through field survey and data on livelihoods which has been presented on throughout the thesis is that Domban community is far from the kind of development definition which Sen had envisaged. The process of development which involves social freedom which leads to political freedom and then to economic freedom is not materialized in the case of this community. They are excluded from the society. Even, they have not yet formalized their citizenship on the basis of their identity as Domban. They have health issues and the incidence of open defecation is there. Gender discrimination in wage payment is widely prevalent. Their land holdings are very small and lack of physical assets for livelihood and housing conditions are deplorable. They are not aware of their rights and they are not using the platform like Gramsabha where they can express and raise their opinions and concerns. They, don't enjoy social freedom, economic freedom and political freedom. Thus, they are deprived of their rights, far from the main stream development process. They are running backwards actually. These facts should be treated as serious issue as it is reported to have taken place in Kerala which is hailed for falling in conformity with the Sen's developmental paradigm compared to the other states of Kerala.

Conclusion

Majority of the people engaged in casual workers which provide low remuneration and Per capita Consumption expenditure of the Domban people is very low. Most of them have debt. Economic situation and health status of the Domban people are very bad compared to general population.

Most of them do not follow their traditional occupation because this does not provide them adequate income for their consumption needs. So some of the families follow their traditional occupation as a secondary occupation. If this condition prevails further, this will lead the community into an identity crisis.

Obviously, the educational attainment of this community is not better compared to the general population of Kerala. But the dropout ratio, which stood zero for Domban community, is a positive sign. At the same time, the number of illiterates among Domban community is very high compared to the general population of Kerala.

While considering the debt position of the people, the situation is very bad as the people in the community face huge amounts of debt in banks, NBFC, and local moneylenders. Majority of them fall into indebtedness due to the loan taken for meeting the expenses of house construction and marriage of their children.

The people do not have much access to the benefits of the development schemes provided by the government and they usually do not participate in the Gramsabha, which offers the platform where they can address their issues and raise opinions. If they do not participate in that meeting they lose their avenue to avail government benefits. They do receive the benefits from government as the SC community, but do not receive any special consideration as a Denotified tribes.

NOTES

1. In 1871, The Criminal Tribes Act or XXVII of 1871 passed by the British Government.
2. Ayyangar Committee submitted its report in 1950, in which it made several recommendations for the repeal of the Act and gave reason for this.
3. According to Kalelkar Commission report, the 'Criminal Tribes' should not be called 'Tribes' nor should the names 'Criminal' or 'Ex-Criminal' be attached to them. They could be called 'De-notified Communities'.
4. The Criminal Tribes Act was replaced by Habitual Offenders Act in the statute book.
5. Here formalization of citizenship means Possession of various cards.

REFERENCES

Bokil, M. and Raghavan, V. (2016). Women and Children as Victims and Offenders: The Case of De-Notified Tribes in India. In *Women and Children as Victims and Offenders: Background, Prevention, Reintegration* (pp. 755-790). Springer, Cham.

Bokil, M. (2002). De-Notified and Nomadic Tribes: A Perspective. *Economic and Political Weekly, 37*(2), 148-154. Retrieved from: http://iproxy.inflibnet.ac.in:2060/stable/4411599 Accessed on 13/05/2018.

Dandekar, A. (2009). *The Issue of Denotified Tribes in Independent India*, Working paper No. 214. Gujarat, Institute of Rural Management.

Dandekar, A. (2009). *The Issue of Denotified Tribes in Independent India*, Working paper No. 214. Gujarat, Institute of Rural Management.

Devi, M. (1985). The Shavara Tribals of West Bengal? Shavaras of Midnapur. *Economic and Political Weekly, 20*(35), 1467–1469. Retrieved from http://www.jstor.org/stable/4374763 Accessed on 31/05/2018.

Devi, M. (1992). Kheria-Savar Sammelana in Purulia. *Economic and Political Weekly, 27*(41): 41–42. Retrieved from http://www.jstor.org/stable/4398975 Accessed on 31/05/2018.

D'Souza, D. (1999). De-Notified Tribes: Still 'Criminal'? *Economic and Political Weekly*, 34(51) 3576-3578. Retrieved from http://www.jstor.org/stable/4408732 Accessed on 25/02/2018.

Gandhi, M. (2014). "Educational Status of Denotified Tribes in Andhra Pradesh: Attainment and Challenges". *Journal of Rural Development*, Vol. 33(2, April–June), 215–240.

Governemnt of India (2016). *National Family Health Survey (NFHS-5) India.* International Institue for Population Science. Retrieved fromhttp://rchiips.org/NFHS/factsheet_NFHS-5.shtml Accessed on 10/06/2018

Heredia, R.C. (2007). Denotified and Nomadic Tribes: The Challenge of Free and Equal Citizenship [Monograph].

Japhet, S., and Sabharwal, N.S. (2015). Criminal Stigma and Livelihood: Socio-Economic Study of De-notified Tribes in Karnataka.

Kapadia, K.M. (1952). The criminal tribes of India. *Sociological Bulletin, 1*(2), 99-125. Retrieved from http://www.jstor.org/stable/42864482 Accessed on 25/02/2018

Korra, V. (2017a). "Status of Denotified Tribes Empirical evidence from undivided Anddesh". *Economic and Political Weekly, 52*(36): 61.

Korra, V. (2017b). Educational Status of De-notified Tribes: A Study of Telangana. Working Paper No. 139. Hyderabad. Centre for Economic and Social Studies.

Kumar, M. (2004). "Relationship of Caste and Crime in Colonial India: A Discourse Analysis", *Economic and Political Weekly*, Vol. 31(10), 1078-1087. Retrieved from http://www.jstor.org/stable/4414739 Accessed on 28/02/2018 Accessed on 25/02/2018

Ministry of Social Justice and Empowerment. (2008). *National Commission for Denotified, Nomadic and Semi-Nomadic Tribes*. Governemnt of India Retrived from http://socialjustice.nic.in/ViewData/OldArchives?mid=1249 Accessed on 16/01/2018

Radhakrishna, M. (1989). "From Tribal Community to Working Class Consciousness: Case of Yerukula Women", *Economic and Political Weekly*, WS2-WS5. Retrieved from http://www.jstor.org/stable/4394727. Accessed on 03/05/2018

Radhakrishna, M. (2000). "Colonial Construction of a 'Criminal Tribe': Yerkulas of Madras Presidency", *Economic and Political Weekly,* 35(28/29), 2553-2563.

Radhakrishna, M. (2007). "Urban Denotified tribes: competing identities, contested citizenship". *Economic and Political Weekly*, 42(51): 59-64. Retrieved from: http://jstor.org/stable/40276878 Accessed on: 25/02/2018.

Radhakrishna, M. (2009). *Invented Pasts and Fabricated Presents*: Indian Nomadic and Denotified Communities.

Shyjan, D. and Sunitha, A.S. (2009). Changing phases of Kerala's development experience and the exclusion of scheduled tribes: Towards an explanation. *Artha Vijnana*, Vol. L1, No. 4, pp. 340-359.

20

Sarvodaya Approach of Decentralisation

M.R. Biju and *M.R.B. Anantha Padmanabha*

Gandhiji wanted decentralisation of both economic and political power. He contemplated a society in which all would have their rightful place and each would enjoy freedom and participation in the management of the affairs of the community. However it is not possible to say how far he could succeed in implementing his scheme of decentralisation as he had no opportunity to do so because of his assassination only a few months after the attainment of independence of the nation. But after his death his followers took this challenge upon themselves and made sincere efforts to fulfil his mission through various programmes such as the Bhoodan-Gramadan movement, Reconstruction of Indian polity, Panchayati Raj, Total Revolution etc. They met in Sevagram in March 1948 and formed an organisation for the uplift and welfare of one and all. It was called the '*Sarvodaya Samaj*'. At this conference under the guidance of Vinoba Bhave, the word Sarvodaya was accepted as the goal of their movement and all the workers constituted a fellowship called Sarvodaya Samaj with the objective to reconstruct a social order on the basis of truth and non-violence, in which there would be no possibility of exploitation and in which both the individual and society would have an opportunity for fullest development.

Similarly, a Sarvodaya Economic Conference was held in December 1948, which also aimed at establishing a 'Sarvodaya Society'. The Society reiterated its faith in the ideals of the Sarvodaya which had been laid down in the first conference a year earlier.

According to the advocates of Sarvodaya, the principles underlying their view of democratic decentralisation is that the power of the people based on 'Lok-Niti' alone can reduce the interference and coercive role of party politics to the minimum (Jayaprakash Narayan). Vinoba Bhave points out that the real revolution will come only by the power of the people and not by the power of the party as party politics gives the people only by an illusion of security in which they become more and more helpless. Like Gandhi, he believes that concentration of power in a few hands is a negation to democracy. Sometimes the right of voting can be a farce as merely voting does not guarantee the power of the people after the voting is over. It means the real power remains in the hands of a ruling elite and the common people do not have any consciousness of possessing power.

Another objective of the Sarvodayists, to the present system of democracy is that it is impossible to separate politics from life, since the government has the power to control the affairs of every village and every community and the people are not left with any opportunity to take decisions on any matter at all. Vinoba comments that there is no self-government in the villages, as they have no authority in anything that really matters (Vinoba Bhave). But Sarvodayist strive for 'Swaraj'—self-government. Vinoba declares, "I do not want government, I want self-government." It means at what is managed from the centre is government whereas what goes on in village communities where man manages his own life, is real self-government.

Accordingly, Sarvodaya seeks to establish democratic decentralisation in the light of its own view of life. To achieve this end the Sarvodayists lay emphasis on the efforts of the people, on building up popular strength, cultivation sense of the power of the 'self,' creating confidence and courage for managing the affairs of their community. As a matter of fact, Sarvodaya philosophy draws its support from the people and opposes the present Western mechanism of democracy wherein the elections alone bring the people into the picture. On the contrary, Sarvodaya claims to establish a self-Government by the people, for the people and of the people—on 'Gramdan' principles which means a government of the villages, by the villagers and for the villagers as primarily India is made up most of villages.' Under this scheme, the Sarvodayists give topmost priority to the lowest rung of the administrative ladder of the country. Accordingly, each village or unit must be self-sufficient and self-governing. The villages must themselves produce things for their basic needs and must have the right to decide about its imports and exports. To them, this will ensure 'Gram Swaraj' of Gandhi's conception. (Sharma, M.L.).

Sarvodayists claim that their ultimate goal is the creation of a decentralized polity and social order a society free from exploitation and fetters of controls and pressures the crippling influences, which are inherent in the exercise of political power (Danda) and formal organizational structures (Tantra), since they create disability, both social and economic and, more than any other factor, are responsible for perpetuating a class of handicapped population for all times to come.

Democratic Decentralisation through Gramdan

As mentioned earlier, the Sarvodayists had chalked out a unique way of democratic decentralisation, i.e. Gramdan-Gramswaraj to create people's power (Lok Shakti). Most of them put in efforts to realize this ideal. Vinoba Bhave felt that the village Swaraj could be attained only through Gramdan. For, he felt that even after the withdrawal of the British from India, villages had gained neither economic nor political freedom, as they were still languishing in poverty, unemployment, ignorance and disease. Therefore, the villagers had to be taken out of their present flight of despondency and dependence on others to give real content and meaning to freedom. And to him this could be done only through Gramdan (Sarvodaya).

Similarly, Jayaprakash Narayan affirmed that real panchayati raj community development programme could be realized only through Gramdan (Vinoba and J.P.). However, it must be noted here that the original inspiration for the Bhoodan Gramdan movement initiated by Vinoba Bhave, is derived from a desire to solve the age old agrarian problem which in all the underdeveloped country of the world, seems to be a baffling problem. But it does not mean that there is no other factor in its emergence. The poverty of the masses and political exploitation are some other factors.

Meaning and Substance of Gramdan

Generally, Gramdan means the pooling and sharing of the entire land of a village by all its inhabitants equally and impartially. According to its advocate its seeks to establish social order of equality and liberty, of love and sympathy where the rich and the poor will live like friends without any conflict and clash. Vinoba feels that Gramdan opens the door to a new era of social evolution wherein human beings will perceive and realize the higher values and richer relationships of community sharing. Similarly according to Jayaprakash Narayan, Gramdan constitutes the first step towards non-violent social change and the reconstruction of Indian society at the lower levels carrying forward Gandhi's unfinished work, namely, the work of building a non-violent, decentralized social order as it carries forward the process of non-violent social transformation in as much as it entails:

(a) Conversion of private ownership of land into community ownership;
(b) Sharing within a village community of a small part of land, produce, income and labour, as a regular way of life; and
(c) Observance of the principle of consensus in all decision-making.

Working of Democratic Decentralisation Under Gramdan

On March 4, 1968, a draft containing five points was presented to Vinoba. He added a sixth and said that the six together could very well form the basis and substance of Gram Swaraj. These may be discussed as follows:

Autonomous Village Assemblies (Gram Sabhas)

Under the new process, Gramdan visualizes a village assembly (Gram Sabha) comprising all the adults in the village, which shall function on the basis of general agreement amongst the members within the limits of its capacity and considerations for general good, as the basic autonomous unit of village self-rule in the spheres of both internal administration and development, the village people having already vested in it their full legal land ownership (Swaitva Visarjan), as also having placed as its disposal their collective village capital (Gram Kosh).

Here village autonomy implies a two-tier democracy, direct participation at the village level and indirect representative at higher levels. This system is based on the principle of consensus where all its decisions are supposed to be made by unanimity or near-unanimity. However, Sarvodaya philosophy is not clear about the structure and functioning of the bodies at the higher levels.

Partyless Village Representation

Gramdan system rejects the politics of power and government by political parties in any form since their role according to the Sarvodayists, is tragically arising as these area completely engrossed in keeping hold on power bags or in grabbing it. In the lure and craze for political power they seem to have forgotten their basic duty. Empty political slogans befool the electorate and those saddled in power do not display a better appreciation of reality. They do not bother about how to build up a polity and an economy from the grassroots, how to find employment and housing for the poor masses, how to ensure quick delivery of justice to the innocent-illiterate people. These are the most relevant and agitating questions, which are forgotten and ignored by political parties.

Village-oriented Economic Policy

Gramdan polity is opposed to the present official plan and policy of love, the gift of wisdom, the gift of labour, the gift of wealth and the gift of land. The Bhoodan movement had its dramatic and sudden beginning on 18 April, 1951 when a Sarvodaya Sammelan (Conference) was held at Shivarampalli, about four miles away from Hyderabad City. Vinoba hold a meeting at Pochapalli, a town let of about 700 houses and 3000 people, in the Nalgonda district, where some landless untouchables approached him for land and the Acharya (Vinoba) appealed to the landlords of the area to donate him some land for the landless. At his appeal, a rich man of the area, V.R. Reddy, who had hitherto nursed every bit of his property with care, agreed to part with some portion of his surplus land and made it over to the dispossessed (Vinoba Bhave). After getting his first gift of land, Vinoba walked from village to village listening to the problems of the landless labourers. He identified himself with the landless as Gandhi had identified himself with the scavenger.

A Social Order Relatively Free from Police and Law Courts

For peace and order and its own defence, Gramdan village will develop its own peace corps having moral authority. All disputes, instead of going to the law courts, will ordinarily be settled in the Gram Sabha itself by the methods of conciliation and arbitration.

Independent Education

Gramdan rejects the present system of education, as it is controlled by government. Vinoba points out that whatever 'test blood' is prescribed by the government, it has to be studied by every child in the state. That is to say, the government has the power to push its own ideas down the throats of all children. If it is a Communist government it will teach the students socialism. If the government believes in planning, the children will be filled up with propaganda in favour of planning. In short, the children will have no freedom to think for themselves. This is in contrast to the Indian tradition of keeping education free from the control of the state.

Therefore, in Gramdan special order, education develops into a constructive social force, strong enough to replace the present leadership of business and politics. It is completely free from government patronage and control. Accordingly its exponents want that education must become at least as independent as the Judiciary (Sharma, M.L.).

Role of Lok-Shakti (Power of the People) and Lok-Niti (People's Polity) in Gramdan

Lok-Shakti is a concept which is being undertaken to achieve certain goals and the main goal, according to Sarvodaya leaders, is the creation of a new kind of society a new society in which the 'greatest good of all' is attempted to be achieved. It lays greater emphasis on the movement for Lok-Shakti than on Rajya-Shakti or power of the state.

Role and Scope of Shanti-Sena (Peace Corps)

With the emergence of Gramdan movement, Vinoba also felt the need to create an atmosphere for Shanti-Sena (Peace Corps) in India for defence and maintenance of peace and order in society. He argues, "We will have to establish the efficacy of Shanti-Sena in internal affairs. There are so many internal issues in India today. Also one finds much discontent. Again, there party-differences and quarrels and conflicts too. We will have to show that these conflicts do not lead to breach of peace anywhere. For this, there is no other way except Shanti-Sena." Therefore, Vinoba visualises Shanti-Sena on the one hand and Gramdan on the other.

Jayaprakash Narayan (1902-1979) and Sarvodaya

Jayaprakash Narayan was one of the legendary figures of Indian political philosophy. Whatever he thought and did drew the attention and admiration of the serious thinkers of the country. He was a man of the common people who relentlessly worked for their upliftment and few inspiration from them. His writings and activities exhibited his deep concern not only for the freedom of the Indian people but also for the freedom of man everywhere.

According to Jayaprakash Narayan, the existing form of society is so compels. It is under the clutches of bureaucrats and technocrats. He believed that the existing social system is not congenial for the overall well-being of mankind. Man is the product of nature and culture. "Self-government, mutual co-operation, self-management could be practiced and developed far better if man lived in small communities." The harmonious blend between nature and culture is possible only in small village communities.

J.P. urged for the establishment of 'Self-government' in the country. He called it as "Participating democracy". He made self-governing and self-sufficing village communities as the foundation of participating democracy. The family should be the primary unit of self-government. But it will be too small unit. So a number of families should join together and form a village community. Swaraj will become an ultimate reality only if government is brought near to the people.

Jayaprakash's great passion for freedom was responsible for bringing him to Sarvodaya. He felt that the method of Sarvodaya was more effective and original compared to the traditional specialist methods. According to him, this was the practical form of Gandhian philosophy for the realisation of social revolution. He resigned from the Praja Socialist Party in 1957. He wrote: "I decided to withdrew from party and power politics not because of disgust or sense of any personal frustration but because it became clear to me that politics could not deliver the goods, the goods being the same old goals of equality, freedom, brotherhood, peace." He wholeheartedly devoted himself to the work of Bhoodan and Sarvodaya. It became clear to him that a new social order could be worked out through the instrument of party and state power.

Jayaprakash believed that the democratic system should involve the masses. Otherwise, the ideals of liberty, equality and justice cannot be achieved. He agreed with the view of Harold Laski and said that the worth of democracy must be judged by the amount of voluntary activity within it. The formal institutions like Parliament, Assemblies and elected governments along do not constitute democracy. There cannot be true democracy unless it lives in the life of the people. There can be hardly any democracy if differences on the basis of economic status social status and castes persist. In the year 1959, Jayaprakash prepared his thesis "Reconstruction of Indian Polity," which was published by the

journal will stress the following freedom as being essential to any democratic society, freedom of expression, freedom of worship, freedom of peaceful protest, demonstration and of other forms of peaceful social action including Satyagraha." He stressed on the importance of moral values and individual freedom and warned the people against the growing social evils.

Jayaprakash said that Sarvodaya is the people's socialism. He observed: "The remedy is to create and develop forms of socialist living through the voluntary endeavour of the people rather than seek to establish socialism by the use of the power of the state. In other words, the remedy is to establish people's socialism rather than state socialism". He insisted on a band of selfless workers who would be prepared to live and move in the midst of the masses and help them to reorganise their lives on a self-reliant and self-controlling basis.

Criticism

Sarvodaya and Gandhism have been criticised for being an impracticable ideal. The ideas are noble but the ideals are unattainable. Referring to the Bhoodan Movement, it is a method through which land is distributed to the landless without payment of any compensation. One of the major problems of payment of proper compensation and knocking at the doors of the court of law, in appeal against inadequate compensation is most adequately solved. Moreover, the peasants of India, are already hard pressed and have poor economic standard. Here Vinoba touches their conscience and obliges them to part with some of their land which reduces them to still more poverty. Not only this but those who get the land also live in poverty. It is also said that only the barren land is being given in donations and there is no possibility of crops being grown in such a land in the near future. Thus, those who get the land cannot put that to their use. Another problem of the movement is that instead of collective and co-operative farming which is the order of the day and also most essential for excessive production is being said good-bye by this movement. On the contrary land is being divided into fragments and each 'fragment is not producing what it should produce under collective farming. In this way nation on the whole is a great looser.

Further, Sarvodaya is bound to flounder on the rock of human nature. We are expecting too much from human beings as they are. Most of them selfish and it is too much to expect that they will change overnight or change at all. The whole basis of Sarvodaya is the transformation of the present man and if that does not happen the rest of the superstructure cannot be raised at all. The exponents of Sarvodaya stand for the abolition of political parties as they do not work properly. However, that is not the right solution. Political parties are bound to stay so long as there is freedom of thought and human nature is what it is. The solution lies in their reformation and reorganisation and not in abolition. The advocates of Sarvodaya attack the majority rule but the majority does not always and necessarily reduce the minority to a eiper. Moreover unanimity in the field of legislation is an impossibility. It is true that legislation also helps in creating conditions for better living. While decentralisation is a welcome step, it should not be based on the self-sufficiency of the villages. In the present complex, competitive and interdependent world the idea of self-sufficient village republic is only a dream. The concept of non-violent, stateless and partyless democracy is a noble vision but a poor plan. 'The Sarvodaya leaders themselves are disappointed over the concrete results of their movements. Sarvodaya also stands for direct democracy; but that is not suited to modem conditions of society. Sarvodaya does not reorganise the necessity of analysing social development from the scientific point of view. It ignores the reality of class divisions in society and is unrealistic.

In conclusion it can be stated that Sarvodaya is a powerful attempt to build-up a political and social reconstruction on the basis of ethical idealism. It seeks to create a new social, political and economic order. Sarvodaya is an attempt to develop the ideas of Gandhiji in the framework of independent India. It is a dynamic philosophy which can make possible the advent of a radically transformed humanity. Its greatest contribution lies in the assertion of a moral approach to the problems of man. It gives us the message of love for all.

REFERENCES

Arumugam, M., *Socialist Thought in India, The Contribution of Ram Manohar Lohia*, New Delhi, 1978.

Biju, M.R., Gandhiji and Panchayati Raj, *Indian Communicator*, 2-3 October, 1995.

Das, H.H. and Patro, P.S.N., *Indian Political Traditions*, Sterling, New Delhi, 1989.

Jaya Prakash Narayan, *Communitarian Society and Panchayati Raj*, Varanasi, 1970.

Jaya Prakash Narayan, *Towards Total Revolution*, Popular Prakashan, Bombay.

Mahajan, V.P., *Modern Indian Political Thought*, S. Chand & Co., New Delhi, 1987.

Ram Suresh, *Vinoba and His Mission*, Varanasi, 1958.

Sharma, M.L. (1987). *Gandhi and Democratic Decentralisation in India*, Deep & Deep Publications, New Delhi.

Verma, V.P. (1965). *Political Philosophy of Mahatma Gandhi and Sarvodaya*, 1965.

Index